Britain's Trade and Economic Structure

Fifty years ago, Britain was a major manufacturer; now she is predominately a service economy. How far this change is due to her entry to the EU, and how far to the discovery and exploitation of North Sea oil, is just one of the issues discussed in this volume.

Britain's Trade and Economic Structure: The Impact of the EU examines the reasons behind the UK's economic decline since the 1960s. The work provides a new perspective by focusing on the restructuring of British industry and trading policy. The author uses this approach to discuss the causes and effects of deindustrialization and changes to traditional trading patterns. Particular attention is devoted to the impact of the EU. Key areas covered include: the UK's transformation from a manufacturing to a service economy; trade theory, the UK's trade policy and the effect of multinational agreements; monetary integration; the fuel sector and North Sea oil; CAP and its effect on the UK's agricultural position; trade and protection in the motor vehicle industry; textiles and clothing; high-tech and research development; liberalization and growth; and regional policy and taxation.

Twenty-five years after Britain's accession to the EU, this volume provides a very timely and topical assessment of the effect of membership on the UK economy. Written in an accessible and jargon-free style, the work also provides a valuable comparative study of Britain's trading partners and rivals.

Lynden Moore is an applied economist specializing in international trade, the economics of the EU and the textile and clothing industry. She was previously a Lecturer at Manchester University and Senior Associate Member of St Antony's College, Oxford University.

Britain's Trade and Economic Structure

The impact of the European Union

Lynden Moore

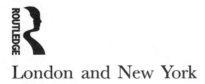

London and New York

330.941
B85b

First published 1999
by Routledge
11 New Fetter Lane, London EC4P 4EE

Simultaneously published in the USA and Canada
by Routledge
29 West 35th Street. New York, NY 10001

© 1999 Lynden Moore

Typeset in Baskerville by The Florence Group, Stoodleigh, Devon
Printed and bound in Great Britain by Mackays of Chatham PLC, Chatham, Kent

All rights reserved. No part of this book may be reprinted or
reproduced or utilized in any form or by any electronic,
mechanical, or other means, now known or hereafter
invented, including photocopying and recording, or in any
information storage or retrieval system, without permission in
writing from the publishers.

British Library Cataloguing in Publication Data
A catalogue record for this book is available from the British Library

Library of Congress Cataloguing in Publication Data
A catalog record for this book has been requested

ISBN 0–415–16920–8 (hbk)
ISBN 0–415–16921–6 (pbk)

To Celia and Ivan

University Libraries
Carnegie Mellon University
Pittsburgh, PA 15213-3890

Contents

List of tables   x
List of figures   xiv
Preface   xvii
List of abbreviations   xviii

1 Introduction   1

2 Britain's comparative position   5

Changes in population, total income, per capita income
Investment and investment ratio
Allocation between industries of employment and output
Changes over time in employment and output

3 The theory of trade, protection, and discrimination   28

Benefits of trade
Theory of tariffs and quotas
Theory of preferential trading systems: Trade creation and
   trade diversion

4 UK trade policy and agreements that have affected trade   63

System of Commonwealth preference
Membership of EFTA
EEC. Anticipated effects of Britain joining
The Uruguay Round Agreements

5 Moves towards monetary integration   93

6 Other EU policies affecting trade 102

Competition policy
Industry policy
*Policies towards the Steel industry and European Computing
and Telecommunications industry*

7 The impact of preferential trading areas and international direct investment on the development of UK trade 119

*Shift from Commonwealth and EFTA to EEC: How much
Trade Creation, how much Trade Diversion*
Effect of EFTA
*Winter's estimate of the effect of membership on British trade
in manufactures. Recent developments in the EC, the Single
European Market*
Distribution of trade between commodities
Distribution between areas

8 The energy sector and the development of North Sea oil 144

*Decline in the use and output of coal – average cost pricing
policy so that lower cost pits subsidizing higher cost ones.
Development of North Sea gas – AC pricing policy – no
economic rent being obtained. North Sea oil – government
endeavours to obtain economic rent*

9 The Common Agricultural Policy and its effect on UK agricultural production, trade and consumption 188

Agricultural Act of 1947 and effects
The Common Agricultural Policy (CAP)
Present position after the Uruguay round

10 Trade and production of motor vehicles 234

Britain's historical position as a major exporter
*Agreement with Japan limiting imports to 11% of market in
cars and commercial vehicles*
*Entry to EEC changed trade with EFTA and led to rapid
increase in deficit with other EEC countries*

Austin Rover obtained assistance of Honda. Greenfield
investments of Nissan and Toyota
Divergence in prices between UK and other countries

11 Textiles and clothing 259

Commonwealth preference, then 'voluntary' exports restraints.
  Cotton re-organization scheme. EFTA
Regional employment premium and its discontinuance
Multi-fibre arrangement
Uruguay round and phasing out the MFA

12 High-technology industries and research
and development 283

Innovation record up to 1970 good. But take up by British
  manufacturing poor. High proportion of R&D financed by
  government. High proportion of this for defence
Thatcher government wished to reduce government expenditure
  and increase commercial orientation of universities. Patented
  innovations and expenditure on R&D fell except in
  Chemical industry
EEC schemes for co-operation in R&D. Not very productive
Only Chemical industries maintain leading edge
EEC schemes to reduce imports − encouraged entry of
  Japanese electronics firms

13 Trade in services: Liberalization and growth 318

Liberalization under the SEM and Uruguay round
Privatization
Growth of alliances

14 Regional policy and taxation 343

Divergent effect on manufactures and services
Emergence of the poverty trap. Reduces any multiplier effect
  in depressed regions

15 Conclusion 372

Index 377

Tables

2.1 Britain's comparative position with respect to income and population 6

2.2 Factors affecting the growth of output, 1955–68 10

2.3 Distribution of civilian employment in 1960 and 1994 for the EU(15) 12

2.4 Value added per person employed in each sector as a percentage of GDP per person employed in the country as a whole in 1968 13

2.5 Trend rates of growth of employment in total and by sector, 1955–68 13

2.6 Trend rates of growth of output per employed person, 1955–68 14

2.7 UK and EU rates of growth, 1960–96 19

2.8 Income levels and growth rates in some European and Asian countries, 1950–92 20

2.9 Crafts-accounting for growth 21

4.1 Distribution of UK merchandise trade by area 65

4.2 Anticipated effects on the balance of payments and welfare of British entry into the EC 73

6.1 Steel products: price differentials between internal and international prices in 1987 108

6.2 Direct effect on the main steel-using branches of a variation of 10 per cent in the price of steel 108

6.3 Steel-making costs in Europe, March 1993 109

6.4 Breakdown of steel-making costs in Europe, March 1993 110

7.1 Distribution of UK exports of goods by product group, 1950–96 120

7.2 Distribution of UK imports of goods by product group, 1950–96 120

7.3 The effects of EFTA on Britain's imports and exports in 1965 125

7.4 Britain's balance of trade and changes in the volume of trade by product, and for exports by destination and imports by origin, 1970–87 129

7.5   Alan Winter's estimates of the effect on Britain's trade in
      manufactures of her entry into the EC   133
7.6   UK's balance of trade in 1987 and 1996 and change in the
      volume of exports and imports   135
7.7   Reddaway Report on the effects of UK direct investment
      overseas, 1955–64   137
7.8   Inward direct investment in the UK by overseas companies,
      1992–95   140
7.9   Outward direct investment by UK companies overseas, 1992–95 140
8.1   Consumption of commercial energy in Western Europe
      in 1950 and 1973   145
8.2   Net effective cost of nuclear and coal-fired generating stations 156
8.3   Output of the UK fuel industries   175
8.4   Unit costs of gas and oil fields on the UK continental
      shelf at 1995 prices   177
8.A1 Domestic expenditure on energy 1963–89: fuel and light,
      and petrol and oil   184
8.A2 Industrial energy consumption   184
8.A3 Energy consumption in transport   185
9.1   Agricultural protection in the EEC: Minimum import price
      divided by the world price   194
9.2   Degree of self-sufficiency for selected commodities   195
9.3   UK prices and the variation throughout the EU in 1996   197
9.4   Quantities and prices of farm products produced in the UK
      in 1970/71 and 1994   198
9.5   UK consumers' real expenditure on food from 1970–94 at
      1990 market prices   199
9.6   EC agricultural trade and self-sufficiency, 1990–91   219
9.7   Target, intervention and threshold prices for cereals,
      1992–96   222
10.1 British motor vehicle production by firms, 1947   235
10.2 Mergers in the British motor vehicle industry, 1945–68   236
10.3 Minimum efficient scale per activity in the car industry   238
10.4 Non-tariff restrictions on imports of cars and commercial
      vehicles into EC countries from Japan before 1993   241
10.5 Structure of the European automobile market in 1986   244
10.6 Comparative unit costs of car manufacture, 1955–77   246
10.7 The cost of employing labour in the automobile industry
      in 1980 and 1989   247
10.8 UK trade in motor vehicles in 1973 and 1995   248
10.9 UK production of cars in 1996 and 1995, and allocation to
      the export and home markets in 1995   252
10.10 UK new car registrations in 1997   255
10.11 Intra-firm trade of multinationals producing cars in the
      UK in 1995   256

11.1   Cost comparisons in the textile and clothing industry   268
11.2   Cost of cotton shirt production   269
11.3   Effective limitation on imports into Britain due to VERs   270
11.4   Hong Kong quota premia on clothing exports to the UK in
        1983 and 1988   271
11.5   Shares of UK import market for clothing   271
11.6   UK changes in production, consumption, imports and
        exports of textiles, 1973–88   272
11.7   EU quotas for clothing imports in Group IB in 1996   278
12.1   Comparative gross domestic expenditure on R&D (GERD)
        in relation to GDP and the OECD total and relative
        employment of researchers of the major participating countries 287
12.2   Relative expenditure on R&D, 1963–64 to 1994   288
12.3   Personnel engaged on R&D within business enterprises,
        in the UK in 1981, 1989 and 1994   290
12.4   1998 Patent applications within countries, and patent
        applications taken out by them abroad, and their share of
        patent applications in the US. Growth rates given for 1984–88 295
12.5   Technology balance of payments in major OECD countries
        in 1990   295
12.6   Intensity of R&D expenditure in the OECD area   296
12.7   R&D intensity ratios for high- and medium-technology
        industries   298
12.8   UK balance of trade in high-tech products in 1994 by area   300
12.9   Import penetration and export sales ratios for high-tech
        industries, 1994   301
12.10   The main EC programmes for promoting new technologies   303
12.11   Community trade in high-tech products: Export/import
        ratio by selected trade partners, 1982–90   305
12.12   Definitive anti-dumping duties and undertakings in force
        on 30 April 1996   310
12.13   1996 plans to build or extend electronics plants in the UK   314
13.1   Geographical distribution of trade in services in 1995   322
13.2   British Airways stakeholding and alliances in 1995   334
13.3   Foreign direct investment flows in services for US, UK,
        and Japan   336
13.4   Outward direct investment in services by UK companies
        overseas   338
13.5   Airline Atlantic alliances   339
14.1   Regional employment changes, 1952–93   346
14.2   Annual growth in real gross domestic product and
        productivity, 1971–92   348
14.3   Composition of regional economies, 1992   349
14.4   Expenditure on research and development, 1995   350

14.5 UK regional unemployment and average weekly
      earnings, 1996   351
14.6 UK employment by region in June 1995   352
14.7 Allocation of EU structural funds   356
14.8 The effect of general government taxation, transfers and
      expenditure on the regions in 1991   357
14.9 Ratio of direct and indirect taxes and social security
      payments to total personal income, 1960, 1970 and 1974   360

Figures

2.1   Changes in nominal GDP, real GDP and inflation:
Year-to-year percentage changes   18

2.2   UK output of non-tradeables, 1948–96   23

2.3   UK output of tradeables, 1948–96   24

2.4   UK de-industrialization in terms of employment and output,
1960 and 1994 (%): (a) employment 1960; (b) output 1960;
(c) employment 1994; (d) output 1994   26

2.5   Employment in Great Britain in 1996   26

3.1   Production and consumption under autarchy and free
trade   31

3.2   Offer curve of a country exporting cars   33

3.3   Consumption and production with free trade and a tariff   36

3.4   Self-sufficiency and free trade: A partial equilibrium analysis   38

3.5   The partial equilibrium analysis of a tariff   39

3.6   A minimum import price   41

3.7   Trade creation and trade diversion   45

3.8   A free trade area   47

3.9   A customs union   48

3.10   The effect of a quota: Multilateral situation and preferential
situation   49

3.11   Economies of scale   52

3.A1   A tariff on imports when the country is facing an
upward-sloping supply schedule   61

4.1   The anticipated effects of Britain joining the Common
Agricultural Policy   74

4.2   The structure of the European Union   77

4.3   Tariffs on manufactured products (EU12), 1995 and 2000   86

7.1   UK imports by commodity group, 1958–96   122

7.2   Trade in manufacturers and fuel   124

7.3   UK commodity groups' balances, 1970–96   124

7.4   UK exports of manufactures, 1970–96   127

7.5   The effects of integration on the origin of manufactures
sold in the UK: (a) imports; (b) home market   132

7.6   UK real current account balance, 1950–96   141
7.7   UK current account balances by zone   142
8.1   International prices of fuel, 1980–95   147
8.2   Marginal cost pricing and deviations from it   154
8.3   UK fuel production, 1950–95   164
8.4   Fuel input for electricity generation   165
8.5   Assistance to UK coal producers, 1982–93   166
8.6   North Sea revenue in real terms   167
8.7   UK domestic fuel consumption, 1960–89   169
8.8   Industrial energy consumption, 1960–89   171
8.9   Energy consumption in transport, 1960–89   173
8.10 UK consumption of primary fuels, 1960–95   179
8.11 Final energy consumption, 1960 and 1995: (a) by final user;
      (b) by type of fuel   174
8.12 The contribution of oil and gas from the continental shelf to
      the GDP of the UK   176
8.13 Real net trade in energy: UK energy production and
      consumption, 1965–95   178
8.14 Net exports of fuels, 1970–95   179
9.1   The CAP when production exceeds consumption at the
      minimum import price   191
9.2   World price higher than the minimum import price   192
9.3   UK food consumption, production and imports, 1970–89   200
9.4   UK producer price and institutional prices for soft wheat   201
9.5   UK wheat prices under the CAP, 1983/84 to 1995/96   202
9.6   UK barley prices under the CAP, 1983/84 to 1995/96   202
9.7   Area under different crops in Britain, 1968–94   203
9.8   UK cereal output and utilization, 1973/74 to 1992/93   204
9.9   Wheat for milling in the UK, 1970–95   205
9.10 UK wheat output and imports, 1970–95   206
9.11 UK wheat exports, 1970–95   206
9.12 UK sugar output, trade and consumption, 1972/73 to
      1992/93   208
9.13 UK oilseed output and uptake, 1981/82 to 1992/93   209
9.14 UK livestock numbers, 1970–95   210
9.15 UK production and trade in beef, 1971–95   211
9.16 UK milk production and use, 1971–95   212
9.17 UK butter production and imports, 1971–95   213
9.18 UK cheese production and imports, 1971–95   213
9.19 UK butter consumption and exports, 1973–95   214
9.20 UK cheese consumption and exports, 1973–95   215
9.21 UK lamb production and trade, 1971–95   216
9.22 UK consumption of fertilizers, 1970/71 to 1993/94   218
9.23 EU consumer subsidy equivalents (CSEs) and producer
      subsidy equivalents (PSEs), 1986–88   220

9.24 EU provisional consumer subsidy equivalents (CSEs) and producer subsidy equivalents (PSEs), 1995 — 225

10.1 The automobile production system — 237

10.2 UK car production and trade, 1946–96 — 239

10.3 UK commercial vehicle production and trade, 1946–96 — 240

10.4 Supply to the UK car market: Domestic production and imports, 1964–95 — 243

10.5 UK car production by firm, 1968–96 — 251

11.1 Clothing production and expenditure, 1973–95 — 273

11.2 Soft furnishings production and expenditure, 1973–95 — 274

11.3 Textile production, 1973–95 — 275

12.1 UK business enterprise R&D, 1966–94 — 289

12.2 Government R&D finance, 1966 to 1994–95. Real terms (1990 = 100) — 291

12.3 Finance of business R&D, 1982–94. Real terms (1990–91 = 100) — 292

12.4 Gross expenditure on R&D (GERD) by sectors in the UK, 1994 — 293

12.5 UK business R&D in 1981 and 1994 — 299

13.1 Volume of trade in services, 1974–95 — 320

13.2 Financial business services, 1984–95 — 320

13.3 Service sector balances, 1985, 1990, 1995 — 321

14.1 Manufacturing and service employment by region, June 1970 and 1995 — 347

14.2 Full- and part-time employment in Great Britain, June 1971, 1976, 1995 — 353

14.3 Male average earnings per region, 1996 — 354

14.4 Female average earnings per region, 1996 — 354

14.5 The effects of tax and inflation on the real disposable earnings of men in Great Britain, 1975–82 — 362

14.6 Differences in net spending power for a £1 increase in gross earnings: As at November 1977 for married couples with two children aged 4 and 6 — 364

14.7 The relationship between net spending power and gross earnings of the husband: As at November 1977 for married couple with two children aged 4 and 6 — 365

14.8 Poverty Trap April 1983. Net weekly spending power: By level of earnings and type of family — 366

14.9 Poverty Trap July 1995. Net weekly spending power: By gross weekly earnings and type of family — 367

Preface

The ignorance of the British about the economic structure of their own country and the dramatic changes that have occurred to it over the past fifty years has been my chief motivation in writing this book. Britain's entry into the EC, far from providing a buttress to British manufacturers as they expected, only increased competition in their home market, which led to a decline in their real manufacturing output. Britain has moved from a manufacturing to a service economy. She has a deficit in all sectors except fuel with the EU; her surpluses in services are earned with the rest of the world, particularly North America. Thus I have endeavoured to show that there is a genuine divergence of interests within Britain in respect to any greater regional preferences, as would be entailed by her membership of the EU monetary union.

I am indebted to John Black for his detailed comments on the entire book, and to the following for reading and commenting on individual chapters: Paul Horsnell on Chapter 8, George Peters on Chapter 9, George Bowen on Chapter 11, and Peter Holmes and Chris Gannon on Chapter 12. My sincere thanks also to Jack Hayward, Rosemary Fennell, Rosemary Clarke, and Robert Baker of SMMT for reading parts of the text. I was also grateful for the sabbatical term from Manchester University in 1991, which I spent at the Wolfson College and the Department of Applied Economics at Cambridge University, researching developments in the UK market for fuel and energy.

Lynden Moore
Oxford

Abbreviations

ACP	African, Caribbean and Pacific
BA	British Airlines
BT	British Telecommunications
CAP	Common Agricultural Policy of the EU previously the EC
CEC	Commission of the European Community now the European Union
CEEC	Central and Eastern European Country
CET	Common External Tariff of the EU
dcw	dead carcase weight
EAGGF	European Agricultural Guidance and Guarantee Fund
EC	European Community
ECSC	European Coal and Steel Community
ECU	European Currency Unit
EFTA	European Free Trade Association
EU	European Union
FDI	Foreign direct investment
FTA	Free trade area
GATT	General Agreement on Tariffs and Trade
GDP	Gross Domestic Product
GNP	Gross National Product
GSP	Generalized System of Preferences
HDTV	High Definition Television
ILO	International Labour Organisation
LAC	Long run average cost
LDC	Less developed country
LTA	Long Term Arrangement regarding Cotton Textiles
MCA	Monetary Compensatory Amount
METS	Minimum efficient technical scale
MFA	Multi-Fibre Arrangement
mfn	most-favoured-nation
MRS	marginal rate of substitution
MRT	marginal rate of transformation
NAFTA	North American Free Trade Agreement

NICs	Newly industrializing countries
NTB	non-tariff barrier
OECD	Organization for Economic Co-operation and Development
OEEC	Organization for European Economic Co-operation
ONS	Office of National Statistics
OPT	Outward processing traffic
PPP	purchasing power parity
PSE	Producer Subsidy Equivalent
SEA	Single European Act
SEM	Single European Market
TEU	Treaty of European Union – Maastricht Treaty
VER	Voluntary Export Restraint
VIL	variable import levy
WTO	World Trade Organization

1 Introduction

Britain approaches the millennium with some trepidation; a succession of bright promises, of the new world that was going to be built after the Second World War, the great opportunities provided by entry into the EC, and the wealth of North Sea oil seem a distant memory. Even the 'peace dividend', that is, the reduced requirement for defence expenditure with the ending of the Cold War, seems to have been dissipated.

The return of a Labour government after the election in May 1997 raised hopes that the harsher aspects of the legacy of Margaret Thatcher, British Prime Minister from 1979 to 1990, might be ameliorated. But the Labour government has pledged to retain the previous Conservative government's spending plans. Furthermore privatization, which was the outstanding feature of the Thatcher 'revolution', is now being copied by other EU countries. The relatively low social security payments and the removal of restrictions on the employment of labour that she introduced are also being studied by other EU countries as a means of reducing unemployment. The UK has one of the lowest rates of unemployment and the highest rates of labour participation in the EU. Thatcherite policies, far from being abandoned, are presented both by Britain and the Commission of the EU (CEC) as the way forward for the other Member States.

High unemployment in Western Europe has been the effect of government endeavours to keep down the rate of inflation in the context of lowered rates of growth and inflexible labour markets. The other large Member States of the EU are refraining from any addition to their expenditure to increase employment in order to conform to the Maastricht requirements for monetary union.

At present Britain's economic performance in terms of unemployment and even in terms of growth compares favourably with that of other members of the EU. This is in contrast to her situation in most of the post-Second World War period when she has appeared a laggard in terms of economic growth. Britain's gross domestic product (GDP) increased on average at 2.3 per cent per annum in real terms between 1960 and 1994, with the result that her economy doubled in size over the period. Most of this was due to an increase in productivity because her population was almost static, increasing at only 0.3 per cent per annum and employment 0.1 per cent from 1960 to 1994. But this rate of growth of GDP was lower than that of the other Western European countries and less than half that of Japan.

This poor economic performance meant that she became a much smaller economy in relation to the rest of the world. In 1950, in the immediate aftermath of the Second World War, the UK was the second largest western manufacturing nation after the US. Until 1960 Britain's total output, that is, her GDP, was the largest in Western Europe; at current prices and exchange rates it was 63 per cent greater than that of the Japanese economy but only 14 per cent of that of the US, then by far the largest economy in the world. The position in 1994 was that the British economy was smaller than that of Germany and France in Europe, 22 per cent of the size of the Japanese economy, and 15 per cent of the size of the US economy (which had also been growing relatively slowly), when measured at current prices and exchange rates. This indicates the decline in the UK's importance in the world economy.

The UK's macroeconomic fluctuations and monetary situation have been described by numerous economists. This book will be concerned with the change in structure of her economy. Although structure is sometimes thought of in terms of the division of activity between the public sector and the private sector, in this book the emphasis will be on structure in terms of industries. Britain has exhibited the phenomenon of 'de-industrialization', that is, the decline in the relative size of the manufacturing sector. This has been due to the transfer of factors of production, labour and capital away from manufacturing to other areas of the economy. Employment in manufacturing began to fall in 1966 at an accelerating rate, from 1973 to 1979 by 1.3 per cent per annum, from 1979 to 1989 by 3.3 per cent per annum, and from 1989 to 1993 by 5.5 per cent per annum. The reduction in employment was partly compensated by a more rapid increase in productivity in manufacturing than in other sectors of the economy. Nonetheless output in manufacturing was lower in the mid-1980s than it was in 1973.

This change in the composition of her output is associated with the change in her trading position. In 1950 Britain was the paradigm of an industrial power exporting manufactures for food and raw materials. Four-fifths of her exports were manufactures; she was the second largest exporter of manufactures after the US, accounting for 26 per cent of world trade in them. Obversely she was the largest importer and net importer of agricultural products in the world. Imports of food, beverages and tobacco accounted for 40 per cent of her imports in 1950 and agricultural raw materials for 18 per cent. Fuel in the form of petroleum products accounted for 7½ per cent (Mansell 1980).

Yet by 1980 she had moved into deficit in her trade in manufactures. Why has this radical shift in specialization occurred? Was it due to the development of North Sea oil in the mid-1970s and her shift from a position as a net importer of fuel to the position of net exporter? Does this represent a shift in her comparative advantage?

How far was it due to changes in her preferential trading arrangements, first as a member of the Commonwealth Preference Scheme to which she belonged until 1973, second the formation of the European Free Trade Association (EFTA) in 1959, and finally her membership of the EC in 1973? This represented a shift from a preferential position in her export markets for manufactures to greater and greater direct competition with her manufacturing rivals. As a member of the EC she also acceded to the Common Agricultural Policy (CAP), which entailed the imposition of substantial levies on imports from Commonwealth countries.

She now appears in the drag of a continent whose economic performance is in decline, having cut her preferential links with the Commonwealth, in particular the Asian countries, which have been growing far faster. In 1970 roughly a fifth of her merchandise trade was with the EC(6) and a fifth with the Commonwealth. But by 1994 approximately half UK trade was with the EC(15) and 10 per cent with the Commonwealth. There remains the question that dogged the previous Conservative government, that is, whether Britain should integrate more closely with the EU by joining a monetary union.

In Chapters 3 to 7 of this book Britain's preferential agreements concerning trade and other EU policies that affect it are considered. The indirect effect of EU trade policy on inward foreign investment into the UK will also be discussed.

Then in Chapter 8 the fuel sector and the impact of government policies towards it is examined. The shift from the consumption of coal, the extraction of which was labour intensive, to North Sea oil has had significant effects both on employment and on government revenue. The EU has only had a marginal influence on this sector.

In Chapters 9 to 12 individual sectors which are subject to considerable EU or government intervention are discussed. The most notable of these is agriculture, discussed in Chapter 9.

Finally, the implication of these changes in specialization and trade for the regional disparities in employment and income is considered in Chapter 14, together with the UK government's and EU policies towards the poorer areas. Associated with this is the problem of alleviating poverty without incurring ever greater government expenditure on social security. A brief mention will also be made of the change in the system of taxation which was required for EC entry.

We shall begin by looking at the UK's comparative position more closely, and then consider why trading agreements can affect a country's specialization.

REFERENCES

Mansell, K. (1980) 'UK visible trade in the post-war years', *Economic Trends*, Central Statistical Office, October.

2 Britain's comparative position

The UK is one of the most populous countries in Western Europe with 58 million people in 1994, almost the same as France and Italy; only unified Germany with 81 million people is appreciably larger (see Table 2.1). But in terms of geographical area the UK is considerably smaller than they are, and her density of 238 people per square kilometre is exceeded only by the Netherlands and Belgium.

In the immediate aftermath of the Second World War Britain was also the second largest industrial economy in the world after the US. When Germany recovered, however, this position was ceded to her. By 1960, as can be seen in Table 2.1, Britain's GDP was less than that of Germany but greater than that of France and Italy. The Netherlands had the highest GDP per head in terms of 1990 price levels and exchange rates, but it was not much higher than those of Germany, Britain, and France.

In this chapter the transformation Britain has undergone from being a major industrial country and the second largest exporter of manufactures to a predominately service economy will be related to developments in the world as a whole. We shall begin by considering her position up to 1970 within the framework of the international financial system. As her financial position in relation to the rest of the world is shown by her balance of payments a brief explanation of this term will now be given.

BALANCE OF PAYMENTS

The balance of payments of a particular country is a summary of all the transactions between its *residents* and the *residents of the rest of the world* over a period of time, here taken to be a year. These must logically add up to zero because this is a form of double-entry bookkeeping. An item is regarded as being positive if it adds to the country's supply of foreign exchange, and negative if it uses it up – exports are therefore positive and imports negative.

The balance of payments is divided into the *current account* and the *capital account*. The current account is a record of the value of goods and services

Table 2.1 Britain's comparative position with respect to income and population

	Population (000s)	GDP at current prices and exchange rates (US$bn)		GDP per head at current prices and exchange rates ($)	GDP per head PPP rates ($)	GDP per head at 1990 price levels and exchange rates ($)		
	1994	1960	1994	1994	1994	1960	1970	1994
Britain	58,366	72	1,020	17,468	17,650	8,928	11,120	17,297
Original EC								
West Germany	81,410[U]	81	2,046[U]	25,133[U]	19,675[U]	9,008	13,001	21,528
France	57,903	61	1,329	22,944	19,201	8,857	13,700	21,336
Italy	57,190	40	1,018	17,796	18,681	6,948	11,290	19,710
Belgium	10,124	11	228	22,515	20,166	7,817	11,987	19,850
Netherlands	15,382	12	334	21,733	18,589	9,108	13,146	19,803
Luxembourg	397	1	14	35,281	29,454	12,714	16,593	28,262
EU(15)	349,023	329	7,344	19,798	17,914	7,879	11,693	18,923
US	260,651	515	6,650	25,512	25,512	12,259	15,724	23,123
Japan	124,960	44	4,590	36,732	20,756	5,005	12,161	24,810

Source: OECD (1996a) *National Accounts, 1960–1994*, Paris: OECD.

Note: U = United Germany.

traded and income payments. Visible, or merchandise trade, refers to trade in goods, and invisibles to all the other items. The latter includes trade in services described in Chapter 12. There is also the receipt of interest and dividends by British residents from their ownership of foreign assets, and the payment of these to foreigners because of their ownership of assets involved in production in the UK. Generally Britain earns more than she pays out, that is, she has a net positive balance of interest, profits, and dividends. In addition there are transfers, that is, payments made without any goods or services received in exchange. These include all foreign aid, both that provided by the government and that by private persons or agencies. They also include government subscriptions to international agencies and the EU. Transfers could be put into a separate account but in Britain they are included in the current account. The total balance of the current account must be equal and opposite to the balance of the rest of the account.

The other major account is of *investment* and other capital transactions which we will call the capital account. Within it certain subcategories are distinguished, such as direct investment, which involves some control of assets acquired abroad; in the UK this is defined as a holding of 20 per cent or more in a foreign enterprise. This is distinguished from portfolio investment, which is carried out just for profit. There is import and export credit associated with sales of goods and services. Then there is what is referred to as 'hot money', namely, the short-term international lending or borrowing that may involve speculation on the value of the currency or exchange rates. Finally there is the central bank's intervention in the market, that is, the Bank of England's net sale of foreign exchange to support the price of sterling in terms of other currencies and vice versa.

The sum of these transactions should be zero. However, there is generally a discrepancy, the net errors and omissions term, which is called the *balancing item*.

EARLY POSTWAR PERIOD

First, let us consider the changes in the macroeconomic environment in which Britain has been operating, although this is not the subject of this book. Britain emerged from the Second World War having had to sell off most of her foreign assets, the interest and dividends from which had paid prewar for a quarter of her imports. US finance in the form of Lend-Lease was stopped immediately the war ended in 1945. Britain desperately needed additional foreign exchange – in particular, dollars – to rebuild her war-battered economy, but found it very difficult to increase her supply of manufactures from factories in which there had been scarcely any investment in civilian production in the previous six years and, in some cases, for very much longer. In negotiating a loan with the US she had to accept a condition of convertibility for current account transactions. As a result of introducing this in 1947 she lost £50m of her foreign exchange reserves in a month before abandoning it (Pollard 1969: 360). This eventually led to a UK devaluation in 1949 from $4 to $2.8 to £1.

The US was the only large economy to be unscathed by the Second World War and was the source of investment goods badly needed for the rebuilding of war-devastated Europe. The US eventually realized how difficult it was for the Western European countries to earn enough foreign exchange to purchase such goods and in 1948 instituted the Marshall Plan. This Marshall Aid was allocated in accordance with the anticipated deficits of individual European countries, and was conditional on them extending aid to each other. The distribution of aid under this plan was carried out by the Organization for European Economic Co-operation (OEEC), which insisted that the European countries removed trade barriers between themselves as a condition of receiving aid.

From 1946 to 1958 US aid and government loans to Europe amounted to $25 billion (Maddison 1965: 162). The US also agreed to, and indeed encouraged European countries to discriminate against US goods in favour of imports from each other, as an additional means of alleviating the 'dollar shortage'. In the initial postwar period this is how Western European countries identified their balance of payments problems, that is, an inability to earn enough dollars to re-equip themselves.

THE BRETTON WOODS SYSTEM OF FIXED EXCHANGE RATES

This situation must be seen in the context of the system of fixed exchange rates which had been agreed at the conference at Bretton Woods in 1944. The conference had set up two financial institutions, the World Bank for Reconstruction and Development concerned with long-run loans for development, and the International Monetary Fund (IMF) concerned with tiding countries over short-run balance of payments difficulties. Each member of the IMF had to fix the exchange rate of its currency in terms of gold, or, in actual practice, dollars because the gold value of the dollar was fixed. It was allocated a quota which the member financed by supplying the IMF with a quarter in gold and the rest in its own currency. When the member was in balance-of-payments difficulties it could borrow against its quota, on increasingly onerous terms the more it wanted to borrow. It could only alter its exchange rate when it was in 'fundamental disequilibrium' in its balance of payments, which was not defined in the rubric.

Equilibrium in a country's balance of payments was initially thought of in terms of the 'basic balance'. This was the balance of autonomous items, transactions undertaken for their own intrinsic profitability and without regard to the state of the balance of payments, that is, not for the purpose of speculating on the value of the currency or acting against speculation.

They were regarded as including all current account items and long-term capital investment ('long-term' being defined as being held for longer than a year). A country was regarded as being in equilibrium in its balance of payments if the basic balance was zero, and in deficit if it was negative.

However, in the 1960s, because of the growing importance of export and import credit and the lengthening terms for which they were offered, it became increasingly difficult to distinguish between long-run and short-run capital movements, and eventually these were put together with the current account transactions and labelled the 'balance for official financing'. If this was negative, the balance of payments was in deficit, and the central bank had to use up its foreign currency reserves in order to prevent the currency from depreciating.

DEMAND MANAGEMENT

In setting their macroeconomic policy the governments of western indus-trialized countries were reacting against the high rates of unemployment of the interwar years. The macroeconomic objectives of the UK governments of all persuasions were to maintain full employment, to encourage and increase the rate of growth, and to keep down inflation. Keynesian theory implied that these could all be achieved if demand was controlled so that it did not exceed the productive capacity of the economy. Demand manage-ment was aimed at maintaining full employment. Indeed, for most of the 1950s and 1960s unemployment was very low, between 1.3 per cent and 4 per cent. Fiscal policy was regarded as the appropriate method of control-ling (consumers') demand. There was a disinclination to raise the rate of interest when demand appeared excessive because this would discourage investment and growth was regarded as dependent on investment. However, in practice, the rate of interest was raised when the country encountered balance of payments difficulties.

As the Western European recovery got underway Britain's problem then became one of her exports not increasing as fast as her imports. Her output was growing, but neither in total nor per head was it growing as fast as it was on the Continent. The constraint on the government raising the rate of growth appeared to be the balance of payments. An expansionary fiscal policy in the form of a reduction in taxation or an increase in government expenditure, or a lowering of the bank rate, to which monetary policy was geared at the time, could be used to induce an expansion in output. But very soon the country ran into balance of payments difficulties, that is, the combined deficits on the current and long-term capital account grew so large that it led to a speculation against sterling. The government's reluctance to devalue not only because of its adherence to the fixed exchange rate system of the IMF, but also because it did not wish to undermine the role of sterling as a reserve currency meant that devaluation was only undertaken as a last resort in 1949 and 1967. The general response was a raising of the bank rate and a contraction of fiscal policy. However, the type of policy pursued was also affected by the government's position in the electoral cycle; it would pursue an expansionary policy just before elections were due to take place, and then the successor government would have to take any corrective action required. Thus 'demand management' tended to produce fluctuations in economic activity, rather than smoothing them out.

THE OECD'S ANALYSIS OF ECONOMIC GROWTH 1955–68

The Organization for Economic Co-operation and Development (OECD) investigated why developed countries experienced such different rates of growth. Taking the period 1955 to 1968 it divided the economies of industrialized countries into three main sectors: (1) agriculture; (2) industry, which included public utilities and the construction industry plus the subsector, manufacturing; and (3) the service sector. It separated out the elements contributing to growth into, first, the expansion in overall employment, secondly, the shifts in employment between sectors, and thirdly, the growth in productivity within sectors. The contribution of these different factors to the overall growth in output of Britain, other European countries and the US is shown in Table 2.2.

Table 2.2 Factors affecting the growth of output, 1955–68 (percentages)

	Source of growth					
	Growth in employment	*Sector shift*	*Growth in industrial productivity*	*Growth in productivity in services*	*Growth in agricultural output*	*Total percentage increase*
Britain	5.0	2.0	20.1	10.0	1.4	38.4
EC(6)						
France	8.0	16.8	40.4	22.4	4.1	91.7
West Germany	10.1	12.6	44.0	15.8	2.3	84.8
Italy	−7.0	36.2	34.8	27.4	6.8	98.3
Belgium	5.7	7.5	27.7	15.9	1.5	58.2
Other European						
Austria	2.3	19.4	39.2	16.6	2.6	81.2
Denmark	21.1	17.9	15.4	16.0	4.6	74.9
Finland	5.0	26.8	26.2	8.0	4.0	70.0
Ireland	−0.4	20.5	20.2	18.1	7.5	65.9
Norway	6.7	16.5	23.7	25.2	−0.4	71.7
US	27.1	7.1	14.7	13.7	0.5	63.1

Source: OECD (1980) *The Growth of Output, 1960–1970*, Paris: OECD, p. 39, table 9.

The growth in employment (see Table 2.2, col. 2) depends partly on the increase in population of working age, and partly on changes in the rates at which the population of working age 'participated' in employment. Ireland, traditionally a country of emigration, had a negative rate; so did Italy for reasons that are not clear. For the other countries the rate was positive: in particular, it contributed 27 per cent to the US, a country of immigration. It contributed only 5 per cent to Britain's growth in output because, as mentioned in Chapter 1, her population was increasing very slowly, and because her participation rates were already very high with, for instance, more than 50 per cent of women of working age employed.

The distribution of employment between the different sectors in 1960 is shown in Table 2.3. Britain had by far the lowest employment in agriculture at 4.7 per cent compared with an average for the EU(15) of 21 per cent. In Italy it accounted for a third of employment and even more in Finland, Ireland, Spain, and Portugal. Britain appeared the most industrialized country with 48 per cent of employment in industry and 38 per cent in manufacturing. The next most industrialized was West Germany with 47 per cent and 34 per cent respectively. The average for the EU(15) was 40 per cent and 29 per cent respectively.

The contribution of the sector shift to growth is due to labour moving from sectors of low productivity to ones of high productivity. This was generally from the low productivity agricultural sectors to the industry and service sectors. As can be seen from Table 2.4, even by the end of the period (1968 for most countries) the productivity of the agricultural sector was much lower than elsewhere. Only in Britain and Belgium was agricultural productivity as high as in one or both of the other sectors.

The rate of change in employment by the different sectors between 1955 and 1968 is shown in Table 2.5. There was a decline in employment in agriculture throughout the developed world and the British rate of decline was similar to that in other European countries. Where did this labour go? Some of it went into industry, particularly in countries with low levels of industrialization in the first place such as Italy, Ireland and Denmark. But for most countries the greatest increase in employment took place in the service sector.

The total contribution of this shift in employment out of agriculture depends on how relatively low agricultural productivity was and also on the proportion of employment in the agricultural sector in the first place. It was therefore an extremely important source of growth to Italy, accounting for 36 per cent, and also to Ireland, Finland, and, to a lesser degree, Austria, Denmark, France and Norway (see Table 2.2, col. 3). Unfortunately, information is not available on all countries for Table 2.3. But such labour movements provided very little growth for Britain and Belgium because their productivity in agriculture was about the same as in the rest of the economy and, in any case, a very small proportion of employment was in agriculture.

Table 2.3 Distribution of civilian employment in 1960 and 1994 for the EU(15) (percentages)

	1960				1994			
		Industry				Industry		
	Agriculture	Total	Manufacturing	Services	Agriculture	Total	Manufacturing	Services
Original six countries								
West Germany	14.0	47.0	34.3	39.1	3.3	37.6	25.6	59.1
France	22.5	37.6	27.3	39.9	4.8	26.9	19.0	68.4
Italy	32.6	33.9	24.2	33.5	7.9	32.4	22.9	59.7
Belgium	8.7	45.0	37.7	46.6	2.9	28.9	20.7	68.2
Luxembourg	16.6	44.9	32.4	38.4	2.9	30.3	19.7	66.8
Netherlands	9.8	40.5	29.7	49.7	2.9	23.0	15.5	73.0
Entrants 1973								
UK	4.7	47.7	38.4	47.6	2.3	24.1	18.0	72.4
Denmark	18.2	36.9	25.1	44.8	5.1	26.8	20.8	68.1
Ireland	37.3	23.7	17.2	39.0	12.0	27.6	18.2	60.4
Entrant 1981								
Greece	57.1	17.4	11.6	25.5	20.8	23.6	15.3	55.5
Entrants 1986								
Spain	38.7	23.0	23.0	31.0	9.8	30.1	16.8	60.2
Portugal	43.9	31.3	22.6	24.8	11.5	32.8	20.4	55.7
Entrants 1995								
Austria	22.6	40.3	31.3	37.1	7.2	33.2	23.5	59.6
Finland	35.2	32.6	27.9	32.2	8.3	26.8	22.0	64.9
Sweden	15.7	40.3	31.5	44.0	3.4	25.0	17.3	71.6
Total EU(15)	21.3	39.7	28.9	39.0	5.5	30.1	20.2	64.2

Source: OECD (1992, 1996b) *Historical Statistics, 1960–1990, 1960–1994*, Paris: OECD.

Table 2.4 Value added per person employed in each sector as a percentage of GDP per person employed in the country as a whole in 1968

	Agriculture	Industry	Services
Britain	102.4	101.8	98.3
EC(6)			
France	48.7	114.9	104.4
West Germany	45.7	107.6	104.3
Italy	50.4	94.4	135.6
Belgium	100.4	94.2	105.0
Other European			
Austria	43.8	130.7	97.5
Denmark	72.8	106.4	102.2
Finland	60.3	117.4	110.5
Ireland	66.9	119.5	109.5
Norway	45.2	105.0	113.0
Greece	47.5	121.7	175.6
Portugal	60.6	120.1	115.8
Spain	52.0	93.9	152.5
US	68.5	116.8	93.8

Source: OECD (1980) *The Growth of Output, 1960–70*, Paris: OECD, table 8.

Table 2.5 Trend rates of growth of employment in total and by sector, 1955–68 (average annual percentage rates)

	Total	Agriculture	Industry	Services
Britain	0.5	−3.0	0.2	1.0
EC(6)				
France	0.3	−3.6	1.2	1.6
West Germany	0.6	−3.9	0.7	1.9
Italy	−0.5	−4.7	1.3	1.3
Belgium	0.4	−4.5	0.1	1.5
Other European				
Austria	0.1	−3.3	0.4	2.1
Denmark	1.3	−2.8	3.0	1.7
Finland	0.4	−3.7	1.3	3.3
Ireland	0.1	−2.6	2.8	0.8
Norway	0.4	−3.2	0.6	1.8
US	1.5	−4.1	1.0	2.4

Source: OECD (1980) *The Growth of Output, 1960–1980*, Paris: OECD, p. 31, table 5.

The OECD took the increase in output in agriculture as the extrapolation of a trend, independent of employment in it (see Table 2.2, col. 6). The rest of the increase in output was attributed to the growth in labour productivity in industry and the service sector (see Table 2.2, cols. 4 and 5). The growth in productivity is shown in Table 2.6. The growth in output per employed person was generally much greater in industry than services. The increase in labour productivity in industry was very much less in Britain, at 2.9 per cent per annum, than it was in most of the European countries. Therefore, although she had the highest proportion of employment in industry it only contributed 20 per cent to her growth (see Table 2.2, col. 4). Her growth in productivity in the service sector was also lower and therefore contributed only 10 per cent to her overall growth, compared with 27 per cent in Italy and 22 per cent in France.

Why was Britain's productivity growth so much lower? Did this in any way reflect her lack of membership of the EC? It should be pointed out that the productivity growth in industry of the other European countries shown in Table 2.6 appeared to be somewhat lower than those of the EC countries, but they were all greater than that of Britain.

Part of the divergence in the rates of growth of industrial countries can be attributed to their ratio of investment (I) to their GDP (Y), that is, the difference in their investment ratios I/Y, the proportion of income that they spent in increasing their productive capacity. In the period 1960–67, Japan invested a third of her GDP, most European countries invested around a quarter, but Britain invested only 17.8 per cent (OECD 1987). The OECD estimated the marginal return to capital to be 0.3, that is, £1 of investment

Table 2.6 Trend rates of growth of output per employed person, 1955–68 (average annual percentage rates)

	GDP	Agriculture	Industry	Services
Britain	2.4	5.8	2.9	1.4
EC(6)	5.0			
France	5.1	6.1	5.3	3.4
West Germany	4.4	6.1	5.0	2.5
Italy	6.0	7.8	5.8	3.7
Belgium	3.5	5.8	4.4	2.3
Other European				
Austria	4.5	5.1	4.4	3.1
Denmark	3.7	4.3	3.0	3.0
Finland	3.9	4.6	4.1	1.5
Ireland	3.3	3.3	3.4	2.2
Norway	4.1	2.5	3.9	3.4
US	2.5	5.4	2.9	1.7
Japan	8.6	—	—	—

Source: OECD (1970) *The Growth of Output, 1960–1980*, Paris: OECD, p. 35, table 7.

would lead to £0.3 extra output (OECD 1970: 257). Interestingly, a more recent study of growth suggests a similar elasticity of output with respect to investment of 0.33 (Crafts 1996). But this then begs another question: why was British investment so low? One explanation was that the share of profits in the earnings of business was relatively low and the gross rate of return on investment was low. So the situation was that the low rate of growth in Britain was partly due to her low investment ratio, which appears due to the low returns on investment, which in turn was ascribed to her low rate of growth – a vicious circle.

The other problem that emerged during the 1960s was a rising rate of inflation. During the 1950s and 1960s, external factors did not appear as an important contributor to inflation. The most important exogenous shock was at the beginning of the period in the form of the Korean War boom in commodity prices in 1951. Some economists regarded an increase in trade union militancy as an exogenous factor contributing to inflation. However, this is generally subsumed into the general problem of maintaining full employment.

Research by Phillips (1958) on UK data suggested that there was a trade-off between inflation and unemployment. The monetarists contested this, saying that this could only be obtained in the short run. In the long run, they argued, there was a 'natural' rate of unemployment and any government efforts to reduce unemployment below this would lead to constantly increasing inflation as workers built into their wage demands the existing rate of inflation. There appeared general agreement that this 'natural' rate increased during the 1960s, 1970s and 1980s, but there was no generally agreed explanation for this. Nor was there any explanation of why the 'natural' rate should have such a large regional variation.

Towards the end of the 1960s a number of developed countries were finding it increasingly difficult both to control inflation and to maintain balance of payments equilibrium. In the UK a large basic balance deficit mounted up during the election of 1964. The incoming Labour government endeavoured to correct it by reducing government expenditure and increasing taxation, but found it impossible to damp down the ensuing speculation against sterling and was eventually forced to devalue the pound in 1967 from $2.8 to $2.4. This put pressure on the dollar, and in 1971 the US concluded the Smithsonian agreement under which it devalued the dollar from $35 to $38 per ounce of gold but also removed its convertibility. Then, in 1972 Britain abandoned the system of fixed exchange rates and allowed the pound to float, with stabilizing intervention by the Bank of England. The US followed with a similar 'dirty float' in 1973.

In the 1970s the Organization of Petroleum Exporting Countries (OPEC), faced with a continuing rise in the price of imports of manufactures, which represented a decline in the real unit value of their exports of oil, began to use their power as a cartel to raise prices. There was a small rise in 1971, then a quadrupling of the oil price between 1973–74 after the Yom Kippur war, and finally a doubling from 1978 to 1980, followed by an erratic decline. Furthermore, by the 1970s, as will be described in Chapter 7, the industrial countries were very heavily dependent on imports of oil. The adverse movement of the terms of trade associated with the oil price rise from 1973 to 1974 represented a 2 per cent reduction in the real income of the Western European countries (Bank of England 1980). It threw into disarray their macroeconomic policies; on the one hand, they were anxious to maintain employment, while on the other hand, they wished to control inflation. The phenomenon of 'stagflation' was identified, that is, high inflation associated with high unemployment. One of the worst sufferers was Britain.

Britain had entered the EC at the beginning of 1973 and thus was simultaneously removing her tariffs on imports from other EC countries while imposing the Common External Tariff (CET) on imports from third (i.e. non-member) countries, and adjusting to the high price level of the Common Agricultural Policy (CAP), as well as to the rise in price of oil. For most of the period she had high but variable unemployment and high and erratic inflation. The Conservatives led by Margaret Thatcher, elected in 1979, made the reduction of inflation their top priority. The Keynesian approach of demand management was abandoned and monetarist approaches were employed. Initially, endeavours were made to control various measures of money supply but eventually reliance was placed on the rate of interest. The Conservative government, avowedly determined to reduce taxes, relied on its control of the Bank of England's minimum lending rate (bank rate), which set the level of interest rates throughout the economy, to alter the level of activity in the economy. An interest rate rise induces an inflow of lending from abroad which raises the exchange rate and therefore leads to a fall in demand for goods that can be exported and imported (tradeables). The higher cost of borrowing reduces the demand for goods purchased on credit, investment goods such as plant and machinery, and consumer durables. It also reduces the demand for mortgages and thus construction in the housing market. Initially, the level of inflation fluctuated and unemployment remained high. Monetarists have argued that the high rate of unemployment is voluntary or structural.

Margaret Thatcher's government was also determined to reduce the role of government in the economy. It reduced and eventually removed the deficits in the coal and steel industries by scrapping plant and reducing employment in them. It began a programme of privatization which led to most nationalized firms being sold to the private sector, as will be described in subsequent chapters. It also scrapped a large number of regulations governing employment, limited the trade unions' ability to strike, and forbade their engagement in sympathy strikes.

This did not appear to have any immediate effect in raising investment or growth. Indeed initially, as will be described, there was a dramatic fall in the output of manufactures. But, as the most laissez-faire economy in the EC from the mid-1980s, the UK did attract the most foreign investment, and in particular, 40 per cent of that from the US and Japan.

The slow rate of growth therefore continued even with successive governments declaring their intention to increase it, or boasting about how fast it had been increasing, as did the Prime Minister, Margaret Thatcher, as the economy emerged out of the deep recession of the early 1980s, and as the recent Prime Minister, John Major, did in comparing it with other European economies. Such claims simply show that the economy has not only expanded slowly, but also very erratically, as can be seen for the period 1960–94 in Figure 2.1. The total length of the bars shows the change in the monetary value of the British GDP from year to year. But most of this has been due to a rise in prices shown by the grey bar below the abscissa. Real growth is shown by the black bar; this has generally been positive, but in 1974, 1980–81, and 1991–92 it was negative.

Macroeconomic instability has therefore been a major feature of the British economy, particularly recently. But even earlier, in the 1950s and 1960s, because Britain was growing more slowly the fluctuations of output around trend appeared more disturbing than for other European countries. The instability appears to have affected some sectors of the economy more than others.

Growth rates both of total UK GDP and GDP per head of population have been lower than the average for the EU(15) and they have not improved over time. The OECD averages for the identifiable periods are shown in Table 2.7. The highest rates of growth were achieved for the earlier period 1960–73 at 3.1 per cent per annum on average for total GDP and 2.6 per cent for GDP per head. By 1989–94 they had dropped to 0.8 per cent and 0.4 per cent respectively.

Taking the period 1960–94 as a whole the UK's real GDP has increased on average at 2.3 per cent per annum, with the result that the British economy has doubled in size since 1960. However, this rate of growth is lower than that of the other industrial countries. Thus by 1994 the British economy was smaller than that of Germany and France, and the same size as that of Italy (see Table 2.1). It was only 15 per cent of the size of the US economy and 22 per cent of that of the Japanese when measured at current prices and exchange rates. Furthermore these relationships are not changed much by measuring them in terms of purchasing power equivalents. They indicate the decline in the UK's importance in the world economy.

However, if concern is with the standard of living – that is, income[1] per head of population – Britain's relative performance does not show up so badly, because, unlike other countries, the size of her population has remained relatively static, having increased by only 0.3 per cent per annum from 1960 to 1994. Her GDP Per head in 1994 at $17,468 was somewhat less than the EU average, and was 68 per cent of that in the US and 48 per cent of that in Japan at current prices and exchange rates. But if allowance is made for the purchasing power of different currencies differing from their exchange rates the disparity in per capita incomes between Britain and the other industrial powers is reduced (see Table 2.1).

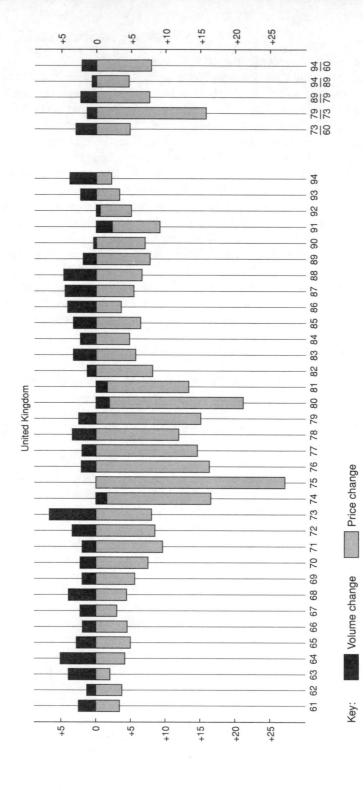

Figure 2.1 Changes in nominal GDP, real GDP and inflation: Year-to-year percentage changes
Source: OECD (1996b) *Historical Statistics*, 1960–1994, Paris: OECD.
Note: The increase in nominal GDP is given by the sum of the two bars

Table 2.7 UK and EU rates of growth, 1960–96

	Average yearly percentage increase						
	1960–73	1973–79	1979–89	1989–94	1995	1996	1960–94
Real gross domestic product (GDP)							
UK	3.1	1.5	2.4	0.8	2.5	2.2	2.3
EU(15)	4.7	2.5	2.3	1.3	2.5	1.6	3.1
Real GDP per capita							
UK	2.6	1.5	2.2	0.4			2.0
EU(15)	14.0	2.2	2.0	0.9			2.6

Sources: OECD (1996b) *Historical Statistics 1960–1994*, Paris: OECD, tables 3.1 and 3.2; 1995 and 1996 figures from Office of National Statistics, *Economic Trends*, No. 520, March, 1997.

In accounting for differences in economic growth the major problem for economists is how to model the process. Initially it was regarded as a function of investment, or rather the rate of accumulation of physical capital. Then there was the question of whether there were constant or diminishing returns to additional investment, which in turn determined how difficult it was to permanently increase a country's rate of growth. Sometimes it was also assumed that investment in new machines embodied new technology and thus raised the rate of growth even further. However, in contrast, technical change is often regarded as an exogenous factor. But when it became clear that a country's ability not only to innovate but also to adopt innovations depended on the skill and education of its workforce, the concept of capital became extended to include human as well as physical capital.

Nick Crafts (1996), taking the periods 1950–73 and 1973–92, calculated the growth rates of real income per head for the major European countries and three Asian ones (see Table 2.8). He calculated the actual growth rates over the two periods and then adjusted them to take account of the change in working hours. Over the period 1950–73 the UK had the lowest actual growth rate at 2.5 per cent per annum; it was half that of Germany and Italy and an even smaller proportion of that of Japan, Korea and Taiwan. When adjustment is made for the change in working hours the growth rate of the European countries goes up, that is, working hours have fallen; in other words, workers have taken some of the fruits of their increased earning power in the form of leisure. But in the Asian countries the reverse has occurred. This suggests that some of the growth in Asian countries was due to a reduction in underemployment, as has been argued elsewhere (Krugman 1996). The growth in the second period 1973–92 was lower for the European countries and Japan. The UK's actual growth rate declined to 1.4 per cent per annum, still lower than that of all the countries shown.

Table 2.8 Income levels and growth rates in some European and Asian countries, 1950–92

	Income per head ($)			Growth rate per cent per annum			
				1950–73		*1973–92*	
	1950	*1973*	*1992*	*Actual*	*Adjusted[1]*	*Actual*	*Adjusted[1]*
France	5,221	12,940	17,959	4.0	5.0	1.7	2.7
Germany	4,281	13,152	19,351	5.0	6.0	2.1	2.7
Italy	3,425	10,409	16,229	5.0	5.8	2.4	2.4
UK	6,847	11,992	15,738	2.5	3.1	1.4	2.2
Japan	1,873	11,017	19,425	8.0	7.7	3.0	3.1
Korea	876	2,840	10,010	5.2	4.1	6.9	5.2
Taiwan	922	3,669	11,590	6.2	5.6	6.2	5.3

Source: Crafts, N.F.R. (1996) '"Post-neoclassical endogenous growth theory": what are its policy implications?', *Oxford Review of Economic Policy*, **12** (2), table 1.

Note: [1] Adjusted growth rates allow for changes in hours worked.

In order to account for these differing rates of growth Crafts (1996) used the equation:

$$\dot{Y}/Y = a\ \dot{K}/K + b\ \dot{L}/L + TFPGR$$

where:

$\dot{Y}/Y$ = increase in income per annum;

$\dot{K}/K$ = increase in capital stock per annum;

$\dot{L}/L$ = rate of growth of labour, taking some account of quality as well as quantity of factor input growth, i.e. human capital inputs; and

$TFPGR$ = total factor productivity growth: the residual.

Applying this to the data, Crafts obtains the results shown in Table 2.9. Taking the average investment ratios over the period as shown in column 2, it can be seen that in both periods the UK with 18 per cent had a lower investment ratio than any of the other countries shown, although it was the same level as in the US. But because the UK had a lower capital stock the proportional addition to it was similar to that in the other European countries. Britain's TFPGR at 1.2 per cent from 1950 to 1973 is less than half that of the other countries and with France is the lowest at 0.6 per cent from 1973 to 1992.

Interestingly, nothing is said about the contribution to growth of the sector shift of labour out of agriculture, which was identified as an important component of growth of the continental European countries (apart from Belgium) by the OECD in its study of 1955–68, the results of which were shown in Table 2.2. In the Crafts study this would all come under TFPGR.

The most recent figures for 1995 and 1996 show the UK growth rates of GDP comparable with and in 1996 exceeding the average for the EU. This must be seen in the context of a general slowing down of growth in

Table 2.9 Crafts-accounting for growth

	I/Y^*	$\dot{K}/K$	Growth due to capital	TFPGR	$\dot{Y}/Y$
1950-73					
UK	18.3	5.5	1.6	1.2	3.0
France	23.8	5.3	1.6	3.1	5.0
Germany	26.9	7.3	2.2	3.3	6.0
Italy	24.6	5.2	1.6	2.5	5.0
Japan	32.6	10.2	3.1	3.6	9.2
1973 92					
UK	18.1	3.1	0.9	0.6	1.6
France	21.6	4.2	1.3	0.6	2.3
Germany	22.2	3.1	0.9	1.5	2.3
Italy	21.9	3.2	1.0	1.1	2.8
Japan	30.3	6.6	2.0	1.2	3.8
1966 90					
Korea	28.4	13.7	4.1	1.7	10.3
Taiwan	26.9	12.3	3.2	2.6	9.4

Source: Crafts, N.F.R. (1996) ' "Post-neoclassical endogenous growth theory": what are its policy implications?', *Oxford Review of Economic Policy*, **12** (2), table 2.

Note: * I/Y = proportion of income invested.

Europe and a general decline in investment ratios. This stagnation on the Continent is partly due to the other EU countries trying to meet the Maastricht conditions for monetary union. In Britain the boom appears once more to be associated with the run up to a general election. This was held in May 1997, but not withstanding the acceleration in economic growth it led to a fall of the Conservative government and its replacement by a Labour government pledged to keep a very tight control on inflation. One of its first moves was to raise the rate of interest by ¼ per cent to 6¼ per cent and then to transfer the responsibility for setting the rate to the Bank of England.

This book is mainly concerned with the sectors that are affected by international trade, that is, those sectors whose output is exported or competes with imports. These industries are competing with those of foreign countries both abroad and in the domestic market. Macroeconomic factors determine the terms under which they compete, that is, the exchange rate and their relative rate of inflation. If we assume that Britain is now small enough on the world stage not to be able to affect international prices, a devaluation of her currency will appear beneficial to the export industries, as the domestic price of her exports will have gone up by the same amount. It will also appear beneficial to her import-competing industries in so far as the price of imports will also have gone up by the amount of the devaluation. There will be an increased demand for her exports and import substitutes. This will expand output and lead to greater employment, but if the latter is above the 'natural' rate of employment it will also lead to inflation. Monetarists argue that this inflation will eventually offset the effect of the devaluation. Thus any benefits of devaluation will be short term and will have been achieved at the expense of output and employment in other countries.

This is one of the reasons that the government decided to join the EU's Exchange Rate Mechanism (ERM) in 1990. In so doing it limited the fluctuation of the sterling exchange rate in relation to other EU currencies. However, Britain's deficit on current account went on increasing, inflation remained high at around 4 per cent, and the massive speculation against sterling eventually forced her to leave the ERM in September 1992. Between 1992 and 1993 Britain's effective exchange rate fell by 8 per cent. But in relation to the Deutschmark it started rising after 1995 and now exceeds the level in 1992. Recent exchange rate rises (July 1997) appear mainly the result of speculation on further rises in the rate of interest as it is used as the main lever to control the expanding economy and inflation, which is regarded as its inevitable concomitant.

CHANGES IN ECONOMIC STRUCTURE

Construction, the industry with the least participation in international trade, has been the sector showing the greatest instability from year to year (see Figure 2.2). Taking an index of real output with the 1990 level as 100, it has fluctuated between the 1948 low of 41 and the maximum output it reached in 1990. The sector's fluctuations are almost entirely the result of government policy: on the one hand, the changes in government investment, which are largely accounted for by expenditure on housing and roads, and on the other hand, monetary and interest rate policy, which affects the private housing market. The construction industry has become an indicator of the state of the economy. This is because almost all the output of the construction industry is for the domestic market and virtually all its raw materials are purchased from it, and therefore the multiplier associated with it is high.

In Figure 2.2, indexes of the real output of the other major non-tradeable sectors are also shown from 1948 to 1996. Non-tradeablity is a matter of degree rather than an absolute definition. The indexes are based on relative production in 1990 and are linked backwards to 1948. Services, the main non-traded sector, have shown a fairly steady expansion, and since the mid-1960s their output has been growing at a somewhat faster rate than the GDP of the UK as a whole. In 1996 the output of services was three times its level in 1948.

The third non-tradeable sector is electricity, gas and water, the output of which has been increasing considerably faster than GDP; its output is now six-and-a-half times its level in 1948. These used to be public utilities but

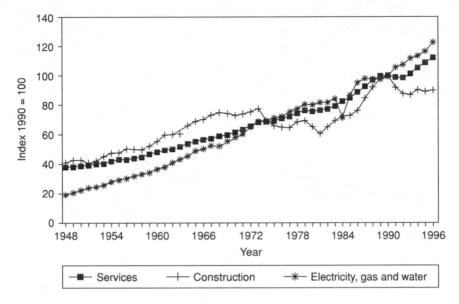

Figure 2.2 UK output of non-tradeables, 1948–96
Note: 1990 = 100.

now the industries have been privatized. Furthermore, as barriers to trade in services are lifted, in particular by the provisions of the Single European Market (SEM), and privatization is extended to the public sector in other EU Member States, these last two sectors are becoming increasingly open to trade.

The indexes of real output of the main tradeable sectors are shown in Figure 2.3. The output of manufacturing, the main tradeable sector, has not only been affected by UK macroeconomic policy but also by the preferential trade arrangements that she concluded, which will be discussed later in Chapters 3 and 4. Manufacturing output increased erratically from 1948 to reach a peak in 1973 and then equally erratically declined (see Figure 2.3). Between 1979 and 1980 it fell by 9 per cent and then by another 6 per cent by 1981. Many firms closed down. The level of manufacturing output in the early 1980s was at about the same level as the late 1960s; only after 1982 did it begin to increase, and only in 1988 did it reach the level of 1973. In the early 1990s, manufacturing output fell again, but then after 1992, partly as a result of the expansion of exports brought about by the devaluation associated with Britain leaving the ERM, it began again to increase. In 1996 it was 8 per cent above its level in 1973.

The output of the agriculture, forestry and fishing industry (which will generally be referred to just as agriculture) increased at about the same rate as GDP up to the 1960s. Then, after 1970, apparently in anticipation of entering the EU and the UK acceding to the Common Agricultural Policy

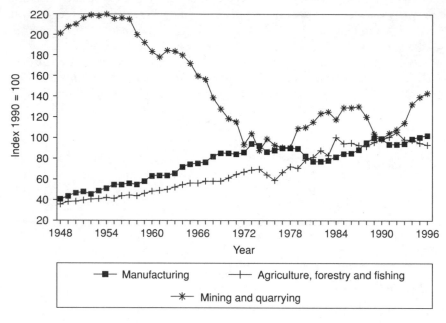

Figure 2.3 UK output of tradeables, 1948–96
Note: 1990 = 100.

(CAP), growth began to accelerate. There was a fall back in 1975 and 1976 and then its growth accelerated again to reach a peak in 1984. It exhibits a certain volatility associated with production which is heavily dependent on the weather. Recently it has been adversely affected by the BSE crisis. In 1996 output was 94 per cent of its level in 1984 and 52 per cent above its level in 1970.

The greatest changes have been shown by the last sector, mining and quarrying. The initial massive contraction from the early 1950s to the 1970s was due to the closure of the high-cost coal mines as Middle Eastern oil became available. Then, in the 1960s natural gas and oil were discovered in the North Sea. In the late 1960s the nation shifted to the use of natural gas in place of that extracted from coal. Oil also began to be brought ashore in the 1970s and OPEC's raising of its price of oil made North Sea oil more profitable to extract. As can be seen from Figure 2.3, there was a dramatic rise in output after 1978 such that it had increased by 43 per cent by 1987, but this was of gas and oil, as coal continued to decline. Between 1987 and 1990 output declined, but has now started to increase again so that in 1996 it was 44 per cent greater than in 1990.

These shifts in the use of energy resources have affected not only British growth, but also its specialization vis-à-vis the rest of the world. In 1960 three-quarters of energy consumption was of home-produced coal. Then there was the shift from the use of coal to imported oil as the Middle Eastern reserves were discovered and exploited at a falling real price (discussed in Chapter 8 and illustrated in Figure 8.10). By 1970 less than half total energy consumption was of coal, 5 per cent was of natural gas, and 45 per cent was of oil. All the oil and some other fuel was imported, such that in the early 1970s imports accounted for over half UK energy consumption. The OPEC price rises were an inducement to the development of supplies of North Sea oil and encouraged the further exploitation of natural gas. By 1981 Britain was a net exporter of fuel and by 1983 her net exports were equivalent to 18 per cent of her consumption. Since then her exports of oil have fluctuated, partly because of the reduction in production due to the Piper Alpha disaster. Since 1986 she has became a net importer of electricity on a minor scale. In total, in 1995 she was a net exporter of fuels equivalent to 17 per cent of her consumption. The energy sector accounted for 5 per cent of GDP and employment, and 8 per cent of total investment and 30 per cent of industrial investment.

However, this does not show up very well in the comparative work on structure carried out by the OECD because it is included in the larger category of industry. We have already considered the OECD analysis of growth from 1955 to 1968, before Britain joined the EC. What did not show up in that analysis was the phenomenon of de-industrialization that had begun to emerge in all the major European countries. The proportion of employment in manufacturing started to decline in the 1960s in most of the major Western European countries – the Netherlands after 1955, Britain after 1961, France after 1964, Germany after 1966 (Brown). However, as labour productivity in manufacturing was increasing very fast, approximately 1½ times the rate for the EU(15) economies as a whole, manufacturing output for EU countries other than Britain generally continued to increase; only in the 1990s has it clearly begun to fall. The price of manufactures has also not increased as fast as for other products. The general phenomenon of de-industrialization in terms of the proportion of employment and output provided by the manufacturing sector is illustrated for Britain in Figure 2.4.

In Britain, de-industrialization was intensified by her entry to the EC. Absolute employment in manufacturing declined precipitously over the three years from 1979 to 1982 when a fifth of manufacturing jobs disappeared. On average it declined from 1979 to 1989 by 3.3 per cent per annum and from 1989 to 1993 by 5.5 per cent per annum. Thus by 1994 industry in total accounted for only 24 per cent of British employment and manufacturing 18 per cent. This was considerably less than in West Germany with 38 per cent and 26 per cent respectively and below the average for the EU(15).

The sector that has grown in importance has been services. As a proportion of civilian employment in Britain it increased from 48 per cent in 1960 to 73 per cent in 1994. This is similar to the situation in the Netherlands.

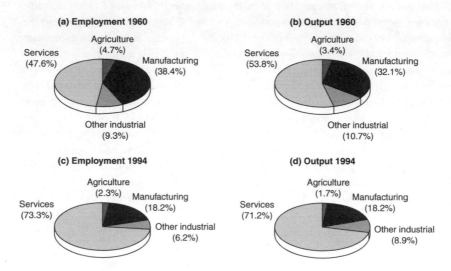

Figure 2.4 UK de-industrialization in terms of employment and output, 1960 and
1994 (%): (a) employment 1960; (b) output 1960; (c) employment 1994;
(d) output 1994

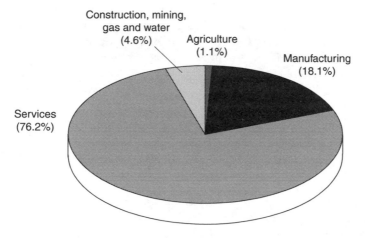

Figure 2.5 Employment in Great Britain in 1996 (%)

It has been the result of an absolute increase in service employment of 1.4
per cent a year compared with a decline in the other sectors.

The most recent more detailed breakdown of employment in Great
Britain[2] in 1996 is shown in Figure 2.5. Manufacturing accounts for 18 per
cent, construction, mining, gas and water 4.6 per cent, and agriculture a
mere 1 per cent. Great Britain is now overwhelmingly a service economy,
with 76 per cent of those in employment in that sector.

This long-run shift in specialization, with people moving out of agriculture and industry into the service sector and with a corresponding change in output of the different sectors, is a feature of many developed countries. Why should it be so important to Britain? Clearly in so far as it reflects a change in Britain's comparative advantage due to the development of North Sea oil the change is to be expected and may be welcomed. The problem then is that it may be a short-term bonanza. It may also be due to a lack of innovation by British firms. The change in her trading position may also reflect not only changes in her comparative advantage, but may be the result of government policy both internally and in the form of trade agreements with other countries. Furthermore, such policies have not necessarily had beneficial effects on either total real income or its distribution.

NOTES

1 GDP is here taken as a proxy for income as being more easily obtainable and measurable.
2 This excludes Northern Ireland, but as it is so small with less than 1 million employees it would not make much difference to the overall distribution.

REFERENCES

Bank of England (1980) 'The North Sea and the United Kingdom economy: some longer-term perspectives and implications', *Bank of England Quarterly Bulletin*, December.
Brown, C.J.F. (n.d.) 'De-industrialisation in the UK: background statistics', NIESR Discussion Paper No. 23, National Institute of Economic and Social Research, London.
Crafts, N.F.R. (1996) '"Post-neoclassical endogenous growth theory": what are its policy implications?', *Oxford Review of Economic Policy* **12** (2), summer.
Krugman P.R. (1996) *Pop Internationalism*, Cambridge, Mass.: MIT, ch. 11.
Maddison, A. (1965) *Economic Growth in the West*, New York: Twentieth Century Fund.
OECD (1980) *The Growth of Output, 1960–1980*, Paris: OECD.
—— (1987) *Historical Statistics, 1960–1985*, Paris: OECD
—— (1992) *Historical Statistics, 1960–1990*, Paris: OECD.
—— (1995a) *Regional Integration and the Multilateral Trading System: Synergy and Divergence*, Paris: OECD.
—— (1995b) *Historical Statistics, 1960–1993*, Paris: OECD.
—— (1995c) *National Accounts, 1981–1993*, Paris: OECD.
—— (1996a) *National Accounts, 1960–1994*, Paris: OECD.
—— (1996b) *Historical Statistics, 1960–1994*, Paris: OECD.
Phillips, A.W. (1958) 'The relationship between unemployment and the rate of change of money wage rates in the United Kingdom, 1861–1957', *Economica* **25** 283–99.
Pollard, S. (1969) *The Development of the British Economy, 1914–1967* 2nd edn, London: Edward Arnold.

3 The theory of trade, protection, and discrimination

In using the tools developed by economists to analyse the effect on a country of adopting protection or becoming a member of a preferential trading area it is essential to be aware of the vantage point taken. The traditional approach is to assume that the only international transactions are of trade in goods, and to compare a situation of protection or preference with an ideal allocation of resources, as under perfect competition and free trade. The latter is regarded as the world order in which output can be maximized with the available inputs and therefore one in which real income can also be maximized.

This has been modified to take account of imperfect competition, as, for instance, in calculating the effect of the introduction of the Single European Market (SEM) by the EU.

In addition, the overall impact on the balance of payments should be considered. This is particularly important in the EU because transfers are so important; 90 per cent of all tariff revenue and levies collected on imports from third countries has to be transferred to the EU Commission. It also receives a certain percentage of value added tax (VAT). In turn countries receive subsidies and grants under the Common Agricultural Policy and various development funds. If membership of a customs union leads to an increase in a country's deficit on current account the country will need to devalue. However, as Britain's entry to the EC involved a complicated change in her preferences, consideration of this will be left until Chapter 5.

Traditional theory

Let us begin our exposition with the orthodox approach to the consideration of protection and discrimination. The traditional rationale for free trade is the theory of comparative advantage, namely, that it benefits a country to specialize in producing the product in which it has a lower relative cost of production in relation to the rest of the world and to export it in exchange for a commodity in which it has a higher relative cost; by doing so, total world output and therefore income are increased. It is not absolute costs but relative costs that matter. The theory of comparative advantage can be illustrated with a very simple example, as shown below, taking two countries such as Britain and Australia, two products (wheat and cars), and labour as the only factor of production:

	Output per man per year	
	Wheat (tonnes)	Cars
Australia	10	30
Britain	12	60

Britain has a higher level of productivity than Australia in both lines of production, but her *comparative advantage* is in cars. Full employment is assumed, and therefore it is only possible to increase the number of cars produced by a reduction in the amount of wheat produced and vice versa. If one man were to be transferred from wheat production to car production in Britain, and two men were to be transferred from car production to wheat production in Australia, the world output of cars would have remained the same but there would be 8 more tonnes of wheat. It would therefore be possible for both countries to be better off than before, with Britain exporting cars in exchange for wheat from Australia.

The cost of other factors of production such as capital and land can be included by using the concept of opportunity cost, that is, the marginal cost of producing one additional item in terms of the amount of the other product forgone. In the above example the opportunity cost of producing a tonne of wheat in Australia is 3 cars (30/10), and in Britain it is 5 cars (60/12); therefore, as before, Australia has a comparative advantage in wheat production. We will generally assume that the opportunity cost of producing cars in terms of wheat forgone will rise as more cars are produced. However, we will also consider a situation in which there are economies of scale.

The ideal allocation of resources

The theory of comparative advantage remains logically irrefutable. It has been used in turn as a first step in the construction of international trade theory, only a section of which we will consider here. Most of this theory takes as the touchstone the ideal allocation of resources as represented by perfect competition. This ideal world is one in which there is perfect knowledge on the part of consumers and producers. Factors of production – let us assume for the moment only two, labour and capital – are generally assumed immobile as between countries, but perfectly mobile between industries within a country. With a given amount of capital in, say, the car industry, the number of extra cars an additional worker will produce is assumed to fall as more workers are employed (the law of diminishing returns). The wage paid is equated with the value of the product of the last worker – the marginal product of labour. In equilibrium the return to labour must be the same in both industries, otherwise workers would move to the higher paying one. These conditions ensure full employment. The cost of producing one more car, the marginal cost, is the additional payments that have to be made to factors of production to do so. Under perfect competition, producers are assumed to expand production of cars until the marginal cost of an additional car is equal to its price.

A consumer is assumed to expand his purchases of a product until the value of the last unit to him is equal to the value of the money he spends on it. The value of money is thought of in terms of its purchasing power over other goods. An industry faces the aggregate of consumer demands.

The simultaneous satisfaction of consumers and producers is achieved when the market price is equal, on the one hand, to the value consumers place on the last unit they purchase, and, on the other hand, to the marginal cost of producing it. This situation, with an equality between marginal cost and benefit, is regarded as an optimum allocation of resources.

Let us begin by considering a general equilibrium analysis in which the economy is considered as a whole and therefore also the interaction between the different sectors. In so far as we are concerned with the general change in specialization of the British economy, this analysis would appear to be the most appropriate. However, it is difficult analytically and requires a great deal of information. Later, therefore, we will consider a partial equilibrium framework in which the market in one particular product is considered and it is assumed that any changes in it do not have an appreciable effect on the rest of the economy. In that case it is possible to analyse the situation using market demand and supply curves.

General equilibrium analysis

In order to consider the situation diagrammatically we will take the initial model in which only cars and wheat are produced. The production possibility curve TT' in Figure 3.1 describes the outer limit of the country's production, along which it will be operating under perfect competition. The marginal cost of producing an additional car, in terms of the wheat forgone, is shown by the slope of the production possibility curve at this point; this is called the marginal rate of transformation (MRT). As can be seen from the diagram, it has been assumed that the marginal cost of production, or the MRT, increases as more cars are produced, that is, the production possibility curve has been drawn concave to the origin. Therefore, a country's comparative advantage depends not only on its production possibilities (i.e. its supply side), but also on whereabouts it is producing, which depends on domestic demand.

Domestic demand is introduced into the picture by the use of community indifference curves such as i_1, i_2, and i_3. Each indifference curve connects all combinations of cars and wheat between which the community would be indifferent; in other words, it represents a contour line of community

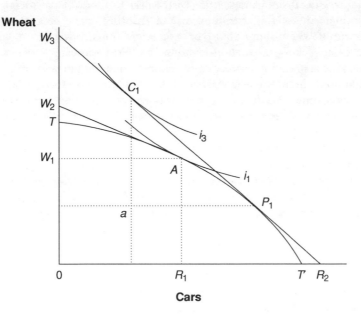

Figure 3.1 Production and consumption under autarchy and free trade

Notes:

Autarchy The highest community indifference curve the country can reach is i_1 at A. Production of OR_1 cars and OW_1 wheat is equal to domestic consumption. The domestic price is given by the slope of the price line W_2A which is equal to MRT, the slope of the production possibility curve TT', and this, in turn, is equal to the slope of the community indifference curve i_1 which touches it, which is the MRS.

Free trade The international price of cars in terms of wheat is equal to the slope of C_1P_1. The country can reach a higher indifference curve i_3 by increasing its production of cars and trading them for wheat. Its exports of cars equals aP_1 and imports of wheat are equal to C_1a.

welfare. The higher the indifference curve – that is, the further away it is from the origin – the greater the welfare it represents. It is assumed that it is logically impossible for the community indifference curves to cross. A community indifference curve map, therefore, is taken to represent levels of welfare and also to show the reactions of the community to changes in prices and incomes. There has been considerable controversy about the use of indifference curves in so far as they weight an additional £1 of expenditure equally as between consumers regardless of their incomes, and they also entirely ignore the effect of income distribution. However, they will be used, in spite of these drawbacks, because they are very useful tools.

The highest community curve that can be reached in the absence of trade will be the one that just touches the production possibility curve. At this point A, the MRT will be equal to the marginal rate of substitution (MRS), that is, the rate at which consumers are willing to trade the products at the margin. The equality is achieved through the market, with producers altering production until, for example, the extra cost to them of producing one more car in terms of the output of wheat that has to be forgone is equal to the rate at which these could be exchanged on the market, that is, the market price. Likewise, consumers adjust their expenditure until the amount of wheat they would be willing to trade to acquire an additional car is just equal to the rate at which they could be exchanged on the market. The market price before trade is therefore shown by the slope of TT' and the community indifference curve where they touch at A, that is, the slope of W_2A.

If the country then becomes open to foreign trade and the world market price is different from its previous domestic one, it can benefit by specializing according to its comparative advantage. In this case, if the relative price of cars on the world market, shown by the slope of W_3R_2, is greater than the previous domestic price, the country can benefit from *both* the reallocation of consumption away from the more expensive cars into cheaper wheat *and* specialization, that is, the reallocation of productive factors out of growing wheat and into the production of cars. The optimum point of consumption will be C_1, and the optimum point of production will be P_1, where:

MRT = MRS = international price of cars in terms of wheat

The excess production of cars, aP_1, can now be exchanged for aC_1 of wheat so that consumers can move from consumption at A to C_1. The move from indifference curve i_1 to i_3 represents an improvement in consumers' welfare, which can be measured in terms of either cars or wheat, and at either the pre-trade or post-trade prices. The greater its price of exports relative to imports – that is, the better its 'terms of trade' – the greater are the benefits a country derives from trade in comparison with autarchy. In Figure 3.1 the steeper the international price line, the higher the community indifference curve that can be reached.

Offer curves

From Figure 3.1 it can be seen that, given a country's production possibility curve, it has a comparative advantage in cars compared with the rest of the world, and that the better the terms of trade – that is, the steeper the international price line – the greater its specialization in cars and the lower its production of wheat.

The position of the country in relation to the rest of the world can also be shown by means of an offer curve $0R$ (see Figure 3.2). This is a general equilibrium device which shows how much a country is willing to trade at various prices. At the price given by the slope of $0E$, which is the same as that of C_1P_1 in Figure 3.1, it exports $0X_1$ and imports $0Y_1$, which are equal to aP_1 and aC_1 respectively in Figure 3.1.

What then determines a country's comparative advantage?

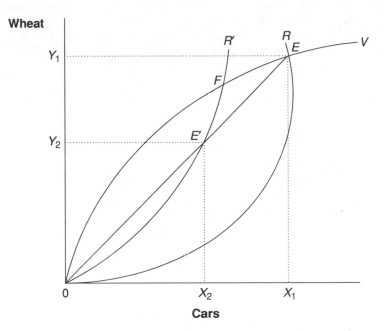

Figure 3.2 Offer curve of a country exporting cars

Explanation of comparative advantage

An important branch of international trade theory is the Heckscher–Ohlin theory, which explains the direction of a country's trade in terms of its relative endowment with factors of production. A country that is relatively well endowed with land will have a comparative advantage in wheat that uses land relatively intensively at any given factor prices. A country that is well endowed with labour will have a comparative advantage in labour-intensive goods, in this case cars. Factors are assumed to be of the same quality in the different countries. For the theory to be logically watertight it is necessary to assume that demand functions are the same in the different countries, and that the income elasticities for the products are one in order that differences in the relative demand for the products do not outweigh the relative factor endowment in determining what a country will trade. There must be perfect competition so that countries are operating on their production possibility curves and so that the returns to factors of production are equal to the value of their marginal products. Perfect knowledge is assumed and therefore that countries are operating on the same production functions. It must be possible to order commodities according to their factor intensity and there must be no factor intensity reversal, that is, it must not be possible for a product to be relatively labour-intensive at one set of factor prices and relatively capital-intensive at another. In the case where all the commodities continue to be produced in all countries – that is, there is no complete specialization – and the number of commodities (assuming more than two) is greater than the number of factors, free trade in goods will lead to factor price equalization; in other words, the return to labour and capital will be the same in each country (Samuelson 1949).

Thus the Heckscher–Ohlin theory connects the product market to the factor market and, as such, has provided a tool for analysing the effects of economic expansion in the form of an increase in the labour supply or an inflow of direct investment.

There have been criticisms of the Heckscher–Ohlin theory from a theoretical point of view, particularly with respect to the concept of a given return on capital, with which I shall not be concerned. There have also been various attempts to test it empirically, the most famous of which is that of Leontief (1968). He assumed there to be two factors of production, labour and capital, and took the relative capital intensity of products to be shown by the capital–labour ratios calculated from the input–output table of the US for 1947. This showed that US exports were relatively labour-intensive and her imports relatively capital-intensive, which appeared a paradox in so far as all economists were agreed that the US was relatively well endowed with capital compared with other countries.

There has been little econometric testing of this theory in relation to the trade of the UK, although her initial position, importing food and raw materials and exporting manufactures, would appear to be consistent with her factor endowment of having relatively little agricultural land and raw materials in relation to labour and capital. The free trade policy she pursued from the abolition of the Corn Laws in 1846 to the First World War would have maximized her income, and should have meant that the returns to her abundant factor labour and to a lesser extent capital should have been higher in relation to land than they would have been otherwise. Conversely, her subsequent protection of agriculture from the 1930s onwards would have been expected to raise the price of land and lower the return to labour.

Furthermore the discovery of North Sea gas and oil was equivalent to an increase in Britain's natural resource endowment. Under the Heckscher–Ohlin theory and the Rybczynski's theorem developed from it, with full employment and constant commodity prices and, therefore, factor prices, the output of the sector using this natural resource most intensively would be expected to increase and the output in the rest of the economy would fall (Rybczynski 1955). This situation in which the development of a natural resource has led to a decline in other sectors of the economy producing tradeables, notably manufactures, is often called the 'Dutch disease' as it was evident not only in Britain with the exploitation of North Sea oil, but also previous to that with the exploitation of natural gas in the Netherlands.

Another development of the Heckscher–Ohlin theory was to consider not only physical capital as a factor of production but also human capital, that is, the education and training of the workforce.

The problem in applying the Heckscher–Ohlin theory is that it is really a theory of specialization rather than trade: that is, it is concerned with a country's net exports or import position in relation to the rest of the world and the effect of this on the allocation of resources and the returns to factors of production. It provides no explanation at all for the rapid expansion of trade between industrial countries, often in goods which are classified as being of the same industry. The assumption of perfect competition precludes a consideration of innovation as part of the competitive advantage of a firm.

The question then is what is the cost of any deviation from free trade? Again this question can be broached in terms of either a general equilibrium or a partial equilibrium model. A common form of intervention is a tariff, and most other forms of intervention can be converted into tariff equivalents.

A tariff is a tax that discriminates according to the origin of the product. It can be quoted at a specific rate – a monetary value per physical unit of the product – or it can be stated in proportional terms. The latter, an ad valorem tariff, is generally used in economic theory.

General equilibrium analysis of tariffs

In a general equilibrium analysis, as previously depicted, because there are only two commodities the concern is with their relative price, not their money price. In that case a tariff on imports of, say, wheat has the same effect as a tariff on exports of cars. They both increase the relative price of wheat to cars.

Let us take the free trade price of cars in terms of wheat as shown by the slope of the line $W_4 P_1$, equal to that of $W_3 P_2$, in Figure 3.3. The initial point of production is P_1, and the initial point of consumption is C_1. Exports of cars are initially $a P_1$ and imports of wheat $a C_1$. A tariff on imports of wheat at a proportionate rate t raises the relative domestic price of wheat in relation to the international price. This, in turn, leads to an increase in the output of wheat at the expense of car production, with the point of production moving to P_2. The relative domestic price is shown by the slope of the line $W_2 P_2$. This appears to be the limit of consumption possibilities at domestic prices. However, as the country can still engage in trade on the international market, the boundary of actual consumption possibilities is given by the line $P_2 C_2$, the slope of which is equal to the international price.

Consumers will be operating on this line $P_2 C_2$, if the Meade assumption is made, namely, that tariff revenue is distributed back to consumers so that they are compensated for the loss of income which it entails. Then they will be at a point such as C_2 where their MRS equals the relative domestic price. Therefore, expressing the price of wheat in terms of cars:

Domestic price of wheat = international price of wheat $(1 + t)$

Wheat

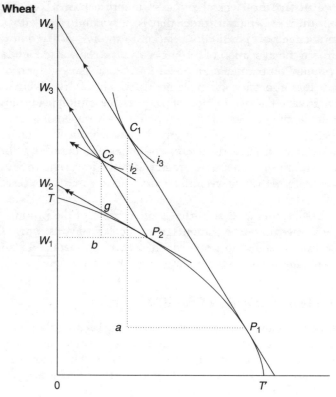

Cars

Figure 3.3 Consumption and production with free trade and a tariff

Notes:

Free trade The price of cars in terms of wheat is equal to the slope of C_1P_1. Exports of cars are equal to aP_1. Imports of wheat are equal to C_1a.

With a tariff on wheat and the tariff revenue redistributed back to consumers, the domestic price of cars in terms of wheat is equal to the slope of W_2P_2, and thus:

$$\text{the domestic price of wheat with the tariff} = \frac{W_1P_2}{W_1W_2}$$

$$\text{the international price of wheat} = \frac{W_1P_2}{W_1W_3}$$

Let the tariff be a proportion t. Then:

$$\frac{W_1P_2}{W_1W_2} = \frac{W_1P_2}{W_1W_3}\ (1 + t)$$

$$t = \frac{W_1W_3 - W_1W_2}{W_1W_2} = \frac{W_2W_3}{W_1W_2} = \frac{C_2g}{gb}$$

Exports of cars will be bP_2. Imports of wheat will be bC_2.

The tariff revenue in terms of wheat is C_2g. It is redistributed back to consumers. C_2b of wheat is imported in exchange for exports of bP_2 of cars.

However, this is not the only possibility. The government may require the revenue for projects of its own such as building an army or airforce; under this Lerner assumption the government is regarded as having its own separate preferences. It is also possible, as with the EC, that tariff revenue is not appropriated by a country's own government, but by an external organization such as the EC Commission.

From the point of view of the rest of the world the home country's offer curve appears to move inwards from $0R$ to $0R'$ as it is now willing to export and import less at any given international price (see Figure 3.2). If the country is small and therefore facing an infinitely elastic offer curve on the part of the rest of the world, this will not affect its 'terms of trade' which remain at $0E$; the equilibrium position just moves from E to E'.

But a large country which can affect the international price by changes in its own trade such that it is facing an offer curve on the part of the rest of the world of $0V$, will generally find that the effect of the tariff is to improve its terms of trade as depicted from the slope of $0E$ to the slope of $0F$. If the Meade assumption is made, consumers then benefit from the higher income this entails, while they lose from the economic inefficiencies at the margin that result from the tariff. The tariff is described as optimal when these two effects are equalized at the margin; at this point, the MRT is equated with the MRS and they are both equal to the *marginal* rate at which the rest of the world is willing to supply wheat for cars.

Partial equilibrium analysis

If we wish to consider a situation in which there are not just two but numerous commodities produced, the situation is best depicted using a partial equilibrium analysis. Let us assume that the country is small, that is, it cannot affect the international price. The market demand schedule D_H in Figure 3.4 represents the quantities of the product, say, wheat, that would be purchased by consumers at different prices assuming their income and tastes remained the same. Prices are given in monetary terms and are regarded as representing opportunity costs in terms of possible expenditure on other products. Consumers are assumed to go on purchasing the product until the value to them of the last unit is just equal to the price. The demand curve therefore also represents the valuation that consumers place on each of the units they purchase. The difference between their total valuation of the quantity they purchase, which is the area underneath the demand curve, and their actual expenditure, which is equal to the price times the quantity they buy, is called the consumer surplus.

There is also a domestic supply schedule S_H which shows the quantity that producers would supply at any given price (see Figure 3.4). Under competitive conditions producers will expand production until the extra cost of a unit of

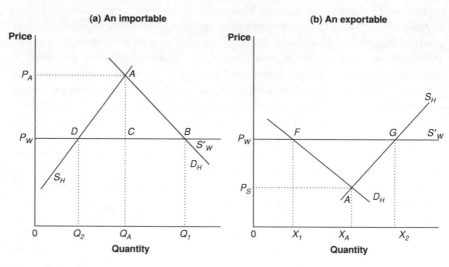

Figure 3.4 Self-sufficiency and free trade: A partial equilibrium analysis

output is equal to the price they receive for it. The supply schedule therefore traces out the costs of producing each unit of output. The area under the supply schedule to the point of production therefore represents the total cost of production, whereas the revenue earned is the price times the quantity produced. The difference between these is the producer surplus or profit.

With no trade, domestic demand must equal domestic supply. However, if the country becomes open to trade it then faces the international price. If the price on the international market is lower than the domestic self-sufficiency price P_A (Figure 3.4(a)), the product is one in which the country has a comparative disadvantage, that is, it is an importable. Assume that the foreign supply schedule to this market is infinitely elastic, say, S_W. As the country becomes open to foreign trade the domestic price will fall until it reaches the international price level P_W. This will lead to a reduction in domestic production to Q_2 and an increase in domestic consumption to Q_1. Imports will therefore be $Q_1 Q_2$.

In this partial equilibrium analysis the benefits of trade are considered in terms of the total changes in consumer and producer surplus. The consumers gain surplus of $P_W P_A AB$, whereas producers lose surplus of $P_W P_A AD$. Thus the net gain to the economy is ABD. This can also be considered as an efficiency gain due to $Q_2 Q_A$ being obtained more cheaply from abroad than at home at a saving in real resources of ACD, plus the consumer surplus gained on the increase in consumption of $Q_A Q_1$ of ABC.

In contrast the country is shown to have a comparative advantage in the product if the international price is above the self-sufficiency price P_S (see Figure 3.4(b)). Opening the country to trade leads to an expansion of production from X_A to X_2 and a contraction of consumption to X_1 with exports X_1X_2. There is a gain in producer surplus P_WGAP_S which is greater than the loss in consumer surplus P_WFAP_S, and therefore an efficiency gain.

Clearly, which commodities a country exports and imports will partly be determined by the foreign exchange rate, which translates international prices into domestic ones. We are implicitly assuming here that the exchange rate is such as to achieve balance of payments equilibrium.

The argument so far is that a country will benefit by moving from a position of self-sufficiency to one of free trade. The country benefits from the reallocation of production and consumption in response to the international price. The international price thus represents the opportunity cost, to the economy as a whole, of obtaining goods.

Partial equilibrium analysis of tariffs

The effect of a tariff on imports can be seen in Figure 3.5. Under free trade the price on the domestic market is the world price P_w. Domestic consumption is Q_1 and domestic production is Q_2 with imports of Q_1Q_2. If a tariff is imposed on imports of t in percentage terms or d in absolute terms with:

$$t = P_W P'_W / OP_W \text{ and } d = P_W P'_W$$

it appears to domestic consumers and producers that foreigners are now only willing to supply the domestic market at P'_W, that is, it looks as if the foreign supply schedule has shifted upwards to S'_W. Consumers and producers

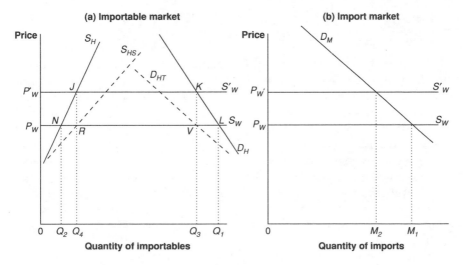

Figure 3.5 The partial equilibrium analysis of a tariff

respond by reducing consumption to Q_3 and increasing production to Q_4 respectively. Imports fall to Q_3Q_4, *both* because production has increased by Q_2Q_4 *and* because consumption has fallen by Q_1Q_3. The welfare cost of this is regarded as being the loss in consumer surplus of $P_WP'_WKL$. Set against this is the gain in producer surplus of $P_WP'_WJN$ and the gain of tariff revenue of $JKVR$. The net result is a welfare loss of the two triangles JRN, which is the additional cost of obtaining the extra output Q_2Q_4 from domestic sources instead of from the international market, and KLV, which is the consumer surplus lost on the reduction in consumption Q_1Q_3.

The impact of a tariff can also be considered as a combination of a subsidy on production, such as to shift the domestic supply schedule to S_{HS}, and a tax on consumption so that the demand schedule appears to have shifted to D_{HT}. The OECD has found this useful in presentating the degree of protection afforded by the wide variety of devices that countries use to foster their industries. It introduced the concepts of consumer and producer subsidy equivalents. A consumer subsidy equivalent (CSE) for a crop such as wheat is the difference between the world and domestic price paid by consumers multiplied by the quantity consumed C, which, if domestic prices are higher than world prices, is negative, plus any subsidy G they receive. A negative subsidy is a tax. The producer subsidy equivalent (PSE) is the difference between the world price and the price received by producers P_D multiplied by the quantity produced Q plus any net direct payments for production F; it is regarded as measuring the incentive effects of government intervention. The world price P_W is taken as the opportunity cost (OECD 1987). Thus:

Total PSE $= Q(P_D - P_W) + E = P_WP'_WJR$ in Figure 3.5(a)
Per unit PSE $=$ Total PSE$/Q = P_WP_{W'}$

Total CSE $= C(P_W - P_D) + G = -P_WP'_WKV$ in Figure 3.5(a)
Per unit CSE $=$ Total CSE$/C = P_WP_{W'}$

An alternative presentation of this situation is to look solely at the import market (see Figure 3.5(b)). The demand schedule for imports D_M is obtained by taking what would be domestically supplied from the amount that would be domestically demanded at each price. Thus the price elasticity of demand for imports – the percentage change in quantity of imports demanded for a 1 per cent change in price – is greater than the elasticity of demand for the product itself (see Appendix 3.1). The foreign supply schedule is the same as before. With free trade the domestic price is the same as the international price P_W, and imports are $M_1 = Q_1Q_2$ in Figure 3.5(a). As before, the foreign supply schedule appears to rise with the imposition of a tariff in accordance with it, reducing imports to $M_2 = Q_3Q_4$ in Figure 3.5(a).

However, if the country imposing the tariff is facing an upward-sloping supply schedule on the part of the rest of the world, the tariff makes it appear to the latter as though the import demand for the product had fallen. The price in the home market does not go up by the full amount of the tariff because the foreign supplier is forced to pay part of it (see Appendix 3.1).

A minimum import price

A variation on a tariff is a minimum import price. This system of protection is used in the Common Agricultural Policy and also in some of the anti-dumping agreements entered into by the EU. The situation is illustrated in Figure 3.6. With domestic supply and demand schedules of S_H and D_H and the world supply schedule S_W as before, if the tariff distorted price is $P*$ consumption will be Q_3, home production Q_4, and imports will be Q_3Q_4 with tariff revenue *ABCD*. But in this case the minimum import price $P*$ is fixed regardless of the price on the world market. So long as the country or EU remains an importer it ensures absolute domestic price stability. Changes in the world supply schedule – for instance a movement from S_W to S_W' – do not affect the domestic price. It only affects the tariff revenue, in this case reducing it to *ABFE*. By removing all response of the domestic market to changes in world prices, a minimum import price contributes to instability on the international market.

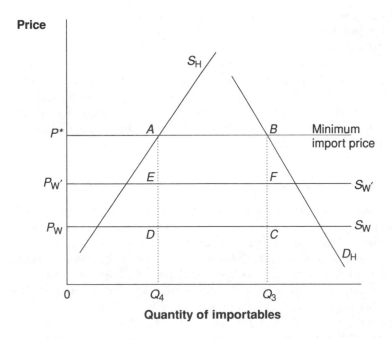

Figure 3.6 A minimum import price

Imposition of a quota on imports

An alternative form of protection is by the imposition of a quota, that is, a physical limit on imports. To have any effect a quota must reduce the quantity of imports below their free trade level. The situation is described in more detail below in 'The analysis of quotas under a preferential system'. It has similar effects to the imposition of a tariff, and the proportional rise in price is described as the tariff equivalent of the quota, except that as a tariff has not been imposed, the government does not automatically gain tariff revenue. Who gains the surplus due to imports being supplied at a lower price than they are sold on the home market depends on the institutional arrangements.

There was a shift away from the imposition of tariffs to 'voluntary' export restraints, which were negotiated bilateral quotas, in the 1960s, 1970s and 1980s, even though it increased the welfare loss to a country because of the loss of tariff revenue. This was partly because industrialized countries tied their hands by their rounds of tariff reductions under GATT. Industries also appear to prefer quota protection because it insulates them against the downward shift in foreigners' supply schedules.

The beneficiaries of protection

So far we have taken a simple supply schedule for which factors of production and also raw materials have been assumed implicitly to be obtained domestically. But which factors of production benefit most from protection? The argument is that it will always be the factors in the most inelastic supply to the industry (Corden 1971). For agriculture it will be par excellence land; that is, the benefits of agricultural protection are always capitalized in higher land prices. Labour hardly benefits because its supply to the agricultural industry is very elastic. For manufacturing, the most inelastic factors are likely to be labour with non-transferable skills and industry-specific capital, the owners of which benefit.

Product differentiation

We have thus far considered the analysis of industries producing fairly homogenous products such as wheat. In a competitive market, differences in quality are reflected in price differentials, but these are not associated with any particular producer. But say, as is the case with branded manufactures, that each type of good is associated with an individual producer so that he or she is faced with their own individual demand curve. The elasticity of the demand schedule will depend on how substitutable consumers regard the output of different producers in the industry. Monopolistic competition is the term used to describe the situation of a large number of producers. Oligopoly with price differentiation is the term used to describe a market with few producers where each producer has to take the reaction of the others into account when setting his or her price or output.

In the analysis of the effect of a tariff the differentiation is generally taken to be associated with the origin of the goods. Let us assume that consumers regard imported TVs as distinct from EU-produced ones. If a tariff is imposed on imported TVs their price will go up by the amount of the tariff if they are in infinitely elastic supply. This will lead to an increase in demand for home-produced ones. The increase in price of the home-produced TVs will depend on what proportion of home sales they account for and the elasticity of supply of home producers and demand for home-produced goods. If the elasticity of supply of foreign producers is less than infinite the price of imports will go up by less than the tariff, that is, the foreigner will be forced to pay for some of the tariff in the form of lower prices.

Effective protection

The other problem is that trade takes place not only in final goods but also in the intermediate goods used in their production. Assuming that the world supply of the intermediate good is infinitely elastic, its cost to the industry will be the tariff-distorted world price. The whole benefit of protection will then go to the factors of production employed in the later stages of processing. Let us say that the world price of a passenger car is £6,000 and it requires £2,000 of imported components. If the tariff, the nominal rate of duty, on cars is 20 per cent, and on components is 10 per cent, then the domestic price of a car with protection will be £7,200 and the price of the components incorporated into it will be £2,200. *The effective rate of protection* – that is, the increase in the value added by car manufacturers because of the protection – will be £(7,200–2,200) – (6,000–2,000) = £1,000. Divided by the free trade value added of £4,000 this represents an 'effective rate of protection' to the car manufacturers of 25 per cent, higher, it might be noted, than the nominal tariff of 20 per cent. It would only be the same if the nominal rate on the car and components were the same. But there is a tendency for tariffs or tariff equivalents on manufactures to increase with the degree of processing. Tariffs on raw materials have generally been very low or zero.

These aspects of protection, namely, product differentiation and trade in intermediate products, we will bear in mind, although it is too complicated to include them in the succeeding discussion on preferential trading.

Preferential trade agreements: Partial equilibrium analysis

A preferential trading area is one in which members give each other special privileges that they do not extend to third (i.e. non-member) countries. Generally these privileges consist of having no import duties or quotas placed on your exports to another member: that is, barriers on trade between member countries are removed.

If a common external tariff (CET) is imposed on imports from outside the area, as for the EU, the preferential area is a *customs union.*

If each member country is allowed to decide its own level of tariff on imports from third countries, the preferential area is a *free trade area.* In order to avoid all imports coming through the member countries with the lowest external tariff, such an agreement limits free trade status to member countries' products. These are specified by its rules of origin. In the European Free Trade Area (EFTA), a product was accorded free trade status if 50 per cent of its value was accounted for by production within EFTA or certain processes had been carried out within EFTA.

Although customs unions and free trade areas (FTAs) appeared to conflict with the principle of non-discrimination, they were favourably regarded as leading on to greater liberalization of trade. But under Article XXIV of GATT they were required to comply with certain provisions; they should cover 'substantially all the trade between constituent territories', 'the (external) duties . . . shall not on the whole be higher or more restrictive than . . . prior to the formation of such a union' and they 'shall include a plan and schedule for [their] . . . formation within a reasonable length of time' (GATT 1986a).

The formation of a customs union or free trade area was initially regarded as a movement towards free trade. But Viner pointed out that it also included an element of greater discrimination between member and non-member countries. He distinguished two aspects of the situation. First, one in which production is transferred from a higher-cost to a lower-cost source of production, from, say, the home country to the partner country because tariffs have been removed from the latter country's products; this he termed 'trade creation'. The second occurs when production is transferred from a low-cost source to a higher-cost source of production, from, say, a third country to a partner country because tariffs are no longer imposed on products from the latter; this he termed 'trade diversion'. Trade creation he regarded as always beneficial, and trade diversion as detrimental (Viner 1950). This is to look at benefits and costs entirely from the production point of view – he assumed that the commodities were always consumed in the same proportion. It was left to Lipsey to point out that there was also a consumption angle. Indeed, consumer benefits occurred in both cases and might even outweigh the losses in the case of trade diversion (Lipsey 1957).

The effect on the market for a particular importable of a country becoming a member of a free trade area or customs union will be illustrated with a diagram used by Kindleberger (1973) (see Figure 3.7). The country is assumed to be 'small' and therefore faces an infinitely elastic supply schedule from the rest of the world S_W; with a tariff $P_1 P_2$ or at a rate $P_1 P_2 / O P_1$ this appears as S_W'. The partner B's supply schedule is also assumed infinitely elastic at S_B; with a tariff it would be above S_W', and is not shown. The domestic

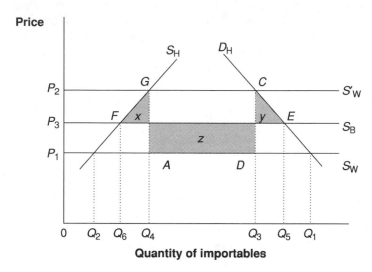

Figure 3.7 Trade creation and trade diversion

supply schedule is assumed to be upward sloping. The domestic demand schedule is D_H. Consumers are assumed not to differentiate according to the origin of the product.

Before the formation of the customs union, all imports come from the rest of the world, as they appear the cheapest. The price on the domestic market is equal to the world price P_1 plus the tariff P_1P_2 and is thus $0P_2$. Consumers purchase a quantity $0Q_3$ and the output of domestic producers is $0Q_4$. Q_4Q_3 is imported from the rest of the world, requiring a foreign exchange expenditure of ADQ_3Q_4 and providing a tariff revenue of $GCDA$.

If a customs union or free trade area is formed, the tariff is removed on the partner's goods but not on those from the rest of the world, and thus goods from the partner country appear cheaper at $0P_3$. If P_3 is less that P_2, prices on the domestic market fall. All imports are then acquired from the partner country and are greater at Q_6Q_5. There is therefore a diversion in the purchase of imports of Q_4Q_3 from non-members to the partner country. There is also trade creation of Q_6Q_4 which is now supplied by the partner country instead of domestic producers. In addition, there is an increase in consumption of Q_3Q_5 which is supplied by the partner country. There is a gain in consumers' surplus of P_2CEP_3 and a loss in producers' surplus of P_2GFP_3 due to the lower price, and also a loss in tariff revenue of $AGCD$. In total this is equal to a net gain of $x + y - z$. z can be regarded as the cost of trade diversion, that is, of transferring purchases from a low-cost producer W to higher-cost producer P. x and y are the familiar efficiency gains obtained from the reduction in tariffs.

Cooper and Massell (1965) challenged the assumptions underlying this particular argument. The comparison was being made between the pre- and post-customs union's position in order to assess whether it was beneficial. They argued that a comparison should be made between a discriminatory reduction of tariffs, as in a customs union and free trade area, and a non-discriminatory removal of tariffs. A non-discriminatory removal of tariffs was always superior and avoided any trade diversion.

Nevertheless, most economists carrying out applied work have continued to use the original framework and compared the situation of the country before and after it joined the customs union. This, then, is a theory of second best. It is clear from looking at Figure 3.7 that the benefits are likely to be greater the higher the original level of the tariff and thus the greater the size of x and y. The losses due to trade diversion are likely to be lower the smaller the differences in the costs of production between the partner countries and third countries – in the diagram the smaller the difference between the supply schedules of the partner country and the rest of the world and therefore the smaller z.

Initially, a union between complementary economies – that is, ones producing a different range of products – was regarded as the most beneficial. However, Viner argued that such a union would provide the least scope for trade creation and the most for trade diversion. But with a union of competitive economies, producing the same range of products, there is scope for the low-cost producers to oust the higher-cost producers when barriers to trade are removed (i.e. trade creation). The benefits of such trade creation will be greater the greater the difference in costs between the two countries.

Greater realism can be introduced by dropping the assumption of an infinitely elastic supply schedule of the partner country. The implicit assumption in the previous analysis, that the CET was the same rate as the previous tariff, can also be dropped. In that case, the country with the higher tariff is assumed to have the higher marginal cost, because producers are assumed to produce to the point at which their marginal costs are equal to the tariff-distorted price.

Let us analyse the situation for a preferential agreement between two countries, the home country H and partner country B. Let us assume that marginal costs of production are greater in H than in B, corresponding to the higher level of protection in the former. Let us also make Robson's simplifying assumption that at the initial level of protection in P it is just self-sufficient. We will follow Robson's analysis and consider the final price and equilibrium that is established, the changes in welfare, and the effect on trade with the rest of the world (Robson 1984).

Free trade area

Each member country can retain its previous tariff on imports from outside the area. However, it is now possible for H, with a high tariff at a rate $TT_H/0_H$ and price level initially at $0_H T_H$, to import goods duty free from the lower-

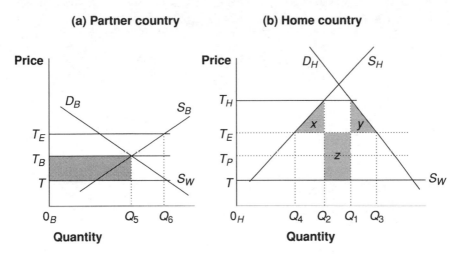

Figure 3.8 A free trade area

priced B with an initial price level $0_B T_B$. The maximum that H can import from B will be the whole of the latter's *production*. The price in H will come down to the world price plus tariff in B, $0_B T_B$, if B's production is greater than the amount H wishes to import at that price. The excess demand of B's consumers will be supplied by imports from the rest of the world.

The overall effect depends on the relationship between the supply schedule of B, S_B, and the import schedule (demand minus supply) of H. If equilibrium can only be achieved at a price above that initially existing in B, such as T_E as shown in Figure 3.6, then B's producers will expand output from $0_B Q_5$ to $0_B Q_6$ and will gain from extra profits; the consumers will purchase $0_B Q_5$ as before because they can import any amount at the world price plus tariff $0_B T_B$. Tariff revenue will be earned, indicated by the crosshatched area, due to switching consumption from home to third country sources.

The net effect in the home country is that it obtains the efficiency gains of x and y due to the trade creation and consumption effects respectively, but with the loss of z due to the trade diversion effect of obtaining $Q_2 Q_1$ imports from the partner country rather than from the rest of the world.

As the partner country now imports $0_B Q_5$, the imports of the free trade area as a whole from the rest of the world have increased by $0_B Q_5 - Q_2 Q_1$. There has been trade creation through the intermediation of the partner country. Only if B cannot supply all H's requirements, even at price T_H, will H continue to import from third countries.

Customs union

To comply with GATT rules the level of protection in a customs union should be no greater than before. Thus the EC decided to set its CET at

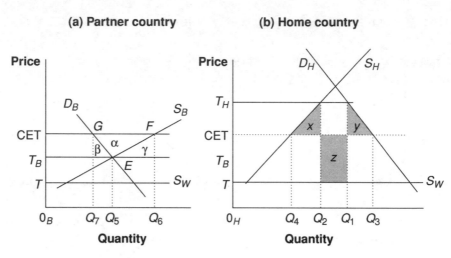

Figure 3.9 A customs union

the arithmetic average of the previous tariffs of member countries. This therefore raised the level of protection against third countries in those members with liberal trade regimes and lowered it in the more protectionist ones.

Let us return to the analysis of the two countries and assume that the CET is the average of previously existing tariffs (see Figure 3.9). The ceiling price becomes that at which imports can enter – that is, the world price plus CET – throughout the union, which is shown as CET in Figure 3.9.

In the home country H with the high level of tariffs the reduction in apparent price of imports from $0T_H$ to the CET level will lead to an increase in imports from Q_2Q_1 to Q_4Q_3, all of which will now be obtained from B, the partner country. This will lead to the familiar trade creation gain of x and consumption gain of y, and the trade diversionary cost z of transferring Q_2Q_1 purchases from the rest of the world to B.

In B, the partner country with initially low tariffs, prices will rise due to increased protection. The gain in producer surplus will be greater than the reduction in consumer surplus, leading to a net gain α. Although there will be marginal efficiency losses of β and γ. The ruling price will be at the ceiling CET price if B cannot supply, or can only just supply the amount required by the home country, $Q_6Q_7 = Q_4Q_3$. In the former case, there will be fewer imports from the rest of the world, and none in the latter. However, the equilibrium price may be below the ceiling, with B supplying all the imports of H and cutting out all imports from the rest of the world.

This analysis suggest that customs union is inherently more likely than a free trade area to reduce trade with third countries. This is because of our assumption about the CET, which although it reduces protection in one country raises it in another, whereas in a free trade area the trade deflection effect lowers the price in the highly protected market without increasing the price to consumers in the other.

The analysis of quotas under a preferential system

Figure 3.10(a) and (b) illustrates the situation for a non-discriminatory impo-sition of a quota on imports, that is, the multilateral situation. Let us assume for the sake of simplicity that the importing country H is small and there-fore cannot affect the world price $0P_W$. With a home supply schedule S_H, and demand schedule D_H, the resulting demand schedule for imports, the difference between demand and supply at domestic prices, is D_M. With free trade, domestic consumers and producers are operating at the international price; $0Q_2$ will be supplied and $0Q_1$ consumed and $Q_2Q_1 = 0M_1$ will be imported from what we will take to be a traditional supplier T. To be effec-tive any quota must be smaller than the present level of imports; let it be equal to $Q_2Q_3 = Q_5Q_4 = 0M_2$. The aggregate supply schedule on the domestic market becomes S_A and in terms of imports S_M. This reduction in imports raises the price on the domestic market to P_Q.

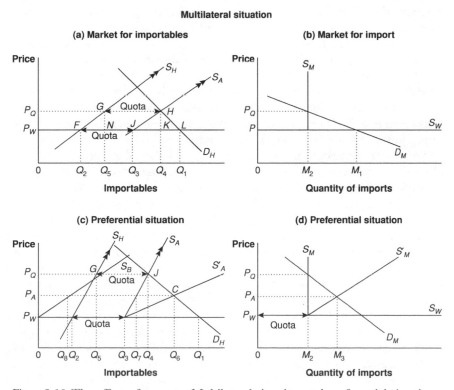

Figure 3.10 The effect of a quota: Multilateral situation and preferential situation

From the point of view of the exporting country it has lost in quantitative terms $Q_3Q_1 = M_2M_1$ of exports, Q_4Q_1 because of a reduction in consumption, and $Q_3Q_4 = Q_2Q_5$ because of trade diversion, that is, the substitution of higher-cost home country production for its exports. The price on the domestic market is higher and this provides an economic rent associated with the quota of *GHKN*. This is the surplus value of imports on the home country market over and above the opportunity cost of procuring them on the world market. It is generally assumed, because the US and EC allocate the quotas they impose on imports from developing countries to the governments of those countries, that the latter gain the economic rents associated with them. This provides the developing countries with some compensation for the reduction in the physical quantity of their exports. Indeed, if the elasticity of demand for imports was -1, their foreign exchange proceeds would be the same as before.

Now let us modify this scenario to allow for another trading partner *B* in a preferential position with respect to *H* (see Figure 3.10(c) and (d)). Let us assume that *B*'s costs are so high that it does not export at world prices; its supply schedule is shown by the line P_WS_B. Now if the quota is imposed on imports from the traditional supplier, as before, the aggregate supply schedule S'_A is more elastic because of supplies from the partner country, and therefore the equilibrium price P_A is lower than before. In this case, in comparison with the non-preferential situation there is less of a reduction in consumption. The increase in the production of the home country is lower, at Q_3Q_7, but there is also an increase in output of the partner country of Q_7Q_6; in other words, there has been a reallocation of production not only to the home country, but also to the partner country. Exports from the traditional supplier are not only limited by the quota, but it also gains a lower economic rent from the quota than before, $P_AP_W \times$ quota instead of the previous $P_QP_W \times$ quota.

To make the situation more realistic we could also allow for the existence of tariffs. If these tariffs are not imposed on imports from *B* this acts as an additional element of discrimination in favour of imports from *B*. Let us assume for the sake of simplicity that the tariff is at a rate of $P_WP_A/0P_W$. In that case, the equilibrium price and the quantity of imports from the traditional exporter *T* and the partner country *B* are the same as before, but the whole of the quota rent is creamed off by the government of *H* in the form of tariff revenue. If the tariff is any lower the quota is the effective restraint, but some of the rent from the quota is creamed off. If the tariff is any higher it becomes the effective restraint and there is no quota rent. The higher the tariff above $P_WP_A/0P_W$, the higher the price on the domestic market of *H* and the more the partner country's products are substituted for those of the traditional supplier. Consumers and producers in *H* are only concerned with the rise in price on their domestic market, that is, in percentage terms, the tariff equivalent of the effective constraint. It might be noted that the protective effects of a tariff and a quota are not additive.

These comparisons are all implicitly made with a free trade position. The analysis gives an indication of the relative effects of different forms of intervention.

ECONOMIES OF SCALE

It is widely held that an additional benefit from the formation of customs unions is that they enable firms of member countries to further exploit their economies of scale. Scale economies exist if average costs fall in the long run, when a firm increases its output by investing in greater productive capacity, that is, by increasing its scale of operations. There may also be economies of scale external to the firms that are associated with the expansion of the industry, such as the greater ease of marketing products.

The general approach in the theory is to assume that the firm discussed has only one plant and is the sole domestic producer of the product. Implicitly, the economies of both plant and firm are being considered.

Traditional analysis – model T

With the traditional analysis technological knowledge and the price of factors of production are assumed constant. The firm is faced with two exogenous prices: on the one hand, the world price at which it can export the product; on the other hand, the tariff-distorted price at which products can enter the market from abroad. These represent its minimum and maximum prices respectively (Mead 1968; Corden 1972).

The general argument is that if the country's average cost curve falls below the world price, then it will expand production and export and will not need a preferential system to exploit economies of scale. Therefore this situation need be discussed no further. On the other hand, if costs are above the tariff-distorted price, the market will be supplied by imports.

A customs union will only enable a firm, in, say, country H, to exploit economies of scale if its costs of production lie between the world price and the CET-distorted price, and this will represent the degree of economies of scale that can be exploited. When H forms a customs union with B it appears to the firm in H as if its home market has been expanded because of B's removal of tariffs. It can therefore expand its output, moving down its average cost curve. The equilibrium position is difficult to identify. Because the marginal cost is falling, the rule of profit maximization adumbrated above is difficult to apply; at the point where marginal cost equals marginal revenue no profits may be being earned. The price must fall between two extremes: either (1) that of average cost pricing at which no supernormal profits are earned, that is, the firm is just earning enough to stay in the industry; or (2) a firm will maximize it profits by charging the maximum price, that is, the price at which the product from abroad will just enter. If it can cover costs at this price it will produce, otherwise it will not.

The lower the price and the nearer the firm gets to (1), the greater the exploitation of economies of scale and the more consumers benefit. If, on the other hand, the firm charges the maximum price as in (2), the consumers do not benefit at all.

Let us consider two possibilities: first, the situation in which country H produces the good and country B does not; and secondly, one in which both H and B have producers before they form a customs union.

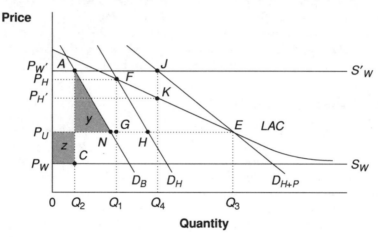

(a) Prior-to-entry production in home country (*H*) only

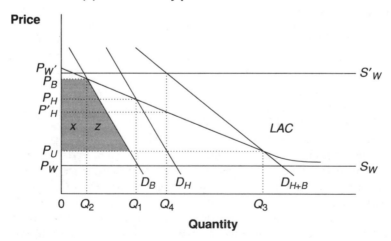

(b) Prior-to-entry production in both countries

Figure 3.11 Economies of scale

Production prior to entry in home country H, but not in partner country B

This situation is illustrated in Figure 3.11(a). Prior to entry the partner country will import all its supplies $0Q_2$ from third countries at a foreign exchange price P_W, which with its tariff will appear as a price P_W'. Tariff revenue will be $P_W P_W' AC$.

For country H, before and after entry there are the two extreme possibilities:

1 If average cost pricing is assumed prior to entry, country H will produce all its requirements $0Q_1$ at a price $0P_H$. On entry, H will expand its output to $0Q_3$ at a price P_U, that is, its costs of production will have fallen from P_H to P_U.

There will be a gain to consumers in both countries. The partner country will gain consumer surplus of $P_W' ANP_U$. This must be set against its loss of tariff revenue of $P_W' ACP_W$. Thus it shows a consumption gain of y and a trade diversion loss of z.

The home country gains the benefit of a *cost reduction* due to the expansion of its industry. Thus $0Q_1$ is now obtained at a lower cost – that is, P_U compared with a previous P_H – and the whole of this benefit is passed on to consumers. In addition, consumers gain a surplus of *FHG* on the expansion in their consumption. The home consumers therefore have a clear gain and there are no trade diversion losses to set against them.

2 If prices remain at P_W', there are no benefits to consumers. If the partner country B transfers its purchases $0Q_2$ to the home country it sustains a loss of tariff revenue and welfare of $P_W' ACP_W$. Country H will expand production to $0Q_4$. Its cost of production will now be P_H' and producers will make profits of $P_W' JKP_H'$.

Production prior to entry in both countries

Figure 3.11(b) illustrates this situation. Even if the average cost curve of the two countries is the same the cost of production will appear lower in the larger country because its producer is operating further down his AC curve, assuming the same pricing policies in the two countries.

1 If the prices in both countries are equal to their LAC, then prior to entry the price in the partner country will be P_B and quantity produced and purchased Q_2, and in the home country the price will be P_H and quantity produced and consumed Q_1. There will be no imports into either country.

With the formation of the union, assuming that it is the firm in H which expands to supply the customs union market, the price will fall to P_U. Country H will produce Q_3. Consumers in H will benefit from the *cost reduction* effect $P_H P_U.0Q_1$ on the amount H was originally supplying plus the additional consumer surplus on the increase in consumption that takes place because of the fall in price.

The industry of the partner country B completely disappears due to the expansion of it in H. There appears to be an efficiency gain due to trade creation equal to the crosshatched area x, and a gain in surplus on additional consumption z. Thus, country B appears to show gains without any losses.

2   If the prices charged are equal to P'_W, then the initial production in both countries would be lower and so would the production after entry at $0Q_4$. The final cost of production would be P_H' and the difference between this and the price $P'_W P'_H. 0Q_4$ would go entirely to the producers in country H.

Conclusions from the traditional analysis, model T

If a country is initially importing from third countries, entry into the customs union will always involve it in making a loss due to trade diversion. Thus the only circumstances in which trade diversion costs are not incurred is when both countries are initially dependent on home production. In that case, expansion of production in one country leads to the disappearance of the industry in the other. This is not regarded as a loss in this type of marginal welfare analysis, but clearly, if this involved a number of industries in B or was important to country B's economy, some adjustment to exchange rates would be required.

Because of the assumption that the long-run average cost curves are the same in both countries, the direction of trade is inherently indeterminate – although the country that can produce in the larger market will appear to have lower costs of production.

In all cases shown, the countries would be better off if they imported from the rest of the world.

Imperfect competition and economies of scale – model M

So far we have analysed the effect of a customs union in a market in which consumers do not distinguish between the goods of the different producers. Let us now investigate how this changes if there are imperfections in the market. Imperfection may be reinforced by the existence of economies of scale. A large firm, then, is at an advantage, and this increases the difficulty for a new firm entering the market because it has to reach a high level of production in order to compete. Technological knowledge and the price of factors of production are assumed constant.

The Emerson Report (CEC 1988), on the benefits the EC would obtain by removing their non-tariff barriers to trade by the end of 1992, approached the problem using an imperfect competition model developed and applied by Smith and Venables (1988a and 1988b). In the Smith and Venables model, Model M, each EC firm is assumed to produce in only one EC country, but each country may have several firms. Each firm may produce several varieties of product; those varieties, however, are peculiar to that firm and cannot be produced by any other firm. The firm discussed has only one plant and is the sole domestic producer of the product. Implicitly, the economies of both plant and firm are being considered. The products of different firms within the same industry are imperfect substitutes.

The empirical basis of the Emerson Report was a series of studies by Pratten (1988). Much of the data referred to the 1960s. Pratten identified various factors which contributed to economies of scale and then listed the 'engineering' estimates. Most of these were associated with the size of plant or production runs, but some were also attributed to the spreading of research and development (R&D) expenditure over more units. The minimum efficient technical scale of plant (METS) is defined as where production is increased costs cease to fall rapidly. The measurement of economies of scale is the percentage increase in costs at half or a third of the METS.

Each firm can produce for its home market or can export its product; it will receive the consumer price in the former, but only $(1-t)$ multiplied by the consumer price in the latter, where t represents the selling costs associated with exporting. It is assumed that because of selling costs the firms will account for a smaller proportion of their export than home markets. A reduction in selling costs, such as those associated with the removal of non-tariff barriers to intra-EC trade, will lead to greater exports and thus induce greater competition and lower prices in all markets. This will expand consumption and allow firms to further exploit their economies of scale.

Each producer is assumed to maximize profits by equating marginal cost with marginal revenue. This is achievable because there are a number of producers which each individually face an elasticity very much greater than the elasticity of demand for the product itself. Smith and Venables (1988a and 1998b) considered the firms either to be making the 'Cournot' assumption in which each firm regards the sales of other firms as fixed, or the 'Bertrand' assumption in which each firm regards the prices of other firms as fixed. In both cases, the elasticity of demand that the firm faces in its export market is assumed to be greater than that in the home market, and therefore marginal revenue is a greater proportion of price in the former.

As sales expand so does output and therefore there is a greater exploitation of economies of scale. If the less efficient firms are forced out to close down by the increased competition, this will enable those remaining to still further exploit their economies of scale.

The removal of non-tariff barriers with the introduction of the Single European Market, discussed in the next chapter, were regarded as being equal to a tariff equivalent reduction of between 2.5 per cent and 13.5 per cent. This was then regarded as a reduction in the selling cost of exporting to other EC countries.

Using these calculations, the Emerson Report shows the percentage reduction in cost from exploiting economies of scale and from restructuring, that is, the disappearance of the less efficient firms. The greatest welfare gains were expected from the chemical industry (7.7bn ECU), electrical goods (5.4bn), motor vehicles (4.7bn), and mechanical engineering (4.6bn) (CEC 1988: table A.7).

Comparison of model T and model M

Clearly the assumptions underlying the two analyses of economies of scale, Model T and M, are entirely different. In Model T one industry or firm is assumed for each country, the production functions for different firms are the same (although this assumption could be modified), and the benefits and costs from the formation of a customs union depend on the reduction in the average cost obtained and the pricing policy pursued. The absolute height of the tariff (or the tariff equivalent of non-tariff barriers) determines the maximum exploitation of economies of scale that can occur due to the customs union, because at the tariff-distorted world price imports could enter and at the world price the country could export.

In Model M, however, because of the heterogeneity of product there is no 'world price'. Model M allows for several firms in each country and for differentiation of products. But these advantages of approximation to reality are thrown away by substituting a number of representative firms for the actual number and size distribution of firms. There is also a very limited concept of differentiation.

From the point of view of trade theory the question is whether in the long run the initial advantages of a country or firm are sufficient to determine trade flows. Where individual firms appear to have advantages specific to themselves, if these are specific to the firm as distinct from the country it is not clear why the firm should not relocate its production to the cheapest location within the EC or maybe abroad. This is precisely what worries trade unionists in the countries with higher wages and social security contributions.

Another aspect of the situation is the identification of economies of scale. The implicit assumption appears to be that a one-plant firm is being considered; in particular, the Emerson Report (CEC 1988) is perpetually slithering from a discussion of the METS and economies of scale of a plant to that of a firm without distinguishing between the two. However, Smith and Venables (1988a and 1998b) discount economies of scale assocated with plant size by assuming that their representative firms are at the METS; it is not clear whether their cost function, which appears to allow for the further spreading of fixed costs, and which they discuss in terms of R&D, is therefore only an economy of scale of a firm. If it is specific to the firm, then the argument in the previous paragraph applies.

In the Emerson Report (CEC 1988), one of the advantages that is said to accrue from further exploitation of economies of scale is that as costs fall European firms will become more competitive and thus will increase their exports to the outside world. But surely in this case they will already be exporting. Furthermore there are considerable exports to non-member countries of all the products considered by Smith and Venables. This suggests that economies of scale of the most efficient firms are already being exploited.

The model entirely ignores the flows of international investment and the multinational nature of the firms operating in the industry. In so far as these producers straddle national boundaries, the assumptions about the bases of the competing firms do not hold. For instance, the choice is not so much whether the French and Germans buy French or German cars, but where the Germans wish to produce their cars. The concept of differentiation being associated with a firm producing in a particular country, which then determines trade, collapses. The location of production becomes determined by costs.

CONCLUSIONS

The traditional analysis of the exploitation of economies of scale in a customs union has been in terms of a homogeneous product. In this case a firm may benefit and expand its output if its potential long-run average cost of production lies somwehere between the international price at which it could export and the tariff-distorted price at which imports can enter the union. The actual distribution of costs and benefits depends on which firms produce before and after the formation of the union, and the pricing policy being pursued.

The imperfect competition approach pursued by Smith and Venables (1988a and 1988b) for the Emerson Report (CEC 1988) eschews all consideration of the level of protection. It is solely concerned with firms within the customs union. Each is assumed to be based in its home country producing and exporting from it. In the Emerson Report the economies of scale of plant are not distinguished from those of the firm. The more efficient firms are regarded as expanding at the expense of the less efficient. Thus it takes account of the effect of increased competition on increasing efficiency, which has been regarded as the most important effect of the formation of the EC by J. Tinbergen and Robert E. Baldwin.

However, it ignores the possibility of a firm choosing to shift production from its domestic base to a lower-cost location within the EC, which has occurred. Multinationals are always in favour of customs unions and free trade areas because by their very nature they are used to relocation and can exploit this facility in supplying the EC. Furthermore, foreign firms can take advantage of this just as much as indigenous firms.

Contingent protection and cartels

Many multinationals now take a global view in locating production. The EU is one regional area and the degree to which they locate production there will depend on costs and the impediments to supplying markets from the various areas. As tariffs are negotiated downwards they become an insignificant hinderance. Contingent protection in the form of voluntary export restraints (VERs) and anti-dumping duties have become much more important, as will be described in succeeding chapters. They enhance the oligopoly power of firms within the customs union and anti-dumping duties have been associated by Messerlin (1990) with the creation of cartels. Cartels are agreements between firms to restrict output or limit the sales of a firm to particular areas, and/or to keep up prices. They are devices for raising prices to consumers and are therefore economically inefficient. They are anti-competitive and, as such, are banned by the EC (see Chapter 4). They are easiest to form and maintain when (1) the industry is dominated by a few firms, generally because there are significant economies of scale in production, and (2) they receive some quantitative or minimum price protection from imports from outside. Thus the products quoted by Messerlin are a number of basic chemicals, glass, cement, steel, and wood pulp. However, by the mid-1980s there were also rulings on CDs and in 1987 on colour films, photocopiers, and printers.

Developing countries are also concerned that this type of contingent protection may be attracting to the EU, or to Eastern European countries that have special preferential terms with the EU, foreign direct investment that would otherwise go to Asian developing countries. That is, investment as well as trade is subject to diversion. Of course, trade diversion in goods does imply some implicit diversion in investment.

Criticisms

A more persistent and growing criticism is that the establishment of the EC, its enlargement, and the way it has signed a whole series of preferential agreements has induced a similar response on the part of other countries, with the US establishing the North American Free Trade Area, and a series of preferential agreements in Asia and Latin America. In other words, the signing of preferential trade agreements is not leading on to free trade but to the breakdown of the multilateral trading system. The completion of the Uruguay Round, discussed in the next chapter, has put some of these fears to rest. There remains the anxiety on the part of the rest of the world, however, that the discrimination exercised by the EU is encouraging inward investment that, with free trade, would have taken place in developing countries. Also, there is the nagging fear of the developing countries that the distribution of EU aid to poorer countries within the EU is at the expense of its distribution to very much poorer countries outside.

The long run

The analyses outlined above have been in the form of comparative statics with technology and generally incomes assumed constant. Only in the general equilibrium analysis have the direct effects of trade on income been considered. But in the long run the growth in demand for goods due to changes in income becomes very important, particularly if the product is in limited supply such as fossil fuels. The relationship of an increase in the demand for a product J to an increase in income is called the income elasticity of demand e_{iJ}.

$$e_{iJ} = \frac{\text{percentage change in quantity of } J \text{ demanded at constant prices}}{\text{percentage change in real income}}$$

This can be measured in total or per capita; if the latter the change in population also has to be taken into account to calculate the total growth in consumption due to higher incomes. 'Real' means that the effect of inflationary price increases has been removed.

Alternatively when analysing consumer expenditure it is sometimes easier to calculate an expenditure elasticity for the product J whereby

$$e_{xJ} = \frac{\text{percentage change in quantity of } J \text{ demanded at constant prices}}{\text{percentage change in expenditure on all goods and services}}$$

As described in Chapter 2 the increase in income is partly attributed to investment and the relocation of labour. However, the major feature of the long run is technological change, now occuring faster than ever. The revolution in computing and telecommunications has provided the foundation for increases in productivity in services and manufactures. Improved communications have also expanded the markets that individual firms can effectively supply. Associated with this has been the introduction of a vast range of electronic products – word processors, electronic printers, facsimile machines, mobile telephones, camcorders – which did not exist a few decades ago. In this book trade in high-tech products is considered in Chapter 12, and the growth in services associated with them in Chapter 13.

APPENDIX 3.1

A tariff on imports when the importing country can affect the world market price

Elasticities

The demand schedule for *imports, D_M*, represents the net result of the change in the quantity of importables demanded by home consumers and supplied by home producers in response to changes in price. Thus the elasticity of demand for *imports*, e_m, depends on the elasticity of home demand and supply of importables, e_{dm} and e_h. That is:

$$e_m = \frac{e_{dm}D - e_hH}{D - H}$$

where D is the original quantity consumed domestically and H is the quantity originally supplied by home producers. That is, the elasticity of demand for imports is lower (or in absolute terms without regard to the sign, greater) than for importables because it is the net result of changes in both the quantity demanded and supplied to the home market.

If, for instance:

$$e_{dm} = -0.5$$
$$e_h = 2.0$$

and the initial consumption D is 100 units, of which 50 are supplied by home producers, then:

$$e_m = \frac{-0.5 \times 100 - 2.0 \times 50}{100-50} = -3.0$$

Likewise with the export market, if there is some domestic consumption of the exportables, the elasticity of supply of *exports*, e_x, will depend on the elasticity of supply of exportables, e_s, and the domestic elasticity of demand for exportables, e_d. As the commodity is exported, the original amount of the commodity produced domestically, S, must be greater than the quantity consumed domestically, D. Thus:

$$e_x = \frac{e_sS - e_dD}{S - D}$$

and e_x will be greater than e_s.

When the home country is not in a perfectly competitive market

The overall demand schedule for imports, M, should be used for analysis when the country is facing a less than infinitely elastic supply schedule in the world market. In that case, some of the cost of the tariff is borne by the foreigners in the form of lower prices (see Figure 3A.1).

If H is an importer, under free trade the price on the domestic market $0P_1$ will be the same as that on the international market and imports will be $0M_1$. If a tariff is imposed proportionately equal to $P_2P_3/0P_2$, the demand schedule for imports M appears to shift to M'. The price in the home market

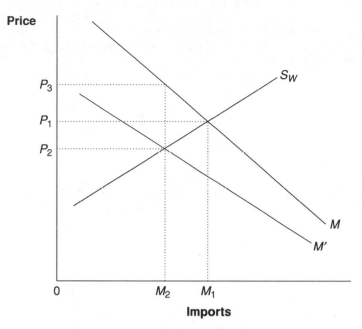

Figure 3.A1 A tariff on imports when the country is facing an upward-sloping supply schedule

rises to $0P_3$ that is, by less than the amount of the tariff. Part of it is borne by the foreigners in the form of the lower price $0P_2$ that they receive for their exports.

REFERENCES

CEC (1988) 'The economics of 1992' (The Emerson Report), *European Economy*, **35**, March.

Cooper, C.A. and Massell, B.F. (1965), 'A new look at customs union theory', *Economic Journal*, **75**.

Corden, W.M. (1971) *The Theory of Protection*, Oxford: Oxford University Press.

——(1972) 'Economies of scale and customs union theory', *Journal of Political Economy*, **80**.

GATT (1986a) *The Text of the General Agreement on Tariffs and Trade*, Geneva: General Agreement on Tariffs and Trade.

——(1986b) *The Texts of the Tokyo Round Agreements*, Geneva: General Agreement on Tariffs and Trade.

Kindleberger, C.P. (1973) *International Economics*, 5th edn, Homewood, Ill: Irwin-Dorsey.

Leontief, W. (1968) 'Domestic production and foreign trade: the American capital position re-examined', in American Economic Association, *Readings in International Economics*, London: Allen & Unwin.

Lipsey, R.G. (1957) 'The theory of customs unions: trade diversion and welfare', *Economica*, **24**.

Mead, D.C. (1968) 'The distribution of gains in customs unions between developing countries', *Kyklos*, **21**; repr. (1972), in P. Robson (ed.), *International Economic Integration*, Harmondsworth: Penguin.

Messerlin, P.A. (1990) 'Anti-dumping regulations or pro-cartel law', *The World Economy*, **13** (4).

OECD (1987) *National Policies and Agricultural Trade: Study on the European Economic Community*, Paris: OECD.

Pratten, C. (1971) 'Economies of scale in manufacturing industry', Occasional Paper No. 28, Department of Applied Economics, Cambridge University.

——(1988) 'A survey of the economies of scale', Study No. 17 in Commission of the European Communities, Documents Research on the *Costs of Non-Europe: Basic Findings*, vol. 2, *Studies on the Economics of Integration*, Brussels: CEC.

Robson, P. (1984) *The Economics of International Integration*, 2nd edn, London: Allen & Unwin.

Rybczynski, T.M. (1955) 'Factor endowment and relative commodity prices', *Economica*, **22** (84); repr. (1968), in American Economic Association, *Readings in International Economics*, London: Allen & Unwin.

Samuelson, P.A. (1949) 'International factor-price equalization once again', *Economic Journal*, **59** (234), June; repr. (1968), in American Economic Association, *Readings in International Economics*, London: Allen & Unwin.

Smith, A. and Venables, J. (1988a) 'The costs of non-Europe: an assessment based on a formal model of imperfect competition and economies of scale', in Commission of the European Communities, '*Cost of Non-Europe: Basic Findings*, vol. 2, *Studies on the Economics of Integration*, Brussels: CEC.

——(1988b) 'Completing the internal market in the European Community', *European Economic Review*, **32**.

Viner, J. (1950) *The Customs Union Issue*, New York: Carnegie Endowment for International Peace.

4 UK trade policy and agreements that have affected trade

The previous chapter outlined the benefits to be expected from trade and how these are reduced by tariffs and quotas. It must be emphasized that this rationale for free trade is implicitly assumed in the constitution of the international organizations set up by the Allies, with Britain as an important participant, after the Second World War. The Allies were very concerned to get away from the instability and unemployment, and the transmission of unemployment through competitive devaluations and protection, which had been such a feature of the international economy in the interwar period. As described in Chapter 2, they established the International Monetary Fund to assist with short-run balance of payment problems, and the World Bank to provide loans for reconstruction and development.

General Agreement on Tariffs and Trade (GATT)

They also wanted to set up an institution to govern and liberalize international trade in goods, particularly manufactures. The General Agreement on Tariffs and Trade (GATT) was signed in 1947 as an interim agreement to lower tariffs and regulate trade between some of the major countries. A conference was then held at Havana in 1947–48 which put forward a plan for an International Trade Organization (ITO) and a (Havana) Charter which outlined the objectives and provisions for such an organization. But the US Congress failed to ratify the ITO. The GATT therefore took over its role and most of its provisions.

The most important of these provisions were those concerning access and non-discriminatory treatment. The member countries of GATT extended most-favoured-nation (mfn) status to each other: that is, they allowed imports into their markets from other member countries at the lowest tariff rate they imposed on imports from any country. This is termed multilateralism. Quotas, regarded as the most pernicious form of protection, were to be phased out, except when required for short-term balance of payments reasons. Certain already existing preferential trading schemes were permitted and the system of Commonwealth preference was one of them.

Customs unions and free trade areas were regarded favourably under article XXIV of GATT because they were seen as a move towards trade liberalization, but they had to comply with certain conditions. They were required to cover a substantial part of the trade of the participating countries, and their duties and other regulations concerning trade with third countries – that is, countries not party to the preferential agreement – were not to be higher or more restrictive than before. Such agreements – were also to include a schedule for the completion of the customs union or free trade area within a reasonable period of time (GATT 1986).

This is the international framework within which countries have conducted their trade policies. Under GATT auspices there have been eight rounds of negotiations to reduce tariffs and other trade barriers; the latest and most important of these was the Uruguay Round, which will be discussed later. Britain has participated in all of them, although latterly as a member of the EC.

As mentioned in Chapter 2, in Western Europe in the late 1940s and 1950s the OEEC negotiated away many barriers to trade as a condition for the distribution of Marshall Aid. Thus trade liberalization was taking place at an international and regional level even before the formation of the EC.

Merchandise trade with the US and Western Europe

Let us consider this in relation to Britain's distribution of trade by area. In 1950 the US as the industrial hegemonic power accounted for 6 per cent of British exports and 8 per cent of her imports. She then became an even more important trading partner with shares of 11 per cent and 12 per cent respectively by the mid-1960s (see Table 4.1). As Table 4.1 shows, UK trade with the whole of Western Europe was relatively low, accounting for only 25 per cent of her exports and imports in 1950, but this rose to 43 per cent and 33 per cent respectively by 1965.

The measures of liberalization under the OEEC and later GATT were mainly directed at trade in manufactures. This was because imports of raw materials had very low or zero tariffs in most countries. Thus the system of tariffs tended to escalate, with tariff rates being higher the more processed the product, and so the *effective rates of protection* for manufactures were even higher. With liberalization, trade in manufactures increased very fast, far faster than in other commodities. However, products of declining industries were often excluded by the members of GATT from the rounds of tariff reductions; these 'sensitive' products comprised cotton textiles and often footwear, and agriculture was always excluded.

Agricultural protection

The major industrial countries other than Britain all protected their agriculture. The developed countries with the lowest levels of protection were

Table 4.1 Distribution of UK merchandise trade by area (% OTS basis)

Area	1950	1960	1965	1970	1975	1979	1987	1996
Imports								
EC Total		15	15	18	34	45	53	54[a]
EC(6)	13[a]	15	15	18	30	38	44	40[a]
Rest of Western Europe	12	15	16	16	15	17	14	6
North America	15	20	20	21	13	13	12	14
United States	8	12	12	13	10	10	10	13
Other developed countries	16	12	12	9	8	6	9	8
Oil exporters	9	11	10	9	14	7	2	2
Other developing countries	30	22	19	15	11	11	11	15[b]
Commonwealth	40	31	29	23	14	11	8	
Exports								
EC Total		15	19	21	32	42	50	57[a]
EC(6)	11[a]	15	19	21	20	34	39	41[a]
Rest of Western Europe	14	14	17	20	17	14	9	4
North America	11	16	18	18	12	12	17	13
United States	5	9	11	12	9	10	14	12
Other developed countries	21	15	15	12	9	6	5	7
Oil exporters	6	7	6	6	11	9	7	5
Other developing countries	29	25	20	17	15	16[b]	13[b]	14[b]
Commonwealth	38	34	26	20	16	12	11	

Sources:
ONS, *Monthly Review of External Trade Statistics*, MM24, February 1997.
CSO, *Monthly Review of External Trade Statistics*, Annual Supplement No. 11, 1990.
DTI, *Overseas Trade Statistics of the United Kingdom*, various years.
K. Mansell, 'UK visible trade in the post-war years', *Economic Trends*, October 1980 (for most Commonwealth figures).

Notes: [a]Includes all Germany. [b]Rest of the world.

the exporters Australia, New Zealand and Canada, which were all heavily dependent on the British market for their exports. Britain had been pursuing a free trade policy with respect to agriculture ever since the abolition of the Corn Laws in 1846. This policy had been slightly modified in the 1930s to maintain some stability by giving traditional exporters quotas, but there were very few tariffs on imports of agricultural products. In fact, Britain was pursuing what was termed a 'cheap food policy'; she also introduced a subsidy to home producers with the Wheat Act of 1933. After the Second World War, agricultural subsidies were put on a systematic basis with the Agricultural Act of 1947. Britain allowed in imports of most of the major agricultural product duty free; there were only duties on some of the minor horticultural products during the British season. However, she guaranteed prices for her farmers for the major cereals and livestock products; the differences between these guaranteed prices and the actual market prices were made up to farmers in the form of deficiency payments, a form of subsidy. Therefore Britain certainly intervened in the agricultural market, but in so far as she did not raise prices to consumers she remained much more liberal than the other major European countries.

Let us now consider the succession of preferential agreements in which Britain has participated. It will be argued here that the shifts from one to the other, although maybe inevitable from a political point of view, have not only led to alterations in her specialization, but have also contributed to increasing economic inequality between regions and social groups.

COMMONWEALTH PREFERENCE

Britain was the first country to industrialize and then followed a policy of free trade. But the exigencies of the First World War led her to introduce the McKenna duties in 1915 on luxuries such as cars in order to save shipping space. Then, under the Safeguarding of Industries Act 1921 she instituted high import duties on products such as precision instruments and synthetic organic chemicals, the domestic production of which she wished to foster after finding during the First World War how dependent she was on imports from Germany.

However, the Great Depression that succeeded the Wall Street crash of 1929 induced the government to enter into the Ottawa Agreements of 1932 under which Britain formally abandoned free trade and instituted (mfn) tariffs that increased with the degree of processing of the product, but with reciprocal preferences for Commonwealth countries. Thus food and raw materials continued to enter duty free, but tariffs on other imports from the Commonwealth were either zero or four-fifths the mfn rate. In return, she was given preferential access in Commonwealth markets by which she hoped to protect herself from competition, particularly from Japanese exports of textiles.

Among Commonwealth countries Britain was the dominant industrial power; thus the Commonwealth Preference Scheme was a preferential trading scheme between complementary countries, Britain exported manufactures and imported food and raw materials. In 1950 Britain's ties and preferential agreements with the Commonwealth meant that 38 per cent of her export and 40 per cent of her import trade was with the Commonwealth (see Table 4.1). However, these channels of trade became transformed by the industrialization of other Commonwealth countries. This was partly their response to being cut off from British supplies during the Second World War. In addition, all British colonies on reaching independence wanted to hasten their industrialization, and this generally involved raising their tariffs on imports of manufactures and reducing Britain's preference in their markets.

There was also a reversal in the direction of trade, as India, Pakistan and Hong Kong increased their exports of cotton textiles to Britain. By 1959 Britain's imports of cotton textiles were greater than her exports. Instead of accepting the shift in her comparative advantage she endeavoured to limit these imports by negotiating 'voluntary' export restraints (VERs) with these

Commonwealth countries. When other developing countries rushed to take advantage of this, VERs were also extended to them.

EUROPEAN INTEGRATION

The movement for European integration was a reaction by politicians and combatants to the devastation of the Second World War and the realization that three wars in the past hundred years had been started by nationalistic conflicts between European countries. It was also regarded as a method of buttressing democracy in Western European countries, which had seen the Eastern European countries taken over by the USSR, and many of whom faced large Communist minorities in their own countries. Political integration was to be achieved by economic means.

Before the war a customs union had been negotiated between Belgium, the Netherlands and Luxembourg (Benelux) and this was put into effect in 1948.

Treaty of Paris establishing the European Coal and Steel Community (ECSC)

The first fruit of the European movement, however, was really the Treaty of Paris, signed in 1951 by France, Germany, Italy and Benelux, establishing the European Coal and Steel Community (ECSC). The objective was to open up the markets in coal and steel between member countries and to remove discrimination by ECSC producers – whether that discrimination was exercised by direct or by indirect means (e.g. via distorted transport cost schedules). The basic aim of the signatories was to integrate the German steel industry so completely with the rest of Europe that Germany would never again be able to use it as the base for a large armaments programme. However, because these industries were so important, a high degree of government intervention was assumed in its provisions. For instance, Article 2(2) of the treaty states:

> The Community shall progressively bring about conditions which will of themselves ensure the most rational distribution of production at the highest possible level of productivity, while safeguarding continuity of employment and taking care not to provoke fundamental and persistent disturbances in the economies of Member States.
>
> (cited in Glais 1995)

In 1957 the same six countries signed two further treaties, one establishing the European Atomic Energy Community (Euratom) and the more important Treaty of Rome establishing the European Economic Community (EEC). A treaty amalgamating these three European Communities – ECSC, EEC and Euratom – was signed in Brussels in 1965 (Leonard 1993: 36).

Treaty of Rome establishing the European Economic Community (EEC)

The main trade provisions of the EEC were as follows:

I   *Trade in Manufactures*

1) Elimination of tariffs on trade in manufactures between Member States.
2) Elimination of quotas on trade between Member States.
3) Establishment of a common external tariff on imports from non-member countries. This tariff calculated as the unweighted average of Member States, already existing external tariffs.

II   *Agreement with Associated Territories* [i.e. former colonies]

The EC Member States were also to gradually abolish tariffs and quotas on the imports from the Associated territories. The Associated territories were gradually to remove any element of discrimination between the imports of the Member State that they were formerly associated with and other Member States. They did not, however, have to reciprocate by removing the tariffs on imports of Member States completely, that is, they could retain tariffs to protect 'infant industries' and for revenue purposes.

III   *Free Movement of Factors*

There were also provisions for the free movement of labour and also of capital between Member States.

IV   *Trade in Agriculture*

Agricultural policy was separated from that governing trade in manufactures; there was to be a common market for agricultural products but with protection from imports from third countries. Common prices were agreed in 1967.

(Treaty of Rome Part 3, 1957)

The EC was thus a customs union aspiring to be a common market, with special provisions for agricultures. However, it also laid the foundation for a panopoly of supranational institutions which have been able to develop policies for further integration.

The Common Agricultural Policy (CAP)

Agriculture policy was conceived in terms of the interests of home producers: this sector was to be protected from free trade. The initial structure of intervention was established under a system of fixed exchange rates, which was necessary for it to function properly. A 'target price' was to be set for the main agricultural products at the location of maximum deficiency in the EEC; for cereals, for example, this was at Duisburg in Germany. The aim was then to achieve this target price by the imposition of variable import levies on imports in order to bring them up to a minimum import price, variously described as a 'threshold' or 'sluice gate' price. If this was not sufficient to keep up the price of these products because EEC supply was greater than demand at this price, there was for some products a further degree of intervention, that is of purchases for stockpiling. This was at a price below, but related to, the target price. Clearly, under this scheme the consumers paid more than world prices. However, the cost to them depended on the level of protection. This caused a great deal of controversy among the six, partly because the level of protection was different among them: the Netherlands was relatively liberal, whereas Germany still had the relic of the monopoly trading system established by the Nazis in the 1930s. Furthermore, in most countries the price of bread grains, generally wheat but also rye in Germany, was kept at a much higher level than that of the other cereals, although on the world market the unit price of wheat and barley were almost the same.

Agreement on actual target prices was not reached until 1967, and only under great pressure from France. In general it represented an upward movement in prices. Italy in particular was faced with a 40 per cent increase in the price of feed grains. More importantly, it represented a general increase in prices in France, the major agricultural producer. This inevitably encouraged an expansion of production. With prices kept high to consumers this just as inevitably led to the accretion of stocks. The initial idea was that the CAP would be self-financing, with the revenue from import levies when the harvests were bad financing the purchase of stocks when the harvests were good. However, the high prices provided a strong inducement both to expand and to maintain high levels of production, and this led inevitably to the accumulation of stocks.

Furthermore, because the CAP was regarded as one of the foundation stones of the EC it received considerable protection within the EC constitution. Once the prices had been agreed by the Council of Ministers, the Commission had an open-ended commitment to finance it. The result was that soon the CAP accounted for two-thirds of the expenditure of the EEC.

The revenue of the EEC was also a matter of contention. The EEC was very anxious to establish its 'own resources', or in other words, its own taxable base. Initially this consisted of all customs duties – that is, all revenue from tariffs and variable import levies – and, in addition, a proportionate value-added tax, but it also had to be supplemented by transfers from the governments of Member States.

Britain's reservations

The CAP was one of the main stumbling blocks to Britain joining the EC. It involved her abandoning the free trade in food and the associated cheap food policy that she had been pursuing since her abolition of the Corn Laws in 1846. With the high levels of protection envisaged she would also become a net contributor to the funds of the EC.

Becoming a member of the EC customs union also meant her abandoning the system of Commonwealth preference, a trading system which had in most cases been reinforced by the sterling area. Members of the sterling area, kept their reserves in sterling, with the gold and dollar reserves backing sterling kept on behalf of members at the Bank of England.

Last, but not least, Britain feared the loss of sovereignty involved in becoming a member of the EEC with its supranational institutions.

For all these reasons she was not willing to sign the Treaty of Rome.

European Free Trade Association (EFTA)

As a counterweight to the EEC Britain in 1959 founded EFTA which was a free trade area in manufactures between herself and six other European countries, Sweden, Switzerland, Austria, Denmark, Norway, and Portugal. Finland became an associate member in 1961. It thus included some of the most advanced industrialized countries such as Sweden and Switzerland, and also one of the least advanced, Portugal. Britain with a population of 52 million was by far the largest country. She accounted for more than half EFTA's population and income. EFTA had a secretariat but no supranational institutions.

Because EFTA was a free trade area it required no adjustment of tariffs on imports from non-member countries though in fact due to GATT negotiations a certain lowering did take place. However, as they varied greatly between the members, rules of origin were necessary. These were that 50 per cent or more of the value of a product had to be accounted for by production within EFTA, or certain processes had to be carried out within EFTA for the product to be freely traded between Member States. Tariffs between Member States were removed in stages and even by 1965 there were still some low tariffs on intra-EFTA trade (EFTA 1969).

Effect of EFTA on trade

Between 1959 and 1965 Britain's exports increased by 39 per cent in terms of value and 30 per cent in terms of volume (EFTA 1969: 137, table 8), but as this was at a slower rate than world trade her share of it continued to decline.

British imports of manufactures from the world as a whole had increased by 114 per cent between 1959 and 1965. Imports from EFTA had grown somewhat faster at 127 per cent, and those from the EEC more slowly at 91 per cent. This should be put in perspective by the very much greater increase in imports from the US of 196 per cent and from Japan of 340 per cent, with whom Britain had no preferential arrangements.

Furthermore, because EFTA was comparatively small, although the proportion of exports and imports it accounted for was increasing over time, UK trade with the EEC was becoming steadily more important.

British producers felt that they were competing on unfavourable terms in a large, rapidly expanding market. The financial sector also thought it would benefit and was anxious to be inside the EEC before it began to draw up financial regulations. Thus there was mounting political pressure to join the EEC. The political objection that it would involve a loss of sovereignty was dismissed by those in favour as representing the view of Little Englanders, that is, very parochial people. The system of Commonwealth preference was regarded as a relic of Britain's colonial past and, in any case, the value of the preference to British exporters in Commonwealth markets was declining at about 4 per cent a year. The Common Agricultural Policy was acknowledged as a cost.

BRITAIN'S APPLICATION FOR ENTRY TO THE EC

Britain's two initial applications for entry in 1963 and 1968 were vetoed by President de Gaulle of France. Then, after intensive negotiations a third application was agreed to in 1971 (Leonard 1993). France, however, insisted that accession to the CAP was a condition of British entry. This was partly because she did not want competition from a country whose wages were lower because of lower food prices, but chiefly because Britain, a net food importer, was regarded as a potential absorber of the CAP surpluses. Thus much of the intensive negotiations were devoted to trying to secure markets for Britain's traditional suppliers of agricultural products, and in particular, the Commonwealth developing countries, New Zealand and, to a lesser extent, Australia. Special arrangements were drawn up for the entry of sugar from developing countries, but not Australia, and also for imports of butter, cheese and lamb from New Zealand (Young 1973).

Negotiations also took place with respect to the entry of other products from Commonwealth developing countries. The EC would not extend to India, Pakistan and Hong Kong the same privileges that had been given to former French dependencies under the Association Agreements. In 1971 the EU agreed to a Generalized System of Preference under the auspices of UNCTAD by which she allowed imports of manufactures duty free from developing countries up to a certain limit. The terms for this had to be negotiated each year with each exporting country. Commonwealth developing countries were generally included in this, except for imports of textiles and footwear from Hong Kong. In fact, imports of textiles and clothing were to be restricted by a more extensive scheme, the Multi-Fibre Arrangement of 1974 (see Chapter 10).

Entry was supported by all the quality newspapers. There was some dissent, most noticeably within the Labour Party, but it received very little publicity. The Communists were the only political party officially against it. Economists as a group appeared equally divided. Those in favour brushed aside the anticipated cost on the grounds of the opportunities that would be provided by entry.

Britain's anticipated economic cost of entry to the EEC

However, the costs loomed larger to those who calculated the effect of entry. The estimates of Kaldor, Miller and Spencer, Josling and Williamson and those presented in the government White Papers of 1970 and 1971 were compared and summarized by Marcus Miller (1971). Miller distinguished between the effect on trade in manufactures, trade in agricultural products and official transfers (see Table 4.2).

The CAP was described by all agricultural economists as both a very bad policy and one which would be very expensive to Britain. The estimated costs varied according to the assumptions made of the elasticities of demand and of supply. But the chief variation between the official estimates as presented in the White Papers of 1970 and 1971 were due to the increase in world prices of food that began in the early 1970s, which lowered the apparent protective effect of the CAP. For a very short period of time the variable import levies became negative. For most of the time, however, they have been high and positive.

In Figure 4.1 there is a modified version of Marcus Miller's diagrammatic presentation. Initial consumption at 1969 prices was assumed to be £2,000 million and production £1,770 million at 1969 prices. In the 1970 White Paper the level of protection in the EEC was regarded as yielding prices 25 per cent above the world level. The price to consumers rose by this full amount and even though the elasticity of demand was assumed to be very low, at 0.16, it was calculated that this would lead to a reduction in food imports equal to £150 million. The increase in prices to British farmers, who already received production subsidies of 15 per cent of world prices, was only 10 points (see Figure 4.1) and their increase in output at low elasticities was assumed to be 3 per cent and at a higher elasticity 10 per cent, leading to a reduction of imports of respectively £50 and £170. Thus the net effect on the balance of payments of changes in consumption and production was £200 million with an inelastic supply and £320 million with a higher elasticity of supply.

As world prices had risen by the time of the 1971 White Paper it took the increase in prices to consumers to be 15 per cent. However, because it assumed that demand was totally inelastic with respect to price this did not lead to any reduction in purchases. The reduction in imports was assumed to be entirely due to the increase in production.

Other estimates were made of the response of consumers to these higher prices; in most cases the calculations were heavily dependent on the assumptions made as to the cross-elasticity of demand between butter and margarine.

Table 4.2 Anticipated effects on the balance of payments and welfare of British entry into the EC (£m at 1969 prices)[a]

	Kaldor		Miller–Spencer	Josling–Williamson	1970 White Paper		1971 White Paper
	'High'	'Low'			Inelastic	Elastic	
1. Trade creation			*56*	75		−35	—
2. Trade balance in manufactures	−275 *−50*	−125 *−20*	−151	−100 *−25*	−58 *−70*	−12	−190
3. Effect of rise in price of imported food	−200 *−267*	−200 *−267*	−167 *−206*	−110 *−131*	−255 *−485*	−235 *−294*	−238
4. Import saving on food	—	—	480 *118*	301 *75*	200 *240*	320 *107*	140 *47*
5. Net effect of change in trade	−475 *−317*	−325 *−287*	162 *−32*	91 *−6*	−113 *−315*	50 *−199*	−50 *−191*
Transfers							
6. Levies and duties on food	−200 *−267*	−200 *−267*	−282 *−350*	−136 *−162*	−176 *−334*	−167 *−209*	−80 *−100*
7. Other customs duties	−240 *−320*	−240 *−319*	−222 *−275*	−240 *−285*	−240 *−456*	−240 *−300*	−240 *−300*
8. Value-added tax	−230 *−306*	—	—[b]	—[b]	—[b]	—[b]	−75 *−94*
9. Receipts from the EC	50 *66*	100 *133*	—[b]	—[b]	—[b]	—[b]	100 *125*
10. Total of transfers	−620 *−827*	−340 *−453*	−504 *−625*	−376 *−447*	−416 *−790*	−407 *−509*	−295 *−369*
11. Total effect of trade and transfers	−1095 *−1144*	−665 *−740*	−342 *−657*	−285 *−453*	−529 *−1105*	−357 *−708*	−345 *−560*

Source: M.H. Miller (1971) 'Estimates of the static balance of payments and welfare costs of United Kingdom entry into the Common Market', *National Institute Economic Review*, **57**, August.

Notes:
[a] The figures in roman print are for the effect on the balance of payments and those in italics are for the effect on welfare. The estimates refer to the period after transition.
[b] Nil for rows 8 and 9 together.

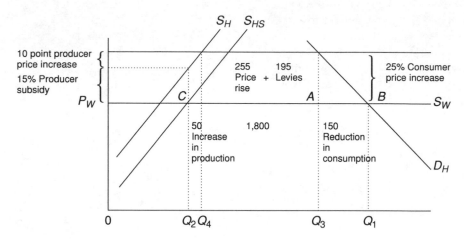

Figure 4.1 The anticipated effects of Britain joining the Common Agricultural
Policy: An interpretation of the 1970 White Paper (at 1969 prices and
a low price elasticity of supply)

Source: M.H. Miller (1971) 'Estimates of the static balance of payments and welfare
costs of United Kingdom entry into the Common Market', *National Institute
Economic Review*, **57**, August.

Notes:

Let S_H be the British supply schedule for food and S_{HS} the supply schedule allowing for a
15% subsidy on production. Let D_H be the British demand schedule for food. Imports are
assumed to come from third countries whose supply schedule is given by S_W. But membership of the CAP involves the imposition of variable import levies on them.

The initial quantity of British Food Production is $0Q_2$ and its value $0P_WCQ_2$ is
£1,770m. The initial quantity of Food Consumed is $0Q_1$ and total expenditure is $0P_WBQ_1$
which is £3,770m. Britain initially imports Q_2Q_1, which in value is Q_2CBQ_1 equal to
£2,000m.

The effect of joining the CAP is assumed to be a rise in prices to consumers of 25%.
But producers already receive a 15% subsidy so the rise to them is only of 10%.

The reduction in the value of consumption according to the 1970 White Paper would
be £150m; this is consistent with a price elasticity of demand of 0.16 and a resulting
reduction in quantity of 4%. The increase in production depends on the elasticity of
supply. The White Paper gives a low estimate of 3% and a high one of 10%. Taking the
lower one, this is consistent with a supply elasticity of 0.32 and an increase in output at
the initial prices of £50m.

Thus the total reduction in the quantity of imports at the initial prices is £(50 + 150)m
reducing them to £1,800m. Their price goes up either because they continue to be
imported from third countries and variable levies are imposed on them, or alternatively,
they are purchased from the higher-cost producers within the EC. The White Paper
assumes an increase of £255m due to the price rise and £195m due to levies.

The CAP price of butter was about six times the world price, and the more consumers transferred to margarine, the greater the import saving.

All agreed that there would be an import saving due to the increase in production and maybe also to the reduction in consumption. However, in addition, the food that continued to be imported would cost Britain more. This was *either* because it would be imported from other EEC countries at the higher CAP price, *or* because even if it continued to be imported from third countries at international prices the variable levy would have to be paid on it and 90 per cent of the revenue from this would go to the Commission, not the British government.

Thus in the 1970 White Paper the balance of payments cost of the CAP due to levies plus changes in imports (lines 3 + 4 + 6, Table 4.2) was estimated at between £231 and £82 million at 1969 prices and in the White Paper of 1971 at £130 million. This was considerably less than the welfare loss, which was due to the loss in consumer surplus offset by only 10 per cent of the revenue from the variable import levies.

Financial transfers

In so far as the CAP was the largest item of expenditure the question of EEC finance was intimately tied up with it. Because agriculture is such a small part of the British economy it was assumed that Britain would have to be a net contributor to the Community. These contributions were in the form of the variable import levies already discussed. In addition, because she conducted a high proportion of her trade with non-EC countries she would collect a considerable amount of customs revenue, 90 per cent of which would have to be transferred to the Commission. An additional contribution was expected by Kaldor to come from a value-added tax. Economists' estimates as collated by Marcus Miller are given in Table 4.2.

Trade in manufactures

The changes in tariffs on manufactures which would result from entry were complex. Britain would remove all tariffs on imports from other members of the EC and she in turn would get free access to their markets. On the other hand, membership meant that she would lose her preferential position in the markets of EFTA countries and Ireland if these joined at the same time as she did. The Common External Tariff she was due to impose on imports from non-member countries was for many commodities lower than her mfn tariff and therefore involved a reduction in tariffs on imports from developed countries such as the US and Japan; conversely, it was greater than her Commonwealth Preference tariff, which was often zero, so she was raising her duties on imports from Commonwealth countries.

As can be seen from Table 4.2, the economists and the 1970 White Paper anticipated that the effect of British entry into the EEC would be to reduce her balance of trade in manufactures, that is, the value of imports would increase more than the value of exports. Only the 1971 White Paper assumed that there would be no effect.

Total anticipated cost of British entry

In conclusion, the estimated effect on trade in manufactures of British entry, contrary to public perception, was that it would contribute a deficit – again, only the White Paper of 1971 thought not – and this would have a negative effect on welfare. The major cost to Britain, however, was that of the CAP, due partly to the higher prices of imported food and to the levies and duties on food. These two factors were anticipated to amount to £500 million or more in welfare terms, that is, between 1 and 2 per cent of GNP.

The overall effect of UK entry into the EC on her balance of payments was assumed to be negative. Different estimates placed the cost to the balance of payments at between £285 and £1,095 million. This represented a welfare loss, as Britain would have to increase exports and/or reduce imports in order to correct it. The welfare cost, which was even greater than that of the balance of payments, was placed at between £453 and £1,144 million at 1969 prices. Direct transfers accounted for a major portion of this cost. This may be compared with a GNP of £50 billion at 1969 prices (Miller 1971).

The service sector was the only one that was regarded as being a clear beneficiary.

BRITAIN'S ENTRY

Thus the government was aware that entry into the EC involved a clear cost due to the CAP. The manufacturing sector appeared unlikely to gain much, apart from ensuring that the UK remained an important base for foreign investors concerned with access to the EC. It was also thought that the service sector would gain, although this was not quantified. Nonetheless, in spite of the evident costs involved the British governments persisted with negotiations for entry. Political advantages were clearly thought to outweigh the palpable economic costs (although the governments of the next twenty years would endeavour to negotiate a reduction in the transfer costs).

In order to get the Bill of Accession through Parliament the Conservative government under Ted Heath had to rely on the support of pro-European members of the Labour opposition. To limit the scope for opposition the Bill consisted of a few clauses referring to other Acts; on reading it, it appears incomprehensible. The result of this ruse is that to this day the average Member of the UK Parliament and the public at large appear ignorant of the provisions and structure of the EC. It is the House of Lords through its Select Committee on the European Communities that keeps track of EC legislation.

Britain entered the EC – that is, the three communities of the ECSC, the EEC and Euratom – at the beginning of 1973, together with Denmark and Ireland. Norway rejected entry in a referendum, and, with the other members of EFTA, then formed a free trade area in manufactures with the EC. So from 1973 manufactures have been freely traded across Europe, with a few qualifications discussed in the commodity chapters.

INSTITUTIONAL STRUCTURE OF THE EC

In becoming a member of the EC Britain joined a political organization which operated in an entirely different way from her national one. In particular, this is because the body which initiates legislation is the Commission of the EC (CEC), its civil service.

However, the power to make final decisions lies with the Member States, through the Council of Ministers which comprises representatives, from each of the Member States. The actual ministerial representative varies according to the subject under consideration. The intermediate standing body which co-ordinates action between the CEC and the Council of Ministers is the Committee of Permanent Representatives (COREPER) whose members are drawn from the civil services of the Member States (see Figure 4.2). In addition, since 1974 the European Council has become an increasingly important

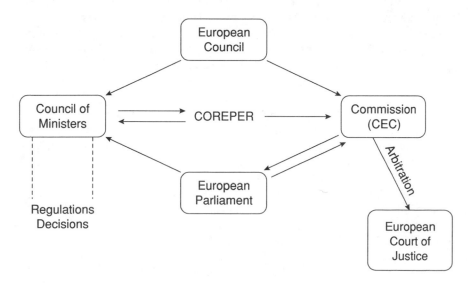

Figure 4.2 The structure of the European Union

body, setting the overall political objectives of the EU and resolving problems which the Council of Ministers finds intractable. It comprises the heads of governments and the foreign ministers of the Member States plus the EU President and one additional commissioner of the CEC, and it meets at least twice a year.

The European Parliament is a successor to the Assembly of the ECSC, which was a purely advisory body. However, since its members became elected in 1979, its power has been increasing, and this was assisted by provisions of the Single European Act of 1987 and the Maastricht Treaty, which took effect in 1993, but it is still largely a consultative body. It now helps to select the Commission, can question the CEC, and can veto trade treaties and new membership. The budget, which is proposed by the CEC, and amended by the Council of Ministers, then has to be laid before Parliament. The Parliament may propose modifications to the compulsory part of the budget (66 per cent largely for agriculture) and amendments for the non-compusory part. This budget with amendments is then referred back to the Council of Ministers which may or may not accept them. The resulting budget is then returned to the Parliament to be adopted. It may decline to do so by a two-thirds majority of the votes cast. This has happened three times and in each case Parliament has finally accepted a revised draft (Leonard 1997).

Members of the European Parliament (MEPs) severely criticized the CEC over its handling of the BSE crisis, accusing it – British readers may be bemused to hear – of acting in collusion with the UK Ministry of Agriculture (further details are given in Chapter 9). Parliament cannot dispose of individual Commissioners but it has the power to dismiss the whole Commission, which in this instance it threatened to do. However, the CEC succeeded in mollifying its critics sufficiently to avoid a motion of censure being passed. For such a motion to succeed requires a two-thirds majority of the votes cast; it is such an extreme measure that it has so far not been employed.

In addition, there is the European Court of Justice (ECJ), which arbitrates on the interpretation and application of all the EU treaties, and there is also the Council of Auditors, which has the task of examining all the revenue and expenditure accounts of EU institutions. The Council of Auditors has grown in importance and is now of equal status to the ECJ and the CEC.

The structure of the EC, with its central administrative body, the CEC, responsible for initiating legislation, ensures constant pressure for further integration and greater powers for the CEC. The degree and form it takes depends partly on the President of the CEC; Jacques Delors (1985–94) was, for instance, a very active President, and tended to be in favour of industrial intervention. But it also depends on the Commissioners who are heads of the various Directorates General, the units into which the CEC is divided. However, in the Maastricht Treaty recognition was given to the principle of subsidiarity by asserting that decisions should be 'taken as closely as possible to the citizens' (Leonard 1993: 73).

There are several types of Community decision:

- a *regulation* is generally and directly applicable as it stands;
- a *directive* is binding in objective on Member States but not in method attainment;
- a *decision* is binding on those to whom it is addressed.

This body of law, built up over time, is termed the *acquis communautaire*. It takes precedence over national law and has to be accepted by all new members.

PROGRESS IN THE LIBERALIZATION OF INTRA-EC TRADE

Initially, the EC Commission's efforts were mainly directed at achieving a greater degree of integration between the economies of the existing Member States. It wanted to establish a 'level playing field' such that EC firms could compete with each other without assistance from their national governments. The Commission was also concerned that national restrictions or requirements should 'not be used as a means of arbitrary discrimination nor as a disguised restriction on trade between Member States' (Article 36). Articles 100–102 provided the legal framework for 'harmonizing' these national restrictions if they affected trade.

Not only were all tariffs and quotas to be abolished, but so was any national regulation that interfered with intra-EC trade. Thus was the EC Commission set upon the road to 'harmonization', which proved to be very slow and arduous.

Soon after Britain joined the EC in 1973 instances of 'harmonization' aroused the ire of the British populace, as one consumer product after the other appeared under threat, as, for instance, in the case of British chocolate because British manufacturers were not required, as on the Continent, to include cocoa butter and generally used a cheaper vegetable oil as a substitute. The CEC's compromise directive to allow chocolate to contain up to 5 per cent of vegetable fats as in Britain, Denmark, Ireland, the Nordic countries, Austria and Portugal was thrown out by the European Parliament in response to an emotional debate led by the Belgians (Maitland 1996; Tucker 1997).

This process culminated in a case brought by a German company, Rewe-Zentral, which was trying to import the French blackcurrant liqueur 'cassis', which had a lower alcohol content than required by German law. In 1978 the European Court ruled that consumer protection could have been achieved by a label indicating the alcohol content: the German requirement was not essential. The 'Cassis de Dijon' principle, essentially one of

mutual recognition of standards, has become increasingly important
ever since.

There are areas in which the process of harmonization has been fruitful,
in particular with regard to the safety requirements for motor vehicles: the
harmonization of technical requirements for passenger cars was completed
in 1992, accepted in 1993 and became mandatory in 1996, and is due to
be extended to other vehicles (WTO 1995b, 2: 44). There are other areas
where agreements on standards have become very important and sometimes
essential to communication, as for instance in the case of electronics, and
they will be discussed later.

But great difficulties have been encountered within the EU with respect
to the standardization of *electrical equipment*. In particular, there has been no
agreement on a harmonized European plug and socket system. The German
electrical accessory makers objected to the proposals put forward in 1995
on the grounds that the system was inferior to their own, while

> the UK was worried about 'dangerous compatibility' between the new
> plug and some of the British sockets with their three rectangular holes.
> But it also believed the proposed plug was too simple technically,
> increasing the risk of market penetration by cheap imports from Asia.
>
> (Baxter 1995)

Thus protectionism, officially disavowed in the choice of standards in the
GATT Tokyo Round, reared its head. The producers of electrical goods
lobbied for the proposals because if they had been accepted the same
moulded plug could have been put on every electrical appliance produced.
Needless to say, the plug and socket manufactureres lobbied against it. The
outcome was that the proposals were thrown out (op.cit.).

By the 1980s there were still perceived to be a large number of non-tariff
barriers to trade in goods. The Commission was also concerned with the
obstacles to the sale of services between Member States, particularly as
services were accounting for an ever larger proportion of GDP. In the Single
European Act (SEA) of 1986 it was specified that the EC internal market
should comprise an area *without internal frontiers*; in particular:

1   Non-tariff barriers to trade in goods *and* services were to be removed by
    the end of 1992. Services included transport, banking, and insurance.
2   There should be a mutual recognition of national *technical standards* for
    manufactures pending the adoption of European standards, and an
    adoption of a community trade mark system.
3   There should be a liberalization of *public procurement* so that contracts
    were not awarded solely to national firms.

The question of public procurement was important, particularly as the
Continental countries were slower to engage in privatization than Britain.

In 1987, public procurement accounted for 16 per cent of GDP (GATT 1991, 1: 15), and in 1984 a third of this was for manufactures (CEC 1988: 55). Traditionally, national firms had considered they had a right to supply their own government or nationalized industries and the proportion supplied by imports was very much less than in the private sector. This was inconsistent with the ethos of the EC. Under the SEA, orders above certain magnitudes have to be submitted for tender available to all Member States. Potentially this represented an important breakthrough in the market for telecommunications equipment, which is growing fast but which in many European countries is under the control of a nationalized industry.

Secondly, non-tariff barriers to intra-EC trade had arisen when Member States had imposed their own individual non-tariff barriers on imports from third countries. The most noticeable of these was in the car industry, where there was a wide variation in the restrictions imposed by Member States on imports from Japan. These restrictions have now been replaced by an EC quota and this quota itself should be lifted by 2000.

Non-tariff barriers

Let us now briefly consider these non-tariff barriers (NTBs) to trade which have been widely used as an additional form of protection, although they will be discussed in more detail in the chapters devoted to particular commodities. One commonly used device was the 'voluntary' export restraint (VER) by which the importing country negotiates a physical limit on exports from a particular country. The VER is in effect a bilateral quota. It has a similar effect to a tariff in raising the price of the product on the market of the importing country (see the analysis in Chapter 3). But no tariff revenue is gained; instead there is an 'economic rent' associated with the quota due to the fact that the product is sold on the domestic market at a much higher price than it can command on the international market. Who gains the economic rent depends on how the quota is allocated. When VERs are imposed on developing countries those countries are generally given the entitlement to export and are therefore generally regarded as acquiring the rent from the quota. When the VER is imposed on imports from Japan the importing country retains the right to the quota and therefore may gain the economic rent, or alternatively, if it allocates the right to importers, the importing firm will gain the rent. The imposition of a VER was entirely inconsistent with the ethos and legal requirements of GATT, and yet, as will be described in Chapter 10, it became an institutionalized feature of trade in textiles and clothing. VERs were also used by certain Member States to control imports of footwear, and imports of cars and machinery from third countries, in particular Japan. After 1983 Japan also 'monitored' its exports to the EC of colour TV sets, colour TV tubes and video tape recorders: that is, it restrained its exports of these items in order to avoid the imposition of a VER or anti-dumping duty (GATT 1991, 1: 211–17). With the institution of the SEM such

VERs could only be maintained at an EU level, and all those of the individual Member States had to be phased out.

There has also been widespread use by the EU of countervailing and anti-dumping duties. Dumping is defined as the situation in which a product is sold in a market at less than its 'normal' value which is regarded as being either 'the comparable price ... when destined for consumption in the exporting country, or, in the absence of such domestic price is less than either the highest comparable price ... [of the] product for export to any third country ... , or, the cost of production of the product in the country of origin plus a reasonable addition for selling cost and profit' (GATT 1986: Article VI). The importing firm or country can levy an anti-dumping duty not greater than the margin of dumping on the exports of the firm. Alternatively, if the difference is due to a government subsidy, a countervailing duty may be imposed to offset it. Sometimes firms avoid anti-dumping duties by accepting a 'price undertaking' – that is, a minimum import price, by which the exporting firms lose their competitive advantage but gain a higher price. In the year to June 1995 the EU led the field, initiating thirty-seven anti-dumping actions, but EU companies themselves were the targets for eight started by other countries (Williams 1995).

The problem with these non-tariff barriers is their arbitrary nature, that is, the way they not only discriminate between countries, but also, in the case of anti-dumping duties, between firms, penalizing the most efficient producers. In calculating the size of anti-dumping duties the EC is also accused of the misleading use of statistics. Increasingly, as the CET is reduced, the main trade advantage of joining the EU is to avoid these NTBs or, as they are often described, 'contingent protection'.

ENLARGEMENT OF THE EU AND PREFERENTIAL AGREEMENTS

Over time, the area of preference has been steadily extended, as the EC continued its process of enlargement with new entrants:

1981 Greece
1986 Spain and Portugal
1995 Austria, Finland and Sweden (previously members of EFTA and thus countries which already had free trade in manufactures with the EU).

The major changes, however, have been due to the collapse of Russian power in Eastern Europe. Eastern Germany was reunified with West Germany in 1990, making the unified Germany by far the largest member of the EC, with 80 million people and the largest economy by a wide margin.

The Eastern European states that acquired independence in 1990 – the Central Eastern European States (CEECs) of Poland, Czechoslovakia,[1]

Rumania, Hungary, Bulgaria, and the smaller Baltic states of Estonia, Latvia, and Lithuania – are all queuing up to join. This presented the European Union with a quandary. On the one hand, it was anxious to assist the rehabilitation of these newly democratic states into the free markets of the Western world. On the other hand, the industries in which the CEECs appeared most competitive were the 'sensitive' ones, that is, the declining industries that the EU was doing its best to protect, in many cases by the imposition of quotas. Horticulture and textiles and clothing were the most important, but so also were coal and iron and steel.

The EU moved tentatively at first, extending to the CEECs the generalized system of preference provisions it had instituted for developing countries. Then, between 1991 and 1993 the EU negotiated with each of the six countries broadly similar agreements termed the Europe Agreements. The objective of these was the establishment of a free trade area in goods and services between the EU and these countries within ten years. Quotas and tariffs were removed on industrial products *except* for those listed in the annexes. There is very little liberalization of agriculture, which is a major problem; the Common Agricultural Policy of the EU will have to be scrapped in it present form before the CEECs can become members, otherwise the EU's financial burden will become too great (Winters and Wang 1994).

The Baltic republics – Latvia, Lithuania and Estonia – signed free trade agreements with the EU in July 1994. The agreements provided for free trade in industrial goods and the EU granted limited concessions in agricultural trade (Enders and Wonnacott 1996).

Mediterranean countries

The CEC considers that the Mediterranean countries need to obtain 'comparable accords', similar but not identical to the Europe Agreements. In 1995 it approved a plan to progressively establish a free trade area in manufactures by 2010, and to liberalize trade in agriculture, services, capital (WTO 1995, 2: 23). Cyprus and Malta have already applied for membership.

At the beginning of 1996 the EU entered into a customs union with Turkey. She has become part of the SEM and has adopted EU trade legislation and its common external tariff. However, there appear to be qualifications with respect to textiles, and free trade in agricultural products is not anticipated to be achievable until 2005 (Barham and Southey 1995).

Developing countries

At the outset the EC formed bilateral free trade areas with the 'overseas territories', mainly former colonies and territories of the six original Member States. The membership of this scheme has been steadily increased by a succession of Lomé Agreements to seventy African (excluding South Africa),

Caribbean and Pacific (ACP) countries. However, despite this preferential access to the EU market, the ACP's proportion of EU imports has fallen significantly since the 1980s (WTO 1995, 1: 27).

Generalized system of preference

In response to the developing countries in the United Nations Conference on Trade and Development (UNCTAD) the EC also established in 1971 a generalized system of preference (GSP) by which they were permitted to export their manufactures tariff-free to the EC up to a certain limit (tariff quota), but this had to be renegotiated each year. At the beginning of January 1995 this was replaced by a *revised GSP scheme* covering 145 countries and the entire industrial sector except for armaments, whereby tariff quotas are scrapped to be replaced by a degree of tariff preference which depends on the 'sensitivity' of the product being imported and the 'development index' of exporting countries. There are four categories of sensitivity:

1   *'very sensitive' products* (textiles, clothing and ferro-alloys) for which the preferential rate of duty is 85 per cent of the regular duty;
2   *'sensitive' products*, which include footwear, electronics and motor vehicles, and for which the preferential duty is 70 per cent of the regular duty;
3   *'semi-sensitive' products*, for which the preferential duty is 35 per cent of the regular duty; and
4   *'non-sensitive' products*, for which the preferential rate is 0.

However, the least developed countries and the Andean Pact countries gain more favourable treatment.

Although this is not due to be reviewed before January 1999, under certain conditions a country can be 'graduated' out of the GSP. These depend, first, on the beneficiary country's *development index*,[2] which is dependent in turn on its per capita income as a percentage of that of the EU, and on the value of all manufactured exports from the beneficiary country as a proportion of total EU manufactured exports. The second criterion is the *specialization index*[3] in the product category being considered (WTO 1995b, 1: 28–37). These conditions tend to have most effect on large countries and those that specialize in their exports.

We have now covered just a few of the twenty-six EU trade agreements in force in February 1996, many of which have been signed in the last five years (Southey 1996). It should be borne in mind, however, that many of these agreements overlap so that, for instance, the Lomé countries do not receive any additional benefits from the GSP.

Nonetheless the EU gives the impression of entering into preferential schemes as a means of placating neighbouring countries or as a means of exerting political influence with others, but then modifying a beneficiary country's access immediately it begins to show success in its exports. Nowhere is this better exemplified than in its provisions for 'graduating' countries out of the GSP. This contributes to the uncertainty of its trading partners and is likely to discourage marginal suppliers to the EU market. Although intra-marginal exporters to the EU may benefit from preferences, it is not clear how much effect they have had on the overall pattern of trade. The uncertainty also discourages trade links. It is noticeable that although Asia is the EU's largest export market, its share of that market is shrinking (Montagnon and Bardacke 1996).

THE INTERNATIONAL CONTEXT

Although many of the EU measures such as the SEM represent milestones in the removal of barriers to intra-EU trade, a whole series of international negotiations were taking place in tandem under the auspices of GATT for a further multilateral liberalization of trade. The most important of these has been the Uruguay Round.

The Uruguay Round and the World Trade Organization

The Uruguay Round of negotiations to reduce or eliminate barriers to international trade (begun in 1986 and ending with the Agreement signed in Marrakesh in April 1994) was more ambitious than previous ones. It included two 'sensitive' sectors – agriculture, and textiles and clothing – which had been previously excluded by the industrial countries from negotiations, and it was also extended to cover services. All three areas posed great problems, which is why the Round took so long to complete. It also comprised negotiations on trade-related investment measures (TRIMS) and trade-related aspects of intellectual property rights (TRIPS). Provision was made for the establishment of the World Trade Organization (WTO) in 1995; this took over the previous and extended functions of GATT.

The Commission negotiated on behalf of the EC. There was some problem with services, but in 1994 the ECJ ruled that the Community had exclusive competence with respect to trade in goods (with some qualifications with respect to products covered by the ECSC) and this extended to *trade* in services. However, this did not extend to the situation in which the service was provided physically within a state, nor did it extend to transport services. The EU's common commercial policy did extend to intellectual property rights. Nevertheless, the Commission still had difficulties when faced with the entrenched interests of particular members such as France with respect to agricultures.

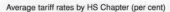

Average tariff rates by HS Chapter (per cent)

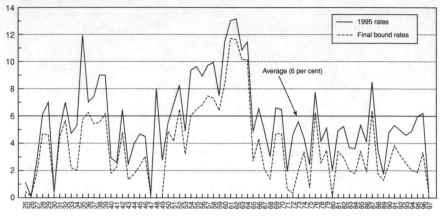

HS Chapter

Chapter	Description	Chapter	Description	Chapter	Description
25	Salt; sulphur; earths and stone, etc.	48	Paper and paperboard, etc.	72	Iron and steel
26	Ores, slag and ash	49	Printed books, newspapers,	73	Articles of iron and steel
27	Mineral fuels, mineral oils, etc.		pictures, etc.	74	Copper and articles thereof
28	Inorganic chemicals; organic or	50	Silk	75	Nickel and articles thereof
	inorganic compounds of precious	51	Wool; fine or coarse animal	76	Aluminium etc.
	metals, etc.		hair, etc.	78	Lead and articles thereof
29	Organic chemicals	52	Cotton	79	Zinc and articles thereof
30	Pharmaceutical products	53	Other vegetable textile fibres	80	Tin and articles thereof
31	Fertilizers	54	Man-made filaments	81	Other base metals, etc.
32	Tanning or dyeing extracts, etc.	55	Man-made staple fibres	82	Tools, implements, cutlery,
33	Essential oils and resinoids;	56	Wadding, felt and non-wovens;		spoons and forks, etc.
	perfumery, cosmetic or toilet		special yarns; twine, cordage, etc.	83	Miscellaneous articles of
	preparations	57	Carpets; other textile floor		base metal
34	Soap, organic surface-active		coverings	84	Nuclear reactors, boilers,
	agents, washing preparations, etc.	58	Special woven fabrics; lace, etc.		machinery, etc.
35	Albuminoidal substances;	59	Impregnated, coated, covered or	85	Electrical machinery and
	modified starches; glues, etc.		laminated textile fabrics, etc.		equipment, etc.
36	Explosives; pyrotechnic products;	60	Knitted or crocheted fabrics	86	Railway or tramway
	matches, etc.	61	Articles of apparel and clothing		locomotives, etc.
37	Photographic or cinematographic		accessories, knitted or crocheted	87	Vehicles other than railway
	goods	62	Articles of apparel and clothing		or tramway rolling-stock, etc.
38	Miscellaneous chemical products		accessories, not knitted, etc.	88	Aircraft, spacecraft, etc.
39	Plastics and articles thereof	63	Other made-up textile articles;	89	Ships, boats, etc.
40	Rubber and articles thereof		sets, worn clothing, etc.	90	Optical, photographic, etc.
41	Raw hides and skins and leather	64	Footwear, gaiters, etc.		apparatus
42	Articles of leather, etc.	65	Headgear and parts thereof	91	Clocks and watches, etc.
43	Furskins and artificial fur;	66	Umbrellas, walking-sticks, etc.	92	Musical instruments, etc.
	manufactures thereof	67	Prepared feathers and down, etc.	93	Arms and ammunition, etc.
44	Wood and articles of wood, etc.	68	Articles of stone, plaster, etc.	94	Furniture, bedding, etc.
45	Cork and articles of cork	69	Ceramic products	95	Toys, games, etc.
46	Manufactures of straw, of	70	Glass and glassware	96	Miscellaneous manuf. articles
	esparto, etc.	71	Natural or cultured pearls, precious	97	Works of art, antiques, etc.
47	Pulp of wood or of other		or semi-precious stones, precious		
	fibrous cellulosic material		metals, etc.		

Figure 4.3 Tariffs on manufactured products (EU12), 1995 and 2000

Source: World Trade Organization (1995) *Trade Policy Review: European Union, 1995*, vol. 1, Geneva: WTO.

Note: In the Uruguay Round negotiations, certain items in chapters 25 to 97 were classified as 'agricultural products'.

Provisions of the Uruguay Round

Tariff reduction

With respect to tariffs the overall result for manufactures will be a reduction in the EU's unweighted average CET from 6 per cent in 1995 to 3.7 per cent in 2000. But there will still be a considerable variation in the degree of tariff protection for different product categories, as can be seen from Figure 4.3. The tariffs on construction equipment, agricultural equipment, medical equipment, pharmaceuticals, most steel categories, paper products, furniture, selected toys and soaps and detergents will be eliminated. The highest tariffs in 2000 will be on textiles and clothing, aluminium, and passenger cars (at 10 per cent), all of which are now regarded as the products of 'sensitive' (i.e. declining) industries, but also radio and TV sets at 14 per cent (WTO 1995b, 1: 52, 94 and 104).

Agriculture

The objective 'is to establish a fair and market-orientated agricultural trading system' and 'to provide for substantial progressive reductions in agricultural support and protection sustained over an agreed period of time, resulting in correcting and preventing restrictions and distortions in world agricultural markets' (GATT 1994: 39). Members undertake not to provide export subsidies. A member shall not provide support to its agricultural producers in excess of its commitment levels; this is defined in terms of the 'aggregate measurement of support', which is 'calculated as the sum of all aggregate measurements of support for basic agricultural products, all non-product-specific aggregate measurements of support and all equivalent measurements of support for agricultural products' (GATT 1994: 41). There are many qualifications.

Textiles and clothing

It was agreed to phase out the Multi-Fibre Arrangement (MFA) to achieve full liberalization of this sector within twelve years, as described in Chapter 11.

Trade-related investment measures

The TRIMS to be banned include those which require:

a) the purchase or use by an enterprises of products of domestic origin or from any domestic source, whether specified in terms of particular products, in terms of volume or value of products, or in terms of a proportion of volume or value of its local production; or

b)   that an enterprise's purchases or use of imported products be limited to an amount related to the volume or value of local products that it exports.

(GATT 1994: 167)

That is, all TRIMS which refer to quantitative restraints. Thus local content requirements as required or desired by members of the EC and also the US would be disallowed. Also to be banned would be discriminatory tax treatment of foreign subsidiaries in comparison with national firms.

But export performance requirements, which most developing countries have within their export processing zones, would be allowed.

Agreement on trade-related aspects of intellectual property rights

This agreement covers the protection of *copyright, patents, industrial designs, and trademarks. Copyright protection is extended to expressions and not to ideas, procedures, methods or mathematical concepts as such.* Mfn treatment is to be applied to the granting of rights, that is, there is to be no discrimination between members of the WTO.

Industrial countries – in particular, the US and the EC – were very anxious to have this agreement, and the developing countries were worried that it would involve them in extra costs. It is clear that some developing countries are too poor to finance compliance and policing of such an agreement (e.g. Bangladesh).

Trade in services

A separate treaty on the *General Agreement on Trade in Services (GATS)* was concluded.

'*Services*' exclude services supplied in the exercise of government authority. It includes the sale of a service:

1   from the territory of one member into the territory of any other member;
2   in the territory of one member to the service consumer of any other member;
3   by a service supplier of one member, through commercial presence in the territory of any other member;
4   by a service supplier of one member, through presence of natural persons of a member in the territory of any other member.

Trade in services is by its very nature controlled more by government regulation than by tariffs. Under the Uruguay Round agreement, several principles were recognized. First, mfn principles were to be applied, that is, there should be no discrimination between different foreign suppliers of services to the importing country, although certain exceptions were allowed. Second, there should be no distinction made between national and foreign suppliers.

The participant had to provide a list of the services they were willing to liberalize in exchange for the liberalization of the markets for services in other countries. The negotiations proceeded on a 'positive' list principle. They continued long after the Marrakesh Agreement had been signed.

Some of the problems encountered were as follows:

1   In so far as public ownership extends further in some EU countries than others, markets in the latter will be much more exposed to competition, particularly in telecommunications. However, in so far as the EU Member States have agreed to privatize their telecommunications market by 1998 this should not be a problem for long.
2   Developing countries fear that they will face some very large multinationals in the service sector, but it is argued that providing there is competition such countries will not be worse off.

Summary

Thus the protective ring around the EC now consists of the common external tariff (CET), which for industrial products under the Uruguay Round will be lowered to 3.7 per cent by 2000 and under many preferential agreements has been removed entirely. As tariffs are lowered, other impediments to trade become more apparent. The EU retention of the use of 'contingent' protection, (i.e. safeguard and anti-dumping measures) in most preferential schemes adds an element of hazard. However, the Uruguay Round included an Agreement on Safeguards by which the parties agreed to the phasing out of all existing VERs within four years of it coming into force. One exception was allowed to each signatory, the duration of which should not extend beyond the end of 1999, and the EU opted for this to be the VER it had concluded with Japan on automobiles (Mattoo and Mavroidis 1995). The EU has also agreed to more stringent rules for ascertaining dumping.

The Uruguay agreement represented a great step towards the elimination of barriers to trade in goods and services on a multilateral basis and thus introduces the possibility of a more efficient allocation of resources worldwide. To this extent it will reduce the preferential advantage of being a member of the EU in which similar provisions have been negotiated for the Single European Market. In future, it is likely that trade in services will be governed by global agreements. However, both the US and the EU have been slow to put some of the provisions into effect, in particular for agriculture and textiles and clothing. They also seem just as inclined to resort to contingent protection.

DEEPER INTEGRATION: THE TREATY OF EUROPEAN UNION SIGNED AT MAASTRICHT IN 1993

The area of jurisdiction of the EC is determined by the treaties which have consistently extended the purview of the EC. The Maastricht Treaty of European Union 1993 (TEU) distinguished three pillars of EU activities: first, there is the concern with economic integration, comprising the original three treaties establishing the ECSC, the EC, and Euratom enhanced by the TEU itself; second is the common foreign and security policy (CFSP); and third, justice and home affairs, concerned with police co-operation, drug trafficking and fraud.

The first pillar of economic integration is by far the strongest and its scope was considerably reinforced by the TEU. The provisions which are most relevant to UK trade are Article 129b whereby:

1) ... to derive full benefit from the setting up of an area without internal frontiers, the Community shall contribute to the establishment and development of trans-European networks in the areas of transport, telecommunications and energy infrastructures.

2) Within the framework of a system of open and competitive markets, action by the Community shall aim at promoting the interconnection and interoperability of national networks as well as access to such networks. It shall take account in particular of the need to link island, landlocked and peripheral regions with the central regions of the Community.

(CEC 1992, Title XII: 51)

The protocol on social policy which the UK initially refused to sign is vague, except in its clear insistence on equal pay between men and women. Now that the Labour government has opted in to it the extent of the area which can be regulated is becoming clearer, as is described in Chapter 14.

The most important element of the TEU were the provisions for monetary policy which will be discussed in the next chapter.

CONCLUSION

Britain's attitude towards Europe is still causing political ructions. An argument used by those opposed to the EC is that it is leading to a loss of UK sovereignty. In fact it was a condition of membership that EC law had precedence over UK law: that is, Britain has already lost her legal sovereignty. Greater awareness of this arises because of the extension of EC law, *acquis communautaire*, not only for manufacturing, but also to labour relations and the service sector. It remains to be seen whether the EU will be successful in instituting a common currency.

Many economists have questioned the advantages of having large preferential areas of trade – they may lead to a reduction in trade barriers between their members, but a multilateral system without the possibility of trade diversion would be better. In the EC, trade diversion is not only due to the CET, but also to the inward investment that takes place to produce goods and avoid the contingent protection in the forms of VERs and anti-dumping duties that are imposed when they are imported. An additional problem is that the attraction of the EU for many aspiring members is often the prospect of benefiting from transfers from the richer members of the EU, either through the CAP or through some of the EU schemes for regional or social assistance. Do these schemes lead to aid being diverted to members of the EU such as Portugal and Ireland and away from the much poorer countries outside the EU? If so, from the point of view of third countries, diversion may not only mean diversion of trade, but also of investment and aid. South Asian countries have already raised their concerns in this connection. The implications for trade of this enlargement will be considered in the chapters on commodities.

NOTES

1 Now the Czech and Slovak Republics.
2 Mathematically, the development index is equal to half the sum of the logarithm of relative income plus the logarithm of relative manufactured exports.
3 Algebraically, the specialization index is equal to the ratio of the sectoral share in EU imports to the global share in EU imports.

REFERENCES

Barham, J. and Southey, C. (1995) 'Turkish–Eu customs union wins backing from MEPs', *Financial Times*, 14 December.
Baxter, A. (1995) 'Deadlines draw closer – electrical harmonisation efforts may finally be scuppered', *Financial Times*, 13 October.
CEC (1988) 'The economics of 1992' (The Emerson Report), *European Economy*, **35**, March.
—— (1992) *Treaty on European Union* (The Maastricht Treaty), Brussels: CEC.
DTI (1994) *The Uruguay Round of Multilateral Trade Negotiations 1986–94*, Cm. 2579, Department of Trade and Industry, London: HMSO.
EFTA (1969) *The Effects of EFTA on the Economies of Member States*, Geneva: European Free Trade Association.
Enders, A. and Wonnacott, R.J. (1996) 'Liberalization of East–West European trade', *The World Economy*, **19** (3), May.
GATT (1986) *The Text of the General Agreement on Tariffs and Trade*, Geneva: General Agreement on Tariffs and Trade Secretariat.

—— (1991) *Trade Policy: Review The European Communities 1991*, 2 vols, Geneva: General Agreement on Tariffs and Trade Secretariat.

—— (1994) *The Results of the Uruguay Round of Multilateral Trade Negotiations: The Legal Texts*, Geneva: General Agreement on Tariffs and Trade Secretariat.

Glais, M. (1995) 'Steel industry', in P. Buigues, A. Jacquemin and A. Sapir (eds), *European Policies on Competition, Trade and Industry*, Aldershot: Edward Elgar.

Leonard, R. (1993; 5th edn, 1997)*The Economist Guide to the European Community*, London: Economist Books.

Maitland, A. (1996) 'European Commission grapples with the content of chocolate', *Financial Times*, 20 March.

Mattoo, A. and Mavroidis, P.C. (1995) 'The EC–Japan consensus on cars: interaction between trade and competition policy', *The World Economy*, **18** (3).

Miller, M. (1971) 'Estimates of the static balance of payments and welfare costs of United Kingdom entry into the Common Market', *National Institute Economic Review*, **57**, August.

Montagnon, P. and Bardacke, E. (1996) 'Door open to wider Europe-Asia links', *Financial Times*, 26 February.

Moore, L. (1985) *The Growth and Structure of International Trade Since the Second World War*, Brighton: Harvester Wheatsheaf.

Southey, C. (1996) 'EU under fire for trade pact proliferation', *Financial Times*, 16 February.

Treaty of Rome (1957), trans. (1962) as *Treaty Establishing the European Economic Community*, London: HMSO.

Tucker, E. (1997) 'MEPs reject chocolate compromise', *Financial Times*, 24 October.

Williams, F. (1995) 'WTO chief tries to avoid confrontation', *Financial Times*, 14 December.

Winters, L.A. and Wang, Z.K. (1994) *Eastern Europe's International Trade*, Manchester: Manchester University Press.

WTO (1995a) *Trade Policy Review European Union*, vol 1, Geneva: World Trade Organization.

—— (1995b) *Trade Policy review European Union*, vol. 2, Geneva: World Trade Organizations.

Young, S.Z. (1973) *Terms of Entry*, London: Heinemann.

5 Moves towards monetary integration

It has long been recognized that the formation of a free trade area or customs union might involve balance of payments difficulties for the countries concerned. Removal of trade barriers between two countries A and B may lead to an increase in the relative demand for goods from A compared with those from B. This could be corrected by revaluing the currency of A in relation to B (Meade 1957). Adjustments of this kind have implicitly been assumed to have taken place in the discussion of trade creation and trade diversion in Chapter 3.

Even when countries are already in a preferential area a similar situation may occur, especially if there is a discovery of natural resource in A, say, gas or oil. The increase in the demand for the product will tend to lead to an appreciation of A's exchange rate. This is known as the problem of asymmetric shock, that is, a shock that does not affect all members of the preferential area. It may also occur if one member country is more exposed to the rest of the world, or if it is more dependent on a particular commodity market, than other members of the preferential area.

However, if the countries have established integration not only in trade but also in their factor markets, adjustment may proceed by the migration of labour and capital from B to country A.

Furthermore, if supranational fiscal and monetary institutions have been established it is also possible for adjustment to be assisted by direct money transfers. Adjustment may then proceed as if A and B were regions within a country such as the UK, or states of the US.

Free trade areas and customs union do not usually involve monetary integration, although an effort is generally made by the member countries to keep their currencies in a stable relationship with each other. For instance, the US and Canada have had close economic relations for a long time, which culminated in their signing the North American Free Trade Agreement (NAFTA) in 1987. The values of their currencies fluctuate to some degree in relationship to each other and to a much greater degree in relation to the rest of the world.

Since the 1960s, however, the EC has been endeavouring to obtain a system whereby not only are EC cross exchange rates stabilized, but full monetary integration is also achieved. The pressure for this seems to have come originally from the French, who felt it was a necessary condition for the CAP to work effectively. Later, as Germany emerged as the dominant economic and financial power in the EC, it became a means of controlling this and harnessing it to the interests of the EU.

Although outside the purview of this book, a summary will be given of the moves towards monetary integration and Britain's participation in them. As Britain was about to join the EC in the early 1970s the Bretton Woods system of fixed exchange rates broke down. The EC thereupon introduced a system for restricting the fluctuation of EC currencies between each other by ± 2½ per cent. This was termed 'the Snake'; the EC currencies in turn fluctuated as a group in relation to the dollar, 'the tunnel'. Britain participated very briefly in the scheme before she put sterling on a managed float in June 1972. Turbulence in the foreign exchange market meant that many EC countries found it difficult to keep within the snake, and at the end of 1977 only Germany, Denmark, the Netherlands, Belgium and Luxembourg remained in it.

In 1979 this system was replaced by the European Monetary System (EMS). This was organized round a basket of EC currencies which comprised the European Currency Unit (ECU), the numeraire of the Exchange Rate Mechanism (ERM). The ERM entails a central rate for each of the participating countries and a permissable band of fluctuation for bilateral exchange rates initially set at ± 2.25 per cent for most countries. Until 1990 Italy was allowed a wider band of ± 6 per cent. When Spain entered in June 1989 and Portugal in April 1992, this wider band was extended to them.

Sterling had been included in the basket of currencies of the ERM from the outset but Britain did not join the ERM initially. The government argued that with British exports of oil, sterling had become a petro-currency, dependent on the price of oil, and quoted in dollars on the world market, which fluctuated considerably. However, while Nigel Lawson was Chancellor of the Exchequer a policy of 'shadowing the Deutschmark' was pursued for a period.

The objective of the ERM was to keep exchange rate movements to a minimum, and, in particular, to prevent competitive devaluations. When a currency diverged from its central rate by the amount permitted by its band of fluctuation the central banks of the strongest and weakest currencies within the system were obliged to intervene in order to stabilize their exchange rates. This was assisted by the capital controls that had been retained in most Continental EC countries, but these were reduced following the EC's Capital Liberalization Directive of 1988, and finally removed by 1992. Over the period 1979 to 1995 there were a number of realignments of the central rates, with the Deutschmark and currencies such as the Danish krone and Dutch guilder which attached themselves to it going up, and the Italian lira depreciating (Bladen-Hovell 1997).

The dominant country was Germany, and, through the intermediary of the EMS, other countries were very anxious to share in the reputation of the Deutschmark for stability in purchasing power, which it had acquired because the primary objective of the Bundesbank, the central bank of Germany, was to avoid inflation.

Britain eventually entered the ERM in October 1990 with a ± 6 per cent band of fluctuation. But the market regarded the central exchange rate at which she entered as too high and, after massive speculation, she was eventually forced to withdraw in 1992. The lira had previously been devalued and after sterling left the ERM it had to follow suit. By the end of 1992 sterling had depreciated by 15 per cent and the Italian lira by 16 per cent. Pressure was also exerted on other currencies; the attack on the French franc was fought off, but the Spanish peseta and Portugese escudo were devalued in November 1992 by 6 per cent. The pressure on non-Deutschmark currencies continued the following year, and after a series of devaluations the EC finance minister agreed in August 1993 that the margin of fluctuation of the currencies around their central rate should be raised to 15 per cent for all except the Dutch guilder, which was to retain its ± 2½ per cent band against the Deutschmark (Bladen-Hovell 1997). The EMS had barely survived.

Nonetheless, in spite of the near failure of the EMS, which allowed for some flexibility in central exchange rates over time, the Member States have continued to press for the implementation of the Maastricht Treaty provisions for monetary union. This involves much tighter links between the Member States.

MONETARY UNION

A European system of (independent) central banks and a European Central Bank (ECB) were to be established with the primary objective of maintaining price stability and instituting monetary union, which involves the establishment of a common currency. Certain requirements such as the removal of all restrictions on capital and current account payments between Member States had been established in the UK since 1979. However, having left the ERM in 1992 she cannot comply with the requirement of fixity of 'the observence of the normal fluctuation margins provided for by the exchange-rate mechanism of the European Monetary system, for at least two years, without devaluing against the currency of any other Member State' (CEC 1992b: 41). Nor can she fulfil another requirement, namely, an independent central bank. However, Gordon Brown, the Chancellor of the Exchequer of the Labour government that came into power in May 1997 has taken a preliminary step towards making the Bank of England independent of the government by relinquishing to it responsibility for setting the rate of interest. Britain might also fulfil the other requirements, as follows:

1   A high degree of price stability, that is, a rate of inflation that does not exceed by more than 1½ percentage points that of the three best performing Member States over a period of a year before the examination.

2   A ratio of planned or actual government deficit to GDP at market prices of no greater than 3 per cent.

3   A ratio of government debt to GDP at market prices no greater than 60 per cent (CEC 1992a).

These conditions required for membership are very strict, and EU governments' endeavours to comply with them appear to be adding to deflation in continental Europe where unemployment is already very high. They are necessary in order to avoid a great deal of subsidization between countries, although some provision is already made for this with the setting up of a Cohesion Fund to assist Member States with a per capita income of less than 90 per cent of the EU average (ibid: 203). In order to comply with these conditions, Member States have been trying to cut back on their more extravagant social security and pension schemes.

A common currency would reduce the costs of trading with other Member States, which in 1996 accounted for 57 per cent of British exports and 54 per cent of her imports of merchandise (see Table 4.1). It would provide a more stable environment for UK manufacturers, particularly multinationals, who have their production processes distributed throughout Europe. Thus they are anxious for Britain to join the common currency. Occasionally it is suggested that the US and Japan would be less likely to invest in Britain if she does not join EMU. However, although variation in exchange rates may be an inconvenience, the cost advantages to Britain in relation to other western Member States have so far not been removed even when the £ sterling reaches a high of 3 Deutschmarks. If investment is transferred elsewhere it is much more likely to be to eastern European countries that are not members of EMU.

A common currency will make costs and prices transparent and would thus be a spur to more competition and therefore greater efficiency. It may be expected that production will gravitate towards the cheapest location, and this may lower the costs of production. However, some of the divergence in prices is due to differences in excise duties and in the rates of VAT between the different countries. Already this has led to shopping expeditions by UK residents to France to purchase cheaper alcohol and cigarettes, thus eroding part of Britain's taxable base. Greater transparency due to a common currency would aggravate this and would lead to greater pressure on the governments of Member States to standardize their VAT rates and excise duties. As a result, they would then lose an element of discretion in tax policy, having already lost their control over monetary policy.

The difficulty of monetary unification can be illustrated by the unification of Germany. In spite of the advantages of a common language and culture, German unemployment is still high, particularly in Eastern Germany where it is expected to be around one-fifth of the labour force in 1998 (Norman 1997). This was partly the result of integrating East Germany at too high a rate for its currency. The rebuilding of the eastern sector has required a massive financial transfer from the west amounting to 4 per cent of West Germany's GDP per annum (Siebert 1998). The rise in interest rates induced by the fiscal deficit was a contributing factor to the recession in the rest of Europe. This illustrates what the potential difficulties of monetary integration are, even when it involves a wealthy country willing to make massive transfers. (Yet the German Chancellor Helmut Kohl is one of the ardent supporters of EMU.) The economies of Member States may not be in such a bad state as that of East Germany, but neither will they receive financial assistance on the same scale if their industries start closing down.

Another problem is the nature of the liabilities the governments of Member States face with their unfunded pension schemes. Almost all EU Member States have ageing populations in which the ratio of old age pensioners to earners is increasing. To retain pensions at the present level the social security provisions paid by each worker must go up or the country must borrow. Alternatively, the pension provision must change by lowering the level of pensions or raising the retirement age. The problem with joining a monetary union in this situation is that it might make it easier for the country to pass on part of that cost to other countries by borrowing and thus raising the rate of interest throughout the Union. This would represent a form of crowding out of investment in the other Member States.

It is in order to limit the extent to which one Member State can pass on its financial problems to another that such strict limits are being imposed on budget deficits and government debt in relation to GDP. The European Central Bank will also not be allowed to lend to the Member States.

Within this straitjacket scenario it will be interesting to see how the EU deals with its main macroeconomic problems. The first problem is the very high rates of unemployment on the Continent. Concern has been expressed in Germany that EMU, by increasing the transparency of wage levels, may in the short run make this unemployment worse by encouraging firms to move away from Germany to the lowest wage cost areas in the EU. The Keynesian fiscal policy of increasing government expenditure is ruled out by the budget requirements. Macroeconomic policy is expected to be exercised by the use of interest rates by the European Central Bank. Its sole economic objective is the control of inflation. However, because there is a wide difference between the economies and structure of Member States an interest rate of, say, 3 per cent that could be combined with low inflation in France and Germany may lead to inflation in Britain. In other words, the fixing of interest rates for the whole of the EU may lead to inappropriate ones for individual Member States. The French were unsuccessful in their endeavours to broaden the Central Bank's mandate to take account of unemployment and growth.

Because the Member States are so heavily dependent on each other's markets, in a situation of unemployment it is very difficult to stimulate demand through additional exports. Convergence would only make this worse; if all Member States are at a point of deflation in the trade cycle, no country is able to provide the impetus to get past that point.

The high unemployment may not by cyclical. The British government has argued that it is due to regulation of the labour market and high social security payments. The latter are highest in Germany where they accounted for 42 per cent of gross wages in 1997 – half paid by employees and half by employers. Indeed, Wilhelm Nolling, formerly of the Bundesbank's central council, said it would be extremely risky for countries such as Germany, France and Italy, with massive structural problems, to enter EMU in the hope that their problems will sort themselves out automatically; EU economies had only succeeded in converging towards high unemployment and high levels of public debt (Münchau 1997a)

There are other fundamental problems. There is a wide divergence in income levels (GDP per head) both between Member States and within Member States. There are provisions for transfers through the regional aid funds, as will be described in Chapter 14, but demand is likely to increase with the accession of new members, so that the CEC under its new Agenda 2000 proposals is endeavouring to restrict such transfers.

Thus the conditions for becoming a member of EMU limit government deficits and debt, although one of the chief methods of correcting divergences between Member States, by monetary transfers, involves a recipient country engaging in them – unless, that is, the transfer is regarded as the recipient country's income.

This raises major problems of equity and democracy. The equity problem arises if there is discrimination in the treatment of a person of a given age and income according to whether or not he or she is in an assisted region.

The problem of democracy arises because taxation policy is frequently part of the agenda of a political party running for election, but presented as if it involves transfers between groups *within* a Member State. There is often great reluctance on the part of citizens of one country to subsidize other countries, and there would be even greater reluctance if the subsidy were known to be going to people in another country who were better off than some of those in the Member State itself.

At the moment, citizens of a Member State continue to identify with others within it, rather than as a citizen of the EU. Except in political propaganda, there appears to have been very little transfer of allegiance from the nation state to the EU. Changes in political identification that have taken place tend, if anything, to be to smaller units rather than larger ones: the establishment of the Scottish Parliament and Welsh Assembly illustrates this point. However, in the long run, as the taxation and financial power of the governments of Member States within the European Monetary Union decline in relation to the centre, it may be expected that firms and citizens will cease to relate as before to their nation state.

This trend will intensify if adjustment is reached by greater factor mobility. At present less than 2 per cent of the EU's working-age population consists of people from one Member State working in another. This is partly because of the different languages and partly because workers are unable to carry social security entitlements, such as supplementary pension rights, across national borders. The CEC is endeavouring to remove these obstacles and make information on vacancies and training across the EU more freely available (Tucker 1997).

Nonetheless, in spite of the apprehension and doubts of citizens in both Germany and France, agreement has been reached that EMU will be launched on 1 January 1999. One of the major problems in establishing EMU is setting the exchange rates at which the countries join without encouraging speculation. It has been agreed that the bilateral conversion rates of the participating currencies will be announced in May 1998, they will probably be near the central rates of the ERM. The core EMU group – Germany, France and Benelux – have identical short-term interest rates of 3.3 per cent, so no problem is anticipated with their currencies, and the Austrian schilling and Italian lira, since rejoining the ERM, have fluctuated without trend. So the actual establishment of the Euro may proceed smoothly. It is expected that EMU will start with eleven members, the others being Spain, Portugal, Ireland and Finland.

Britain, Sweden and Denmark have chosen not to be among the first entrants, nor will Greece because she will be unable to satisfy the requirements. Gordon Brown, the UK Chancellor of the Exchequer, indicated that the British government was in principle committed to EMU membership but would not join during the life of the current parliament, which must end by the spring of 2002.

The reason put forward for Britain not joining was a lack of convergence. She was on a different part of the trade cycle from other countries and therefore the same interest rate policy would not be appropriate for her. The Treasury identified four factors that made Britain more susceptible to external (asymmetric) shocks and interest rate changes than the rest of Europe:

1   The UK has been a substantial net exporter of oil since 1980 and is likely to remain so.
2   The UK trades relatively less with other European countries and therefore is more affected by changes in demand elsewhere and less by those in Europe.
3   In the personal sector, mortgage debt is equal to 57 per cent of GDP compared with an EU average of 33 per cent, so it is more affected by changes in interest rates.

4   In the corporate sector, big companies rely more on the stock market than banks for finance than elsewhere in Europe. Small firms rely more on variable interest loans (Chote 1997).

Additional reasons for not joining are that trade in services is becoming increasingly important and much of this is with non-EU countries (see Chapter 12). Furthermore, the fastest rates of growth of income have recently been in Asia, the US and Latin America, and they represent a greater potential for the expansion of trade than the relatively stagnant EU. Thus trade links are not a sufficient argument for the UK joining the EMU.

As with entry to the EC, Britain's chief interest appears to be a desire for political participation and influence rather than any economic returns from joining. Tony Blair, the UK Prime Minister, initially insisted that the UK should be included in the discussions of the EuroX club of single currency countries, even though Britain had not joined. Eventually, it was agreed that the EuroX finance ministers would meet alone to discuss matters of specific interest to those in EMU such as the euro's exchange rate, the operation of the fiscal stability pact and appointments to the central bank. But they could not exclude the others from discussion of wider economic issues such as tax and labour markets. Ecofin, the club of the finance ministers of all fifteen members, would remain the sole decision-making forum. (Barber and Peston 1997; Stephens 1997).

REFERENCES

Artis, M.J. and Lee, N. (eds) (1997) *The Economics of the European Union*, 2nd edn, Oxford: Oxford University Press.

Barber, L. and Peston, R. (1997) 'EU agrees deal in dispute over access to EMU members' "club"', *Financial Times*, 13/14 December.

Bladen-Hovell, R. (1997) 'The European monetary system', in M.J. Artis and N. Lee, *The Economics of the European Union*, ch. 12.

CEC (1992a) *Treaty on European Union* (The Maastricht Treaty), Brussels: CEC.

——(1992b) 'Protocol on the convergence criteria referred to in article 109j of the Treaty establishing the European Community', in *Treaty on European Union* (The Maastricht Treaty), Brussels: CEC.

Chote, R. (1997) 'Britain out of step with European partners', *Financial Times*, 28 October.

Meade, J.E. (1957) 'The balance of payments problems of a European free trade area', *Economic Journal*, **67**.

Münchau, W. (1997a) 'Life will not be the same under EMU', *Financial Times Survey*, 'Economic and monetary union', 21 November.

——(1997b) 'Government awaits a swing in public opinion', *Financial Times Survey*, 'Economic and monetary union', 21 November.

——(1997c) 'Risks aplenty when converting 15 into 1', *Financial Times Survey*, 'Economic and monetary union', 21 November.

Norman, P. (1997) 'Calm cloaks a sense of unease', *Financial Times: Survey Germany*, 18 November.

Siebert, H. (1998) 'Model under strain', *Financial Times*, 15 January.

Stephens, P. (1997) 'A foot in the club', *Financial Times*, 15 December.

Tucker, E. (1997) 'Brussels introduces measures to improve worker mobility', *Financial Times*, 12 November.

6 Other EU policies affecting trade

The EU provisions that affect trade are not only those establishing a customs union as discussed in previous chapters but also the 'Rules of Competition' in Part Three of the Treaty of Rome. They form the basis of its competition policy. In addition, the CEC has tried to formulate and put into effect an industrial policy. A resumé of these rules will be presented here and the shifts in industrial policy will be illustrated by an outline of developments in the steel industry, and the 'sunrise' information technology industry. Further references will be made to these policies in the relevant chapters.

COMPETITION POLICY

This policy is concerned with the maintenance of competition, and preventing the formation of cartels and the use of restrictive agreements. Article 85 states that:

> The following practices shall be prohibited as incompatible with the Common Market: all agreements between undertakings ... which are designed to prevent, restrict, or distort competition ... [particularly]
> (a) the direct or indirect fixing of purchase or selling prices ...
> (b) the limitation or control of production, markets, technical development or investment;
> (c) market sharing ... ;
>
> [These] provisions ... may ... be declared inapplicable ... [if it] helps to improve the production or distribution of goods or to promote technical or economic progress, whilst allowing consumers a fair share of the resulting profit and which does not:
> (a) subject the concerns in question to any restrictions which are not indispensable to the achievement of the above objectives;
> (b) enable such concerns to eliminate competition in respect of a substantial part of the goods concerned.
>
> (Treaty of Rome 1957: Art. 85)

Article 86 is concerned with:

> Any improper exploitation by one or more undertakings of a dominant position . . . The following practices, in particular, shall be deemed to amount to improper exploitation:
> (a) the direct or indirect imposition of any unfair purchase or selling prices . . .
> (b) the limitation of production, markets or technical development to the prejudice of consumers; . . .
>
> (ibid. Art. 86)

Article 90 covers public undertakings:

> Member States shall neither introduce nor maintain in force any measure contrary to the rules contained in this Treaty . . .
>
> (ibid. Art. 90)

However, the Treaty did not cover mergers and this was only remedied by the Merger Regulation of 1990 (EEC 1989). This is concerned with large-scale mergers with a 'Community dimension'; it excludes those in which 'the market share of the undertakings does not exceed 25 per cent either in the common market or in a substantial part of it' (EEC 1989: L 395/2):

> . . . a concentration has a Community dimension where:
> (a) the aggregate worldwide turnover of all the undertakings concerned is more than ECU 5,000 million, and
> (b) the aggregate Community-wide turnover of each of at least two of the undertakings concerned is more than ECU 250 million,
> unless each of the undertakings concerned achieves more than two-thirds of its aggregate Community-wide turnover within one and the same Member State [when it is vetted by the national authorities].
>
> (ibid. L395/3)

The Commission requires notification of such mergers. If the CEC decides the merger falls within the scope of the Regulation it then determines whether the merger is compatible with competition in the common market:

> Where the Commission finds that, following modification by the undertakings concerned if necessary, ['the merger does not create or strengthen a dominant position as a result of which effective competition would be significantly impeded'] . . . it shall issue a decision declaring the concentration compatible with the common market.

> It may attach to its decision conditions and obligations intended to ensure that the undertakings concerned comply with the the commitments

they have entered into *vis-à-vis* the Commission with a view to modifying the original concentration plan.

(ibid. L395/3–6)

The Commission is given the power to fine undertakings between ECU 1,000 and ECU 50,000 if they do not supply information or if it is incorrect or misleading. More drastically, it can impose fines of up to 10 per cent of the aggregate turnover of the undertakings concerned if they fail to comply with the Commission's decisions.

The problem for the CEC in instituting its competition policy is that Member States, in particular the UK and Germany, have their own restrictive practices and monopoly legislation and the question has been how to sort out their jurisdiction. This applies particularly to mergers of EU and third-country firms such as BA and American Airlines discussed in Chapter 12.

The CEC's area of jurisdiction becomes even more contentious when the EU endeavours to extend it to cover the merger of two third-country firms such as Boeing and McDonnell Douglas. This proposed merger was approved by the Federal Trade Commission of the US. But under the 1990 Merger Regulation the CEC has the power to investigate big mergers even of non-EU companies, provided the merging companies have a combined global turnover of more than ECU 5bn ($3.3bn) as well as a turnover in the EU's single market of at least ECU 250m as specified above. Karel Van Miert the competition commissioner outlined his three major concerns. First, the merger would extend Boeing's dominant position so that it would control 84 per cent of the world's currently operating jet aircraft. Secondly, Boeing would gain access to McDonnell Douglas's research and development, for which the US government pays as part of its defence budget but which could be used for civilian aircraft. Thirdly, he was concerned that the twenty-year single-supplier deals that Boeing had signed with American, Delta, and Continental Airlines in the US closed too large a section of the market to the European Airbus (Tucker 1997).

If Boeing ignored the CEC's objections and continued with the merger, Brussels could impose fines of up to 10 per cent of the companies' revenues, and could seize Boeing aircraft being delivered to the EU in order to collect the fines. If the CEC declared the merged company illegal, this could also make it difficult for EU companies to sign contracts with Boeing (Tucker and Skapinker 1997).

This display of brinkmanship eventually led Boeing to agree:

1   to make available licences and patents from McDonnell Douglas's military research programmes to rival groups;
2   to establish McDonnell Douglas's civilian operations as a separate legal entity inside Boeing;
3   to promise not to abuse its dominant position to influence the aircraft supplies sector; and

4   to drop the exclusivity clauses from the twenty-year supply deals it had signed with the three US airlines and agree not to sign any more for another ten years.

As a result, at the end of July 1997 the CEC approved plans for the merger. The President of the CEC denied that it had taken into account 'other political interests', although EU Member States were undoubtedly concerned about the effect the merger might have on the sales of Airbus (Tucker *et al.* 1997).

INDUSTRIAL POLICY

Gaul (1995) defines industrial policy 'as the set of government interventions that by way of taxes (or subsidies) and regulations on domestic products or factors of production attempt to modify the allocation of domestic resources that results from the free operation of the market'. The problem for the CEC has been to prevent the governments of individual Member States subsidizing their own industries and thus undermining the operation of free intra-EC trade. Under Articles 92–94 of the Treaty of Rome (1957) the EC Commission forbids national governments from subsidizing the direct costs of its domestic firms in a way which distorts competition between Member States. Export aid is not allowed. Some exceptions are made, most importantly for 'aid intended to promote the economic development of regions where the standard of living is abnormally low or where there is serious under-employment' (ibid. Art. 92). The subsidies that arc allowed are for investment, rationalization, or research and development (R&D) expenditure.

In the CEC's operations, competition and industrial policies have become inextricably interwoven with its trade policy, and these policies in turn have come into conflict with the political objectives of governments in Member States. Furthermore, the orientation of CEC policy has gradually shifted from one of *dirigisme*, which has involved intervention with the use of public money, to competition and liberalization. Jacques Delors, who was President of the Commission from 1985 to 1994, was a socialist and in favour of inter-vention, but the lack of success of this policy, coupled with the appointment of a number of more liberal Commissioners, led to a shift in policies.

The Competition Directorate is constantly upbraiding the governments of Member States for excessive subsidies; generally, this is either for their champions, or for plants in areas of high unemployment. Germany, once the upholder of free market principles, is now regarded as the worst offender after Italy. EU figures show that in 1992–94 German subsidies were 2.6 per cent of GDP and 5.4 per cent of public spending; subsidies to industry were ECU 2012 ($1,812) per employee, pushed up by the massive payments to Eastern Germany. The Kiel Institute of World Economics calculates that the total of direct subsidies and tax breaks is even higher at DM 300bn per year, equal to 8.6 per cent of GDP, and that if you include credits and guarantees from public sector banks, it would be raised to DM 400bn. It questions whether subsidies on this scale are compatible with a market economy. This resort to subsidies represents partly an attempt by the German government to retard de-industrialization and the decline of the coal industry, partly an endeavour to reduce unemployment in eastern Germany, and partly a decline in the status of economics. The competition Commissioner, Karel Van Miert, is still arguing about the aid offered to Volkswagen for two plants in Lower Saxony which amounted to DM 300,000 (around £100,000) per job. Aid to the banking sector and shipbuilding are also being investigated (Tucker and Norman 1997).

In order to illustrate how the shifts in the orientation of industrial policy both by the CEC and the governments of Member States has affected industries, a description will be given of EC policy, first, towards the steel industry, which is now regarded as in decline, and then towards the 'sunrise' information technology (IT) industry.

THE STEEL INDUSTRY

The iron and steel industry has been of major concern to the members of the EC from the outset. Indeed, the Treaty of Paris establishing the European Coal and Steel Community (ECSC) in 1951 preceded the EC, and the ECSC governs trade in steel. The original objective was to remove discrimination by ECSC producers – whether that discrimination was exercised by direct or by indirect means (e.g. via distorted transport cost schedules) – and thus to open up the markets and promote the integration of these industries. This would deprive Germany of the ability ever again to use its own industry as the base for a large armaments programme.

The steel industry has an added political significance in so far as it is regarded as one of the 'commanding heights of an economy', an essential basis for industrialization. All the major countries and many of the minor ones attach great national importance to these industries and much of the steel industry is state-owned. The degree of government involvement has meant that the location of plants has often been determined by political requirements – that is, the need to provide employment – rather than being sited according to considerations of economic feasibility and profitability. A prime example of this was in Britain where instead of a single steel mill being established in the 1960s, one was built in Ravenscraig in Scotland and one in South Wales.

This type of government intervention in location occurs even though the technology used (i.e. for a blast furnace), basic oxygen steel making, is very capital intensive and shows considerable economies of scale. For instance, Pratten calculated that the minimum efficient technical scale was 72 per cent of total production in the UK, with a 6 per cent increase in unit costs for production at half that scale (CEC 1988: 111). This technology is used for 70 per cent of steel production in the EC (Glais 1995: 220). A more recent, less capital-intensive, form of production is the electric arc furnace which melts scrap. It was first used in Italy, and in the late 1970s the investment cost, at $500–700 per tonne, was three times cheaper than for integrated oxygen plant (op.cit.). This process is used to make rods and bars for construction, mechanical engineering and wire drawing (House of Lords 1993).

The problems of the steel industry are long-standing. In the past, EC steel producers have been considerable suppliers in the world market. But steel was one of the first industries to be established by any major developing country starting to industrialize, and consequently a world overcapacity in steel production soon developed. Then, in the late 1950s and 1960s, the Japanese built a number of plants incorporating technological developments such as continuous casting, a more fuel efficient method of production, and computer process control, and this was accompanied by a very rapid increase in labour productivity. Thus Japan became the lowest cost producer of steel (Walter 1983).

The rise in the price of fuel in the early 1970s significantly raised the level of costs in steel production and the downturn in international economic activity in the latter half of the 1970s imposed great competitive strains on all the steel industries. In 1977 Viscount Davignon became the EC Commissioner for industry; his devices for keeping up the price of steel are called the Davignon Plan. He introduced a system of recommended minimum prices for certain iron and steel products which was extended in 1978. Minimum prices were also established for imports, and VERs were negotiated with foreign suppliers (Swann 1992: 325).

When, in 1980, prices resumed their downward slide, production was restricted under 'the manifest crisis' Article 58 of the ECSC Treaty by allocating production quotas to the different firms based on mill capacity. This lasted, with certain misbehaviour on part of participants, from 1980 to 1988. Jonathan Aylen has argued that this effectively ossified the industry. Weaker firms did not go out of business and the German industry remained very fragmented (House of Lords 1993); but all leading European producers cut back and, for the EC as a whole, capacity was reduced by 31 million tonnes between 1981 and 1986.

The Commission tried to reduce state aid and prohibited all subsidization of direct costs and investment. Aid was allowed for the protection of the environment, for research and development expenditure and for closures under strict conditions. The effect of the minimum import prices and production quotas was to keep the price of steel products up to 30 per cent above world prices in 1987, although the price differential was much less for those without quotas, and, indeed, for concrete reinforcing bars and merchant bars it was negative for Germany (*D*), France (*F*) and Italy (*I*) (see Table 6.1) (CEC 1988: 82). In turn a higher price for steel has a knock-on effect for those industries using steel (see Table 6.2).

There was a slight increase in domestic demand in the early 1980s, which then ceased, while exports, if anything, have fallen. From September 1989 to May 1993 steel prices fell by 35 per cent (House of Lords 1993: 27). Demand for steel now tends to be static or to fall (ibid. 77). The items incorporating steel, such as cars and for construction, are becoming lighter, requiring less by weight but of a higher quality.

Table 6.1 Steel products: price differentials (as %) between internal and international prices in 1987 (annual average)

	EUR 4	D	F	I	UK
Products subject to quotas					
Hot-rolled coils	22.8	27.0	17.9	19.7	29.8
Cold-rolled sheet	24.1	25.2	25.2	20.3	24.3
Reversing mill plate	12.8	12.0	4.4	13.3	22.9
Category I beams	35.7	26.2	5.4	33.5	54.3
Products not subject to quotas					
Galvanized sheet	9.8	12.5	3.3	8.8	12.5
Wire rod	15.5	9.9	24.5	7.7	30.0
Concrete reinforcing bars	−16.4	−10.8	−20.5	−21.5	27.9
Merchant bars	−5.1	−0.8	−16.0	−25.8	15.0

Source: CEC (1988) 'The economics of 1992' (The Emerson Report), *European Economy*, **35**, March, p. 83.

Notes: Internal prices (or market prices) = list prices less rebate for certain user groups. International prices = export prices f.o.b. Antwerp. The two types of price are a weighted average of prices over the four quarters.

Table 6.2 Direct effects (as %) on the main steel-using branches of a variation of 10 per cent in the price of steel[1]

	D^2	F	I	UK
Bars	0.5	0.5	0.4	0.5
Metal products	1.8	0.9	2.0	1.5
Construction	0.2	0.1	0.4	0.1
Electrical equipment	0.5	0.1	0.3	0.2
Agricultural and industrial machinery	0.5	0.5	0.8	0.5

Source: CEC (1988) 'The economics of 1992' (The Emerson Report), *European Economy*, **35**, March, p. 83.

Notes: [1]The calculation involved multiplying the price differential (10%) by the share of the inputs of steel products in the branch in question with respect to output. Headings 135 (iron and ECSC products) and 136 (non-ECSC steel products) in the input–output tables were used in determining the steel industry's share of the output of the user branch concerned.

[2]Data not comparable with data in other countries since inputs of steel products are classified together with inputs of non-ferrous metals.

Adjustment to this long-term downwards trend in the demand for steel involves closing down capacity and reducing employment. The political problem arises because in the UK, Italy and Spain, the steel mills were deliberately established in areas of high unemployment, and it is in these areas that steel making has become most unprofitable.

The Conservative government under Margaret Thatcher carried out the rationalization of the UK industry, which involved drastic cuts in capacity and employment, prior to its privatization. Over the period 1975 to 1992 UK cut capacity by 19 per cent. Further contraction then took place with the closure of Ravenscraig in Scotland in 1992, which reduced production of crude steel by an additional 3 million tonnes. This contraction in capacity was associated with a massive reduction in employment from 250,000 in the 1970s to 41,800 in 1993: that is, employment is now 17 per cent of what it was earlier (House of Lords 1993: 10). Britain has recently been the most profitable and the lowest-cost producer in the world in terms of the integrated steel-making route of blast furnace–basic oxygen steel making, and also with the electric arc 'mini' mills using scrap. Her productivity is the same as in France and Germany in terms of hours of labour per tonne of steel, but her labour costs are lower (lower wages and social security contributions) and her depreciation charges are lower (though this may be due to the writing off of debt prior to privatization) (see Tables 6.3 and 6.4). But Britain has only 12 per cent of EC capacity. Recently production has fallen slightly and British Steel has continued with redundancies. There has been some Brussels aid for cuts in the steel industry.

The Italians, with a larger capacity, and the Spanish are finding it very difficult to close down their high-cost plants, which appear to be being heavily subsidized by their governments. Germany in total has about a third of EC capacity; parts of the West German as well as the East German industry also appear to be making losses.

Table 6.3 Steel-making costs in Europe (March 1993)

	US $ per tonne CRC shipped
United Kingdom	413
France	493
Germany	558
Japan	572
United States of America	513
South Korea	511
Taiwan	511

Source: Peter Marcus and Donald Barnett, *World Steel Dynamics*, New York: Paine Webber, 1993, exhibit 14.

Quoted in House of Lords Select Committee on the European Communities (July 1993) *Restructuring the EC Steel Industry*, London: HSMO.

Note: Assumes 90 per cent capacity utilizations. Exchange rates: $ = £0.7; $ = DM 1.64; $ = FF 5.56.

Table 6.4 Breakdown of steel-making costs in Europe (March 1993)

	US$ per tonne CRC shipped		
	UK	France	Germany
Materials			
Coking coal	41	41	44
Iron ore	62	61	69
Scrap (gross)	39	39	38
All other materials	153	160	179
Total materials	295	301	330
Labour			
Cost per hour	18.0	27.5	33.0
Hours per tonne	5.4	5.2	5.3
Total labour	97	143	175
Financial costs			
Depreciation	20	36	42
Interest	1	13	11
Total financial	21	49	53
Total pre-tax cost	413	493	558

Source: Peter Marcus and Donald Barnett, *World Steel Dynamics*, New York: Paine Webber, 1993, exhibit 14. Quoted ibid.

Note: Assumes 90 per cent capacity utilization.

During 1993 the EC Commission was trying to persuade the industry to close 30 million tonnes of excess crude steel capacity – the problems it encountered in doing so are related in the *Financial Times*[1] – but it found it difficult to get the co-operation of the private producers, British Steel and the German companies Thyssen and Krupp-Hoesch, without some reduction in the subsidies paid to the state-owned producers in Spain and Italy. Such a reduction involves a 50,000 cut in the labour force, which would require compensation. It was suggested that a levy be put on the firms remaining in the industry to finance the social costs of those closing down capacity, but this would reduce the profits of a not very profitable industry. Alternatively, the fund collected by the ECSC could be used for this purpose.

By December 1993 the Commission appeared to have given in to the political exigencies of governments involved in steel production. Industry ministers unanimously approved state subsidies for public sector production in east Germany, Italy, Spain and Portugal worth ECU 6.79bn (£5.17bn), involving only a 5 million tonne reduction in capacity, and a restructuring of Ekostahl, the east German producer, which involved an expansion in production. This is a derogation under Article 95 of the ECSC Treaty, which otherwise bans such subsidies. The Commission hoped that the other

25 million tonnes reduction in capacity would be contributed by the private sector in exchange for assistance in financing redundancies and limitations on imports from eastern Europe. Although the Commission's long-term aim was to abolish subsidies and allow trade in steel to take place on the basis of relative cost advantage, in the short term this appears to have been abandoned.

Italy wanted to give ECU 415m (£319.55m) in state aid to Brescia for the reduction of steel capacity. But there was a question as to whether this would be acceptable if the companies did not close down completely. Leon Brittan, concerned with EC trade policy, was worried that the US would regard it as an additional subsidy. Mr Karel Van Miert, the Commissioner concerned with EC competition policy, regarded it as necessary if the EU was to reach its target of reducing EU steel-making capacity by 19m tonnes. The plan then collapsed.

In September 1995, Ispat International, an Indian firm, agreed to take over Irish Steel for a nominal I£1. It involved the Irish government writing off I£17m of debt and injecting I£10m into the company. British Steel, opposing this move, said the Irish taxpayers would be paying I£27m for 300 jobs – but indirect jobs were involved. British Steel then argued that the plan would force it to close a plant in Shelton, near Stoke-on-Trent, involving the loss of 400 jobs directly and 600 jobs indirectly if the plan goes ahead. The international steel market is glutted.

This subsidization by EC governments provided a pretext for the US to impose countervailing duties on steel, and, in January 1993 the US duly imposed dumping duties of up to 110 per cent on imports of carbon steel from the EC.

At the same time the EC's net exports to Eastern Europe went into reverse, and the EC has trying to prevent an anticipated flood of low-quality steel from Eastern Europe, while at same time anxious not to discourage producers too much. For Poland, Hungary, and Czechoslavakia trade has been completely liberalized, but VERs have been negotiated with the other countries of Central and Eastern Europe (CEC 1993: 34). At the end of 1992 the EC imposed anti-dumping duties on imports from Eastern Europe while pressing governments there to agree to minimum import prices. The actual level of imports from Eastern Europe has been kept low; in 1992 it was only 4 million tonnes compared with an EC production of 132 million tonnes (House of Lords 1993).

Thus the situation in the steel industry is confused, with many EU member countries preferring to subsidize their steel industry rather than incur the political opprobrium of closing plants down. Most of these subsidies appear to be inconsistent with EC policy. They also prevent rationalization and forfeit any benefits to be gained from trade creation and further exploitation of economies of scale. The EU is trying to restrict imports from Eastern Europe and, at the same time, export to the US, where it faces anti-dumping duties because of the subsidies.

EUROPEAN COMPUTING AND
TELECOMMUNICATIONS INDUSTRY

The one consistent assumption underlying EC policy towards the computing and telecommunications industry is that Europe *should* be at the leading edge of the technology. But how this is to be achieved has been a matter of dispute between Member States, and the orientation of the CEC itself has changed over time from one of *dirigisme*, espoused by the French, to liberalism and free markets, as espoused by Germany and in the UK after 1979 when the Conservatives came to power with Margaret Thatcher devoted to free enterprise.

Britain

In the immediate postwar period, Britain was at the forefront of developments in computing, which had been pursued to wage the war and 'crack the code' used by the Germans to transmit messages. But the secrecy surrounding the development of the 'Colossus' machine designed by Alan Turing, which was maintained until the late 1970s, handicapped the rest of her industry, particularly as the methodology had been passed to the US (Gannon 1997). Five commercial computers were developed in the 1950s, but the British companies were very wary of expansion unless supported by government funds and these were very limited. Britain's finances were in a parlous state. Most government subsidies went for defence purposes, although the National Research Development Corporation (NRDC) set up by Harold Wilson, then President of the Board of Trade, in 1949 had £5 million to invest. In the 1960s most of the British firms withdrew from computing, leaving IBM with half the sales. In 1968 a succession of mergers between UK companies under pressure from the NRDC ended in the establishment of ICL, the world's largest non-US company producing mainframe computers (Gannon 1997).

Germany

Computers had also been developed during the Second World War by Germany. But the deprivation of the postwar period and the occupying power's ban on commercial manufacture meant that this progressed little until the ban was lifted in 1955. Most German companies found it difficult to finance development, and eventually Siemens, under least pressure and thus able to rescue other German producers, emerged as the major German computer company. It faced competition from IBM, which had set up a manufacturing plant in Stuttgart in 1956. German firms were much more willing to make use of computers than the British. In 1965 there were 2,300 in use in Germany compared with 1,582 in the UK and 1,500 in France. In the US there were 24,700.

France

In France Bull emerged as the major computer company, but the effort of developing a wholly French and wholly Bull design pushed it into bankruptcy and in 1964 it had to sell its computing interests to General Electric of the US. At that time, the French government did not support the company with finance or orders (Gannon 1997: ch. 9).

IBM came to dominate not only the US market but also the European one. It treated Europe as a single market.

> By the mid-1960s, all aspects of IBM's operations were geared toward a single international market, with research and development, component production, and systems assembly allocated among different units around the globe, based on relative costs and the availability of specialised resources in different geographical locations.
>
> (Flamm, quoted in Gannon 1997: 148).

This dominance by IBM led to a backlash, with the governments of the major EC countries endeavouring to support and subsidize their major firms. France went as far as creating one, Compagnier Internationale d'Informatique (CII), by merging the French firms CAE and SEA with a group of smaller ones. The public sector was forced to buy its machines. In Germany, the subsidy went not only on basic research but also on training.

The support each government gave its national champion meant that European firms found it difficult to export to each other, and also led to the cancellation of a joint supercomputer project between ICT of Britain and CAE of France. The CEC, in endeavouring to develop a policy, was caught between the *dirigiste* policies that most Member States were actually following and the competitive policies adumbrated by the Treaty of Rome. The final communiqué of the Paris summit of 1972 called for 'the removal of fiscal and other barriers to mergers and the creation of European companies; and the promotion of European-scale companies to compete in high technology industries' (Gannon 1997: 170).

The European companies began to move in favour of more co-operation with each other when they saw the great advances being made by US and Japanese companies. The European governments continued to subsidize their 'champions' and France nationalized CII-Honeywell-Bull to become once more Bull. But then the CEC and the industry drew up a programme for research in five areas: advanced microelectronics, advanced computing, software technologies, office automation, and integrated computer systems for manufacturing. It was entitled a 'European Strategic Programme for Research and Development in Information Technology' (ESPRIT) and was agreed to in 1982 after objections from Britain. ECU 11.5 million was put forward as pilot financing by the EC, with an equal amount coming from the companies. The projects all had to be in the 'pre-competitive' basic research stage because the Treaty of Rome, under Articles 85 and 86, forbids collaboration. But the competition directorate gave a 'block exemption' to pre-competitive research. There were many applications for money but most went to the Big Twelve (ICL, GEC and Plessey from Britain, AEG, Nixdorf and Siemens from Germany, Thomson, Bull and CGE from France, Olivetti and Stet from Italy, and Philips from the Netherlands). This Esprit programme was then extended.

In telecommunications, the 'Research in Advanced Communications in Europe' (Race) was also started from 1985–87. After the Single European Act was passed in 1968 a series of mini-programmes were introduced applying computer systems to road transport (Drive), medicine (Aim), education (Delta), and some concerned with electronic trading and the information market (Gannon 1997).

However, the companies that made use of these programmes almost invariably did so in their own home markets. There was little sign of European co-operation. Nor did it appear that the programmes had made the industry more competitive. Indigenous computer and semiconductor manufacturers continued to decline. ICL, the last European mainframe manufacturer, was taken over by Fujitsu in 1990. The production that remained was largely by US and Japanese companies who had been induced to invest in the EU by its EC trade barriers, with 40 per cent of the investment going to Britain.

Leon Brittan was made the competition Commissioner in 1988 and he proceeded to argue for free trade:

> Brittan battled fiercely with Delors and others over whether to allow French government support for Bull. 'I do not understand why lack of competition at home should be thought to help a company's prospects abroad. I should have thought the opposite was the case and so it proves when you look at cases.'
>
> (Gannon 1997: 209)

Standards

The main reason that IBM could maintain its position was because its proprietary standards were taken as the 'de facto' ones. Companies investing in computers generally wanted an IBM to save on training, and if they were upgrading, to save on the conversion costs that would be incurred if they invested in an ICL or Bull. This enabled IBM to earn hefty margins – as much as 300 per cent on its mainframe products (Gannon 1997). As Gannon says:

> Standards are, by definition, an abrogation of competition. They are anti-competitive because they necessarily involve companies doing things

by cooperative agreement, or allow a company to extract monopoly rents from a proprietary standard, that is enjoy the fruits of a 'dominant position'. But standards are inevitable in computing, they define its use by millions of people. They can be public and open, proprietary and closed.

(ibid. 244)

However, in international fora throughout the 1970s a system of open standards was gradually being established. These were negotiated through the International Telecommunication Union (ITU) and the International Standards Organization (ISO). In spite of delaying tactics by IBM these organizations slowly built up networking standards known as 'open systems interconnection' (OSI) standards. The CEC encouraged the European computer companies, then ICL, Bull, Siemens, Nixdorf and Olivetti, to adopt the OSI standards, and standards promotion was incorporated by Esprit. The companies agreed, but each tried to manipulate the standards to favour its own product.

These OSI standards were adopted by public administrations in the US and Europe. The CEC wanted to stop the use of disparate national standards, which it regarded as non-tariff barriers to trade. It adopted OSI for its own computing needs in 1985, and in 1988 the Council of Ministers agreed that OSI standards would be required for all public procurement contracts for computing systems. The CEC tried to develop its own standards to keep up with the rapid development in technology and applications. It did not include the TCP/IP protocols used by the Internet and supported by the US government, and its efforts to back OSI as a broader and technically more powerful set of standards failed, partly because European industry did not support it. The CEC directive with respect to the use of OSI in public procurement was largely ignored.

Thus the CEC's endeavour to establish a 'level playing field' by the use of open standards failed. This was because, although customers appreciated the freedom of not being tied to their supplier, other producers were often interested in having their own standard adopted in order to benefit from the monopoly rents associated with it. Some have argued that the adoption of open standards stifles technological development, but the proprietary standards that are adopted are not necessarily the technologically superior ones.

The personal computer

IBM only began to lose its dominance when, because of the minaturization of components, mini and then 'personal' or 'microcomputers' were developed with the power of mainframe computers of a few years previously. They gained in popularity and IBM contracted an outside company, Microsoft, to write the operating system software for its personal computer (MS-DOS), and Intel to design and manufacture the necessary microprocessor chips. These companies, in turn, sold their product to others, who were then able to produce IBM clones. IBM had then lost control of its own standard, which became available to everyone. The other standards disappeared, apart from that of Apple, which still in 1989 maintained 10 per cent of the micro-computer market.

However, the European firms did not benefit from this development because the national champions focused on mainframe computers in their struggle with IBM. Personal computers were not really within the purview of Esprit or national research and development (R&D) programmes. The European companies were unable to keep up with the pace of technolog-ical change. They also wanted to keep their own systems. Thus Acorn, which was chosen to be the BBC personal computer, refused to incorpo-rate DOS because it thought its own operating system was superior. It had not realized how important standards were to become. In addition, the European manufacturers seldom had the experience to produce such low-cost machines. So both Nixdorf and Olivetti lost their initial positions (Gannon 1997).

Therefore, in spite of EC and national R&D expenditure, European firms had abandoned the production of both mainframe and smaller computers by 1997. They turned their attention instead to telecommunications and software.

Telecommunications

Leon Brittan argued for less research funding of particular sectors in favour of 'horizontal' projects to improve overall efficiency. He was arguing against the interventionists such as Filippo Pandolfi of DGXIII. The latter proposed a series of pan-European administrative and public sector telecommunica-tion networks to be publicly financed. It sounded similar to proposals put forward previously by Bull, Olivetti, and Siemens.

However, Martin Bangemann became the Commissioner for industrial affairs in 1988. He also took over DGXIII. He was concerned with compet-itiveness and an efficient functioning market economy. The Bangemann Group report in 1994 on 'Europe and the Global Information Society' argued that public funds were not needed to help build the 'information superhighway' in Europe. The capital cost of constructing this 'integrated broadband communications' network' was estimated at between $250 billion and $1,000 billion, but public money would not be required if restrictions were removed on new entrants and imposed on the powerful state-owned monopolies. As Bangemann said:

> We don't need public money, we don't even need new technologies . . .
> We must deregulate, liberalise, and privatise . . . If we do not do it,
> others will – and we will be lost.
>
> (quoted in Gannon 1997: 308)

The CEC began pressing not only for voice services liberalization to be instituted by January 1998, to which the post, telephone and telegraph state companies (PTTs) had agreed, but also infrastructure liberalization. Furthermore, this was backed up by the Competition Commissioner, now Karel van Miert, blocking alliances of large groups unless they were accompanied by further measures of liberalization. In this, the rest of the EU was following the lead of Britain and the US. The liberalization of the telecommunications market is discussed further in Chapter 12.

Conclusion

This very brief account of an exceedingly complex subject, largely derived from Gannon (1997), has been given in order to show how difficult the CEC has found it to achieve through its own policies its objective of placing the EU in the forefront of the information technology industries. The US firms retain their dominance in the industry even though their inventions are not necessarily superior to those of European firms. The latter have now withdrawn from the production of mainframe computers, and the production of personal computers appears to be an assembly operation of imported components.

NOTE

1. See *Financial Times*: 1 December 1992; 13 September 1993; 18 December 1993; 20 December 1993; 20 May 1994; 13 June 1994; 16 June 1994; 8 September 1995; and 10 November 1995.

REFERENCES

CEC (1988) 'The economics of 1992' (The Emerson Report), *European Economy*, **35**, March.
—— (1993) 'The European Community as a world trade partner', *European Economy*, **52**.
EEC (1989) Council Regulation No. 4064/89 L395 (The Merger Regulation), 'on the control of concentrations between undertakings', put into effect in 1990.
Gannon, P. (1997) *Trojan Horses and National Champions*, London: Apt-Amatic Books.
Gaul, J. (1995) 'The three common policies: an economic analysis', in P. Buigues, A. Jacquemin and A. Sapir (eds), *European Policies on Competition, Trade and Industry*, Aldershot: Edward Elgar.
Glais, M. (1995) 'Steel industry', in P. Buigues, A. Jacquemin and A. Sapir (eds), *European Policies on Competition, Trade and Industry*, Aldershot: Edward Elgar.
House of Lords (1993) *Restructuring the EC Steel Industry*, HL Paper No. 111, Select Committee on the European Communities, July, London. HMSO.
Swann, D. (1992) *The Economics of the Common Market*, rev. edn, Harmondsworth: Penguin.

Treaty of Rome (1957), trans. (1962) as *Treaty Establishing the European Economic Community*, London: HMSO.

Tucker, E. (1997) 'Brussels commissioners place fingers on trigger', *Financial Times*, 21 July.

Tucker, E. and Norman, P. (1997) 'The EU's bad boy is Germany', *Financial Times*, 7 October.

Tucker, E. and Skapinker, M. (1997) 'Boeing merger faces new Brussels attack', *Financial Times*, 17 July.

Tucker, E., Skapinker, M. and Clark, B. (1997) 'Brussels averts crisis by agreeing Boeing merger', *Financial Times*, 24 July.

Walter, I. (1983) 'Structural adjustment and trade policy in the international steel industry', in W.R. Cline (ed.), *Trade Policy in the 1980s*, Washington, DC: Institute for International Economics.

7 The impact of preferential trading areas and international direct investment on the development of UK trade

In 1950 Britain was a paradigm of an industrial power exporting manu-factures in exchange for food and raw materials. Her position can be seen in Table 7.1. In 1950 four-fifths of her exports were manufactures: machinery and transport equipment, categorized as finished manufactures, accounted for 35 per cent, and the 34 per cent of semi-manufactures included textiles 16 per cent, and chemicals 6½ per cent. The UK and the US each accounted for just over a quarter of world exports of manufactures (Mansell 1980).[1]

Obversely she was the largest importer and net importer of agricultural products in the world. Imports of food, beverages and tobacco accounted for 39 per cent of her imports in 1950 (see Table 7.2), and agricultural raw materials for 18 per cent. Fuel in the form of petroleum products accounted for 7½ per cent. Only 4 per cent of her imports were finished manufac-tures, although an additional 14 per cent were semi-manufactures.

In addition, as she was the major industrial power in the Commonwealth, which was a large preferential area, she had a very wide distribution of trade across the world. Certainly, her trading links were much wider than those of the other EC countries. Although 31 per cent of her exports went to Western Europe and 5.6 per cent to the US, 35 per cent went to developing countries, many of them Commonwealth countries (see Table 4.1). This slant towards the markets of developing countries may have affected the quality of her merchandise in so far as it was designed to be robust and tolerant of variations in climatic conditions from drought to monsoon, rather than to meet the sophisticated requirements of high-income countries. Design was one of the most frequently cited shortcomings of British exports when compared with those of other industrialized countries. Britain's exports of manufactures increased in the 1950s and 1960s, but not as fast as those of other countries and not as fast as her imports. The recovery of Germany and Japan enabled them to re-emerge as major competitors.

Moreover, many of her former customers, either resource rich such as Australia or developing countries, were beginning to industrialize. In so far as this provided a greater demand for investment goods this might

Table 7.1 Distribution of UK exports of goods by product group, 1950–96 (percentages)

	1950	1955	1960	1965	1970	1975	1980	1985	1990	1995	1996
Food, beverages and tobacco	7	6	6	7	6	7	7	6	7	7	7
Basic materials	6	6	5	3	3	3	3	3	2	2	2
Fuels	3	5	4	3	3	4	14	22	8	6	7
Semi-manufactures	40	38	35	35	34	30	29	26	28	28	27
Finished manufactures	41	42	47	49	51	52	45	41	53	55	56
Miscellaneous	2	3	3	4	3	4	2	2	2	1	1

Table 7.2 Distribution of UK imports of goods by product group, 1950–96 (percentages)

	1950	1955	1960	1965	1970	1975	1980	1985	1990	1995	1996
Food, beverages and tobacco	39	37	33	30	22	18	12	11	10	9	9
Basic materials	35	29	23	19	15	9	8	6	5	4	4
Fuels	8	11	10	11	8	17	14	13	6	3	4
Semi-manufactures	14	18	22	24	28	24	27	25	26	27	26
Finished manufactures	4	5	11	15	25	30	37	44	52	55	56
Miscellaneous	0	0	1	1	1	2	1	1	2	1	1

Source: Mansell, Ken (1980) 'UK visible trade in the post-war years,' Economic Trends October for 1950–1965.
CSO (1990) Monthly Review of External Trade Statistics Annual Supplement 1990 N.11 for 1970–85.
ONS (1997) MM24 Monthly Review of External Trade Statistics February 1997 for 1990–96.
1950–65 cif. basis 1970–96 balance of payments basis.

have been expected to benefit Britain. For instance, almost all developing countries established a textile industry that required the purchase of imported machinery. But although British exports of machinery by tonnage increased briefly between 1948–52 it thereafter declined to about the same magnitudes as in the early 1930s (*Tattersall's* 1969). At the same time, Britain lost most of her exports of cotton textiles and in the 1950s faced increasing competition from developing countries in her home market, as will be described in Chapter 10.

There were a number of studies investigating the distribution of British exports by commodity and by area. They generally came to the same conclusion, that neither was sufficient to account for the decline in Britain's position; for instance, the distribution of her exports to areas with a low growth in imports was compensated for by the proportion sent to areas with a high growth in imports.

In an earlier study (Moore 1964), the author investigated the factors affecting the UK's exports of machinery and transport equipment and exports of chemicals to the major countries and areas from 1953–62. The industrial production of the importing region, the British price, and the price of other OEEC countries were taken as independent variables. But the most significant variable was found to be the export proceeds that the importing region gained from Britain, which provided a coefficient of 0.7 to 0.8 for machinery and transport equipment, and 0.3 for chemicals. This was termed the 'reciprocity' effect. Taking the former as 0.8 indicated that a 10 per cent increase in British imports would lead to a 3.8 per cent increase in total exports due to additional reciprocal sales of machinery and transport equipment alone.

This was important because at the time Britain was restricting her imports of food by subsidizing her agriculture, and had also imposed restraints on imports of textiles and clothing from developing countries, in both cases restricting the export earnings of her customers. In other words, by supporting her declining industries she was acting against the interests of her exporting industries.

International institutional developments appeared favourable to an exporter of manufactures, with the liberalization of trade between European countries brought about by the OEEC and GATT trade negotiations, described in the last chapter. Between 1950 and 1970 there was a rapid increase in world trade. In particular, trade in manufactures in real terms doubled between 1953 and 1963 and then again between 1963 and 1970. Manufactures increased as a proportion of world trade from 45 per cent in 1955 to 63 per cent in 1970.

However, Britain's exports did not increase in line with those of the rest of the world so that her proportion of world trade in manufactures declined from 26 per cent in 1950 to 11 per cent in 1970. Her fastest growing exports were of chemicals and machinery. By 1970 the proportion of finished manufactures had risen to account for half her exports (see Table 7.1) and semi-manufactures had fallen to 34 per cent, largely due to a reduction in exports of textiles. Manufactures still accounted for more than four-fifths of the total.

The major changes in UK trade were with respect to her imports. The growth of these at *current prices* is shown in Figure 7.1. There appeared little increase in expenditure on food, beverages, and tobacco (Foodbt) and that on fuel appeared stable between the mid-1960s and 1971. But since the 1950s there has been a consistent increase in imports of manufactures. In *real* terms Britain's traditional imports of food, beverages, and tobacco, increased erratically to the mid-1960s and then remained stagnant. Her imports of basic materials just fluctuated. There was strong growth in her real imports of fuels, and her imports of manufactures increased rapidly. Thus, as can be seen from Table 7.2, her pattern of imports had shifted, with food and raw materials accounting for three-quarters in 1950 and declining to 37 per cent in 1970. Imports of fuel had increased to 10 per cent. The growth in her imports of manufactures meant that by 1970 they accounted for half of her total imports. Imports of manufactures had increased so much faster than exports that there was a slight decline in her real *net* exports of manufactures.

Let us now consider the major exogenous changes that have affected trade. They are, on the one hand, the OPEC price rises and the development of North Sea oil, and on the other hand, the changes in Britain's membership of preferential trading areas. Because Britain's accession to the

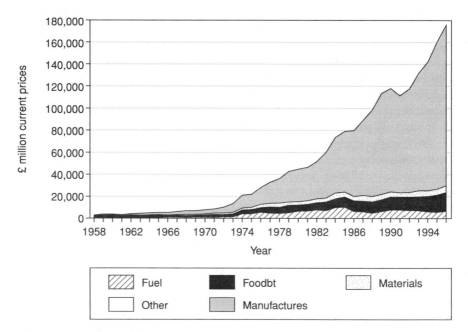

Figure 7.1 UK imports by commodity group, 1958–96 (current prices BOP £m)

EC occurred at the same time as the quadrupling of the oil price between 1973–74 it is difficult to identify their separate impacts.

OPEC PRICE RISE

As will be described in Chapter 8, the combination of the discovery and exploitation of petroleum gas and oil in the North Sea and the OPEC price rises after 1970 contributed to another metamorphosis in Britain's trading position. Her exports of fuel increased, so that by 1983 she had become a net exporter of fuel and had a deficit in manufactures. Looking at this within a general equilibrium framework, the latter is generally attributed to the former. Some idea of the long-run relationship can be obtained from Figure 7.2. Exports and imports of manufactures, and the balance of trade in services and in fuel have been deflated by the unit price index of manufactures exports. The actual price of oil clearly rose far faster than that of manufactures in the 1970s, but this gives an idea of the contribution of trade in fuels to the general equilibrium position elsewhere. As can be seen, in the 1950s, imports and exports of manufactures in real terms were growing at about the same rate. But from the early 1970s imports of manufactures began to accelerate with a slight hump in 1973 until they overtook exports at 1980 prices in the early 1980s. Meanwhile, the fuel deficit that had to be paid for became larger in 1974 due to the rise in the price of oil, but then it declined and reversed itself in 1980. The net balance of the service sector (deflated by the unit price index of manufactures), although small, also began to increase in the 1970s. Thus in the 1980s Britain was paying for her deficit in manufactures and also food (not shown) by a positive balance on services and fuel.

Alternatively, the changes in her balances at current prices for the different categories of goods from 1970 to 1990 can be seen in Figure 7.3. Her fuel balance becomes positive in the 1980s, whereas her balance on both types of manufactures becomes negative and the balance in food becomes increasingly negative.

To use balances in this way is to regard a country as paying for her net imports with her net exports (commodities, the export value of which is greater than the country's imports). In the present situation in which industrialized countries export and import products in the same category, it is the best indication of a country's specialization.

IMPACT OF PREFERENTIAL TRADE AGREEMENTS

An additional explanation of Britain's trading position has been the successive trade agreements which she has concluded, described in Chapter 4. Some of the calculations, first, on the effect of her membership of EFTA, and then on her accession to the EC, will now be described.

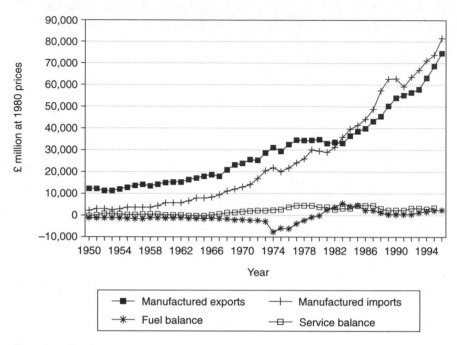

Figure 7.2 Trade in manufacturers and fuel (divided by export UV of manufacturers)

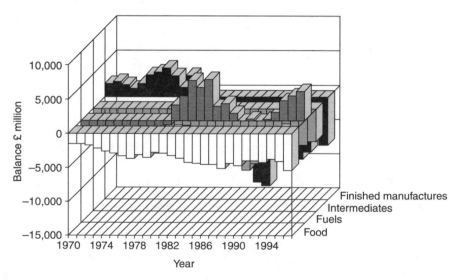

Figure 7.3 UK commodity groups' balances, 1970–96 (current prices £m)

The effect of EFTA on UK trade

Let us begin with the EFTA Secretariat's estimate of the effect of EFTA on British trade. They took as their anti-monde – their alternative scenario – the constancy of the trend in the relation of imports to expenditure: that is, they assumed that the trend from 1953–59 would have continued if Britain had not joined EFTA. Extrapolating the trends for the different commodity categories to 1965 they then compared the results with the actual imports. The results are shown in Table 7.3. Looking at the situation from the British point of view, they estimated that the increase in imports due to trade creation of $72 million was about as great as that due to trade diversion, leading to a total increase in imports from other EFTA countries of $143 million. They then applied the same analysis to the imports of other EFTA countries and concluded that, in the absence of EFTA, UK exports of manufactures to other EFTA countries would have declined far faster than they did, and that in 1965 UK exports to EFTA were $265 million greater than they would have been otherwise. Assuming that supplying EFTA markets would not have involved any diversion from the rest of the world, they then calculated that, taking the effect of the additional imports of $71 million due to trade diversion away from the additional exports of $265 million, EFTA had benefited the balance of payments by around $190 million.[2] This could be compared to the UK deficit at the time of $790 million. In other words, the effect of EFTA was to reduce the UK deficit.

However, because EFTA was comparatively small, although the proportion of exports and imports it accounted for was increasing over time, UK

Table 7.3 The effects of EFTA on Britain's imports and exports in 1965: Calculations of the EFTA Secretariat (US$m)

Commodity group	Import effects		Export effects
	TC	TD	
Leather, rubber and footwear	1	2	14
Wood and paper	39	15	1
Textiles and clothing	21	—	81
Chemical and petroleum products	—	2	28
Non-metallic mineral manufactures	—	—	1
Metals and metal manufactures	3	24	35
Machinery	—	22	46
Land transport equipment	—	4	50
Watches, clocks and instruments	8	2	—
Beverages, tobacco and miscellaneous	—	—	9
Total	72	71	265

Source: EFTA (1969) *The Effects of EFTA on the Economies of Member States*, Geneva: European Free Trade Association, 161.

Notes: TC = trade creation; TD = trade diversion.

trade with the EEC was becoming steadily more important. In 1965 the proportion of total merchandise exports to EFTA was 12 per cent, to the EC(6) 19 per cent, and to the Commonwealth 26 per cent, and the proportion of imports was 11 per cent from EFTA, 15 per cent from the EC, and 29 per cent from the Commonwealth (Table 4.1).

Changes in UK trade after 1970

Area distribution

We shall begin by looking at the change in trade that occurred after 1970, which has been taken as the base year before the anticipations of British accession to the EC and the disruptions of the oil price rises; 1987 is taken as another benchmark, and 1996 is the final year.

Let us refer back to Table 4.1 (p. 65). The EC total represents the preferential area as it was constituted at the date considered. As can be seen, even before Britain's entry the proportion of her trade with the EC(6) was increasing and the proportion with the Commonwealth was falling. By 1970 her imports and exports were distributed, with approximately one-fifth each with the Commonwealth, the EC(6) and the rest of Western Europe. In 1975, two years after Britain's accession, the EC accounted for just over one-third of her imports and exports. By 1996 this had risen to 54 per cent of her imports and 57 per cent of her exports. This increase was due to an increase in EC membership as well as the effect of preferences. Trade with the original six members of the EC has fluctuated around 40 per cent, which tends to bear out Winters' (1984: app. 2) contention that the effect of obtaining EC preference should be conceived of as a once-and-for-all parametric shift, rather than an increase in the income elasticity of demand for imports, as Balassa argued. Because so many EFTA members joined the EC, trade with the rest of Western Europe had contracted by 1996 to less that 10 per cent.

Changes in trade since 1970 by commodity category

As mentioned previously, UK manufacturers were very anxious to join the EC to improve their access to this rapidly growing market. However, reality did not live up to their expectations, as can be seen from Figure 7.4. This shows volume indices of the main categories of UK exports of manufactures from 1970 to 1996, that is, values have been deflated by commodity price indices. There was barely any increase in the volume of road vehicles and mechanical machinery until the end of the period. There was a consistent increase in exports of electrical machinery, and a general increase in exports of instruments and clothes and shoes. However, as imports of many of these products have also increased rapidly it is more revealing to look at the trade balances.

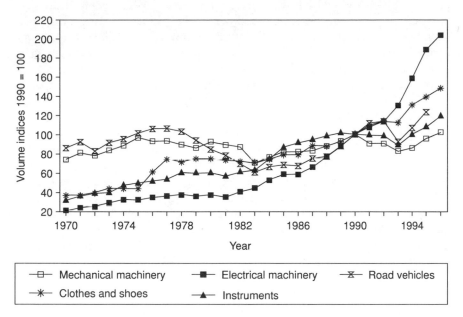

Figure 7.4 UK exports of manufactures, 1970–96 (volume indices = 100)

Before considering the situation in more detail, let us first survey the changes that occurred in the different preferential areas. As related in Chapter 4, Britain's move from being a member of EFTA to membership of the EC was a complicated change, with Britain losing her preferential position in the Commonwealth, EFTA and the Irish market. Commonwealth countries were then faced with the imposition of the CET on their exports of manufactures to the British market, which in the past had often not borne any duty. They were also faced with a variety of restrictions on textiles and clothing and other manufactures described in succeeding chapters. Ireland and Denmark became members of the EC at the same time as Britain, and from then onwards Britain faced direct competition from other EC members in their markets, just as they did in hers. The remaining members of EFTA, who formed a free trade area in manufactures with the EC, were in a similar position, facing direct competition in each other's markets. But in addition, as the CET was sometimes lower than Britain's mfn tariff, other developed countries such as the US had easier access to the British market.

In a previous exercise the author calculated the changes in trade with each of the three groups, standardized by number of countries, that is the EC(12), EFTA(6) and the Commonwealth between 1970 and 1987 (Moore 1989). Thus in Table 7.4 the main commodity categories are listed with some further breakdown for major products. Columns (2) and (3) show the overall trade balances at current prices for 1970 and 1987 on an overseas trade statistics basis (OTS) whereby the value of imports includes the cost of insurance and freight. (In the following, the SITC categories are given in square brackets.) In 1970, in the traditional mode of an industrial power Britain exported manufactures, and was a large net exporter of machinery and transport equipment [7]. She was also a net exporter of chemicals [5] and semi-manufactures [6] and miscellaneous manufactures. In exchange, she was a net importer of food [0], raw materials [2 and 6], fuels [3] and animal and vegetable oils and fats [4].

A considerable number of the subsequent changes in the value of trade have been due to inflationary price increases. In order to remove this from the value of trade overall and in each of the three areas, imports and exports were deflated by the unit price index for the commodity category as a whole. Comparing the resulting changes in trade with the different preferential areas it can be seen that between 1970 and 1987 the most rapid increase in the volume of trade was with the EC(11), columns (6) and (7). Imports of all goods from EC Member States were 250 per cent greater in real terms, and imports of manufactures were 418 per cent greater; imports of passenger cars were $7\frac{1}{2}$ times their level in 1970. British exports of manufactures also increased faster to the EC – by 172 per cent between 1970 and 1987 – than they did to the other groups of countries.

Exports to the EFTA market, in which Britain had lost her preferential position, increased at a much slower rate, by only 18 per cent for manufactures as a whole. There was a more rapid increase in imports, with the greatest increases for metal manufactures [69], electrical goods [75–77], and scientific instruments [87 and 88].

As might be expected from the change in the pattern of preference, trade with the Commonwealth declined; exports as a whole [0–9] fell by 28 per cent, and imports fell by 37 per cent in real terms. There was a decline in imports of food of 50 per cent and imports of fuel and raw materials also fell. But imports of machinery, particularly electrical machinery [75–77], increased, and so did those of scientific instruments and photo apparatus [87–88]. Imports of textiles [65] remained stagnant, but imports of clothing [84] increased by 430 per cent.

The resulting overall increase in her real exports X and imports M between 1970 and 1987 are shown in columns (4) and (5). They display a rapid increase in her exports of primary products; the 236 per cent increase in the quantity of food [0] exported and the 651 per cent of animal and vegetable oils and fats [4] are the result of the CAP, which will be discussed in Chapter 9. It is noteworthy, however, that *imports* of food hardly increased. The increased quantity of fuel [3] exported of 372 per cent, arising from the exploitation of reserves in the North Sea, will be discussed in Chapter 8.

The most significant change occurred in manufactures [5–8]. Exports increased, but not nearly as fast as imports. Exports of manufactures classified by material [6] increased by 33 per cent, but imports increased far faster,

Table 7.4 Britain's balance of trade and changes in the volume of trade by product, and for exports (X) by destination and imports (M) by origin, 1970–87

| | | Overall balance | | Volume increase 1970–87 | | Estimated volume increase 1970–87 | | | | | |
| | | | | | | EEC | | EFTA | | Commonwealth | |
Category	SITC (R2)	1970 (£m)	1987 (£m)	X (%)	M (%)	X (%)	M (%)	X (%)	M (%)	X (%)	M (%)
0	Food	−1,609	−4,964	236	5	439	90	20	21	0	−50
1	Beverages and tobacco	76	431	62	206	252	399	4	−80	28	0
2 and 6	Crude materials, textile fibres	−1,059	−3,251	102	−1	102	141	80	−24	19	−32
3	Fuels	−740	2,648	372	46	487	−34	28	2,181	690	−86
4	Animal and vegetable oils and fats	−92	−194	651	70	1,892	480	0	−38	−25	−53
5	Chemicals	242	2,194	207	252	340	339	62	104	17	−59
6	Manufactures by material	57	−5,077	33	116	70	375	−14	167	−19	−59
65	Textiles	158	−1,638	13	289	91	424	−45	38	−51	3
67	Iron and steel	126	285	79	112	135	337	−17	8	−5	−70
68	Non-ferrous metals	−260	−441	10	21	24	409	35	92	−31	−71
69	Metal manufactures	165	−335	14	418	66	740	3	1,126	−47	198
7	Machinery and transport equipment	1,822	−4,017	60	422	111	450	8	132	−28	307
71–77	Machinery	1,044	−2,074	77	451	128	392	47	167	−18	382
71–74	Mechanical[1]	871	1,194	14	198	12	163	−12	71	−26	87
75–77	Electronical[2]	173	−3,269	222	800	512	1,154	189	442	−2	841
78	Road motor vehicles	700	−3,933	−10	640	(56)	(922)	(−65)	(121)	(−70)	(59)
781	Passenger cars	244	−3,044		665	6	650	−84	74		
8	Miscellaneous manufactures	137	−2,598	183	423	97	453	88	130	54	173
84	Clothing	−13	−2,396	149	454	410	393	46	19	16	193
85 and 88	Footwear					−73	400	−60	−22	−53	−29
87 and 88	Scientific instruments and photo apparatus	55	54	214	475	279	563	100	202	−42	430
5–8	Manufactures	2,258	−9,482	82	271	142	418	18	144	−12	−4
0–9	Total	−1,017	−14,164	109	107	172	250	24	97	−28	−37

Source: L. Moore (1989) 'Changes in British trade analysed in a pure trade theory framework', in D. Cobham et al., Money, Trade and Payments, Manchester: MUP.
Notes: EEC = France, Belgium, Luxembourg, Netherlands, West Germany, Italy, Ireland, Denmark, Greece, Spain and Portugal in 1970 and 1987. EFTA = Iceland, Norway, Sweden, Finland, Switzerland and Austria in 1970 and 1987.

by 116 per cent, and in particular, imports of textiles, iron and steel, and other metal manufactures. The most striking developments were in trade in machinery and transport equipment [7] where exports increased by 60 per cent and imports by 422 per cent. Particularly noteworthy is the increase in imports of passenger cars of 665 per cent. But there was also a rapid increase in imports of machinery, particularly electrical machinery [75–77] with an increase of 800 per cent. There was also a rapid increase in imports in the final category of miscellaneous [8], in particular of clothing and shoes, and scientific instruments.

The net effect of these changes was that by 1987 the positive balance in manufactures of £2 billion in 1970 had been converted to a negative one of £10 billion in 1987. Road motor vehicles [78] with a turn round from a positive £700 to a negative £3,933 million accounted for 38 per cent of it, and within this category passenger cars [781] from a positive £244 to a negative £3,044 million, 27 per cent of the deficit. Miscellaneous manufactures [8] had also changed from a surplus of £137 to a deficit of £2,598 million. But the positive balance in chemicals [5] had increased from £242 to £2,194 million. Britain had also converted her deficit on fuels [3] to a positive balance of £2,648 million.

Thus Britain had shifted away dramatically from her traditional position. Her exports of primary products had increased far faster than her imports, whereas her imports of manufactures had increased for most categories faster than her exports. Overall, Britain's *balance of merchandise trade on a balance of payments basis* – that is, *excluding* insurance and freight included in the OTS cost of imports in Table 7.4 – had moved from a deficit of £14 million in 1970 to £11 billion in 1987, that is, it was some 800 times greater. However, this is in terms of a depreciated currency; measured in terms of US dollars, it was 548 times greater (CSO 1990).

The question then is how much of this change in direction was due to the formation of the EC and the other changes in trading arrangements, and how much of it would have happened anyway? After all the proportion of trade with the Commonwealth was declining just as the rate of Commonwealth preference was declining. The actual measurement of this depends on what is selected as the 'anti-monde', that is, the alternative scenario of what would have happened in the absence of these changes.

The apparent effect on Britain of joining the EC

A number of economists endeavoured to calculate the effects of British entry into the EC on trade by extrapolating shares or trends in markets prior to entry and comparing this 'anti-monde' with what actually happened. Mayes (1983) considered the markets in eight categories of goods. He estimated an increase in imports from the EC of £5 billion in 1981, of which about £1.5 billion was of non-manufactures. In calculating the effect on exports he considered two ratios: the EC(6) share in UK exports, and the UK share of EC(6) imports. From the former he estimated an increase in exports to the EC of £4.75 billion in 1981 and from the latter £7 billion.

Other economists have generally taken the whole category of manufactures, although Morgan (1980) split them into finished and semi-finished manufactures. In the UK import market she applied price elasticities to the known tariff reductions and estimated increases in imports by 1977 due to tariff reductions associated with accession of £500m (finished manufactures) and £250–£350m for semi-manufactures. She calculated the effect on exports by taking the UK share of export markets in 1968–72 as her anti-monde to the period 1972–76 for the EC(6), EFTA, Ireland, Canada, New Zealand and Australia. She then updated it for 1977 by allowing for Britain's improved export performance in that year, and estimates an increase in total manufactured exports of £1,075–£1,125m.

Winters (1987) said that the effects of accession were apparent in the shares of countries in one another's markets for manufactures; the EC(6) share of the UK import market had risen to nearly a half by 1982–84, whereas imports from EFTA and Ireland which had previously had an advantage had fallen to 17 per cent. The proportion of the rest of the world had fallen from 46.5 per cent in 1970–72 to 36.7 per cent in 1982–84. As might be expected, the distribution of Britain's exports had also changed; the proportion going to the EC(6) had risen, as can be seen from Table 4.1, whereas the proportion going to EFTA and Ireland, where she was no longer in a preferential position in relation to the EC(6), had declined slightly. The proportion going to the rest of the world declined from 61 per cent to 53.3 per cent over the same period. The question was how to measure the effect of this.

Using an 'almost ideal demand system approach', Winters (1984) estimated that accession to the EC had led to an increase in the British share of the EC market, but also that home producers had lost an even greater share of the British domestic market in manufactures. In Figures 7.5 and 7.6 the anti-monde scenario, represented by the dotted lines, is compared with the actual trends of the UK, EC(6) and non-EC suppliers to the UK market. Imports are higher from both the EC and non-EC countries than they would have been otherwise, as can be seen from Figure 7.5(b). The increase in imports from non-EC countries might be external trade creation due to the reduction in external tariffs on third countries, as described earlier. But imports from the EC have increased far faster, and thus, as can be seen from Table 7.4, they represent a much higher proportion of imports than they would have under the anti-monde. The most striking effect was the decline in UK domestic production for its own home market of £12.2 billion. In terms of the economic analysis in Chapter 3 this would be regarded as trade creation, the supplanting of high-cost or inferior domestic production by imports.

Winters (1987) surveyed and criticized other economists for calculating the effects of British accession by residual imputation, that is, by attributing all the difference between the anti-monde and actuality to British accession

(a) Share of EC(6) in UK imports of manufactures ('imports only')

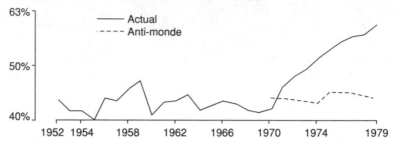

(b) Share of EC(6), non-UK and UK in UK sales of manufactures ('complete model')

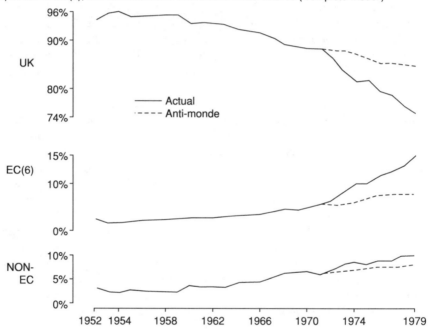

Figure 7.5 The effects of integration on the origin of manufactures sold in the
UK: (a) imports; (b) home market

Source: L.A. Winters (1984) 'British imports of manufactures and the Common
Market', *Oxford Economic Papers*, **36**, pp. 103, 118. By permission of the
Oxford University Press.

to the EC. He considered this more appropriately modelled by including a
specific dummy variable for the effects of accession. The results of this calculation are shown in Table 7.5. He estimated that by 1979 as a result of
accession, Britain's exports of manufactures to the six other EC countries
had increased by £4.5 billion, but £1.7 billion of this was obtained by a
reduction in exports to non-EC countries such as Japan and the US. He

Table 7.5 Alan Winter's estimates of the effect on Britain's trade in manufactures of her entry into the EC

Trade with:	Change in trade due to accession, 1979			
	Imports		Exports	
	£m	As % of actual	£m	As % of actual
France	1,934	62	540	25
Belgium–Luxembourg	1,745	89	n.c.	
Netherlands	1,315	70	n.c.	
West Germany	3,748	69	1,611	57
Italy	1,332	66	663	55
Sweden	−120	−9	n.c.	
Switzerland	542	21	n.c.	
Japan	722	49	−259	−48
Canada	−232	−44	n.c.	
USA	1,186	32	−1,249	−44
UK (change in home sales)	−12,171	−17	n.a.	

Source: L.A. Winters (1987) 'Britain in Europe: a survey of quantitative trade studies', *Journal of Common Market Studies*, **25** (4).

Notes: n.c. = not calculated; n.a. = not applicable.

also estimated that over half the imports from the EC countries were due to accession; this is regarded as gross trade creation. The only observable trade diversion appeared to be in a reduction in imports from Sweden and Canada.

If the net increase in exports of £2.8 billion is taken away from the reduction in home sales of £12.2 billion, this leaves the net effect of a reduction in sales and therefore output of British manufacturers of £9.4 billion. Winters qualifies this in various ways, but then states:

> The unavoidable conclusion is that British accession to the EC worsened her trade balance in, and reduced her gross output of, manufactures quite substantially. Even on the most conservative estimate it reduced output by at least £3 billion, about 1.5 per cent of GNP, and the effect could easily have been twice that.
>
> (Winters 1987: 328)

Thus one of the assumptions implicit in the theory of customs unions, that resources are easily transferable from the production of one product to another and there is always full employment, did not apply to Britain. After accession Britain's output of manufactures fell and so did her GDP. Winters' calculations were carried out for 1979. But largely because of the monetarist macroeconomic policy pursued by the government, output of manufactures and GDP fell even further in the subsequent two years. Productivity per person employed in manufacturing increased, but the 1973 level of manufacturing output was not regained until 1988. The optimism of the British manufacturers about their competitive position and the gains they were going to make appeared to be based on pure illusion.

The welfare effects of a reduction in income and employment may have been modified by the gain in consumer surplus discussed in the previous chapter. However, the entry to the EC also entailed the costs of the CAP, as discussed earlier.

RECENT CHANGES IN THE VOLUME OF TRADE

In Table 7.6 the volume increases in exports and imports between 1987 and 1996 are shown for the major commodity categories. The growth in trade is much lower and the relative performance of UK's trade in manufactures has partially reversed itself. For instance, exports of electrical machinery and road vehicles, especially cars, have both increased faster than imports. This is partly attributable to flows of inward direct investment, which will now be discussed.

International direct investment

Much is now said about the globalization of economic activity, that is, how firms are organizing their production and purchases on a worldwide basis. Some British firms have always conducted their affairs in this way. For instance, the British textile firms were concerned about their raw materials and thus established cotton plantations in various parts of the Commonwealth, including the Sudan. Unilever, an Anglo-Dutch firm initially producing soap and then margarine, and now a wide range of soaps, detergents, and foodstuffs, had oil-palm plantations and also engaged in retail distribution in West Africa. As territories gained independence the British firms were generally forced to relinquish these assets. However, British firms continued to invest abroad. The importance of these assets can be gauged from the calculation of Jack Revell that at the end of 1961 the net worth of overseas subsidiaries etc. of British companies at market values was £8.1 billion, almost equal to a fifth of the net worth of all British companies, and about 9 per cent of the total 'wealth of the nation' (Reddaway *et al.* 1967).

Britain was the second largest foreign direct investor for most of the period since the Second World War. The US was by far the largest foreign investor until the 1980s. Japan and Germany have recently become very large investors.

Table 7.6 UK's balance of trade in 1987 and 1996 and change in the volume of exports (X) and imports (M)

	Category SITC (R2)	Overall balance OTS		Volume increase	
		1987 £m	1996 £m	1987–96 X%	1987–96 M%
0	Food	−4,964	−7,538	50	33
1	Beverages and tobacco	431	1,497	51	55
2	Crude materials	−3,250	−3,662	4	−100
4	Animal and vegetable oils and fats	−194	−512	−39	5
3	Fuels	2,648	5,229	13	−1
5	Chemicals	2,193	3,903	60	72
6	Manufactures by material	−5,077	−5,620	45	40
65	Textiles	−1,638	−1,690	40	23
67	Iron and steel	285	611	62	89
68	Non-ferrous metals	−441	−1,109	66	74
69	Metal manufactures	−336	−167	46	42
7	Machinery and transport equipment	−4,016	−5,001	91	71
71–74 (less 716)	Mechanical machinery	1,193	3,872	24	18
716, 75–77	Electrical machinery	−3,269	−3,093	209	139
78	Road vehicles	−3,933	−7,521	99	49
781	Passenger cars	−3,043	−4,018	203	45
8	Miscellaneous manufactures	−3,062	−4,673	42	69
84 and 85	Clothing and shoes	−1,975	−4,091	68	131
87 and 88	Scientific instruments and photographic apparatus	55	503	25	45
5–8	Manufactures	−9,961	−11,391	68	63
0–9	Total	−14,177	−17,362	54	50

Source: ONS (1997) MM24 *Monthly Review of External Trade Statistics*, February; CSO (1990) *Monthly Review of External Trade Statistics Annual Supplement*, No. 11.

Reddaway Report

Let us begin by considering a study of the effect of direct investment carried out by Brian Reddaway. This was in response to the concern of UK governments of the 1950s and 1960s that some of the British balance of payments difficulties could be attributed to the size of her foreign investment; for instance, taking the record deficit of 1964, almost half was due to the long-term capital account. British firms, on the other hand, argued that Britain benefited overall from the foreign investment. In an endeavour to establish this the CBI set up the research project headed by Reddaway (Reddaway *et al.* 1967 and 1968). By chance, the US government instituted a similar project headed by Hufbauer and Adler (1968) to examine the effect of US overseas investment in manufacturing.

Both exercises were directed at the *marginal* effect of a change in direct investment rather than an all or nothing scenario. They also distinguished the immediate, 'initial' effect of foreign investment and the 'continuing effect'. But in other respects they differed, partly because the US investment was so much greater. The US considered the macroeconomic implications of a change in US investment, whereas in the British study some fairly simple assumptions were made:

1   investment abroad did not have any effect on investment at home, that is, it did not reduce it;
2   investment abroad would have been carried out by some other foreign country if Britain had not done so, therefore it did not alter the total amount of investment abroad.

Reddaway covered the period 1955–64. Most firms were no longer interested in the type of 'vertical' investment in raw materials described above. Manufacturing firms might be investing in agencies to import from Britain, but this was generally prior to the establishment of plants to produce the same goods that they had previously imported from Britain. Let us consider £100 worth of investment. The initial effect would be a deficit of £100 on the capital account. If this led to an extra £100 of plant and machinery being exported from Britain the *real* transfer would have been effected; the additional exports of £100 on the current account would entirely offset the deficit on the capital account. However, Reddaway calculated that the extra sales on the current account only amounted to £11 which meant that this investment led to a debt of £89 (see Table 7.7). Thus Britain was lending long term and borrowing short term. The interest on this debt then had to be paid year after year, that is, it was part of the 'continuing effect'.

This investment in the consumer country led to an expansion of the market for the product but imports of it were reduced by £2.5 which was offset by the increased purchase of inputs from Britain of £3.5, a net addition to the current account of £1. In addition there was the purchase of services, say £0.5. Setting this together with the profit against the interest on the debt led to a net gain of £4.25 per £100 of investment (see Table 7.7).

If part of the finance for the project came from the country in question, which Reddaway worked out to be £67 on average for every £100 of investment from Britain, the benefit to Britain was greater at £6.

The Report showed clearly that manufacturing firms were investing abroad to produce the same goods that they produced in the UK. Although all the firms questioned seemed pleased with the returns on their foreign investment, from the UK's point of view the return of £4–£6 appeared low. This divergent assessment may be partly because the firms were comparing after-tax profits in both cases whereas the British government is interested in its taxable base, comparing the pre-tax profits in Britain with

Table 7.7   Reddaway Report on the effects of UK direct investment overseas, 1955–64

(a) Initial effects

	£100 from UK	*£100 from UK, £67 from elsewhere*
Current account		
Effect on exports	£11	£18
Capital account		
Additional debt	£89	£89 + £67 owed by subsidiaries

(b) Continuous effects

	£100 from UK	*£100 from UK, £67 from elsewhere*
Current account		
Profits (after deduction of overseas tax and allowing for stock appreciation)	£5.5	£5.5
External financing charge	£2.75 (£89 at 3%)	£2 (£82 at 3%)
Add additional exports of goods and services – reduction in UK imports due to UK production being lower	£1.5	£2–£2.5
Total gain	£4.25	£6

Source: W.B. Reddaway with S.J. Potter and C.T. Taylor (1968) *Effects of UK Direct Investment Overseas: Final Report*, Cambridge: CUP, esp. 234.

the profit that is returned and is taxable from abroad. Thus the official response was to place some restrictions on British investment in foreign developed countries.

Britain was also the recipient of foreign direct investment and some of her best established firms were foreign: for instance, in the car industry, Ford, Vauxhall and Chrysler. Dunning (1981) put forward a theory that a firm's greatest incentive for carrying out foreign investment is if it has some 'specific advantage' which it can only exploit by such investment. But clearly there has to be an additional reason for why it does not simply expand its operations in its home country. This might be the high tariffs it faces in the recipient country and which it avoids by producing there, or it might be the lower wage costs in the recipient country.

In 1973 a report on the inflow of foreign direct investment was carried out by Steuer. He confirmed what had frequently been observed, namely, that foreign firms were more willing than indigenous firms, to invest in the outlying parts of the United Kingdom, that is, Wales and Scotland (Steuer *et al.* 1973). As unemployment rose during the 1970s and 1980s the effect on employment of direct investment became of paramount interest. The most frequently expressed anxiety about foreign investment is that in periods of recession a foreign firm will withdraw from its foreign subsidiaries first, and that the foreign firm will also retain the most highly paid jobs, such as those associated with research and development, in its home country.

One of the arguments for joining the EC was that if Britain stayed out she would lose the direct investment of foreign firms anxious to jump over the common external tariff and supply the EC market directly. At the time, the chief concern was with US firms as the US was the largest investor.

The succeeding pattern of foreign direct investment was not anticipated. First, due to the discovery of North Sea oil there was a large inflow of foreign investment to develop it, so much so that in 1974–75 Britain's inflows were greater than her outflows, that is, she became a net recipient of foreign direct investment. The employment associated with this investment was very small.

Then in 1979 the incoming Conservative government under Margaret Thatcher abolished controls on the capital account. This was partly a recognition of the difficulty of controlling capital flows with the vast surpluses of the OPEC producers flowing through the international private sector. Capital movements dwarfed changes in the current account, but most of this movement was of short-term capital, and even for longer-term transactions it was difficult to separate out direct investment from portfolio investment. In the 1980s the world financial system was tilted in a different direction by the US developing large current account deficits – the US had moved from being the largest lender to the rest of the world, prior to the OPEC surpluses, to being a net borrower – it was disinvesting from the rest of the world.

Japanese firms now began to invest in the British manufacturing sector. This was partly to avoid the non-tariff barriers being placed on their exports by the EU, as described in Chapter 4, particularly in cars and electronics, as will be discussed in Chapters 9 and 11. Japanese firms generally chose greenfield sites, often a long way from the previous centres of production, and wanted 100 per cent ownership. They took great care in the selection of their labour force as they wanted to avoid the difficulties with trade unions that had bedevilled previous British production, particularly of cars. Japanese investment was welcomed by the public, who viewed it as creating jobs in areas where there were very few. They also hoped to learn and benefit from the high-quality standards and control adopted by Japanese firms.

This was not the view of other EU countries. The French in particular regarded the establishment of Japanese subsidiaries as undermining the position of European firms, as will be described in Chapters 9 and 11. Britain attracted 38 per cent of Japanese direct investment in the EC over the whole period 1951–89 – although this rate was variable and, for example, in 1988 amounted to 47.5 per cent. But in the 1980s more than 80 per cent of this investment was in non-manufacturing, with nearly half in finance and insurance (Balasubramanyam and Greenaway 1992). Thus the importance attached to Japanese investment in manufacturing appeared exaggerated.

Other European firms also invested in Britain, often by taking over existing firms. However, as can be seen from Table 7.8, two-thirds of inward direct investment in manufacturing has recently been by the US. Japanese direct investment in manufacturing appears to be negative for 1992–95. Although the revival in manufacturing is often attributed to investment by foreign firms, only 36 per cent of inward investment is in manufacturing, equal on average from 1992 to 1995 to £3.4 billion per annum. This is not the same as an addition to capital stock because in many cases it was just used to take over already existing plant. But as a comparison, it amounted to 25 per cent of gross fixed investment in manufacturing.

At the same time, Britain was investing almost three times that amount in manufacturing abroad: 52 per cent of this was in the US, 29 per cent in the EU(15) and 14 per cent in developing countries (see Table 7.9).

Direct investment is regarded as the conduit by which production is transferred from one country to another. Reddaway's analysis showed that, at the margin, UK firms invested abroad to produce goods that had previously been produced and exported from Britain. Thus it reduced British exports of finished goods but increased those of inputs and services plus providing a profit. Britain has been the second largest international investor for most of the postwar period. However, Britain is also the major EU recipient of investment by Japan and the US. These flows of investment in manufacturing and in services have largely been between developed countries, that is, the US and other members of the EU. The importance for the car industry and high-technology industries will be discussed in Chapters 9 and 11.

CURRENT ACCOUNT BALANCES

Let us just conclude this chapter by considering the balances on the current account as demonstrating Britain's trading position with the rest of the world. As recounted in Chapter 2, the current account is a record not only of visible trade, but also of trade in services, transfers, and international payments of interest and dividends. The balances of these items are deflated by the average price (unit value) of exports in order to remove the element of inflation. The total balance and the balances in the visible trade we have just discussed, services, and transfers is shown in Figure 7.6 for 1950 to 1996. As can be seen, there are large fluctuations in the overall balance which appear to be due mainly to the almost equally large fluctuations in the visible balance, and these have become more exaggerated since 1970. The visible balance is generally negative and recently has only been positive from 1980–82 when the UK was severely depressed.

The balance of transfers was initially occasionally positive, but over the years has become increasingly negative. This does not represent an increase in foreign aid. It is mainly due to an increase in payments to the EU.

Table 7.8 Inward direct investment in the UK by overseas companies (includes unremitted profits), 1992–95 (£m)

	Manufacturing				Services				All industries			
	Total	US	EU(15)	Japan	Total	US	EU(15)	Japan	Total	US	EU(15)	Japan
1992	2,950	1,112	1,102	30	3,286	1,545	963	−51	8,816	3,748	3,433	−21
1993	3,316	1,856	544	−80	5,000	2,423	630	315	9,871	5,142	1,590	277
1994	2,394	1,068	839	101	1,646	418	895	−12	6,046	2,138	3,367	4
1995	4,986	4,684	1,110	−121	6,610	988	4,325	−65	13,331	9,054	4,055	−353
1992–5 (avg.)	3,412	2,180	899	−18	4,136	1,344	1,703	47	9,516	5,021	3,111	−23
1992–5 (%)	100	64	26	−1	100	32	41	1	100	53	33	0

Source: ONS (1995) MA4 *Overseas Direct Investment*.

Table 7.9 Outward direct investment by UK companies overseas (includes unremitted profits), 1992–95 (£m)

	Manufacturing				Services				All industries			
	Total	US	EU(15)	Developing	Total	US	EU(15)	Developing	Total	US	EU(15)	Developing
1992	5,029	1,371	1,991	1,210	5,825	1,739	2,589	705	10,107	1,321	4,613	22,799
1993	4,949	2,544	1,023	1,017	10,926	4,431	4,398	1,200	16,859	7,476	6,147	2,224
1994	13,745	6,515	4,969	1,388	4,418	−1,287	3,347	1,840	19,340	4,905	8,274	3,923
1995	12,518	8,359	2,405	1,409	12,566	2,761	5,989	1,176	26,024	10,364	9,613	3,295
1992–5 (avg.)	9,060	4,697	2,597	1,256	8,434	1,911	4,081	1,230	18,083	6,017	7,162	8,060
1992–5 (%)	100	52	29	14	100	23	48	15	100	33	40	45

Source: ONS (1995) MA4 *Overseas Direct Investment*.

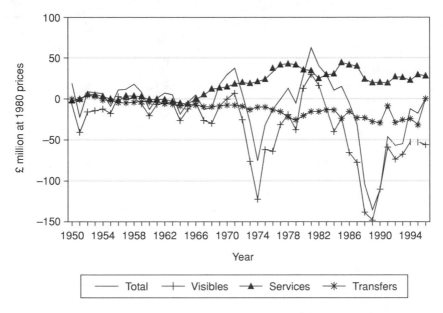

Figure 7.6 UK real current account balance, 1950–96 (deflated by UV of exports 1980 = 100)

These balances are partially offset by the increase that occurred in the balance of trade in services from the late 1960s. This increase did not continue after the late 1970s. Throughout the period there has been a positive balance of investment income (not shown in Figure 7.6), although after the early 1970s it has tended to fluctuate.

We can also consider these balances in relation to the various areas. As can be seen from Figures 7.7, in 1994 Britain had a negative balance with the EC in each category; it is particularly large for goods. Indeed, since accession the only years when she has had a positive balance with the EC in visible trade were 1980 and 1981. However, since 1990 the UK's visible balance with the EC, both in total and excluding oil, has improved, that is, it is less negative than before.

The UK also has a negative balance in goods and investment income with EFTA, but she has a large positive balance in services and investment income with NAFTA and in investment income with the NICs. Thus she is paying off most of the negative balances she is incurring with the EC and EFTA by what she is earning from the rest of the world. This raises serious questions about the advisability of joining a monetary union that would fix Britain's exchange rate to European countries when her surpluses are earned in relation to the rest of the world. The result of doing so would depend on whether the Euro dollar rate tended to rise, and also on the elasticity of demand for UK services by the rest of the world.

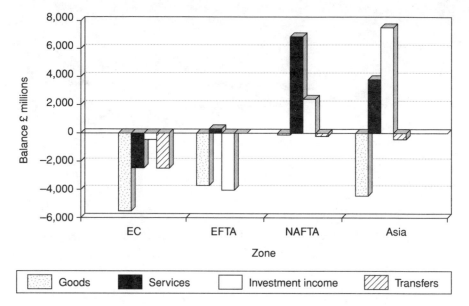

Figure 7.7 UK current account balances by zone (1994 £m)

NOTES

1 Value shares of the main manufacturing countries' exports of manufactured goods. The countries are the UK, West Germany, Belgium/Luxembourg, France, Italy, Netherlands, Sweden, Switzerland, USA, Canada, and Japan.
2. The $265m is measured c.i.f. from the other EFTA countries' point of view. Trade diversion is not regarded by the EFTA Secretariat as having an appreciable effect on the balance of payments in that it just represents a switch of imports from the rest of the world to EFTA.

REFERENCES

Balasubramanyam, V.N. and Greenaway, D. (1992) 'Economic integration and foreign direct investment: Japanese investment in the EC', *Journal of Common Market Studies*, **30** (2).

CSO (1990) *Monthly Review of External Trade Statistics Annual Supplement* (MRAS), London: HMSO.

Dunning, J.H. (1981) *International Production and the Multinational Enterprise*, London: Allen & Unwin.

EFTA (1969) *The Effects of EFTA on the Economies of Member States*, Geneva: European Free Trade Association.

Hufbauer, G.C. and Adler, F.M. (c.1968) *Overseas Manufacturing Investment and the Balance of Payments*, Tax Policy Research Study, No. 1, Washington, DC: US Treasury Department.

Mansell, K. (1980) 'UK visible trade in the post-war years', *Economic Trends*, October.

Mayes, D.G. (1983) 'Memorandum' in House of Lords, discussed in L.A. Winters (1987) 'Britain in Europe', *Journal of Common Market Studies*, **25** (4).

Moore, L. (1964) 'Factors affecting the demand for British exports', Oxford University Institute of Economics and Statistics, *Bulletin*, **26** (4).

—— (1989) 'Changes in British trade analysed in a pure trade theory framework', in D. Cobham, R. Harrington, and G. Zis (eds), *Money, Trade and Payments*, Essays in Honour of D.J. Coppock, Manchester: Manchester University Press.

Morgan, A.D. (1980) 'The balance of payments and British membership of the European Community', in W. Wallace (ed.), *Britain in Europe*, London: Heinemann, discussed in L.A. Winters (1987) 'Britain in Europe', *Journal of Common Market Studies*, **25** (4).

Reddaway, W.B. with Perkins, J.O.N., Potter, S.J. and Taylor, C.T. (1967) *Effects of UK Direct Investment Overseas: An Interim Report*, Cambridge: Cambridge University Press.

Reddaway, W.B. with Potter, S.J. and Taylor, C.T. (1968) *Effects of UK Direct Investment Overseas: Final Report*, Cambridge: Cambridge University Press.

Tattersall's Trade Review (1969) Annual Review, No. 875, Manchester.

Winters, L.A. (1984) 'British imports of manufactures and the Common Market', *Oxford Economic Papers*, **36**.

—— (1987) 'Britain in Europe: a survey of quantitative trade studies', *Journal of Common Market Studies*, **25** (4).

8 The energy sector and the development of North Sea oil

Trade in fuels might be expected to be simply exports from those who have deposits of coal, gas or oil to those who do not. But this ignores the considerable difference in costs of working deposits, which means that prices to producers are important determinants of whether a country is an exporter or importer. It also ignores the great variation in levels of consumption. The US has one of the highest levels of per capita consumption of energy in the world at 7.91 tonnes of oil equivalent (toe) per head in 1994 (UN 1997), and although the US is very well endowed with all the fossil fuels, it is a net importer of energy. Britain, with about half this per capita consumption at 3.99 toe per head – round about the European average – and well endowed with resources, has since 1950 fluctuated between being a net importer and exporter. Oil-exporting developing countries consume on average less than half this, and other developing countries a small fraction of the European levels. Their effective demand is limited by their very low per capita incomes. Furthermore, this divergence cannot all be ascribed to manufacturing usage; much of it is for personal consumption in the form of heating, and for air conditioning and transport. This inequality in the consumption of energy represents a social and ecological time bomb ticking away in the background which has been generally ignored by Western energy economists. They have concentrated on the demand for energy by industrial countries and their access to resources.

As with other products, economic theory indicates that in a competitive market at a low price the fuel is only extracted from fields with the lowest direct cost. As the price rises, sources with higher direct costs are worked; in each case the marginal cost of production is equated with the price. The intra-marginal units all earn economic rent and this rises with the price. However, fossil fuels are an exhaustible resource, that is, in fixed supply; consumption of this stock today precludes consumption in the future. World prices were therefore expected to rise over time. Indeed, with a known stock of an exhaustible resource, economic theory states that in a competitive industry price will rise at an annual rate equal to the rate of interest, and in a monopoly at an annual rate such that the economic rent obtained rises at a rate equal to the rate of interest. If they did not, producers could improve their position by the reallocation of output between time periods.

However, due to the discovery of new oil and gas fields there has been no systematic rise in prices in the postwar period. In the 1950s and 1960s new low-cost oilfields in the Middle East and then North Africa were brought into production. The developing and operating costs of these new fields were lower then those already operating in Latin America (Adelman 1972). The international price fell, but was still considerably higher than costs. Thus, between 1950 and 1970 the real dollar price of oil – that is, the realized price divided by a price index of manufactures – fell until in 1970 it was approximately half its initial level. Because oil is relatively easy to transport, with transport costs accounting for only 10 per cent of the import price of crude oil at Rotterdam (GATT 1980/81), trade increased more than tenfold between 1950 and 1973. Oil became the most important commodity in world trade.

Western European countries had responded to this opportunity to acquire a cheaper form of energy by massive increases in purchases; between 1955 and 1973 their net imports of oil in terms of quantity increased more than sixfold. This entailed, in turn, a large substitution of oil for coal. Total consumption of fuel in 1973 was 265 per cent of its level in 1950 (see Table 8.1), but in 1950 coal supplied 85 per cent of total Western European consumption and oil 12 per cent, whereas by 1973 these figures had changed to 25 per cent and 59 per cent respectively (see Table 8.1). For Germany

Table 8.1 Consumption of commercial energy in Western Europe in 1950 and 1973 (mtoe)

| | 1950 | | | | | 1973 | | | | |
| | Total | Per cent distribution | | | | Total | Per cent distribution | | | |
	mtoe	S	L	NG	H&N	mtoe	S	L	NG	H&N
Western Europe	391	85	12		2.4	1,040	25	59	12	3.5
UK	150	91	9			206	39	47	13	1.3
West Germany	85	96	3		1	246	34	53	12	1.3
France	54	80	17		2.5	158	19	69	9	3.2
Italy	13	49	33	3	15	115	7	76	13	3.3
Netherlands	13	83	17			54	5	38	56	—
Belgium	20	89	11			42	27	55	18	—

Source: L. Moore (1985) *The Growth and Structure of International Trade since the Second World War*, Brighton: Harvester Wheatsheaf, table 12.4; derived from UN Department of International Economic and Social Affairs Statistical Papers (1979) *World Energy Supplies 1973–78* and (1976) *World Energy Supplies 1950–74*.

Note: S = solid fuels; L = liquid fuels (i.e. petroleum); NG = natural gas; H&N = hydro and nuclear electricity.

and Britain the initial dependence on coal was even greater, at 96 per cent and 91 per cent, and the transfer to oil was somewhat lower.

The European Coal and Steel Community (ECSC) supposedly established a free market in coal. It forbade discrimination in the price of coal offered to the six Member States, and also production subsidies, but in the latter it was unsuccessful. Although coal production, employment and the number of pits worked all fell, the Members States with depressed mining areas provided them with state assistance. This was sanctioned by the High Commission of the ECSC because it feared the Member States' very heavy dependence on oil imports (Swann 1988). In the EC as well as Britain the coal miners exercised considerable political power.

The governments of the oil-exporting countries were always endeavouring to get more economic rent from it by claiming royalties and the imposition of taxes. They were also concerned that, as the real price of oil fell, they would be better off keeping more of it in the ground. The Organization of Petroleum Exporting Countries (OPEC), founded in 1960, decided to reverse the decline in the real price of oil; the posted and realized dollar price of oil was raised after 1971, in particular the posted price of oil on which taxation was based. Then after the Yom Kippur war of 1973, from 1973–74 the price of oil was quadrupled, and later from 1978–80 it was doubled. Most of the international oil companies' subsidiaries operating in OPEC were also nationalized. Changes in the dollar price of oil since 1980 are shown in Figure 8.1. It indicates a downward trend.

The international significance of this price was shown yet again by the Gulf War. Saadam Hussein used Kuwait's refusal to raise the price of oil – or more precisely its production in excess of its OPEC quota, which depressed the price – as a pretext for annexing it. Iraq's military arsenal and ability to fight, first, Iran, and then in 1991 the Allies, gave an indication of the vast oil revenues it has acquired from its exports. The co-operation of the Allies under the aegis of the UN may have reflected a determination to prevent unprovoked aggression. But it is unlikely that forces would have been deployed on such a vast scale if Kuwait had not been a major oil exporter.

Natural gas is often found in conjunction with oil. In some countries it is flared off. But in the majority of countries most of it is now either marketed or reinjected. Independent fields of natural gas were discovered in Groningen in the Netherlands, and in Algeria. The Algerians built a liquification plant so that it could be shipped directly. An LNG reception and regassification plant, as at Canvey Island in the UK, is needed at the importing end. But most natural gas is transmitted by pipeline and its location determines the pattern of trade. Generally, the route of the pipeline is determined by negotiations with a trading partner. Negotiations about quantities and price are generally bilateral and thus tend to be confrontational and often tinged with bitterness. The fluctuations in the price c.i.f. of natural gas imported by pipeline into the EU since 1980 are shown in Figure 8.1.

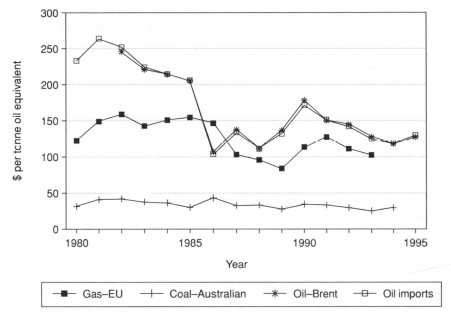

Figure 8.1 International prices of fuel, 1980–95 ($ per toe)

Source: IEA (1996) *Energy Prices and Taxes Second Quarter*, IEA Statistics Paris: OECD/IEA

The international real price of coal has fluctuated (World Bank 1981). Transport costs are important for coal and in Britain this has provided a degree of natural protection for her domestic industry, particularly in supplying inland power stations. But by the early 1970s imports from the US, Australia and South Africa could be supplied to her coastal ports at a lower price than British Coal was charging. The average unit value c.i.f. since 1980 of imports from Australia into the EU of steam coal used in electricity generation is shown in Figure 8.1.

Little account of the reduction in the real price of fuel to the industrial economies in the 1950s and 1960s has been taken when explaining their economic growth (Denison 1967; OECD 1970). Yet when in the 1970s the fall in the price of oil was reversed, it acted as a rapid brake on their expansion. The prices of fuels in terms of $ per tonne of oil equivalent since 1980 are shown in Figure 8.1. The price of natural gas increased to begin with and then began an erratic fall. There appears to be a downward pressure on prices which is even greater in real terms. Since 1980 oil prices have fluctuated downwards; in 1994 they were 5 per cent lower than in 1984, or 37 per cent lower in terms of manufactures (WTO 1995). There was some recovery in 1995 and 1996, but as of December 1996 Iraq's re-entry into the market is likely to lead to a further reduction.

DEFINITION

The energy sector is considered as a whole because although specific fuels are required for certain uses – oil is required for running motor vehicles and aircraft, and coal is required in iron and steel production – at the margin, in the generation of electricity, the fossil fuels coal, oil, and natural gas compete with primary electricity (produced in hydroelectric and nuclear power plants) in the provision of space heating and power.

Problems of measurement

There are certain problems in measuring production and consumption. One is that fossil fuels do not produce the same amount of power per unit of weight. Therefore, in order to obtain a measure of the total quantity consumed or produced they are converted to a standard of, say, a million tonnes of oil equivalent (mtoe), or a million therms.

Secondly, some energy is used up in the conversion of energy into a usable form for the consumer. The most extreme form of this is in the production of electricity. Most of it is supplied by thermal power stations using fossil fuels. The thermal efficiency of these plants is very low, around 36 per cent (*DUKES* 1996: 93): that is, the fossil fuel energy equivalent (FFEE) used up is about three times that of the electricity produced. This is the average figure used, although the modern combined-cycle gas plants have a thermal efficiency of up to 50 per cent.

Thirdly, in addition to fossil fuels some electricity is produced directly by nuclear power and hydroelectric power stations. This poses a problem in the measurement of relative consumption of the various fuels. When discussing the relative contribution of different fuels to *total energy supplies* this primary electricity is generally measured in terms of the fossil fuel equivalent required to produce this electricity. Thus it is multiplied by 1/0.36, approximately three, for the purpose of comparison.

However, when discussing the *consumption of energy by the final user*, the power available is measured directly, so that, for instance, the calorific value of a one kilowatt electric fire can be compared directly with the same calorific value of a gas or coal fire.

UK GOVERNMENT POLICIES

Background

The government has had a direct interest in the energy market ever since Winston Churchill, as First Lord of the Admiralty, converted the navy from being fired by domestically produced coal, to being oil fired. From then on it was concerned to secure a reliable source of oil and thus the UK acquired shares in the Anglo-Persian company, which became the Anglo-Iranian Oil company (now BP) in 1914, and also supported the activities of Royal Dutch Shell. During the Second World War deposits were discovered in Kuwait in which BP had a 50 per cent share. From these holdings arose what the Foreign Office used to describe as Britain's 'strategic' interest in the Middle East. Her contribution to the 1991 Gulf War must be regarded as a relic of this interest.

Government interest in the energy industries was not only due to Britain's reliance on imports, but also because both electricity and gas used a grid system and were widely regarded as 'natural' monopolies, that is, industries in which the economies of scale were so great that monopolies would be bound to develop. Thus the government was expected to be concerned with their pricing and investment policies.

In addition, the extractive industries – coal on the one hand, and natural gas and oil on the other – presented considerable economic and social problems and benefits respectively, as will be outlined.

Nationalizations of the Labour governments, 1945–51

Direct control over the domestic energy market was not secured on a peace-time basis until the Labour government of 1945–50, determined to gain control of the 'commanding heights of the economy', nationalized the fuel industries. The first to be nationalized was the coal industry in 1947, although under the Coal Act of 1938 royalties had already been nationalized (Williams 1981). Then in 1947 the electricity industry was nationalized and in 1948 the gas industry. Both industries were major customers for the coal industry; at that time, all gas was produced from coal or as a byproduct of mining, and was called 'town gas'.

Coal

There had been a great deal of poverty and social unrest in the coal mines in the 1920s and 1930s. The mineworkers supported the Labour Party and hoped for better conditions with the nationalization of the industry. Initially, there was an increase in investment, particularly in mechanized coal-cutting machinery, and great efforts to expand production. In 1952, with employment of 767,000 by the National Coal Board (NCB), a peak production of 225 million tons was achieved. In 1955, power generation, domestic use, and industry each accounted for roughly a fifth of coal consumption and 13 per cent went for gas manufacture. Then, as the price of oil fell, domestic and industrial consumers substituted it for coal. The Central Electricity Generating Board (CEGB) had every economic incentive to substitute oil for coal, as it began to do. The government tried to maintain the market for domestically produced coal by discouraging, and then from 1959–69 banning, imports of foreign coal, and by placing a tax on heavy fuel oil, which effectively increased its cost by 25 per cent (Turner 1984: 4).

But in 1961 the Minister of Power approved the importation of liquified natural gas (LNG) from Algeria. This started to arrive in 1964, and thus began the phasing out of coal for gas production.

Inevitably, there was a reduction in coal consumption in the 1950s and 1960s. From 1950 onwards, although sales revenue was generally sufficient to cover operating costs (*DUKES* 1971), allowing for interest payments, there was a persistent tendency to make losses. This was due to the continued operation of a large number of high-cost mines; in 1959, almost all the Scottish mines and a number of those in Northumberland and Durham were making losses (NCB 1959). From the late 1950s onwards the number of mines was reduced from around 800 to 300 in 1970, while the number of mineworkers more than halved. Due to the increase in productivity, however, production contracted to only two-thirds the 1958 level.

The miners, organized by their union the National Union of Mineworkers (NUM), felt that their wages had lagged behind those of other workers. The miners' strike in pursuit of a wage claim in 1972 placed them in direct conflict with the Conservative government. The latter, in an effort to resist the miners' demands, instituted a three-day working week, but eventually capitulated, granting an estimated increase of between 17 per cent and 24 per cent in average wages. Then in 1974 the miners again went on strike in pursuit of a wage claim. This led to a general election and the return of a Labour government, which settled the wage claim. Anticipating, or maybe just hoping, that the increase in the price of oil in the 1970s would enable coal to regain some of its markets, a committee with representatives of the NCB, coal industry trade unions, and the government put forward an ambitious 'Plan for Coal'. In this plan it was estimated that total energy consumption would be 400 million tonnes of coal equivalent (MTCE) in 1983 and that 120 MTCE would be supplied from the deep mines of the NCB. Targets were set for both output and investment in new capacity, which the government agreed to finance. Subsequent investment exceeded that in the plan, but output and consumption fell short. The additional interest payment and cost of stocks accumulating at pitheads added to the NCB's losses. For a brief period, domestic production remained between 120 and 130 million tonnes, but by that time, foreign coal could be supplied more cheaply than British. From 1977 to 1979 the government put pressure on the CEGB to commit itself to taking given amounts of British coal; the CEGB agreed to do so on condition that it was reimbursed for the higher cost of British coal.

Even the Conservative government established under Margaret Thatcher requested the CEGB in 1981 to stop coal imports (Turner 1985: 4). But in 1983 the government brought in Ian MacGregor to staunch the losses of the NCB by closing down the highly unprofitable mines. This led to a strike by the Welsh miners, and in 1984 the NUM converted this to a general miners' strike, which lasted a year. In this last major confrontation the Thatcher government established its authority and smashed the power of the NUM. This was followed by the closure of ninety-eight collieries, yet the output of deep-mined coal at 82.4 million tonnes remained at almost the same level as before. However, the coal industry continued to make a loss, which forced the Conservative government to enact the Coal Industry Act of 1985 and the Coal Act of 1990. This legislation enabled the government to fund the NCB losses and provide extra finance to compensate redundant miners, which became very important in an industry that had nine pensioners to every man employed (Bailey 1989, 1991). By 1995 deep-mined coal production, at 35 million tonnes, was less than half its level in the late 1980s. Coal from opencast mines, which can be obtained with giant diggers in a less labour-intensive way, accounted for 31 per cent of output (*DUKES* 1996). The number of miners fell by 94 per cent between 1985 and 1995, to 14,000.

Gas

The nationalization of the gas industry in 1948 involved the amalgamation of municipal operators and 509 commercial companies into twelve autonomous Area Boards. However, when natural gas became available it became economic to centralize these operations and a national high-pressure gas transmission system was built to take North Sea gas from beachheads to the off-take point of the regional distribution systems. This structure was formalized by the Gas Act 1972, which not only entrusted the British Gas Corporation (BGC) with the management of the twelve Area Boards, but also gave it the power to search for and extract supplies of gas and oil. In addition, all imports of natural gas had to be offered to the BGC, and exports were effectively prohibited prior to privatization (Vickers and Yarrow 1988).

Electricity

The Electricity Acts of 1947 and 1957 had established a system whereby the Central Electricity Generating Board (CEGB) was responsible for the generation of electricity and its distribution throughout the country via the high-voltage national grid. The twelve Area Boards then distributed it, together with some privately generated electricity, to consumers in England and Wales. In Scotland the South of Scotland Electricity Board and the North of Scotland Hydro-Electric Board each had responsibility for the generation and distribution of electricity in its area.

The sector over which the government has had complete control has been that of atomic power. Nuclear power plants were already being built in the 1950s. They were the original Magnox reactors, which were succeeded by the advanced gas-cooled reactors (AGRs), and then finally the Sizewell pressurized water reactor (PWR), which was brought into operation in 1995. They have involved great technical and managerial problems. They did not supply an appreciable quantity of electricity until the 1960s. By 1970 they supplied 10 per cent of total net electricity supply and 28 per cent by 1995.

Extraction of North Sea oil and gas

Meanwhile the discovery of gas in Groningen in the Netherlands in the 1950s suggested that there might be some below the North Sea. Once the 1958 Continental Shelf Convention establishing international boundaries had been ratified by enough nations, prospecting became feasible. The government divided the UK portion of the continental shelf of the North Sea (UKCS) into blocks, and invited companies to apply for the right to explore them. Exploration licences were granted which were non-exclusive, and then production licences were sold which were exclusive and permitted the extraction of the oil and gas. Drilling began in 1964.

Gas was the first to be found in the UK sector, by BP, in 1965, and was introduced into the gas pipelines in 1967 (*DUKES* 1971). All gas produced from the UKCS had to be brought onshore in the UK. Initially, it also had all to be sold to the British Gas Corporation (BGC), but this statutory requirement was nominally ended in 1982 by the Oil and Gas Enterprise Act (Vickers and Yarrow 1988: 257–9). The BGC as monoposonist was therefore in a very strong position to determine the price.

However, from the outset it was decided that oil would sell at the international price. Some commercially viable fields had been discovered by the early 1970s, but the quadrupling of the oil price by OPEC from 1973–74 greatly assisted their profitability. The government was also concerned to exploit the North Sea in an economic manner: that is, by providing the oil companies with sufficient incentive for exploration while at the same time obtaining as much royalty income as possible.

There was a certain degree of public ownership involved in so far as the government held a stake in British Petroleum (BP) and the British Gas Corporation (BGC). The Labour government also created the British National Oil Corporation (BNOC) in 1975 in order to collect and sell the government's (physical) oil royalites. It was given the right to participate in North Sea developments and to purchase 51 per cent of the resulting output at market prices (Vickers and Yarrow 1988: 319).

Total investment over the period from 1965 to 1989 is estimated to have been about £37 billion; in addition, there has been exploration expenditure of about £12 billion. At 1989 prices this amounted to an investment of £65 billion plus £18 billion of exploration expenditure, £83 billion in total (*Brown Book* 1990). From 1976 to 1989 the real value of investment was falling in oil but not in gas. Then, in the early 1990s total investment rose again; in 1995 it was £4.2 billion, that is, 4 per cent of gross domestic capital investment.

Pricing policy

The energy sector has inspired a great deal of microeconomic analysis and discussion of pricing policies. This is partly because of the degree of state involvement; a private monopolist would have maximized profits, but a government-owned industry was expected to act in the interest of the whole community. It also posed the problems of exhaustible resources and externalities. In the 1950s and 1960s these problems were approached as though domestic output was of non-tradeable products (Eden *et al.* 1981). Oil was considered to be the only tradeable, and therefore, although this was not specifically recognized, the price at which it could be imported represented the opportunity cost of fuel to the British economy.

The pricing policy required of nationalized industries was rather vague; they were initially just expected to break even. This remit allowed a considerable amount of cross-subsidization: for instance, profitable coal mines could subsidize loss-making ones. However, in the 1950s and 1960s there was a gradual closure of loss-making, primarily deep-mined, coal mines. But even by 1970/71, deep-mined coal represented 92 per cent of total British output.

The pricing policy advocated by economists was one of marginal-cost pricing. At any point in time, with a given production capacity, price should be equated with short-run marginal costs. In the long run, industries should invest until the expected long-run marginal cost is equal to the long-run expected price. This was accepted in the White Paper of 1967 (HM Treasury 1967).

Fossil fuels

In the case of fossil fuels, if coal seams or oil wells with the lowest extraction cost were exploited first, this should have led to the earning of a considerable amount of economic rent. However, as already mentioned, the National Coal Board showed a persistent tendency to make losses. Even by the early 1980s the profitable coal mines were still subsidizing the loss-making ones. The economic rent from the lower-cost mines was being used to keep open the higher-cost mines. The situation is depicted in Figure 8.2 where MC is the marginal cost of production at a constant wage rate, and D is the demand schedule. The optimum output Q^* is one where the marginal cost of production is just equal to the price P^*, and at this point an economic rent of P^*EF is earned. However, if the NCB only aims to break even, output will be higher at Q_1, with a lower price P_1, such that the economic rent earned from the low-cost mines, now P_1HF, is just equal to the marginal loss HGJ incurred by high-cost ones. Alternatively, as has been argued by Vickers and Yarrow, some of the rent may be used to raise miners' wages rather than keep open high-cost mines (Vickers and Yarrow 1988).

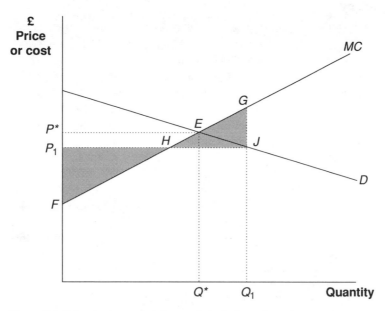

Figure 8.2 Marginal cost pricing and deviations from it

Source: Derived from J. Vickers and G. Yarrow (1988) *Privatization: An Economic Analysis*,
Cambridge, Mass.: Massachusetts Institute of Technology, 327.

In respect to natural gas British Gas was also criticized by a number of
economists for charging average costs rather than the higher marginal costs
(Newbery 1985). Denis Rooke, Chairman of British Gas, stated that BGC
would have earned a further £200 million in the 1970s had it forced
prices up to the full market price (Williams 1981: preface). This gives
some idea of the royalties forgone. This appears due in part to the Gas
Board's use of long-term contracts with the oil companies which extract
the gas from the North Sea, and to the prices associated with the earlier
contracts being much lower than those in the later ones (Vickers and Yarrow
1988: 249).

Only for oil was a clear decision made at the outset that the oil companies would trade freely in the international market and thus charge the
international price.

Electricity

Finally, let us consider electricity. This was a nationalized industry between
1947 and 1990. In both its purchases of fossil fuels and in its sales of off-
peak electricity it has been affected by government policies for the other
fuels. As a capital-intensive industry it has also been constrained by the
government limits on investment. But the aspect of electricity production

that has aroused the most intense debate over pricing policies has been that of catering for a fluctuating demand with a product that cannot be stored, and which must be supplied otherwise the system becomes overloaded and breaks down.

The simplest proposals were those which imposed all the capital costs on the peak-period consumers and only charged the off-peak consumers the direct costs, that is, the costs of the fossil fuel (except when this leads to a greater demand by the off-peak consumers than the peak-period consumers, when the former should be made to pay part of the capital cost). However, in the electricity industry there is also a choice of fuels. Furthermore, they entail different ratios of capital to direct costs; nuclear power has the highest capital cost and the lowest direct cost, coal and oil compete with lower capital costs but higher direct costs, and gas turbines have the highest direct and lowest capital costs. This is what is described as the 'merit' order. The optimum response to fluctuating demand is to work the nuclear plants with the lowest direct costs continuously, then, with increased demand, bring in the oil- and coal-fired plants, and finally, bring in the gas turbines to meet the peak demand.

How then should the state electricity board, the CEGB, decide which type of generator to invest in if it needs to expand its overall productive capacity to meet peak demand? Let us take the calculation made by the CEGB to determine whether to invest in a nuclear plant, Sizewell B, or a coal-fired one, in the early 1980s. Assumptions had to be made about:

1   the future level of demand;
2   the future price of coal and uranium;
3   the discount rate (the government's required rate of return was 5 per cent); and
4   the length of life of a generator over which the capital costs had to be spread (a nuclear plant was assumed to have a life of twenty-five years, and a coal-fired plant, one of thirty years).

Then the net effective cost (NEC) of the new capacity was calculated as equal to the capital cost of the plant spread over its lifetime, *plus* fuel and other costs from operating it, *minus* the saving in fuel costs from displacing other less efficient plant. The CEGB's calculation in £ per kW per year is shown in Table 8.2 (Weyman-Jones 1986: 116). Because of the saving in direct fuel costs the nuclear plant was more profitable and was chosen.

Thus it should be clear that government policy has affected the pricing of coal and gas, and these prices in turn have affected the calculations made in selecting electricity generators. Both affected the relative demand for fuels and thus their production. In addition, a high safety margin of 28 per cent appeared to be built into the CEGB's calculations to allow for failures in generating capacity or unusually high demand (Weyman-Jones 1986: 122).

Table 8.2 Net effective cost (NEC) of nuclear and coal-fired generating stations (£/kW per annum, 1980 prices)

	Nuclear	Coal-fired
Capital charges	77	36
Fuel costs	34	113
Other operating costs	12	10
Total generation costs	123	159
Less fuel saving from displacing less efficient plant	148	143
Net effective cost	−25	16
(Lifetime average load factor)	63%	54%

Source: CEGB *Annual Report and Accounts 1979–80*, quoted in T. Weyman-Jones (1986) *The Economics of Energy Policy*, London: Gower.

Conservative government policies, 1979–96

The Conservative government led by Margaret Thatcher, which came into power in 1979, completely changed the official policy towards the fuel industries. It wished to reduce the role of the government in industry, and wanted it to be more market-orientated and efficient; efficiency was largely considered in terms of profitability. The government also wished to reduce its public borrowing requirement (PSBR), and consequently was very anxious to reduce losses in the state-owned steel and coal industries. Thus it broke the last miners' strike of 1984–85, which enabled the NCB to complete the policy of shutting down high-cost coal mines.

The government began the series of privatizations – the sale of nationalized industries to the public – which contributed to the reduction in the PSBR. The Oil and Gas (Enterprise) Act 1982 established Enterprise Oil to take over the offshore oil interests of British Gas. Then Enterprise Oil and Britoil, the production interests of BNOC, were sold in 1982. This was accompanied by comments by economists that greater efficiency depends more on introducing a greater element of competition than on a change in ownership.

Gas

British Gas was subsequently sold as a single entity in 1986. Thus it was both a monopsony buyer of natural gas from the North Sea, and a monopoly seller on the domestic market. However, the government set up a regulator, Ofgas, to control British Gas's prices and access to the gas grid which it also owned (Vickers and Yarrow 1988).

The market for gas is broadly divided into four sectors:

1   The contract market for industrial consumers requiring more than 25,000 therms a year. Prices are individually negotiated and not published.
2   Industrial and business consumers requiring between 2,500 and 25,000 therms a year. For these and interruptible customers, British Gas has to price according to published schedules.
3   The domestic household market where there are published price schedules.
4   The power market.

Categories 2 and 3 – that is, customers using no more than 25,000 therms a year – are called 'tariff customers'. The rates have to be agreed with the Ofgas regulator and comprise a formula by which the maximum average price per therm M_t for year t is given as:

$$M_t = [1 + (\text{RPI}_{t-1} - X)/100]P_{t-1} + Y_t - K_t$$
$$P_{t-1} = [1 + (\text{RPI}_{t-1} - X)]P_{t-2}$$

Y is the *gas component*, thus Y_t is the beachhead gas cost per therm in year t plus the gas levy. RPI_{t-1} is the increase in the retail price index between October of two years ago and last year. P is the *non-gas* component per therm, changes on which are limited to the percentage change in the retail price index less X. X is the price reduction factor, which was initially set at 2 per cent, but in April 1992 was changed to 5 per cent. K is a correction factor (Vickers and Yarrow 1988: 263). Thus British Gas can automatically pass on to consumers any increase in the average price of gas it procures. The Ofgas formula exerts pressure on the non-gas components. After proposals had been agreed for vertically splitting the industry the Ofgas regulator turned her attention to charges for individual operations. In 1996 she insisted on a 20 per cent reduction in gas transportation charges, allowing TransCo a 7 per cent real pre-tax rate of return on assets (Corzine 1996a). This regulation was required because of the absence of competition.

The Ofgas regulators have been enthusiastic advocates of more competition. This could only be achieved by opening the grid to other suppliers and reducing the monopsony position of British Gas in the purchase of North Sea gas. The Oil and Gas (Enterprise) Act of 1982 made provision for the use of the British Gas pipeline by other suppliers. Initially, this seemed to scarcely affect the monopsony power of British Gas because until 1990 all suppliers were under contract to it (Ofgas 1992). In response to the Monopolies and Mergers Commission (MMC) report in 1988 on the gas contract market large businesses were given the choice of gas supplier. British Gas also agreed in 1992 to reduce its share of its market with industrial and commercial users to 40 per cent by 1995 (Ofgas 1992).

There was another MMC investigation in 1993, which was followed by the Gas Act of 1995. Although the President of the Board of Trade did not accept the Commission's proposals for breaking British Gas up into a number of separate businesses, British Gas eventually decided to split of its own accord. This was partly because Ofgas repeatedly complained about the potential for cross-subsidization in the unified company. In 1997 British Gas was broken up into two companies. Centrica will be the holding company for British Gas distribution to UK domestic consumers, central heating installation and retail businesses; it will also own the North and South Morecambe gas fields. In addition Centrica takes over the 'take-or-pay' gas contracts British Gas negotiated with North Sea gas producers. The second company will be called *BG* and will inherit the heavily regulated pipeline system and the international oil and gas exploration and production business (Corzine 1997). The grid is required to offer exactly the same terms to British Gas trading units as to other suppliers.

Competition is being extended to businesses consuming between 2,500 and 25,000 therms per annum, and British Gas is to enable suppliers other than British Gas to supply at least 45 per cent of this market. By the end of 1995 forty suppliers were active in the contract market, and new entrants had captured from British Gas about 80 per cent of the firm industrial and commercial market, and 70 per cent of 'interruptible sales' (*Brown Book* 1996: 83). By the end of 1996 the share of British Gas in commercial markets had plummeted to about a third (Corzine and Martinson 1996).

Competition is being progressively extended to the market for private householders, and it is anticipated that the move to a competitive market will be completed by 1998. As competition is increased the regulation of the market is being reduced: for instance, British Gas is no longer required by Ofgas to publish its price schedules for industrial and commercial customers using less than 25,000 therms a year (Ofgas 1995: 7).

The real price of gas has been falling, especially to industrial users, to a degree that domestic prices are now among the lowest in Europe. Britain began exporting gas in 1992 and this is expected to increase as more gas pipelines are built to connect Britain to the European gas grids (*Brown Book* 1996: ch. 7).

The fall in the price of North Sea gas placed British Gas in severe difficulties, squeezed between its long-term 'take-or-pay' contracts specifying higher prices while at the same time facing a rapid contraction in its share of the British commercial market. At a cost of £250m in cash or assets BP agreed to terminate some of its supply contracts and to lower prices on others from 16p to 14p a therm (Corzine and Martinson 1996). Mobil agreed to cancel two of its supply contracts in exchange for stakes in two of the gas fields and 2.5 per cent of the Sage offshore gas pipeline owned by British Gas (Corzine 1996b). By the end of 1997 Centrica, the inheritor of the problem from British Gas, had renegotiated most of its contracts, bringing the average price it paid for gas to within 15 per cent of market rates. The last three agreements were with Conoco, Elf and Total for price reductions on 6bn therms in exchange for the payment of £365m in compensation. The total cost to Centrica of renegotiating these contracts was around £750m (Marsh 1997).

Electricity

The electricity industry was privatized in 1990–91. In an endeavour to break up the monopoly power of the CEGB it was split up into two generating companies, National Power and Powergen; an initial 60 per cent of these were sold. So also were the twelve Regional Electricity Companies (RECs), each responsible for distributing electricity within a particular area. The RECs jointly owned the high-voltage national grid, which distributes power throughout the country. From the sale of these the government gained £11bn. The national grid system was to be accessible to all generators of electricity. The two non-nuclear Scottish companies, Scottish Power and Scottish Hydro-Electric, were floated in 1991, and Northern Ireland's four power stations were sold in 1992. The high-voltage national grid was sold in 1995, as was the remaining government stake in the generating companies. The pumped storage plant was separated from the grid and sold to a US company, Mission Energy, in 1995. Since 1989 fifteen new companies have entered electricity generation in the UK; most appear to be gas fired. It seems unlikely that the private sector will build a nuclear plant (*Brown Book* 1996).

Initially, the Regional Electricity Companies (RECs) were made responsible for the distribution of electricity to private households and firms, although large users could be supplied directly by generating companies. The RECs purchased their requirements by the half-hour through the 'Pool' calling on the cheapest generating plant first – thus in merit order. The generators were paid the Pool Purchase Price, which was the price paid to the most expensive generator running in that half-hour, the 'system marginal Price', plus a payment for their capacity. The RECs paid the Pool Purchase price plus a payment for the grid. However, the Electricity Act 1989 also required the RECs to 'contract for a specified minimum of non-fossil fuelled generating capacity'. Most of this is nuclear. As it will cost more, a fossil fuel levy was imposed to compensate the Area Boards for their purchase of non-fossil fuels (IEA 1990). This is due to be phased out.

Economists expressed concern about the safety margin that a privatized industry would carry. By October 1995 the plant margin (the amount by which installed generating plant exceeded forecast peak demand) had been reduced to 15.9 per cent. This was too low, as was demonstrated when overload was nearly reached in January 1996. This was partly because some of the gas-fired turbines were on interruptable supplies and also because the cold weather caused an excess demand for gas. The margin has since been raised to 21.3 per cent (*Brown Book* 1996: 99).

Offer, the industry's regulator, has been concerned about the high prices being charged by the national grid, the one remaining monopolist in the system. In 1996 it was agreed that the grid would reduce its prices to consumers by 20 per cent on 1 April 1997 and by 4 per cent in real terms in the three subsequent years (Holberton 1996a).

The pressure on capacity has also been eased by importing electricity from France, which has a higher proportion of electricity generated by nuclear plants and whose daytime peak periods do not coincide with the British ones. This type of trade is likely to increase if the provision of the Maastricht Treaty of 1993 for establishing Trans-European Networks for energy is put in to effect.

Nuclear power

The government initially retained control of the nuclear power plants, because in 1990 the City baulked at the huge clean-up costs. These nuclear liabilities amount to £14bn. However, in 1996 seven AGR reactors plus Sizewell B, a PWR, were privatized as British Energy for £2.1bn. A special fund was set up with £230m, to which British Energy will contribute £16m a year for nuclear clean-up costs. Magnox Electric was left with the remaining nuclear assets: six operational power stations and three in various stages of decommissioning. It could not be nationalized because its liabilities were £1.3bn greater than its assets, but the government is endeavouring to merge it with Nuclear Fuels Ltd, the state-owned nuclear waste management company (Lascelles 1995, 1996; Holberton 1996b). There is still some controversy as to whether enough finance is being put aside for decommissioning and cleaning up the nation's nuclear industry; a recent report by the Science Policy Research Institute of Sussex University suggests the taxpayer will have to pay for £29.4bn of the industry's officially recognized £42bn nuclear liabilities (Holberton 1997d).

Thus the first step in the privatization of both gas and electricity consisted of selling assets to the private sector. The government is widely regarded as having sold the assets at too low a price. This is because of the profits that were subsequently made, the way the shares rose, and because British Energy was sold for less than the £3 billion cost of building the most recent Sizewell power station (Lascelles 1996). The firms created are also accused of reducing employment while, at the same time, management – in many cases, the same as previously in the state sector – has awarded itself hefty salary increases. The Labour government formed after winning the election of May 1997 kept to its manifesto and imposed a windfall tax on them. The City appeared to have already discounted this and so far it does not seem to have had much effect on the market.

The second stage in privatization, which may be combined with the first, is that of reducing or removing the degree of vertical integration. This was initiated after the main gas sell-off (see above), but, at the outset, in electricity privatization.

The third stage consists of breaking up the large units in order to introduce some competition in production. Because competition was not complete the regulators continued to control both electricity and gas prices, using a formula of the RPI minus a certain percentage.

The fourth and last stage is to introduce some competition for the buyers so that they can choose between different suppliers. This has been done piecemeal in the gas industry, as we have described. In electricity, the market for customers using at least 1 MW was liberalized in 1990 and for those consuming more than 100 kW in 1994. It was proposed by the Offer regulator that the remaining customers could be given a choice of supply by April 1998. But it now looks as if this may be phased in and the promised competitive markets for gas and electricity may not be achieved by 1998.

Use of domestic coal for electricity generation

However, electricity generation has also been affected by the government's protective policy towards the coal industry, and in particular, its efforts to make the CEGB use domestically produced coal. From 1979 to March 1985, sales to the CEGB of steam coal, the variety required for electricity generation, were governed by a non-contractual *Joint Understanding* between the CEGB and the NCB under which they agreed 'to use their best endeavours' to supply and take up to 75 million tonnes annually. The price paid by the CEGB was set roughly equal to the NCB's average operating costs, and was not to rise faster than the UK rate of inflation. Imports were explicitly allowed. But the CEGB's electricity sales fell short of expectations and it did not succeed in taking up that quantity of coal. The *Joint Understanding* was gradually adjusted downwards to 73 million tonnes in 1982, with an initial tranche being purchased at British Coal's average costs, and marginal quantities being purchased at the price of imported coal. This was later adjusted, with the CEGB taking 95 per cent of their estimated coal requirements from the NCB. The *New Joint Understanding*, running from spring 1986 to 1991, divided tonnages and prices into three tranches: the first tranche amounted to 52 million tonnes, the second 12 million tonnes, and there was a third tranche of an additional 10 million tonnes that reflected the price of fuel oil or delivery of imported coal to inland power stations. The prices of the three tranches in the first year were £46.88 ($68.7), £29.5 ($43.2), and £33 ($48.4) per tonne respectively (IEA 1988: 156). Thus, at the margin, prices to British Coal were meant to reflect the opportunity cost to the economy of obtaining coal.

Later, although privatized, National Power and PowerGen had contracts to take almost 80 per cent of British Coal's output, but these ran out in 1993. National Power and PowerGen then concluded five-year contracts with British Coal for the purchase of 40 million tonnes of coal in 1993/4, falling to 30 million tonnes in the next four years, and these contracts were passed on to the successor privatized companies in 1994. The price agreed was £1.51 per gigajoule in 1993/94, falling to £1.33 per gigajoule in 1997/98. This compares with a price of coal imported into the EU of roughly £1.07 per gigajoule at the beginning of 1995, £1.16 in 1996 and £1.00–1.05 at the beginning of 1997. Thus the domestic producers were being paid more than it cost to import the product, but the quantities purchased from them were falling. By 1995 net imports represented a tenth of the total consumption of steam coal. Any renegotiation of contracts will undoubtedly be at a lower price, say, 120p a gigajoule, 11 per cent less than the coal contract in March 1998 (Holberton 1996e, 1997c).

Coal

The privatization of British Coal mines was completed in 1994 with the sale of mining assets, chiefly to RJB Mining, providing the government with £1bn. But, as explained above, the generating companies continued to purchase coal at above market prices. The government subsidized some coal above the base amounts sold in the run up to privatization. By the end of 1997 RJB Mining said that it expected its sales to fall to 20m tonnes, largely due to National Power, the largest consumer of coal, halving the volume of coal it contracted to purchase from it. Closures of deep mines were anticipated, which would lead to a reduction in the underground workforce of up to 5,000. Of the coal National Power bought, 90 per cent would be British. The competition for electricity generation comes not from other coal producers but from gas. Pressure is now being put on the government to deny licences to new gas-fired power stations, but they are cleaner and reduce CO_2 emissions (Holberton and Wighton 1997; Kampfner and Holberton 1997).

Mergers and takeovers

Privatization has opened the door to mergers and takeovers. These began in the distribution of electricity when the government's special share in the twelve RECs expired in March 1995. Each bid is considered by the DTI, which may refer it to the Monopolies and Mergers Commission (MMC). Bids by PowerGen for Midland and by National Power for Southern have been disallowed. They would have re-established an element of vertical integration but without the control over transmission through the national grid, which is the intermediate link between the generation and distribution of electricity. However, Scottish Hydro were allowed to acquire an REC. Some of the RECs have also bought into gas-fired stations, so they are to a small extent integrated. Other takeovers, including those by UK water companies and US energy companies, have been allowed (*Brown Book* 1996, 1: 106). Indeed, one REC after another has been taken over, three of them by US companies with a fourth, the CE Electric bid for the Northern REC, impending (Weston 1996). At the end of December 1996 only two remained as independent companies. There is the question as to whether the regulator Offer can operate in these circumstances, that is, will it be able to obtain information to make meaningful comparisons of different companies?

Although the Offer regulator has tended to frown on bids involving vertical integration, he has not objected to long-term contracts, as, for instance, made by British Energy to supply Southern Electricity for fifteen years. National Power and PowerGen are also discussing arrangements with the supply companies, formerly the RECs (Holberton 1996b). Recently, British Energy has announced plans to build a 50 MW non-nuclear powerplant in England and Wales as a joint venture with Southern Electric.

Future developments

The government appears to welcome the prospect of companies operating to supply both electricity and gas, commenting that all twelve RECs, together with Scottish Power and Scottish Hydro, have gas subsidiaries or interests in gas supply companies. PowerGen has a major stake in Kinetica which both distributes and sells gas. These fifteen companies accounted for about 30 per cent of gas supplies to the industrial and commercial sectors (*Brown Book* 1996: 19). In view of the convergence of the two industries, proposals for the merger of Ofgas and Offer, the respective gas and electricity regulators, appear to be gaining acceptance.

Production of primary energy

Government policy has been one of the factors determining the production of energy in Britain, in particular its protection of the coal industry. The changes in the production of fuel in Britain from 1950 to 1995 can be seen in Figure 8.3. To begin with, the output was entirely of coal, and the initial increase and then decline in production can be seen. By 1970 the output of coal had fallen to 147 million tonnes, by 1980 to 130 million, and by 1995 to 52.6 million.

The main change in Britain's position, however, has been due to the discovery and extraction of, first, gas and then oil from the North Sea, as can be seen from Figure 8.3. Natural gas production has increased from 0.16 mtoe in 1966, to 27 mtoe in 1973, and 71 mtoe in 1995.

A certain amount of oil was produced as a by-product of gas production, but it represented 3 per cent or less of refinery intake. The real expansion in production occurred after the oil price rise of 1973–74. Production increased tenfold to 1.7 mtoe between 1970 and 1975, to 87 mtoe in 1980, and then to a peak of 139 mtoe in 1985. After this, it fell slightly, but after 1991 it began rising again and in 1995 was 144 mtoe.

The production of primary electricity has slowly increased to an 8 per cent contribution of total energy supplies in 1995 in terms of its fossil fuel equivalent (see Figure 8.3).

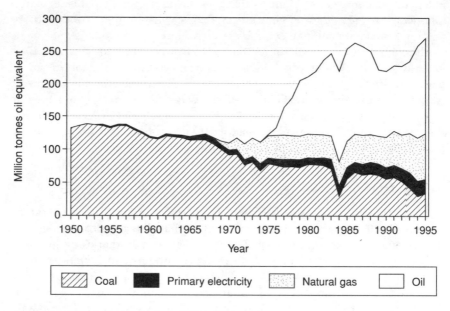

Figure 8.3 UK fuel production, 1950–95 (mtoe)

Production of electricity

Let us turn to consider the input of fuels for electricity generation, as that is where they compete most directly. The contribution of primary – that is, nuclear and hydro – electricity is multiplied up to their FFEEs. As can be seen from Figure 8.4, after 1965 there was a fairly steady increase in the provision of primary electricity from nuclear generators to 28 per cent in 1995. The supply of hydroelectricity from natural flow – that is, excluding pumped storage – did not increase much after the 1950s and just fluctuated around 0.35 mtoe, or 0.6 per cent of the total.

The use of coal has declined from 77 per cent in 1965 to 47 per cent in 1995. However, there were considerable fluctuations in the quantity of coal used; the cutbacks in 1972, 1974 and 1984 all represent the effect of disputes in the coal industry. In each case, greater quantities of oil had to be used instead.

Initially, oil was being used as a substitute for coal, and its uptake in electricity generation increased to a peak of 20 mtoe in 1972. It then fluctuated and eventually declined, so that in the 1980s it was about the same level as in the 1960s, apart from a massive increase in 1984–85 due to the coal miners' strike. It fell in the early 1990s to 3.6 mtoe in 1995.

The most recent development has been the expansion in the use of natural gas; in 1995 it accounted for 16 per cent of inputs (*DUKES* 1996).

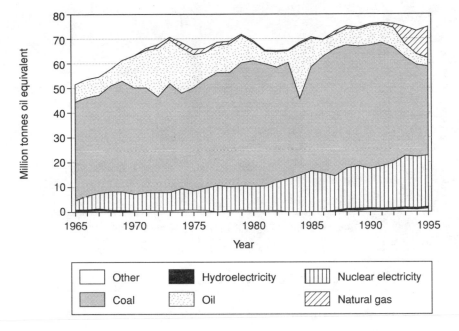

Figure 8.4 Fuel input for electricity generation

Taxation and production subsidies

Before discussing consumption it is appropriate to summarize the government taxation and subsidy policies. So far, we have considered the way in which they have affected the pricing and therefore the production and consumption of the different fuels. Let us now briefly consider government expenditure and the income it has derived from the industry.

We shall begin with the government's support for the coal industry. The market for domestically produced coal was protected by banning imports and by the government insisting that the electricity industry should use a certain proportion of coal as its fossil fuel. The IEA has endeavoured to measure the cost of the support the government provides the coal industry by distinguishing between the assistance benefiting current production, which it terms the producer subsidy equivalent, and 'assistance not benefiting current production' (see Figure 8.5). The producer subsidy equivalent is the direct subsidy paid for current production plus the excess cost charged to consumers. The latter is an efficiency loss, but it is paid by the electricity industry in their purchase of domestic steam coal at above world prices, and not directly by the government. As can be seen, direct production subsidies, which were very large in 1984/85 due to the coal strike and between 1988 and 1990 due to the write-down of assets prior to privatization, have now been phased out. The assistance not

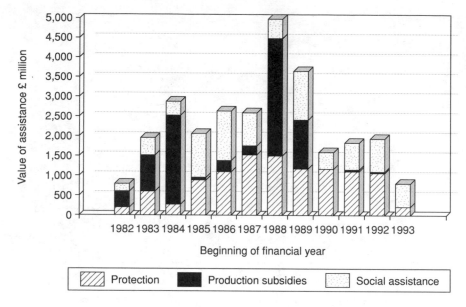

Figure 8.5 Assistance to UK coal producers, 1982–93 (£m current prices)

benefiting production is largely in the form of government and EEC social and readaptation grants.

But government intervention can also be regarded as its 'take', that is, the creaming off of the economic rent from the discoveries in the North Sea. This has consisted of:

1   A 'royalty' equal to 12.5 per cent of the landed value of petroleum less the cost of bringing it ashore and treating it, paid to the government every six months for any field approved before 31 March 1982.
2   A petroleum revenue tax (PRT), introduced in 1975, and paid every six months on profits (i.e. the difference between income and expenditure) from geological and technically determined fields. For fields given approval after 1993 the PRT is zero.
3   The gas levy, introduced in 1981, to capture the rent the BGC was gaining from purchasing PRT-exempt gas under long-term contracts drawn up before a general rise in gas prices.
4   Corporation tax (CT), at present at 33 per cent. For new fields this is now the only tax applicable.

The total revenue the government obtained from the extraction of oil and gas between 1964/65 and 1995/96 in real terms at 1990 prices is shown in Figure 8.6. In relation to GDP it reached its maximum of 3.78 per cent in 1984/5 (*Brown Book* 1996: vol. 2).

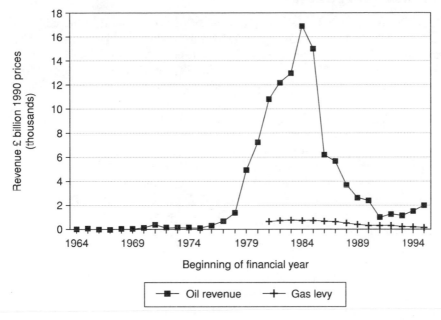

Figure 8.6 North Sea revenue in real terms (£bn 1990 prices)

Indirect taxation

Before discussing consumption, a brief mention should be made of indirect taxation. The government has always taxed petrol. The tax was initially a specific excise duty; in 1954 it represented 56 per cent of the price of four-star petrol and in 1970, 69 per cent. When value-added tax (VAT) was introduced in 1974 it was calculated as a percentage of the total and added as well, but, as the price of oil had risen, tax fell as a proportion of the price of petrol to 51 per cent by January 1975. When the price of oil rose again from 1978 to 1980 the tax fell further to 43 per cent by January 1980. Since then, although the tax in terms of pence per litre has systematically risen, as a percentage it has tended to fluctuate inversely with the price of oil; in January 1995 it was 58 per cent.

From 1961 fuel oil and kerosene were also taxed, although kerosene ceased to be taxed in 1985. Fuel oil, gas oil and kerosene for industrial and commercial users became liable to the standard rate of VAT in July 1990, at 15 per cent to the end of March 1991 and 17.5 per cent since then. Since the beginning of April 1994 an 8 per cent VAT has been imposed on fuel for domestic consumers. In 1997 the Labour government reduced it to 6.5 per cent.

Household expenditure

Before we go on to consider the quantities of fuels consumed in the different outlets, let us first look at the data derived from the household survey. The expenditure by households on energy, measured at constant prices, doubled between 1950 to 1970 (see *Economic Trends Annual Supplement* for 1988). Unfortunately, it is not broken down into fuel and light, and petrol until 1963. Between 1963 and 1970, at constant 1990 prices, expenditure on fuel and light increased by 8 per cent and then by another 23 per cent to 1995. But real expenditure on petrol and oil doubled between 1963 and 1970, and then increased by 76 per cent between 1970 and 1995. Average expenditure on fuel per consuming household per week in 1995 was £12.95 on domestic fuel and £16.62 on motor fuel: that is, the average household with a car spent more on fuel for transport than for cooking and heating. Averaged over all households, this amounted to £23.15 per week (*DUKES* 1996).

A regression analysis, using data from 1963–89 (see Appendix Table 8.A1), of real expenditure related to consumers' total real expenditure, and real price, for fuel and light (F&L) and petrol and motor oil (P&O), showed an insignificant price elasticity of demand. The elasticity with respect to consumers' total expenditure was 0.39 for F&L and 1.03 for P&O and, as the Table shows, this changed little when the price variable was removed. However, because of the considerable divergence between these, with a much higher expenditure elasticity of demand for the highly taxed petrol, there is very little correlation between the index of consumer expenditure on energy, measured at 1985 prices, and the consumption of energy in terms of therms.

Energy consumption

Energy consumption by final user in terms of oil equivalent is generally categorized into that for industry, transport, domestic (excluding transport), and other outlets. We will consider consumption over the whole period, although there is a break in the DTI's recent version of the series after 1987. This break discourages any further econometric calculation, but will be ignored in discussion of changes in quantity consumed because it does not appear to be very large.

Between 1960 and 1970, consumption in all four end uses increased. But the consumption of coal and coke fell in each outlet, whereas the consumption of oil approximately doubled, except in industry where the increase was greater at 174 per cent. Natural gas began to be available at the end of the 1960s and this gradually replaced town gas, particularly for domestic users. The rest of the energy demand is for electricity. This demand has been increasing rapidly; it almost doubled between 1960 and 1970 and then increased by another 55 per cent to 1995.

Domestic consumption

Domestic consumption of energy – that is, by private households excluding for transport – has hardly risen. In mtoe, it was 3 per cent higher in 1973 than 1960 and then rose by another 14 per cent to 1995, see Figure 8.7. This was due to the increased consumption of gas, which rose from 3 mtoe in 1960 to 28 mtoe in 1995. In the 1960s it was gas made from coal, but by 1995 it was entirely natural gas. Consumption of other fossil fuels has fallen: oil to 72 per cent, and coal and coke to a fifth of the 1973 level.

Regression analysis of energy consumption in therms in relation to total household expenditure from 1960–89 provides an elasticity of 0.2, which is half that from the household expenditure survey. This increase in consumption is lower than that indicated by the household expenditure survey. Furthermore, the low increase appears due to a deficiency of effective demand rather than any adequacy of heating. According to the 1991 Home Condition Survey by the Department of the Environment, when outside temperatures fall to 3°C, 50 per cent of all households can no longer maintain minimum acceptable heating standards. This is because of the poor standard of insulation; only 5 per cent of English homes are energy-efficient and one in five are hopeless. Pensioners' homes are in the worst state of all. James McKinnon, the previous gas regulator, concerned about the depletion of North Sea reserves insisted that British Gas invested directly in energy-efficiency measures. His successor, Clare Spottiswoode, did not want

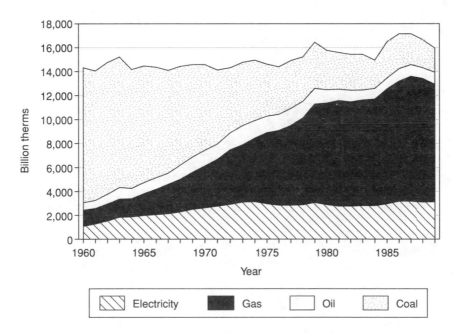

Figure 8.7 UK domestic fuel consumption, 1960–89 (billion therms)

interference with the free market. This is where there appears to be a clear conflict between, on the one hand, imposing regulations which would confer social benefits in the short and long run, and, on the other, the immediate profitability of private firms (Monbiot 1996).

Industrial consumption

The oil price shock of 1973–74 had the most dramatic effects on manufacturing. Suddenly, many heating processes, particularly those using water, which has a high latent heat, became uneconomic. Industrial output fell by 5.8 per cent and consumption of oil by 13 per cent between 1974 and 1975, see Figure 8.8. The next increase in the oil price from 1978–80 was followed, by the 10 per cent decline in industrial output from 1979 to 1981, which was associated with a 32 per cent reduction in oil consumption. Industrial consumption of oil continued to decline until in 1995 it was 28 per cent of its level in 1973. At 8 million tonnes it now represents 22 per cent of industrial energy consumption. On the other hand, there was a rapid increase in industrial consumption of natural gas to a third of the total and an increase in electricity to a quarter of the total. Industrial consumption of energy in 1995 was 55 per cent of its 1973 level and two-thirds of its level in 1960. Industrial output in 1995 was 120 per cent of its 1973 level.

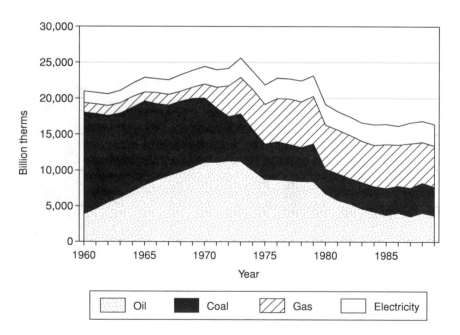

Figure 8.8 Industrial energy consumption, 1960–89 (billion therms)

Regression analysis of industrial consumption of energy from 1960–89 (see Appendix Table 8.A2) shows an elasticity with respect to industrial output of 1.94 and a negative trend of –4.7 per cent per annum. Unfortunately, a satisfactory price index is only available from 1974 onwards. Taking the terms of trade to manufacturing as the price of fuel to producers divided by the price of manufacturing output, the price elasticity is negative but not significant. If it is removed, the R^2 is approximately the same but the elasticity with respect to industrial output rises from 1.35 to 1.49, in both cases lower than over the longer period since 1960. Clearly, this exercise has not properly separated the demand elasticity for fuel from the supply situation in the market for manufactures. However, the estimated trend remains roughly the same at –4.7 per cent per annum.

Transport

Transport has shown the most consistent increase in consumption see Figure 8.9. The level in 1973 was 46 per cent greater than 1960. The oil price rise of 1973–74 led to a temporary dip, but then the expansion continued, so that consumption was 56 per cent higher in 1995 than 1973. A regression analysis of consumption in therms against trend (see Appendix Table 8A.3) shows an increase of 2.5 per cent per annum. Furthermore, this increase was almost entirely of oil. This trend has continued, so that in

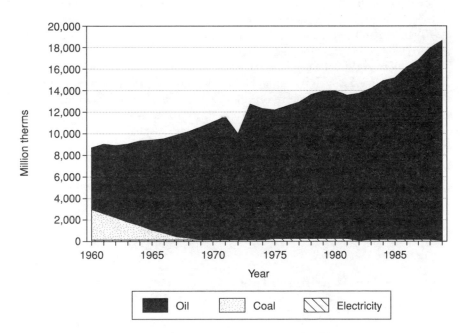

Figure 8.9 Energy consumption in transport, 1960–89 (million therms)

1995, transport accounted for 75 per cent of the total energy use of oil. The increase in consumption from 1973 to 1995 was 78 per cent for air transport and 57 per cent for road transport, but because so much more was initially consumed in road transport – 39.5 mtoe compared with 8.5 mtoe for air – it accounted for 79 per cent of the total increase in oil consumption. Most of this increase for road transport was for passenger cars, and was partly a response to the construction of the motorway network, which greatly cut the time required to get from one part of Britain to another and made road passenger and freight traffic much more competitive with rail traffic.

However, it was intensified by the Conservative governments' reduction in support for the railways. Although the number of passenger kilometres travelled increased from 35 billion in 1979 to 40 billion in 1989, it then fell back to 35 billion in 1994. The number of passenger carriages fell from 17,175 in 1979 to 10,637 in 1994 and seats fell from 1,090,000 to 740,000. Inevitably, this led to overcrowding on the more popular routes, with British Rail not even aiming to provide seats for everyone on the commuter lines. The reduction in traction engines from 8,506 in 1979 to 1,894 in 1993/94 also aggravated the effect of breakdowns. In contrast, the stock of private cars increased by 43 per cent from 14.3 million in 1979 to 20.5 million in 1994.

This has provided a strong incentive for people to travel by road. In addition, a high proportion of cars on the road are supplied by employers. Thus, although there had been a fairly steady increase in travel by car and taxis in the 1960s and 1970s, after 1979 it accelerated, so that passenger miles in 1994 were 60 per cent greater than in 1979. At the same time, there was a considerable transfer in haulage from rail to road; tonne miles going by road increased by 40 per cent, whereas that going by rail fell by a third. The net effect was overcrowding on trains and congestion on the motorways. Petroleum consumption on the railways has been declining, with fluctuations, since 1970, but electricity consumption has been increasing as more lines are electrified: by 1995 it was two-and-a-half times the amount in the late 1970s.

Other outlets

There is also a non-energy use of oil – in, for instance, the production of plastics, synthetic fibres, and chemicals – which has slowly increased by 39 per cent from 1970 to 1995, so that it now stands at 15 mtoe.

Consumption of primary fuels

The total consumption of primary energy (temperature corrected) for all uses increased from 143.5 mtoe in 1950 to 211.9 mtoe in 1970, an increase of 48 per cent. Since then, there have been considerable fluctuations, but in 1995 it was 223.4 mtoe, only 5.4 per cent above its 1970 level. The DTI relates this consumption to real GDP to show that the tonnes of oil equivalent per £1,000 of GDP at 1990 prices has fallen from 176 in 1950 to 95 in 1995 (*DUKES* 1996). This clearly reflects not only an improvement in efficiency, but also changes in the structure of industrial production and thus demand in the British economy.

The total consumption of the different *primary* fuels from 1960 to 1995 is shown in Figure 8.10. In 1960, coal accounted for almost three-quarters and oil a quarter, but, as can be seen, the consumption of coal has fallen steadily until in 1995 it accounted for 23 per cent. The proportion accounted for by oil went up to 35 per cent, natural gas accounted for 32 per cent, and nuclear electricity, in terms of FFEEs, 10 per cent.

The changes in the structure of demand by final user are summarized in Figure 8.11(a). In 1960, with total consumption of 127 mtoe, 42 per cent went into industry, 29 per cent for domestic uses, 17 per cent went into transport and 12 per cent to other final users. In 1995, total consumption had increased by almost a fifth to 151 mtoe, but the proportion going to industry had declined to 24 per cent, whereas that going to transport had increased to 34 per cent.

The change in relative demand of final users is mainly responsible for the proportional change in kind of fuel consumed. Almost all the increase in the quantity of oil consumed and its proportion of the total is due to the growth of road transport, with an additional contribution from airlines.

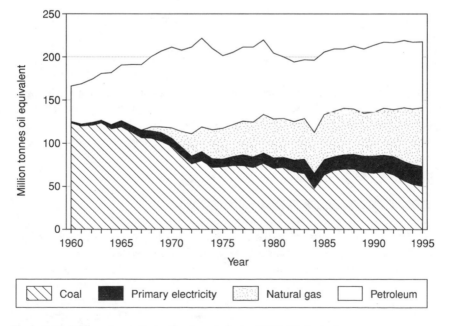

Figure 8.10 UK consumption of primary fuels, 1960–95 (mtoe)

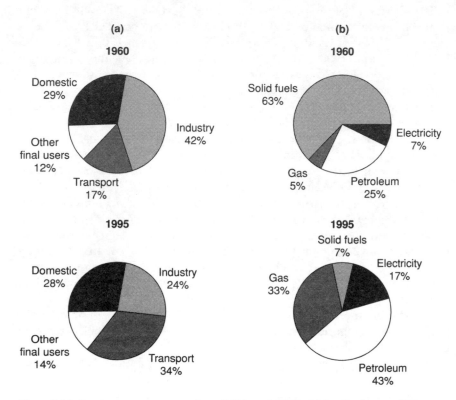

Figure 8.11 Final energy consumption, 1960 and 1995: (a) by final user; (b) by type of fuel
Source: DTI (1996) *Digest of United Kingdom Energy Statistics (DUKES)*, London: HMSO, 139.

Thus, from 1960 to 1995, petroleum as a proportion of the total increased from 25 per cent to 43 per cent (see Figure 8.11(b)). Solid fuels declined from 63 per cent to 7 per cent, gas increased from 5 per cent to 33 per cent (town gas in 1960, but natural gas in 1995), and electricity increased from 7 per cent to 17 per cent.

EFFECT ON THE BRITISH ECONOMY

Since 1950 there has been a massive contraction of the coal industry, which was almost inevitable given the exhaustion of many coal seams and the rising cost of obtaining the remaining deep-mined coal. But this decline was hastened by the increasing supplies of cheap Middle Eastern oil. Employment in the coal industry was more than halved between 1950 and 1970, from 751,000 to 349,000 workers, see Table 8.3. When the general level of unemployment rose in the 1970s and 1980s there was a very high social and political cost to forc-

Table 8.3 Output of the UK fuel industries (gross value-added (GVA) percentage going on wages and net investment)

	GVA £m	GVA per person employed	Wages and salaries/ GVA %	I/GVA %	Employment (000s)[a]
Coal extraction, coke ovens and solid fuel					
1950	398	529	82		751
1970	590	1,693	62		349
1979	2,573	8,803	60	23	292
1980	3,166	10,936	58	22	289
1985	2,696	15,280	67	21	216
1988	2,375	21,207	69	22	112
1993	773	25,000		18	14
Extraction of mineral oil and gas					
1970	51	12,333	14		4
1979	5,729	353,660	2	36	16
1980	8,734	388,191	2	27	22
1985	18,898	609,603	2	15	31
1988	7,770	267,928		20	29
1993	9,521	280,000		49	29
Mineral oil processing					
1950	5	577	72		10
1970	172	9,490	18		18
1979	2,348	97,273	6	13	24
1980	2,017	82,900	9	18	24
1985	1,312	83,229	16	20	20
1988	1,609	102,685	16	17	16
1993	1,618	124,000		22	21
Nuclear fuel production					
1985					15
1993	748	48,000		49	16
Electricity generation and supply					
1985					127
1993	10,577	98,000		26	83
Gas supply					
1985					79
1993	3,125	47,000		32	39
Total energy industries					
1985					488
1993	26,363			35	203
Total production industries					
1993	140,040	31,000		16	

Source: UK Censuses of Production and DTI (1996) *The Energy Report*, vol. 1.
Note: [a] last figure for 1995.

ing mining employment down still further to reduce government subsidies and attain the price and efficiency objectives of equating marginal cost with price. The coal industry was privatized in 1994 and one of the private firms has already gone bankrupt. Employment in 1995 was down to 14,000.

The discovery of North Sea gas and oil made the UK appear a resource-rich country, but this should be seen in the context of the quadrupling of the world price of oil by OPEC from 1973–74 and the doubling from 1978–80, which made it more profitable to extract. The contribution of the extraction of oil and gas from the UK continental shelf to GDP between 1976 to 1995 is shown in Figure 8.12. At its peak in 1984 it accounted for nearly 7 per cent of GDP. The decline after 1985 was partly due to a fall in the price of oil and that in 1988 was due to the disastrous explosion at Piper Alpha, one of the North Sea platforms.

The new fields that were developed in the 1980s appeared to have a higher unit cost (unadjusted for inflation) than those before, see Table 8.4. In the late 1980s and 1990 production was being extended into smaller fields, so that one would expect unit costs to rise. But in fact they have fallen, and that is due to some fairly significant improvements in technology. The average price is £10.5 per barrel of oil and 12.5p per therm of gas (*Brown Book* 1996, 2: 14).

From the outset, oil has been sold at an international price and the government has endeavoured to cream off some of the economic rent by taxation. In contrast, in the 1970s natural gas was sold at a price below its marginal cost, and therefore consumption may have been greater than it would have

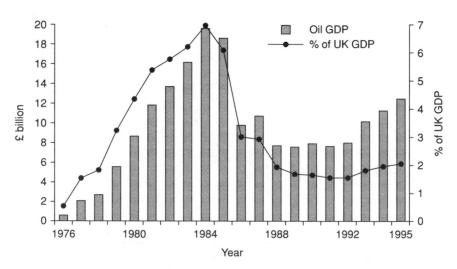

Figure 8.12 The contribution of oil and gas from the continental shelf to the GDP of the UK

Source: *Brown Book* (1996) *The Energy Report: Oil and Gas Resources of the United Kingdom*, Department of Trade and Industry, London: HMSO, vol. 2, p. 9.

Table 8.4 Unit costs of gas and oil fields on the UK continental shelf at 1995 prices

	Oil fields (£/barrel)	Gas fields (p/therm)
Fields starting production before 1980	10	10
Fields starting production 1980–85	14	21
Fields starting production 1986–90	13	18
Fields starting production 1991–95	9	13.5
All fields in production	10.5	12.5
Fields under development at year end	8.5	11.5
Fields approved in year	8	11.5

Source: Department of Trade and Industry (1996) *The Energy Report, Oil and Gas Resources of the UK*, vol. 2: 17.

been otherwise. However, it is more difficult to establish an international price for gas because trade depends on the existence of pipelines or being able to liquify it.

Thus, taking the international price at which goods can be delivered to Britain as representing the opportunity cost of the product to the British economy, the marginal output of the coal industry throughout the period appears to have been uneconomic: that is, GDP would have been greater if more of the marginal pits had been closed down. The output could have been replaced by imports or some other fuel.

Only in oil extraction, where the government had deliberately followed a very liberal policy with respect to the access of foreign investment and sale on the international market, at the same time as it had charged royalties and imposed taxes, did the government earn much economic rent.

These changes in production have represented a decline in a relatively labour-intensive form of extraction, coal mining, to a capital-intensive form of extraction for gas and oil. An indication of the difference in labour intensity is the higher proportion of gross value added (GVA) accounted for by wages and salaries in coal extraction in comparison with the extraction of oil and gas, and mineral oil processing in each year (see Table 8.3). The reduction in the ratio of wages and salaries to GVA in mining suggests that the labour intensity in mining has fallen over time. Unfortunately, there are no figures for capital stock to measure capital intensity directly. The ratio of investment to GVA is shown, but this is likely to vary with the age of the mine or oilfield because most expenditure is incurred when it is first opened up.

In view of the great change in relative prices it is difficult to discuss the real change in GVA. However, the production of primary energy in 1985 was 80 per cent greater than in 1950, but as can be seen from Table 8.3, employment in 1985 was less than half its level in 1950. Almost all of this reduction was in mining, which declined by 564,000, equal to 2 per cent of total UK employment.

Trade in fuel

The net effect of the changes in consumption and production have shown up in trade. Trade in fuel can be considered either in real terms – that is, in terms of coal or oil equivalent or therms – or in monetary terms.

Let us begin by considering the situation in real terms, taking all fuel consumption, production and trade measured in mtoes. In 1950, domestically produced coal accounted for 90 per cent of British fuel consumption and she also exported some. All oil was imported, but her net imports of fuel were only 3 per cent of consumption; she was approximately self-sufficient. The changes since 1965 are depicted in Figure 8.13. By 1970, due to the shift in consumption from coal to oil and with almost all the oil imported, net imports were as large as home production and accounted for half domestic consumption. By 1980, due to the expansion of her domestic production of gas and oil, she was approximately self-sufficient. By 1986, due to the continued expansion in production of oil, she was a net exporter.

Now let us consider the effect of the international price changes on the British economy. As the real price of oil on the international market fell between 1950 and 1970 and Britain imported all her requirements, this represented an improvement in her terms of trade: that is, it meant that

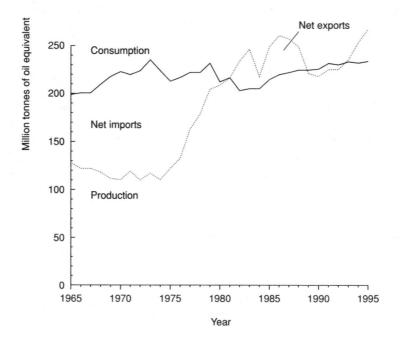

Figure 8.13 Real net trade in energy: UK energy production and consumption, 1965–95 (oil equivalent)

Source: DTI (1996) *Digest of United Kingdom Energy Statistics (DUKES)*, London: HMSO, p. 137.

the cost of obtaining a given amount of oil imports in terms of exports fell. The subsequent rise in price engineered by OPEC after 1971 represented an adverse movement in the terms of trade; in particular, the quadrupling of the oil price from 1973 to 1974 was calculated to represent a 2 per cent reduction in GDP (Bank of England 1980).

However, once Britain became a net exporter of oil, any rise in its relative price represented an improvement in her terms of trade: that is, she could obtain more imports in exchange for her exports of oil than she did before. Thus, whether any price change was detrimental or beneficial to her economy as a whole depended on her trading position, which, in turn, depended on her production and consumption.

So how has this affected the balance of payments? You would expect the monetary balance to reflect the real balance, except in so far as relative prices have changed. But it should be remembered that traded products of the same energy value may represent different degrees of processing, and, in particular, that from 1986 we have had growing imports of electricity. From 1950 to the mid-1970s Britain's *net imports* of fuel increased fairly steadily in terms of sterling, but only slightly in terms of the exports required to pay for them, deflated by the price index of manufacturing exports. The balance of payments position at current prices since 1970 is shown in Figure 8.14. *Net imports* of fuel in terms of sterling increased particularly after 1973–74 to reach a maximum in 1976 (see Figure 8.14). After that, they declined with the extraction of North Sea oil until Britain's position became reversed in 1981. Her positive balance in fuels reached a peak in 1985; it then fell off until 1989 to near zero. But then in the early 1990s it began to increase again.

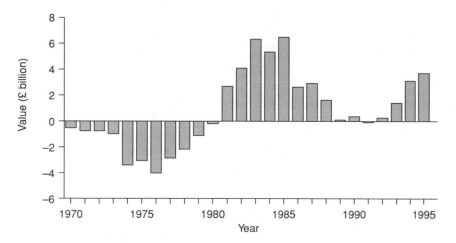

Figure 8.14 Net exports of fuels, 1970–95 (£bn current prices)

Source: DTI (1996) *Digest of United Kingdom Energy Statistics (DUKES)*, London: HMSO, p. 145.

Note: 'Free on board' basis and at current prices.

In addition, there is also the effect of the inflow of foreign investment to develop the North Sea on the capital account, and the subsequent outflow of interest and dividends on the current account.

EU networks

The EU policies which are most relevant to UK trade are, first, the TEU provisions with respect to networks.

Secondly, the EU has been trying liberalize the EU market in energy. It spent eight years in negotiations on the market in electricity, with three main objectives:

1   transparent, non-discriminatory licensing for the construction of generator capacity;
2   mandatory third-party access (TPA) to networks for utility and non-utility producers and consumers; and
3   the unbundling of management and accounts of vertically integrated utilities.

The Directive for liberalizing the electricity industry was accepted in June 1996 and Member States have two years to put it into effect. Objectives 1 and 3 have been achieved with certain qualifications, but very slow progress has been made towards objective 2. The final Directive provides for a progressive opening of national markets to large final consumers only. Each Member State initially has to allow consumers absorbing 40 GWh of electricity per year to seek alternative supplies. After three years this threshold is reduced to 20 GWh, and after six years to 9 GWh; the last is equivalent to opening a third of the EU market to competition (IEA 1996). But as a result of a concession made to France the Member State can choose its method of market opening. Hence, whereas in the UK and Germany customers can buy the electricity from domestic or foreign generators, paying a fee to the distribution network for carrying the electricity, in France all these negotiations are carried out by the sole buyer Electricité de France (EdF). The German generators fear that EdF as a monopoly buyer will learn the price of any competitor and therefore be able to undercut it. EdF will be able to dominate its home market at the same time as being able to compete freely in the other more liberalized markets. Furthermore, while the large consumers will be able to take advantage of the competition, in many cases the same advantage will not extend to small business, let alone the household market. Consumers' associations are afraid that prices may be raised to private households to compensate the suppliers for the lower prices they have to accept in the more competitive markets. The EU electricity industry is worth $175bn per annum and there is a wide variation in prices between Member States, which would suggest considerable scope for trade, but even by 2006 many EU countries will not be as liberalized as the UK was in 1992 (Buckley and Holberton 1996).

Clearly, with the disaggregation and privatization of national industries, trade in electricity will become easier. But it is thought that the more risky markets and the larger share of privately owned generators will discourage the more capital-intensive forms of generation and encourage the use of natural gas. There is the problem of security of supply, which in electricity consists in having a margin for unforseen breakdown in generators or transmission. Competition that makes better use of existing facilities could save $3.76–5.37 billion annually (IEA 1996).

Such liberalization will make it difficult for countries to enforce their environmental standards. On the other hand, the greater use of natural gas will lower the emission of the toxic gases SO_2 and NO_2.

The EU Commission has been less successful with the gas industry. Member States are worried about their dependence on a few remote suppliers such as Statoil in Norway, Sonatrach in Algeria and Gazprom in Russia. Opponents of liberalization argue that the lowering of prices and gas utility profits would limit their ability to import remote and expensive gas and increase their dependence on Middle East oil. The Commission says, 'that necessity of supply shall be ensured through an open market functioning under competitive conditions at all stages from production to transmission in conformity with the Treaty [of Rome]' (IEA 1996). Even if a main source of supply is cut off by political troubles or damage to the pipelines, alternative sources of supply are more easily available through a European grid. This, however, will require the separation of gas transport from supply, so that all gas companies have the right to use pipelines. In addition, just as for Britain, there are many take-or-pay contracts that under liberalization would require renegotiation.

Yet all this is of little benefit to a country such as Britain with sufficient gas resources to supply herself. The real benefit to Britain is that her producers of gas can get more for it now by exporting, particularly when as at present there is a surplus of gas.

As has already been recounted, Britain has led the way in liberalizing its electricity and gas industries; she was the first country to separate out its vertically integrated power industry, distinguishing, as the MMC put it, between 'generation, transmission, distribution and supply' (MMC 1996). But attaching herself to EU networks of countries that are also liberalized is likely to lead to much more trade and greater uniformity of prices throughout Europe.

Already the UK and continental gas grids are being joined by a 150-mile interconnector costing £500m ($776m) between Bacton, Norfolk and Zeebrugge in Belgium, to be completed in 1998. It is being built by a consortium of British Gas (with a 40 per cent stake), Gazprom, BP, and Ruhrgas. Two deals have already been concluded to supply Germany's Wingas utilizing it; one by British Gas for 20bn cubic metres of gas over ten years, and one by the UK subsidiary of Conoco to sell 2bn cubic metres of gas a year (Dempsey and Corzine 1996). Gaz de France may also conclude an agreement (Owen 1997).

CONCERNS ABOUT POLLUTION

Recently, increasing concern has been shown about the externalities associated with energy consumption and production. On the one hand, the concern about the hazards of radiation from nuclear power stations was intensified by accidents at 3-Mile Island in the US and Chernobyl in the USSR. This led to considerable public opposition to the construction of the British nuclear power station at Sizewell in Sussex.

On the other hand, there is concern about the pollution resulting from the burning of fossil fuel. The Scandinavians claimed that 'acid rain', produced by the emissions of SO_2 and NO_x from British power stations, was destroying their forests. In 1994 two-thirds of SO_2 produced by Britain was from power stations: 72 per cent from coal and 21 per cent from fuel oil. Twenty-four per cent of NO_x came from the burning of coal, largely in power stations. But RJB Mining, the main successor to British Coal, complained that the lower emission standards for power generation that National Power, PowerGen and Eastern Group had agreed with the Environmental Agency would lead to a loss of 8,000 mining jobs, that is, 40 per cent of the total. This is because of the high sulphur content of British coal, particularly that from northeast England and the Midlands (Holberton 1997a). An additional 49 per cent of NO_x came from the use of petroleum in road transport.

More recently, there has been growing concern about the production of 'greenhouse gases', which destroy the ozone layer around the earth and raise its temperature. These greenhouse gases occur naturally and, in the case of CO_2, are necessary for life. The problem is their increased concentration due to the burning of fossil fuels. In 1994, 37 per cent of CO_2 was produced from petroleum, largely in road transport, 32 per cent was produced from coal and 26 per cent from natural gas. The source of the emissions was fairly widespread, with power stations accounting for 30 per cent, other industry 23 per cent, road transport 20 per cent, and the domestic sector 15 per cent (*DUKES* 1996).

There is therefore a certain conflict in objectives in so far as nuclear power may involve a risk of radiation pollution but it does not produce 'acid rain' nor does it contribute gases that destroy the ozone layer. Another conflict is that the lowering of energy prices which is likely to result from the liberalization of the trade and industry in the EU may lead to a higher consumption than there would otherwise be and therefore to the production of more 'greenhouse' gases. This could be cancelled out by the application of 'carbon taxes', but in Britain this has proved politically unpopular; thus, at the moment, tax is being levied on household gas and electricity bills at 8 per cent rather than the full VAT rate of 17.5 per cent. Furthermore, Gordon Brown, Chancellor of the Exchequer, said in his budget of July 1997 that he will keep to the Labour Party's pre-election pledge and reduce the VAT on domestic fuel to 5 per cent.

However, although the EU has been unsuccessful in instituting a carbon tax it is anxious to set minimum rates for coal, gas, and electricity, and to extend them to aviation fuel (assuming that the international agreements that prohibit it can be amended). The CEC's objective is to reduce the emission of carbon and other greenhouse gases by discouraging consumption, and to harmonize taxes as the EU markets become more liberalized. At present, the UK rates of tax are above the proposed minimum rates, except for lead-free petrol (Boulton 1996).

CONCLUSION

The policies introduced by Margaret Thatcher of privatizing and breaking up the large firms in the fuel industries in order to introduce competition are now being pursued by most other developed countries, in particular those of the EU. By 1998 the gas and electricity markets in the EU will be partially liberalized and the UK electricity and gas grids will be connected to those of the continent. Trade will increase. Privatization has lowered the price of electricity and domestic fuel in the UK (Holberton 1997b) and it is likely to lower average prices in the EU. Trade and competition may lower still further the price of coal and electricity in the UK. However, it may raise the price of gas in Britain if North Sea firms find it more profitable to export to other EU countries. Britain's experience of privatization suggests that the smaller companies do not remain independent for long; they will be taken over by other energy firms. It is not clear that this type of integration is better or will be more economically efficient than that which existed previously, and certainly it will make monitoring and regulation more difficult than before.

The long-term perspective is being ignored. What happens when the North Sea oil and gas reserves run out? How do you compare the relative merits of a capital-intensive form of production such as nuclear power, with a fossil fuel generator, when the rate of interest is being used as an instrument for short-term macroeconomic policy? How do you reduce the production of 'greenhouse' gases when the major addition to them is coming from motorized transport and there appears to be very little response of consumption to petrol taxes?

APPENDIX 8.1

Table 8.A1 Domestic expenditure on energy 1963–89, fuel and light (F&L) and petrol and oil (P&L) and oil. Household expenditure survey

$$\log = D\ a_1 + a_2 \log \text{Exp} + a_3 \log P.$$

where:

D = Domestic expenditure in real terms that is divided by its price index.

ExP = Total consumers' expenditure deflated by the general retail price index (RP1).

P = Real price that is the retail price index of the product divided by the RP1.

	Expenditure elasticity a_2	Price elasticity a_3	R^2
Fuel & Light			
	0.3880	−0.0393	0.8382
t-stat	(7.94)	(0.42)	
	0.3731		0.8371
t-stat	(11.33)		
Petrol & Oil			
	1.0276	0.0647	0.1691
t-stat	(2.19)	(0.07)	
	1.0311		0.1689
t-stat	(2.25)		

Table 8.A2 Industrial energy consumption

Therms

$$\log C_1 = a_1 + a_2 \log I + a_3 T + a_4 \log P$$

where:

C = Consumption measured in therms.
I = The index of industrial production.
T = Trend.
P = Price of fuel to producers/price of manufacturing output.

Period	Elasticity in respect to I a_2	Trend a_3	Price elasticity a_4	R^2
1966–89	1.9437	−0.0468	−	0.09096
t-stat	(10.80)	(−14.06)		
1974–89	1.3511	−0.0474	−0.0590	0.9719
t-stat	(4.62)	(9.94)	(0.62)	
1974–89	1.4909	−0.0496		0.9710
t-stat	(8.5)	(16.94)		

Table 8.A3   Energy consumption in transport

Therms

$$\log C_{TR} = a_1 + a_2$$

where:
C_{TR} = Energy consumption by transport.

Period	a_2 Trend	R^2
1960–89	0.0249	0.9602
t-stat	(25.98)	

REFERENCES

Adelman, M.A. (1972) *The World Petroleum Market*, London: John Hopkins.

Bailey, R. (1989) 'Coal – the ultimate privatisation', *National Westminster Quarterly Review*, August.

—— (1991) 'Energy policy in confusion', *National Westminster Quarterly Review*, February.

Bank of England (1980) 'The North Sea and the United Kingdom economy: some longer-term perspectives and implications', *Bank of England Quarterly Bulletin*, December.

Bending, R. and Eden, R. (1984) *UK Energy*, Cambridge: Cambridge University Press.

Boulton, L. (1996) 'EU acts on minimum energy tax rates', *Financial Times*, 6 December.

Brown Book (various years) *The Energy Report: Oil and Gas Resources of the United Kingdom*, Department of Trade and Industry annual report, London: HMSO.

Buckley, N. and Holberton, S. (1996) 'Plug for the generation gap', *Financial Times*, 26 June.

CEC (1992) *Treaty on European Union*, Brussels: CEC.

Central Statistical Office (CSO) (1991) *Social Trends 21*, London: HMSO.

Corzine, R. (1996a) 'Final plans presented as "good compromise" ' *Financial Times*, 22 August.

—— (1996b) 'British Gas revises Mobil deal', *Financial Times*, 24 December.

—— (1997) 'Break-up long in the pipeline', *Financial Times*, 11/12 January.

Corzine, R. and Buckley, N. (1996) 'On the front burner', *Financial Times*, 20 November.

Corzine, R. and Holberton, S. (1997) 'Power set for shock to the system', *Financial Times*, 10 November.

Corzine, R. and Martinson, J. (1996) 'British Gas and BP end North Sea row', *Financial Times*, 6 December.

Dempsey, J. and Corzine, R. (1996) 'Britain in big gas supply deal with Germans', *Financial Times*, 26 July.

Denison, E.F. (1967) *Why Growth Rates Differ*, Washington, DC: Brookings Institute.

Department of Energy (1988) *Development of the Oil and Gas Resources of the United Kingdom (Brown Book)*, London: HMSO.

Department of Transport (DOT) (1990) *Transport Statistics Great Britain 1979–1989*, London: HMSO, and previous years.

DUKES (various years) *Digest of United Kingdom Energy Statistics* (previously *Digest of Energy Statistics*), Department of Trade and Industry (previously Department of Energy) annual publication, London: HMSO.

Eden, R. and Evans, N. (1984) *Electricity's Contribution to UK Self-sufficiency* Joint Energy Programme Paper No.11, London: Heinemann.

Eden, R., Posner, M., Bending, R., Crouch, E. and Stanislaw, J. (1981) *Energy Economics*, Cambridge: Cambridge University Press.

GATT (1980/81) *International Trade*, Geneva: GATT.

HM Treasury (1967) *Nationalised Industries: A Review of Economic and Financial Objectives*, Cmnd. 3437, London: HMSO.

Holberton, S. (1996a) 'National Grid will cut £1bn from bills', *Financial Times*, 26/27 October.

—— (1996b) 'British Energy in 15-year deal with Southern Electric', *Financial Times*, 22 November.

—— (1996c) 'Sparking a favourable reaction', *Financial Times*, 29 November.

—— (1996d) 'Waves in the wake of a sell-off', *Financial Times*, 2 December.

—— (1996e) 'Power to the people', *Financial Times*, 4 December.

—— (1997a) 'Air controls may hit coal jobs', *Financial Times*, 1/2 February.

—— (1997b) 'Electricity prices down and gas generation rises', *Financial Times*, 28 February.

—— (1997c) 'RJB loses out on PowerGen coal contracts', *Financial Times*, 21 April.

—— (1997d) 'Nuclear cost may hit the taxpayer', *Financial Times*, 10 November.

Holberton, S. and Wighton, D. (1997) 'Coal industry could receive aid as RJB faces job losses', *Financial Times*, 27 November.

IEA (1982, 1984 and 1988) *Coal Prospects and Policies in IEA Countries*, Paris: OECD/International Energy Authority.

—— (1982) *Natural Gas*, Paris: OECD/International Energy Authority.

—— (1990) *Energy Policies and Programmes in IEA Countries 1989 Review*, Paris: OECD/International Energy Authority, and previous issues.

—— (1996) *Energy Prices and Taxes Second Quarter 1996*, IEA Statistics, Paris: OECD/International Energy Authority.

Kampfner, J. and Holberton, S. (1997) 'Coal crisis puts cabinet unity under strain', *Financial Times*, 1 December.

Lascelles, D. (1995) 'Funeral for the nuclear power industry attracts few mourners' *Financial Times*, 12 December.

—— (1996) 'It's nuclear power to the people', *Financial Times*, 25/26 May.

Marsh, V. (1997) 'Centrica settles inherited "take or pay" contracts', *Financial Times*, 5 December.

MMC (Monopolies and Mergers Commission) (1983) *National Coal Board: A Report on Efficiency and Costs in the Development, Production and Supply of Coal by the NCB*, Cmnd. 8920, London: HMSO.

—— (1996) *PowerGen plc and Midland Electricity plc*, London: HMSO, 3.

Monbiot, G. (1996) 'Bleak house', *Guardian*, 24 December.

NCB (1959) *Report*, vol. 2, London: National Coal Board.

Newbery, D.M. (1985) 'Pricing policy', in R. Belgrave and M. Cornell (eds), *Energy Self-sufficiency for the UK?*, Joint Studies in Public Policy No. 10, London: Gower.

OECD (1970) *The Growth of Output 1960–80*, Paris: OECD.
—— (1992) *Historical Statistics 1960–90*, Paris: OECD.
—— (1994) *National Accounts 1960–92*, Paris: OECD.
Ofgas (1992) *Report of the Director General Gas Supply*, London: HMSO.
Ofgas (1995) *Annual Review*, London: Ofgas, and previous issues.
Owen, D. (1997) 'Gaz de France may take supplies from UK', *Financial Times*, 10 February.
Posner, M.V. (1973) *Fuel Policy*, London: Macmillan.
Robinson, C. and Marshall, E. (1984) *Oil's Contribution to UK Self Sufficiency*, Joint Energy Programme Paper No. 12, London: Heinemann.
Stern, J.P. (1984) *Gas's Contribution to UK Self Sufficiency*, Joint Energy Programme Paper No. 10, London: Heinemann.
Swann, D. (1988) *The Economics of the Common Market*, 6th edn, Harmondsworth: Penguin.
Turner, L. (1985) *Coal's Contribution to UK Self Sufficiency*, Joint Energy Programme Paper No. 9, London: Heinemann.
UN (1997) *1995 Energy Statistics Yearbook*, New York: United Nations.
Vickers, J. and Yarrow, G. (1988) *Privatization: An Economic Analysis*, Cambridge, Mass.: MIT.
Weston, C. (1996) 'Predator grabs Northern Electric', *Guardian*, 27 December.
Weyman-Jones, T. (1986) *The Economics of Energy Policy*, London: Gower.
Williams, T.I. (1981) *A History of the British Gas Industry*, Oxford: Oxford University Press.
World Bank (1981) *Commodity Trade and Price Trends*, London: John Hopkins.
World Trade Organization (WTO) (1995) *International Trade Trends and Statistics*, Geneva: WTO.

9 The Common Agricultural Policy and its effect on UK agricultural production, trade and consumption

As described in Chapter 3, Britain introduced a system of production subsidies for agriculture with the Agricultural Act of 1947. She guaranteed prices for her farmers for the major cereals and livestock products; the difference between these guaranteed prices and the actual market prices were made up to farmers in the form of deficiency payments, a form of subsidy.

The result of this was as might be expected from the analysis in Chapter 3. Consumption was unaffected because consumers continued to purchase food at world prices. But the price British farmers received was relatively stable and higher than the world price and this encouraged them to expand their output, and led to import substitution. This can be measured in a variety of ways. Between 1955 and 1970 Britain's net imports of food declined in monetary terms and even more in real terms. This represented a decline in export earnings of her traditional suppliers and was an element in their decisions to industrialize. Nonetheless by 1970 food still accounted for 20 per cent of her imports; 39 per cent of this came from the Commonwealth and 29 per cent from the EC.

As recounted in Chapter 4, accession to the Common Agricultural Policy was made a condition of British entry to the EC, although it involved Britain abandoning her cheap food policy and making net transfers to the rest of the EC.

THE COMMON AGRICULTURAL POLICY

The Common Agricultural Policy (CAP) was formulated in the 1950s postwar world of recent shortages and high prices. Its main objective was to integrate the markets in agricultural products of the proposed member countries, as for manufactures. But from the outset, agriculture was treated as a special case and a much greater degree of EC intervention was anticipated. This was partly because of the relatively low level of incomes in the agricultural sector and the price instability associated with exogenous fluctuations in output due to variations in the weather, diseases, and so forth. The policy makers were considering the small family farm, although many of the cereal farms in the north of France were large.

Thus Article 39 of the Treaty of Rome 1957 states:

1   The objectives of the common agricultural policy shall be:
(a)   to increase agricultural productivity by promoting technical progress and by ensuring the rational development of agricultural production and the optimum utilisation of the factors of production, in particular labour;
(b)   thus to ensure a fair standard of living for the agricultural community, in particular by increasing the individual earnings of persons engaged in agriculture;
(c)   to stabilise markets;
(d)   to assure availability of supplies;
(e)   to ensure that supplies reach consumers at reasonable prices.

Article 40 states:

2   [A] common organisation of agricultural markets shall be established . . .
3   [It] may include all measures required to attain the objectives set out in Article 39, in particular, regulation of prices, aids for the production and marketing of the various products, storage and carry-over arrangements and common machinery for stabilising imports or exports . . . Any common price policy shall be based on common criteria and on uniform methods of calculation.

(Rome Treaty 1957)

These objectives were elaborated in the Stresa Conference of 1958 which set guidelines for the CAP as follows:

the structures of European agricultures were to be reformed to become more competitive, without any threat to family farms; as production costs were higher in the Community than in the other main producing countries, the common prices must provide adequate earnings and must be established at above world prices, without this being an incentive to overproduction; the common agricultural policy could not be autarkic but must protect the internal market against distortion by outside competition.

(OECD 1987: 60)

Thus from the outset the CAP was designed to countermand the efficient allocation of resources. High production costs were used as an argument for protection and intervention to raise prices, rather than for contracting the industry. The objective was to raise farm incomes with high agricultural prices, but the assistance they provided increased with the output of the farmer. Hence large farmers benefited from high prices much more than small farmers. Consumers and taxpayers paid for the CAP. It was, and is, a thoroughly bad policy.

A market price support system of protection similar to those already existing in most Member States was adopted. This was based on Community-wide '*target prices*', which were objectives set annually by the EC's agricultural ministers. These were to be achieved by the imposition of 'variable import levies', to bring the prices of non-EC products up to a *minimum import price* set below but in relation to the target price. If the price fell below this, buying for stock could be employed as an additional form of support. The objectives, therefore, were both to raise and to stabilize producer prices.

In addition to this Guarantee Section of the CAP there was also a Guidance Section. The latter is concerned with the structure of agriculture, but it accounts for a minor fraction of CAP expenditure and has had little impact in the UK where farms are already large by EC standards, so it will be ignored in this chapter.

The beginning of the CAP

The chief difficulty the six Member States had in opening up their markets and establishing common prices was due to the widely differing levels of protection the Member States had engaged in before entry, with a low level of protection in the Netherlands and a very high level in Germany. Furthermore, in the larger countries the prices of bread grains, wheat and rye were kept above those of the other cereals, although they were at similar levels on the world market. The degree of protection depended on the divergence between the world and EC prices. The EC common prices were not agreed until 1967. They were set nearer to the high German prices than the low Dutch ones, and they actually raised prices, particularly of cereals, to the largest producer, France.

Minimum import prices were set for the major farm products: that is, cereals, wheat, barley, rice, milk and milk products, sugar from sugar beet, beef, and sheep and goat meat. The minimum import price for pig meat comprised a 'sluice-gate price', that is, the price which represented the cost of producing pork in non-member countries using the most efficient methods (OECD 1987: 75) plus an allowance for the higher price of feed in the EC. The levy imposed for poultry also made allowance for this high price of feed.

Intervention

If supply is greater than demand at the minimum import price levies on imports do not hold up the price. Let us use a modified version of Figure 3.3 that was used to illustrate minimum import prices in Chapter 3. In Figure 9.1, at the minimum import price P^* the quantity supplied would be Q_2 and that demanded would be Q_1. The market would clear at the self-sufficiency price of P_S. If a higher price is to be achieved, the surplus at that price must be removed. It could be purchased for storage; the price at which this takes place under the CAP is called the *intervention price*. The intervention price P^I was to a varying degree below the target price and minimum import price. But intervention buying was only employed for cereals, beef, sugar, butter and skimmed milk powder. The last two were used as a proxy for milk, the price of which could not be supported directly because it was so perishable.

It had been hoped that stocks acquired by intervention buying could be sold off on the EC market in years of shortage, but the high prices encouraged such an increase in production that these stocks had to be disposed of. One method of disposal was by denaturing: that is, rendering the product unfit for its primary market and selling it in another one; for instance, at one time sugar was mixed with carbon and then fed to cattle. Alternatively, the surpluses could be exported with a subsidy, an *export restitution*, to compensate exporters for the difference between the EC internal price and the world price.

A similar system of support was set up for fruit and vegetables, although, because of their perishable nature, buying to stockpile was not feasible. The products covered were added to over time and included apples, pears, peaches, lemons, mandarins, oranges, table grapes, vegetables, cauliflowers, apricots, aubergines, and tomatoes (OECD 1987: 78). A 'basic price' is set, and also a 'buying-in price' at which producer groups withdraw the

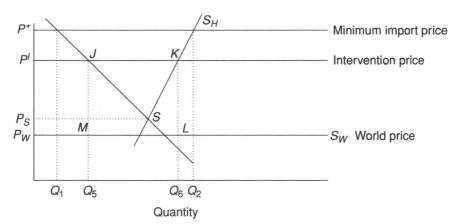

Figure 9.1 The CAP when production exceeds consumption at the minimum import price

Note:
When the EU supply curve is to the right of the demand curve with no interference, price would fall to the self-sufficiency clearing price of P_s. But a higher intervention price P^I, which must be lower than P^*, can be achieved by taking the surplus JK off the market. JK = Q_5Q_6 may be purchased for a stockpile or for exporting to the rest of the world with an 'export restitution' that is a subsidy of $P^I P_W$ per unit at a total cost of $JKLM$.

product from the market, and which may be between 40 per cent and 70 per cent of the 'basic price'. The fruit and vegetables withdrawn were either fed to animals, distilled into alcohol, or destroyed (Fennell 1979; NCC 1995).

When world prices are higher than EC prices

Occasionally the world price is higher than the minimum import price P^*. This rarely happens; only in the early 1970s and the mid-1990s has the world price of cereals exceeded the minimum import price. This is illustrated in Figure 9.2. Let us assume that the EU's supply schedule is S_H and that it would be a small net importer at the minimum import price P^* with consumption Q_3 and production Q_4. If the world price P_W rises above P^*, as can be seen from Figure 9.2, and this is directly transmitted to the home market, consumers will reduce their purchases to Q_7 and domestic producers will expand output to Q_8 thus leading to exports of Q_7Q_8. In that case the EU may endeavour to stabilize price on the EU domestic market by placing a tax on exports. The maximum effective tax it can impose in this case is P_WP_S, which brings it to a point of self-sufficiency Q_9 at a price P_S. When such an export tax is imposed, greater domestic EU stability is being acquired at the cost of increasing instability in the rest of the world by inhibiting an increase in supply from the EU to it.

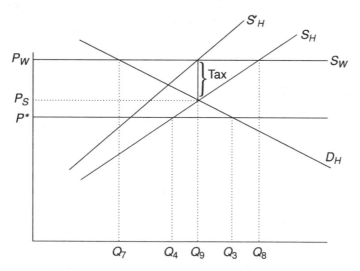

Figure 9.2 World price higher than the minimum import price

Note:
Occasionally the world price is higher than P^*. In that case the EU may stabilise the EU domestic market by placing a tax on exports; this leads to an even greater rise in price in the rest of the world.

The development of the CAP prior to British entry

The degree to which the CAP raised prices above the world level can be shown by dividing the minimum import price by the world price, and thus getting the tariff equivalent of the variable import levy (see Table 9.1). The degree to which the figure is above 100 indicates the percentage protection. The target prices and minimum import price and intervention price associated with it were increased for most products each year, but the degree of protection they afforded depended on world prices. When the EC had a surplus at this minimum import price, domestic prices fell to the market clearing level or the intervention price.

As can be seen, by the late 1960s the EC's minimum import price of butter was round four to six times the world price, the price of sugar three to four times, while wheat, rice and barley were all about double. The world price of cereals and other food began to increase in the early 1970s, thus leading to a reduction in tariff equivalents; this becomes zero when the figure is below 100. That is why estimates of the cost of the CAP to Britain from entry were reduced in the 1971 White Paper as compared with that of 1970.

EC farm output increased by 30 per cent in the ten years after 1963. Because consumption increased much more slowly the EC became self-sufficient in many products, the significant exceptions being beef (see Table 9.2), and fresh fruit and vegetables, oilseeds, and sheep meat (not shown). EC expenditure on intervention purchases and export subsidies for wheat, dairy products and sugar were rapidly increasing (CEC 1994: 13, 57).

BRITISH ENTRY

The French insisted that the British should accede to the CAP as a condition of becoming a member of the EC. They feared that a continuation of the British cheap food policy would enable Britain to have a competitive advantage in lower wage costs. But more importantly, Britain was a large deficit area where in 1970 domestically produced food accounted for only 49 per cent of all food consumed or 62 per cent of temperate food stuffs consumed (CSO 1980: table 9.34). In other words, the French hoped that Britain would absorb some of the surpluses that were emerging.

As a transitional measure, Britain moved from her previous system of production subsidies to tariffs in 1971. In 1973, Britain, the large net importer of agricultural products, joined the EC together with Denmark and Ireland, which were both net exporters. The agricultural sectors in both Britain and Denmark were commercially orientated.

Table 9.1 Agricultural protection in the EEC: Minimum import price divided by the world price per cent

	Soft wheat	Durum wheat	Rice	Barley	Maize	Sugar	Pork[1]	Butter	Skimmed milk	Olive oil	Oilseeds	Beef and veal live animals
1967/68	185	200	117	160	160	438	147	397		166	200	175
1968/69	195	214	138	197	178	355	134	504	365	173	203	169
1969/70	214	230	186	203	159	298	137	613		160	155	147
1970/71	189	232	210	146	141	203	134	481		155	131	140
1971/72	209	254	205	185	176	186	131	171	112	153	147	133
1972/73	153	181	115	137	143	127	147	249	145	125	131	112
1973/74	79	116	60	96	98	66	131	320	156	96	77	110
1974/75	107	120	81	107	106	41	109	316	139	113	80	162
1975/76	124	145	137	117	128	109	113	320	266	217	127	158
1976/77	204	236	166	147	163	176	125	401	571	192	121	192
1977/78	216	218	128	206	203	255	137	388	494	211	153	196
1978/79	193	216	157	225	201	276	155	403	458	200	161	199
1979/80	163	159	131	161	190	131	152	411	379	193	185	204

Source: CEC (1975, 1978, 1980) *The Agricultural Situation in the Community*, Brussels: CEC 1975: 174; 1980: 196. Eurostat (1970, 1972, 1973) *Yearbook of Agricultural Statistics*, Brussels: CEC 1970: 134, 1972: 199, 1973: 183.

Note: 1 The calendar year of the first are given, i.e. 1979 for 1979/80.

Table 9.2 Degree of self-sufficiency for selected commodities

	EUR-6		EUR-12
	1956/60	*1971/72– 1973/74*	*1989/90*
All cereals	85	97	110
Sugar	104	116	123
Wine	89	101	104
Butter	101	120	124
Beef and veal	92	86	107

Source: EC Commission *Agricultural Situation in the Community*, Brussels: (various issues) EC, 187–9; displayed in CEC (1994) *EC Agricultural Policy for 21st Century*, European Economy, No. 4, p. 57.

Exchange and conversion rates

The unit in which the target, minimum import, and intervention prices were set was the agricultural unit of account (AUA) equal to the pre-1971 value of the dollar. They were then converted into the domestic currency of the Member States, using the par value of the currency as agreed with the IMF under the Bretton Woods system of fixed exchange rates. So initially, the *green rates of exchange* for the conversion of CAP prices into domestic currencies were the same as the market rates of exchange.

The French have always regarded fixed exchange rates or a common currency as a prerequisite for the CAP to work effectively. But soon after the price level was agreed, in 1969, the French had to devalue the franc and the Germans revalued the Deutschmark. Both countries were anxious to insulate their farmers from any immediate change in price. So artificial *green exchange rates* were introduced for the purpose of translating the prices of goods subject to intervention or those dependent on them, as, for instance, poultry and eggs are dependent on cereals. To keep the French price level down, agricultural imports into France from other EC countries had to be subsidized and her exports to them taxed, whereas to keep the German agricultural price level up, imports into Germany from other EC countries had to be taxed and her exports to them subsidized. These taxes and subsidies were termed Monetary Compensatory Amounts (MCAs).

This was a temporary measure, but when the Bretton Woods system broke down in 1971, MCAs were introduced on a continuing basis.

The introduction of MCAs to stabilize the agricultural sector within a country meant that it was being insulated from the adjustments required in the other sectors of the economy. Their presence was an indication of the EC's inability to achieve common prices and a common market in agricultural products. They were meant to be neutral in their impact but, in fact, proved an additional form of subsidy.

When Britain joined in 1973 her exchange rate was floating. For CAP conversion purposes it was decided to use the average exchange rate between the pound sterling and the US dollar that existed in early 1973; this was termed the 'representative' rate. This was then extended to the currencies of all Member States (Fennell 1979).

Then a number of the EC countries decided to restrict the variation between their exchange rates to a very limited band, the 'snake', which jointly floated within a wider band, the 'tunnel', against the dollar. The unit of account then became attached to the value of the joint float currencies. Because the 'central' exchange rate and 'green' rate were fixed for each member of the joint float, so were its MCAs. Only Denmark did not apply MCAs.

The problem was that the countries which remained within the joint float were those Member States whose currencies were appreciating against the dollar. In 1979 the EC replaced the snake in the tunnel with the European Monetary System and the European Currency Unit (ECU) which was based on a 'basket' of all currencies of the EC, including sterling, but which was initially equal to the unit of account. All EC Member States except for Britain joined the EMS. It was then discovered that the value of the AUA was a fifth higher than the ECU, which meant that the institutional prices had to be raised by that amount in terms of ECU. Then it was agreed that new MCAs would be phased out over two years provided that this did not mean a fall in price in the country concerned (Fennell 1979: ch.6). However, MCAs were still in existence fifteen years later.

Thus the price structure of the CAP consists of the 'institutional' target, minimum import, and intervention prices negotiated in ECUs each year by the CEC and agreed to by the Council of Ministers. The institutional prices[1] for a product are established not only to protect the industry concerned, but also, in the case of livestock products, to compensate the industry for the higher price of feeding stuffs resulting from the CAP. They determine the range of prices within the EU. For a Member State of the EU, such as Britain, these institutional prices are then translated into the domestic currency using the 'green' rates of exchange, which have generally been different from the market exchange rates and occasionally differ between commodities. The institutional prices in sterling then act as a gate in the trade flows between Britain and the countries outside the EU. Britain has no barriers on trade with other members of the EU, but MCAs have to be applied.

There have been attempts to reform the agri-monetary system. The MCAs were phased out with the introduction of the SEM at the beginning of 1993. However, a 'green ECU' was invented in 1984 by which institutional prices were linked to the rises in the strongest EC currency; this appeared to ratchet the average support price upwards by an additional 15 per cent, but maybe it would have been raised by this amount anyway.

There is still a considerable variation in prices between different countries, as can be seen from Table 9.3. This shows the UK price for major farm products at the end of November 1996 plus the maximum deviation from it shown

Table 9.3   UK prices and the variation throughout the EU in 1996[1]

	Units	UK price	Highest	Lowest
Fat cattle	p/kg	109.70	+89% Spain	−1% Belgium
Fat pigs	p/kg	117.16	UK	−21% Italy
Eggs	p/dozen	41.70	+78% Spain	UK
Broilers	p/live kg	63.38	+57% Spain	−12% Denmark
Butter	£/tonne	2,445.00	+1% Denmark	−6% Spain
Cheese	£/tonne	2,675.00	+179% Italy	−21% Netherlands
Wheat	£/tonne	98.50	+33% Italy	−5% Denmark
Barley	£/tonne	97.00	+24% Italy	−5% France
Potatoes	£/tonne	51.51	+89% Denmark	−57% Germany

Source: *Agra Europe* (1996) 29 November M1.
Note: [1]Data for week ending 22 November 1996.

by other EU countries. Even for fairly standard products such as wheat and barley the range of variation is 29 per cent or more. The widest range in price is shown by cheese, but this probably partly represents a differentiation of product. Potatoes are not covered by the CAP. Their variation in price is because they are the least tradeable; they are the lowest value product by weight and therefore transport costs are relatively high.

The 'green' exchange rates are still used instead of market rates for converting institutional prices into domestic currency. But now there is a two-tier system for direct income supports, with fixed conversion rates for traditionally strong currency countries such as Germany and variable rates linked to the ECU for what were regarded as the weaker currencies such as those of Italy and the UK. Intermittent efforts are made to align the 'green' rates with the market rates of exchange. In January 1997 the UK and Ireland had their green rates revalued because of the rise in their market rates of exchange in relation to the Deutschmark. Indeed the 'green' pound was revalued four times between November 1996 and June 1997 and further revaluation was expected if the £ sterling continued to rise in relation to the other EMU currencies (Urry 1997). These revaluations lowered the domestic intervention prices in terms of sterling.

Overall increase in production and consumption

After entry to the EC Britain's agricultural output increased faster than the EC average. The increase in the production of food from 1970 to 1989 is shown in Figure 9.3. Measured at farmgate 1975 prices it appears to have increased by 25 per cent between 1970–72 and 1987–89.

A more detailed calculation of the changes in home production of food is made in Table 9.4. The output of the major products for which prices are available in 1970, before the movement towards tariff protection in cereals, is compared with that in 1994. As can be seen, the greatest quantitative increase has been in the production of wheat, rye, sugar and

Table 9.4 Quantities and prices of farm products produced in the UK in 1970/71 and 1994

Commodity	Prices		1970/71	Production 1970 (000 t.)	Production 1994 (000 t.)	Weighted by 1970 prices 1970	Weighted by 1970 prices 1994	Quantity 1994/1970
Wheat	Av.exfarm price	£ per tonne	28.08	4,236	13,314	118,948	373,887	3.14
Barley	Av.exfarm	£ per tonne	29.19	7,530	5,945	219,787	173,533	0.79
Oats	Av.exfarm	£ per tonne	25.41	1,217	597	30,929	15,170	0.49
Rye	Av.exfarm	£ per tonne	25.27	13	90	334	2,274	6.82
Hops	Av.exfarm	£ per tonne	30.42	269	4.4	8,189	134	0.02
Potatoes	Av.exfarm	£ per tonne	14.74	7,482	6,531	110,298	96,281	0.87
Sugar beet	Prod price	£ per tonne	7.06	954	1,263	6,736	8,918	1.32
Oilseed rape	Av.market price	£ per tonne	48.77	8	1,254	395	61,155	154.81
Apples	Av.farmgate price	£ per tonne						
Dessert	Av.farmgate price	£ per tonne	75.64	256	168	19,364	12,708	0.66
Culinary	Farmgate price	£ per tonne	38.33	182	130	6,973	4,983	0.71
Pears	Av.farmgate price	£ per tonne	64.31	71	26	4,553	1,672	0.37
Tomatoes	Av.farmgate price	£ per tonne	183.40	108	108	19,752	19,807	1.00
Cauliflowers	Av.farmgate price	£ per tonne	47.28	284	289	13,405	13,665	1.02
Cattle fat	Clean cattle	p per kg live wt	10.68	1,003	945	10,708	10,091	0.94
Sheep fat	Dressed carcase	p per kg	7.94	227	391	1,799	3,104	1.73
Pigs	Deadweight	£ per kg	0.06	895	851	53	50	0.95
Broilers	Av.wholesale price	p per kg	6.02	588	1,222	3,541	7,355	2.08
Milk	Av.net return to producers	p per litre	3.89	12,293	14,302	47,807	55,621	1.16
Eggs	Av.prod.price	p per dozen	14.40	1,257	792	18,101	11,405	0.63
Wool	Av.prod.price	p per kg	8.53	46	66	395	563	1.43
Weighted sum						642,067	872,376	1.36

Source: Ministry of Agriculture, Fisheries and Food (MAFF) (various issues) *Agriculture in the United Kingdom*; CSO *Annual Abstract*.

oilseed rape, all of which have received high levels of protection under the CAP. The output of apples and pears has fallen, and so to a lesser extent has the production of livestock products such as fat cattle, pigs and eggs. If output in the two years is weighted by 1970 prices, the resulting Laspeyres' quantity index shows an increase in output of 36 per cent over the period.

Consumption of food

Farmers are concerned with the total offtake of their product at farmgate prices. Total consumption of food at constant prices fluctuated slightly but only reached its 1971 level in 1987, see Figure 9.3. Taking three-year averages, between 1970–72 and 1987–89 there was an increase of 5 per cent.

However, the expenditure of households on food at a retail level can also be measured; this increased by 14 per cent over the same period. As it also includes processing and distributive margins this shows that they are increasing much faster than the expenditure on food itself. Both series are at constant prices. A regression of household expenditure on food on total consumer expenditure over the period 1970 to 1994, both measured at 1990 prices, gives an expenditure elasticity of 0.3, see Table 9.5. However, over the initial period 1970–72 to 1987–89, total household expenditure increased by 57 per cent, whereas expenditure on food increased by only

Table 9.5 UK consumers' real expenditure on food from 1970–94 at 1990 market prices ($£m$)

$$\log F = a_1 + a_2 \log E + a_3 T$$

where:

F = Food expenditure at 1990 prices

E = Total consumers' expenditure at 1990 prices

T = Trend

With trend

	Expenditure elasticity a_2	Trend a_3	Constant	R^2
	0.4110	−0.0023	5.6172	0.9590
t–stat	(6.7011)	(1.4883)		

Without trend

	Expenditure elasticity a_2	Trend a_3	Constant	R^2
	0.3222			0.9549
t–stat	(22.05826)			

Source: Data derived from the CSO *Annual Abstract of Statistics 1996*, London, HMSO and earlier editions.

13.6 per cent. The shortfall of 3.5 per cent from the anticipated 17.1 per cent increase appears due to the increase in food prices on the UK entry to the CAP; food prices in Britain increased rapidly, faster than any other major category of consumer goods between 1970–77. The increase then slowed down, but over the whole period 1970–85 food prices rose 2 per cent faster than the retail price index.

Self-sufficiency

The effect of stagnant consumption associated with rising home production led to some fall in net imports for consumption of indigenous type products in the early 1980s (see Figure 9.3). But by 1989 they were 4 per cent above their 1971 level. Imports of non-indigenous products fluctuated but between 1983 and 1989 were rising, so that in 1989 they were 15 per cent above their 1971 level at 1975 prices. However, by 1995 UK self-sufficiency in food and feed as a percentage of all food and feed was 59 per cent and of indigenous products was 76 per cent, that is, it was greater than before. The hoped-for outlet for the surpluses of other EC countries never materialized.[2]

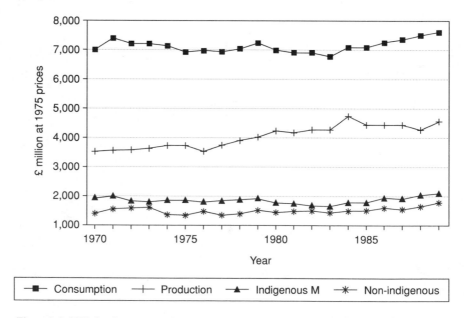

Figure 9.3 UK food consumption, production and imports (1970–89 at 1975 prices)

EFFECT ON BRITAIN OF THE COMMODITY REGIMES

Cereals

The price of cereals

As mentioned earlier the prices of cereals on the world market had soared
in the early 1970s. The market prices of wheat and barley were higher than
the minimum import prices during 1973/74; indeed, for a short period the
EC was taxing exports of grain. The relationship between the producer
price – that is, the market price – of soft wheat and the institutional prices
is shown in Figure 9.4. To begin with, the producer price was fluctuating
around both the threshold – that is, the minimum import price – and intervention prices. But when the world price came down in the late 1970s
the UK market price of wheat fell below its minimum import price to the
intervention price. The intervention price rose until the mid-1980s due to
the combination of a rising AUA price and the depreciation of sterling in
relation to it, but then, as the pound strengthened, the intervention price
in sterling fell slightly. From 1976 until the world price rose again in the
1990s the producer price of wheat stayed very close to the intervention
price: that is, the domestic market price was being kept up by the CAP.

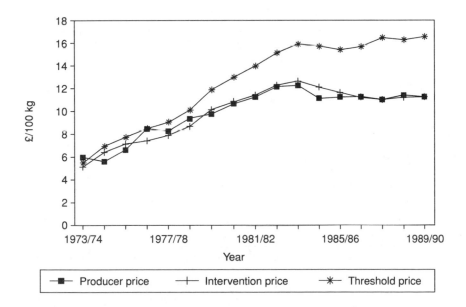

Figure 9.4 UK producer price and institutional prices for soft wheat

Source: S. Tangermann (1992) *Agricultural Price Trends in the EC*, Brussels: EC.

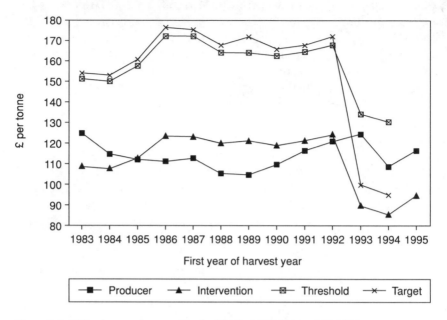

Figure 9.5 UK wheat prices under the CAP, 1983/84 to 1995/96

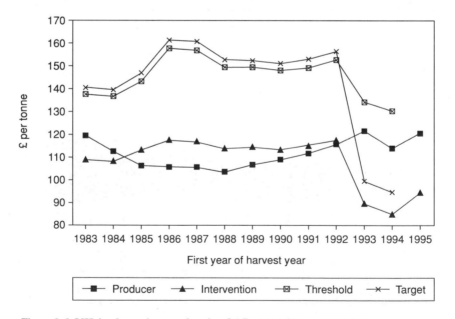

Figure 9.6 UK barley prices under the CAP, 1983/84 to 1995/96

The recent position with regard to the institutional and producer prices for wheat and barley from 1983/84 to 1995/96 are shown in Figures 9.5 and 9.6. For both wheat and barley the producer prices have hovered round the intervention prices. As surpluses mount, the price at which intervention takes place is marginally reduced to a 'buying-in price' not shown on the diagram. The fall in the institutional prices since 1992 is due to the MacSharry reforms which will be discussed later.

Production

On entry to the EC the most rapid increase in British production was that of cereals, which increased by 5.3 per cent per annum compared with the EC average of 3.3 per cent from 1973 to 1985.

The underlying CAP system of protection, with the higher institutional prices for wheat than barley, began to be effective. The yields of wheat also began to increase faster than those of barley. This led to an increasing area devoted to wheat and a decline in the area devoted to barley and other cereals (see Figure 9.7). There was a slight shift from grassland to crops, although the total area utilized for agriculture remained the same until the MacSharry innovations of 1992.

British production of wheat doubled between 1970 and 1980 and then increased by another 42 per cent by 1985. This induced the EC to lower its price for wheat, and the intervention prices for cereals are now all the same.

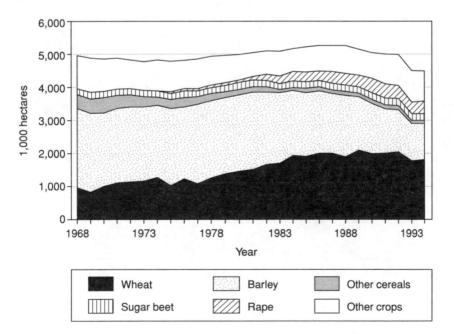

Figure 9.7 Area under different crops in Britain, 1968–94

Utilization of cereals

EC farming is largely a two-stage process, with crops being used to feed livestock. The high price of cereals encouraged their additional production while, at the same time, raising the costs of cereals as inputs into livestock rearing. This increase in home production and a concurrent reduction in the amount going into animal feed is shown in Figure 9.8; the use of barley has fallen fairly consistently since 1971 and of wheat since 1985.

As previously described, the minimum import price for beef and pork was set at a level to take account of the increase in price of feedstuffs due to the CAP. Nonetheless, the high price of cereals induced substitution by other products which had lower levels of protection, namely, the combination of a high-grade protein such as soya bean meal or fish meal plus low-grade feed products such as cassava, bran, maize gluten feed, and so forth, both categories of which faced very low tariffs, 6 per cent or less (Bureau of Agricultural Economics 1985). In other words, there has been a severe distortion in protection in the feed market. One may grimly reflect that the high price of cereals may have been a factor leading the feedstuff manufacturers to use animal protein for herbivores, which was the first step in the downward path towards the emergence of BSE.

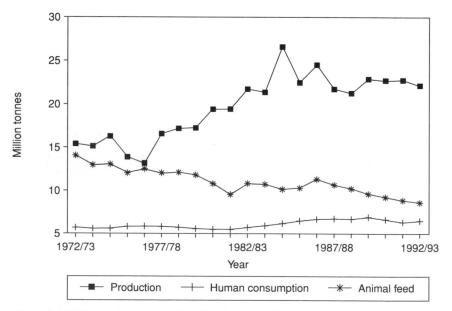

Figure 9.8 UK cereal output and utilization, 1973/74 to 1992/93

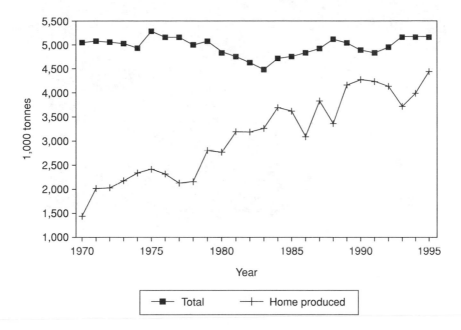

Figure 9.9 Wheat for milling in the UK, 1970–95

The variable levies on imports from third countries also led to their substitution by home grain and sometimes imports from other EU countries. The barley used in brewing and distilling continued, as before, to be home grown. In bread making, in 1970 only 28 per cent of the wheat taken by millers was home produced because imports of hard wheat were required. However by 1995 the home-grown proportion had risen to 86 per cent (see Figure 9.9). This was partly due to the successful development of hard wheat varieties for growing in the UK.

Trade

The combination of increased production and reduced offtake for feed meant that the self-sufficiency ratio – that is, the ratio of production to consumption – had risen by 1986 to 120 per cent for wheat and 162 per cent for barley. Britain began to add to the EC surpluses, particularly of wheat. Her imports of wheat from non-EU countries were squeezed out (see Figure 9.10). She could only dispose of her surplus production by exporting either to other members of the EC or, with the aid of 'restitutions', to the rest of the world (see Figure 9.11). A considerable amount of both wheat and barley was bought by FEOGA but most of this stock pile of cereals has now been sold.

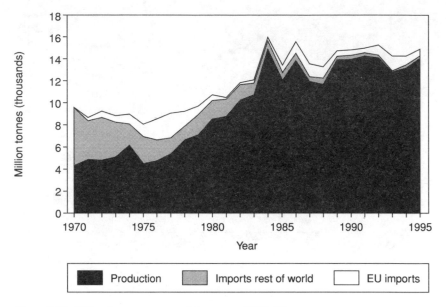

Figure 9.10 UK wheat output and imports, 1970–95

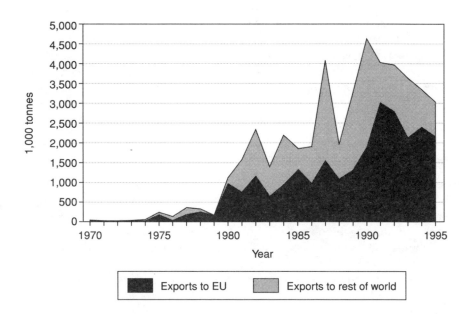

Figure 9.11 UK wheat exports, 1970–95

Sugar

The sugar regime

Sugar produced from beet in the EU is indistinguishable to the consumers from sugar produced from sugar cane. Thus you have direct competition between a temperate and tropical product. Before Britain's entry to the EC her domestic production accounted for 35 per cent of her apparent consumption, and imports of sugar were largely under the Commonwealth Sugar Agreement at a price above the world level. Imports from the other eight members of the EC (as of 1973) accounted for only 2 per cent of consumption. On entry, the developing countries of the Commonwealth joined the other ACP countries under their preferential arrangement for supplying the EU with 1.4 million tonnes of raw sugar. Australia, a former exporter to Britain, was not included in this arrangement.

The system of support was similar to that for cereals, with target, threshold, and intervention prices set for areas of most surplus, and provisions for export restitutions for surpluses to be offloaded on to the world market. But the prices were set differently for each quota. A system of production quotas was established for the individual Member States at roughly the levels existing before the introduction of the Common Sugar Policy in 1968. Each Member State was allocated an A quota on which the full intervention price could be paid and a B quota (originally up to 35 per cent of the A quota) which was subject to a levy to help finance the export of surplus production. Any production above the total of A + B was called C sugar and was exported without any financial assistance. The A quota has increased over time and the B quota has fluctuated.

In an endeavour to make the sugar scheme self-supporting, various clawbacks or levies were imposed on B production and co-responsibility levies were introduced in the 1980s. This was an endeavour to keep up the price of the intra-marginal output of sugar to the benefit of farmers without involving the CAP in any greater expenditure. But between 1989 and 1991 these levies accounted for only half the cost of the sugar regime (CEC 1994: 15).

In Britain in 1983 it was decided to apply a uniform price for all A plus B plus a volume of C beet equal to the B quota. Thus some of the support price for A was transferred to C (Bureau of Agricultural Economics 1985: 201).

The refined sugar equivalent of the sugar imported from the ACP countries is exported with a subsidy financed directly by the EU. The EU by exporting varying amounts of highly subsidized sugar has lowered the world price of sugar and contributed a great deal of instability to the world market. Thus the apparent level of protection also fluctuates. But the world price of sugar has been about a half or a third of the EU price for a number of years. In 1994 the EU spent over 2 billion ECU on supporting its sugar producers, two-thirds of which was on export subsidies; this expenditure amounted to 1,000 ECU (£750) per acre of sugar beet (NCC 1995).

UK sugar production and consumption

As can be seen from Figure 9.12, sugar production has increased, comparing the average of the three years 1970/71–1972/73 with 1992–94, by 51 per cent. Consumption has fallen by 13 per cent and, as a result, net imports have also fallen. Britain's self-sufficiency rate has gone up from 35 per cent to 62 per cent. Almost all her net imports come from third countries; the EU accounts for only 1 per cent.

Oilseeds

Oils and fats is a group of products for which the EU as a whole is in deficit. The EU has a surplus in butter but a deficit in vegetable oils. These are generally joint products with oil cake that can be used as animal feed, for which the EU is also a net importer. Casting around for crops whose production could be expanded without involving subsidized exports, the CEC lighted on oilseeds. But in 1962 the EC had agreed with GATT to impose zero or very low tariffs on oilseeds, so the support given was in the form of subsidies to processors and producers. This proved very expensive and provoked a great deal of argument with the US (CEC 1994: 16–17).

UK oilseed output and consumption from 1981/82 to 1992/93 is shown in Figure 9.13. Consumption initially fell, but has been increasing since

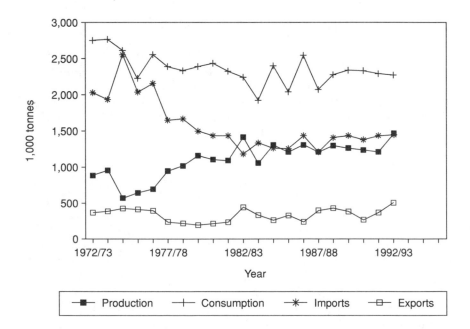

Figure 9.12 UK sugar output, trade and consumption, 1972/73 to 1992/93

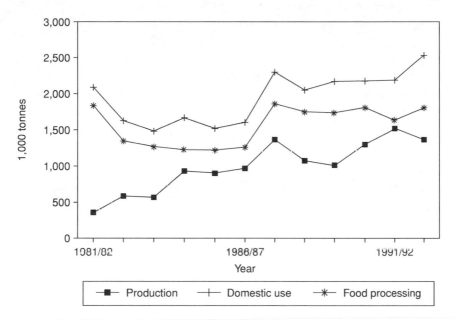

Figure 9.13 UK oilseed output and uptake, 1981/82 to 1992/93

1986/87. Production increased with fluctuations. The EU's introduction of a subsidy for oilseed production led to a rapid expansion in the area under rapeseed in Britain, the main crop grown in the UK. The production of rape has increased nearly a hundredfold, from 11,840 tonnes in 1970/71–1972/73, the period before entry to the EC, to 1,173,330 tonnes in 1992–94. Self-sufficiency in the crop grew from 11 per cent to 86 per cent.

Livestock products

The degree of protection afforded by the CAP for different livestock products has varied considerably. The most systematic support has been given to cattle products, followed by lamb and mutton after 1980/81. As described previously, there is border protection for pig meat and poultry, chiefly to compensate EC producers for their relatively high price of feed. In the UK, between 1970 and 1995 the total numbers of cattle and the subsector, dairy cows, remained more or less the same over the period, as did pigs, see Figure 9.14. But the number of sheep has increased and so has the number of poultry. The poultry shown is only the category of chickens for the table; if turkeys and laying fowl are added the total is almost double.

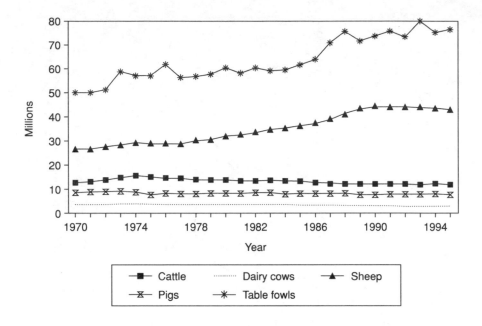

Figure 9.14 UK livestock numbers, 1970–95

Beef and veal

The production of beef and veal was supported with the standard system described above of variable import levies, subsidized exports and intervention buying. In addition there have been special schemes; for instance, in Britain there was a payment for the slaughter of certain full-grown beef cattle. In some years, intervention stocks have been very high due to a considerable oversupply at the EC prices. At the end of 1992 there was a million tonnes of beef in intervention stores, but by the beginning of 1994 this had fallen by half (NCC 1995: 77). Beef deteriorates in storage and when it is sold off it is generally for incorporation in processed products such as pies. In 1994 the cost of EU support for beef and veal production was 3.36 billion ECU; one-third of this went on storage, and a half, 1.7 billion ECU, in export refunds. Exports accounted for 15 per cent of world trade, and there have been complaints from competing South American suppliers. Protests from development charities about EU dumping in West Africa also persuaded the CEC to reduce refunds on exports of beef to that area (NCC 1995: 78–80).

Entry to the EC was associated with an increase in UK production. But over the whole period 1971–95, although output fluctuated there was no marked trend (see Figure 9.15). However, consumption tended to fall; in

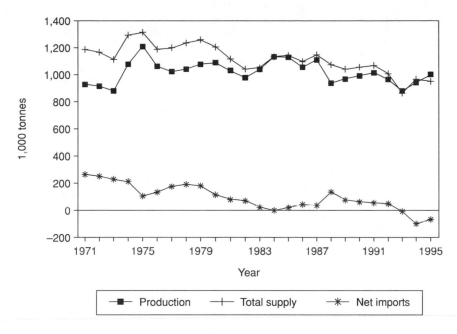

Figure 9.15 UK production and trade in beef, 1971–95

Figure 9.15, ignoring changes in stocks, this is shown by the change in total supply. This decline in consumption gradually squeezed out net imports, and by 1993 the UK was a net exporter. The whole picture has been radically changed by the BSE crisis, which will be discussed later.

Milk

A target price for milk is set each year for delivery to a processing plant. As mentioned previously, the price of milk could not be kept up by intervention buying directly because it was so perishable. Instead, efforts to maintain it have been indirect, by variable import levies on imports of milk products and by intervention buying of butter and skimmed milk powder. There was a persistent surplus of milk. Co-responsibility levies – that is, a reduction in the prices farmers received when surpluses occurred – were imposed in 1977. Then, in 1984/85 these were replaced by a quota scheme on deliveries.

The dairy herd and milk production is associated with beef production. The UK dairy herd did not increase, but the yield per cow rose due to better breeds and the feeding of concentrates. As can be seen from Figure 9.16, the co-responsibility levies appeared to temporarily check the rise in production in the late 1970s. Then, after 1981 milk production

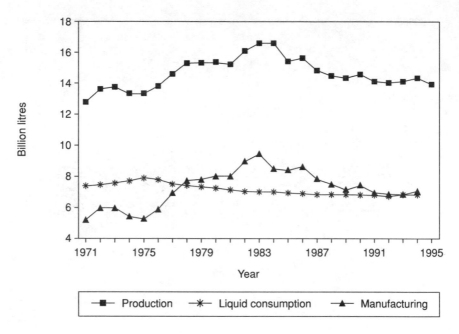

Figure 9.16 UK milk production and use, 1971–95

started to increase again until quotas were introduced in 1984. Thereafter, production began to decline and so did the amount that went into manufacturing. Liquid milk consumption has been declining steadily since 1975.

Butter and cheese

As can be seen from Figures 9.17 and 9.18, the immediate effect of joining the EC was to squeeze imports from non-EC suppliers. In 1969–71, imports of butter from EC(8) and non-EC countries were 144 and 263 thousand tonnes. The former started to rise and the latter to fall in anticipation of entry, and this continued until, in 1975, the EC was supplying 364 thousand tonnes – that is, 2½ times as much – and imports from non-EC countries had halved to 124 thousand tonnes. This is clear trade diversion, because EC imports were much more expensive.

There was a similar change in cheese production; in 1969–71 imports of cheese from the EC(8) and the rest of the world were 57 and 103 thousand tonnes respectively. By 1975 the former had doubled to 119 thousand tonnes, and the latter had fallen by two-thirds to 33 thousand tonnes. Again a clear instance of trade diversion, although the types of cheese involved were rather different – a reduction in imports of New Zealand cheddar and increase in imports of a diversity of hard and soft cheeses from the Continent. Imports

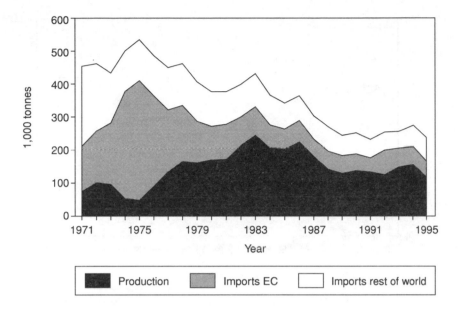

Figure 9.17 UK butter production and imports, 1971–95

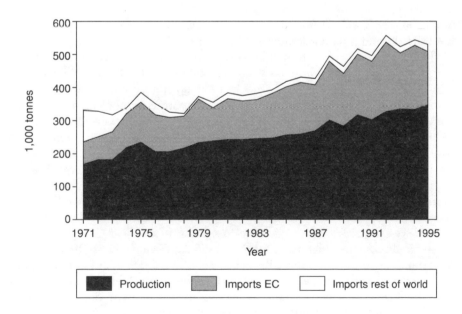

Figure 9.18 UK cheese production and imports, 1971–95

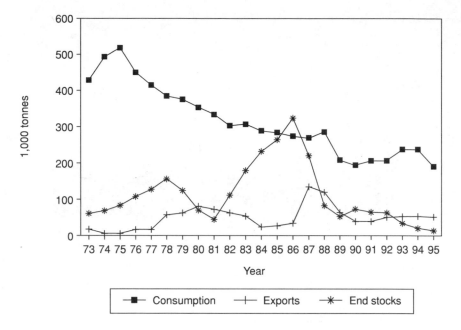

Figure 9.19 UK butter consumption and exports, 1973–95

from the rest of the EC continued to rise with fluctuations to 162 thousand tonnes in 1995, and those from the rest of the world remained at a low level, 22 thousand tonnes in 1995.

Home production of butter fell initially, but after 1975 it began to increase and in doing so reduced imports from all sources (see Figure 9.17). Exports also increased (see Figure 9.19). Stocks built up until, in 1986, they were equivalent to one year's total supply and were considerably greater than annual consumption (see Figure 9.19). After 1983 there was some decline in production, with fluctuations. Meanwhile, domestic consumption was steadily falling, from 477 thousand tonnes in 1969–71 to 190 in 1995 (see Figure 9.19). The degree to which this 60 per cent reduction can be regarded as a response to the high EC prices, thus fulfilling the ex-ante predictions of a high price elasticity of demand for butter due to its substitutability by margarine, and the degree to which it represents a shift in the demand of consumers away from high chlorestrol products, is not clear.

Cheese production increased more steadily and, in 1995, at 348 thousand tonnes, was 2½ times the 1969–71 level (see Figure 9.18). Consumption also rose, so that in 1995, at 480 thousand tonnes, it was 60 per cent greater than in 1969–71 (see Figure 9.20). Imports from the EC have also increased, but since the mid-1970s home producers have held around two-thirds of the market. This may be because imports from their closest competitor,

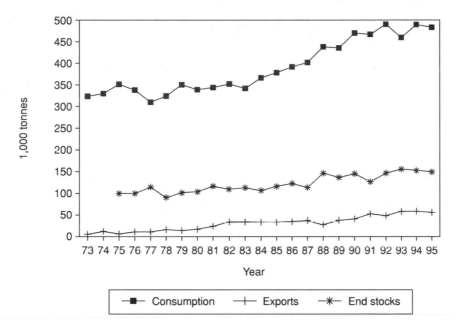

Figure 9.20 UK cheese consumption and exports, 1973–95

New Zealand, are most tightly controlled, and thus represented trade diversion towards the home producers. But it also appears due to the greater efforts made by British producers to market a wide range of differentiated cheeses. Exports have increased to both the EC and the rest of the world (see Figure 9.20). Stocks have risen, so that in 1995, at 148 thousand tonnes, they were almost three times their 1969–71 level.

Sheep meat

When the support scheme was introduced in 1980–81, Member States were given a choice of two methods of support: a variable slaughter subsidy chosen by Britain, and intervention chosen by France. These are related to the basic prices fixed by the Council of Ministers each year (OECD 1987: 75). This appears to have accelerated the upward trend in lamb (and mutton) production; thus, from 1971 to 1981 production increased by 19 per cent, but over the succeeding ten years 1981–91 it increased by 55 per cent (see Figure 9.21). There are few imports from the EC, but imports from the rest of the world declined from 1971 to 1995. There was a slow increase in exports to the EC until the mid-1980s and then they increased faster, particularly when production exceeded the 'new supply' (i.e. consumption) in 1992.

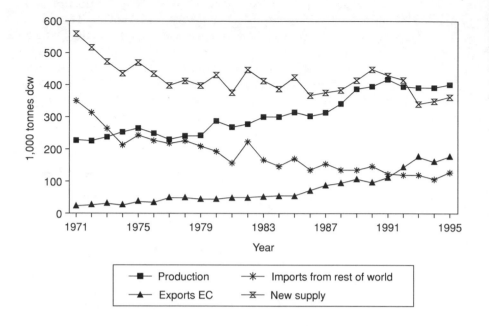

Figure 9.21 UK lamb production and trade, 1971–95

Thus the sheep meat regime has encouraged an expansion of production and led to imports from the rest of the world being squeezed out. This is in spite of the special arrangements made for New Zealand, the chief supplier. Home production as a percentage of 'new supply' was only 41 per cent in 1970; it had risen to 72 per cent by 1981, and 111 per cent by 1995.

INITIAL IMPACT OF THE CAP ON UK AGRICULTURAL TRADE

Thus the immediate impact of entry on the UK was often a substitution of imports of agricultural products from the EC for imports from the rest of the world: that is, for wheat, butter and cheese. The higher food prices retarded an increase in consumption, and the anticipated decline in butter consumption began in the mid-1970s. High prices for cereals also led to a decline in their use for animal feed.

In the longer run, British production increased so much that imports from both sources were being squeezed. The UK began to contribute to surpluses, particularly of wheat, barley, sugar, and milk.

The markets which appeared least affected were those for poultry and pig meat, both having EC border protection but no intervention. There was a steady expansion in the consumption of poultry meat, almost all of which was home produced. The number of pigs remained roughly constant (see Figure 9.14), although production of pork increased somewhat and accounted for all home consumption. The consumption of bacon and ham declined slightly, but home producers retained around 46 per cent of the market – the chief foreign supplier, Denmark, entered the EC at the same time as Britain.

Increased use of factors of production

This increase in output has been achieved using roughly the same quantity of land. For most of the period the area of cultivated land was around 12 million hectares, although in 1992 with the introduction of the set-aside programme discussed later, it has shown clear evidence of decline (see Figure 9.7).

Between 1970 and 1994 there was a reduction in the workforce of nearly a quarter.[3] There was an increase in capital employed, with the rate of investment above the national investment ratio. Technological progress has taken the form of improved breeds of plants and livestock and also the development of pesticides.

There was also an increase in the application of manufactured inputs, namely, fertilizers, lime, and pesticides. As can be seen from Figure 9.22, the greatest increase in the application of fertilizers was of nitrogen, which reached a peak in 1986, since when it has tended to decline. This very heavy application has led to the pollution of some watercourses.

The role of intermediate products such as feedstuffs should also be considered. In 1973/74, feedstuffs were in value equal to about 43–45 per cent of the gross output of livestock and livestock products. By 1995 this had fallen to 32 per cent.

PRESSURE FOR THE REFORM OF THE CAP

Consumers

Consumer groups object to the high food prices entailed by the CAP and the burden it places in particular on the low-income groups in the EU. It was calculated in 1986/87 that the cost of EC agricultural support to consumers was $32.6bn and to taxpayers $15.6bn, whereas the benefit to producers was $33.3bn, which implies a net economic cost of $14.9bn (Rayner *et al.* 1993). The National Consumer Council (NCC) calculated in 1988 that the average family of four was paying £9 a week more than they needed throughout Europe (NCC 1988). By 1994, on OECD calculations,

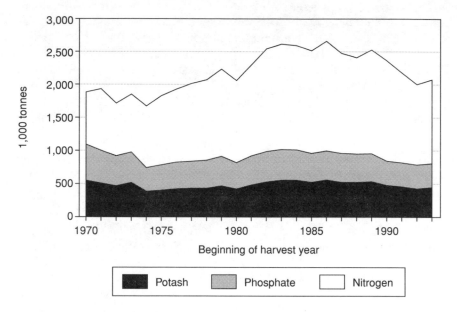

Figure 9.22 UK consumption of fertilizers, 1970/71 to 1993/94

this had risen to £49.2 billion in total, that is, £10 per family of four a week, or £134 per person a year in additional expenditure on food alone due to the CAP (NCC 1995; OECD 1995). The impact is greatest on the poor; in the UK, the poorest 10 per cent of families spent a quarter of their income on food. But at the EU level, consumer pressure groups do not appear to have exerted much influence; the population at large seems scarcely aware of how high food prices are compared with international prices.

Consumers also pay through their additional tax bills. The cost of the CAP to the EU in 1994 was £25 billion in tax, that is, approximately £1.5 per head per week for every person in the EU. But Britain also incurred the *transfer cost* of the CAP across the foreign exchanges: that is, she had to pay in her variable import levies and tariff revenues to the Commission,[4] and because her agricultural sector was so small received very little back. After Germany, she was the major contributor, although her per capita income is below the average for the EU. This is the basis of her claim for a rebate, which, to some degree, she has been granted. This expenditure on agriculture is supplemented by national governments, to the extent of £8.1 billion in 1994. Only now, with Member States endeavouring to achieve the budget conditions required for their entry to a common currency, have they begun to jib at their payments for the CAP.

International pressure

As the EU's increase in production had been so much greater than consumption, by 1990/91 it had become self-sufficient in all its main food products, with the exception of oils and fats and fresh fruit (see Table 9.6). Production of cereals and sugar was more than 20 per cent above domestic consumption, followed by butter, which was 15 per cent higher, and these three surplus products alone accounted for more than $9 billion of exports.

Exports were steadily increasing. The EU has become the largest exporter of food in the world; EU Member States accounted for 43 per cent of world exports and 13 per cent of food exports to non-EU countries in 1994. Its export trade is based on cereals, particularly wheat, wine, sugar, milk powder, butter, cheese and meat. (CEC 1994: 23; WTO 1995). Indeed, exports from the EU have become such a large proportion of the world market that it is misleading now to regard the world price as independently determined.

International pressure for reform came from other agricultural exporting countries such as Australia, New Zealand and the US. The first two have been seriously affected by the loss of most of their markets in the UK and also by the competition they are facing on the world market from the EU's subsidized exports. Developing countries are particularly concerned with the way the EU has undermined the world sugar market. Agriculture was at last introduced into the GATT negotiations with the Uruguay Round of

Table 9.6 EC agricultural trade and self-sufficiency, 1990–91

	Self-sufficiency (%)	Net exports (+) imports (–) (000 t.)	1990 $m
Cereals	120	24,981	4,519
Sugar	128	3,615	1,074
Butter	115	3,362	(3,575)[2]
Wine	103	5,500hl	(7,055)[3]
Fresh fruit	85	–4,417	–9,054
Fresh vegetables	106	1,861	
Meat	120	1,218.4	236
Eggs	103	81.3	2
Oils and fats	70[1]	n.a.	–
All agricultural and food products	—	—	–26,366[4]

Source: EC Commission (1993) *The Agricultural Situation in the Community*, Brussels: EC; CEC (1994) *EC Agricultural Policy for the 21st Century*, European Economy, No. 4, Brussels: CEC.

Notes:
[1] Rapeseed and sunflower seed only.
[2] Milk and eggs together, figure for butter not available.
[3] All alcoholic beverages.
[4] In addition to the deficit shown for fruit, vegetables, and oils and fats, the major contributions to this overall net import figure come from fish (USD –6,611 Mio), coffee, cocoa, tea and spices (–4,174), animal feed (–4,211), oilseeds (–4,198), rubber, timber and natural textile fibres (–14,277).

1986–94. Difficulties in reaching agreement almost prevented the completion of the Round.

But other non-EU developed countries also protect their agriculture. In order to establish a base for negotiations the OECD endeavoured to quantify the support provided by governments to their agricultural industry by calculating consumer and producers subsidy equivalents (CSEs and PSEs, as defined in Chapter 3).

The EU PSEs and CSEs for 1986–88 are shown in Figure 9.23. The negative CSE is shown alongside the PSE to give some idea of the degree to which the consumers were paying for the extra returns the producers were receiving. For most products the producers appeared to be receiving 50 per cent or more above the world price and the consumers were paying for this. In the cases where the negative CSEs were much greater than the positives PSEs (i.e. eggs, poultry and pig meat), it is because of the significance of the high feed costs for those products. The low level of the PSEs for these products is largely because they have no intervention price. For oilseeds, which received a direct subsidy for production, there was no CSE.

Budget limitation

Internal pressure for reform came from the continuous expansion in CAP expenditure and the accumulation of intervention stocks. This was

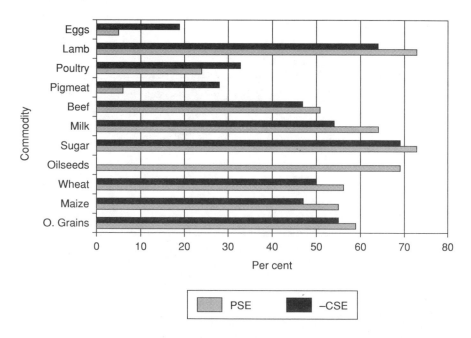

Figure 9.23   EU consumer subsidy equivalents (CSEs) and producer subsidy equivalents (PSEs), 1986–88

because the Council of Ministers appeared politically incapable of reducing prices, and once the prices had been set the Commission initially had an open-ended commitment to support them. Some brakes were placed on this by the Brussels Agreement of 1988 on budgetary discipline, whereby guarantee expenditure should not grow faster than 74 per cent of EC GNP (CEC 1994: 82).

Agricultural economists spent a long time arguing for decoupling, that is, separating the transfer element of price support from actual production and so removing the incentive to increase production. Thus were introduced supply control measures, namely, marketing quotas, co-responsibility levies, and budgetary stabilizers.

In 1984 a delivery quota was introduced for milk from individual farms or co-operatives. In practice, the milk quotas were capitalized with the farm to which they were allocated. Britain is constrained by the quotas to producing only 85 per cent of her dairy needs. In 1996 Britain was pressing to have her quota increased in exchange for a fall in the support price by 5 per cent in preparation for the abolition of dairy quotas in 2000. The Commission was arguing for export refunds for butter and skimmed milk rather than international prices, whereas the French and Danes wanted a two-tier system with higher domestic than export prices (Hargreaves 1996a).

In 1988 'budget stabilizer' mechanisms were introduced for several commodities whereby reductions in 'buy-in' prices were introduced should production exceed certain 'maximum guarantee quantities' (CEC 1994). Thus complexity was added to complexity.

This total support policy is very inefficient; the farmers only receive in benefits a fraction of the costs of the CAP to consumers and taxpayers, around 60 per cent. Furthermore, this is unevenly distributed, with 80 per cent of it going to 20 per cent of the farmers. Because the number of workers in agriculture has declined, the overall payment per worker is large, £12,500 per full-time equivalent (NCC 1995).

The most compelling argument for reform has now become the EU pledge to admit the Central and Eastern European countries (CEECs) – Poland, Hungary, the Czech and Slovak Republics, Slovenia, Romania, Bulgaria, Lithuania, Latvia, and Estonia – to EU membership. The CAP must be reformed and the assistance decoupled before these countries are admitted, otherwise the CEC–EU stock pile will become unmanageable (Southey 1995).

1992 THE MACSHARRY PACKAGE FOR REFORM OF THE CAP

The MacSharry package was agreed to by the Member States of the EC as a response to the internal and foreign pressure for reform of the CAP, but before the conclusion of the Uruguay Round. Its chief provisions were as follows:

1   a decoupling for cereals by reducing the target and intervention prices over a three-year period, beginning in 1995, by 30 per cent from their 1992 levels. The intervention price became 100 green ECU per tonne. But the minimum import price was set at 155 green ECU per tonne.
2   The price support for oilseeds and protein crops was eliminated.
3   At the same time a per-hectare compensatory payment for agreeing to a 15 per cent rotational *set-aside* was introduced to offset the income effects of the price reductions (see Table 9.7). Farmers producing less than 92 tonnes of cereals were excluded from set-aside requirements (Richardson 1996b).
4   The intervention price for beef was reduced by 15 per cent over three years, with some direct payments per head introduced.
5   There was to be a reduction in the ceiling for normal intervention buying of beef from 750,000 to 350,000 tonnes by 1997.

The proposal that small producers should receive proportionally more compensation than large producers was blocked by the British, who were afraid that because they had relatively more large farms they would receive less compensation.

Blair House/Uruguay Round Agreement

On the basis of the MacSharry package the EU tried to limit its concessions under the Uruguay Round. This was done by negotiating a division of the various types of agricultural support into different 'boxes'. The red box contained policies which were to be fully dismantled, the amber box those subject to a monitored reduction. The green box contained policies that did not stimulate additional production and therefore were not 'trade distorting'; the EC regarded all direct compensating payments to farmers as being in this category. The Blair House Agreement was negotiated

Table 9.7 Target, intervention and threshold prices for cereals, 1992–96 (ECU per tonne)

Marketing year	Target price	Intervention price	Threshold price	Compensation rate per tonne[2]
1992/93[1]	206.16	155.33	201.37	
1993/94	130	117	175	25
1994/95	120	108	165	35
1995/96	110	100	155	45

Source: CEC (1994) *EC Agricultural Policy for the 21st Century*, European Economy, No. 4, Brussels: CEC.

Notes:
[1] Barley, rye and meslin. Support prices for common wheat in 1992/93 were some 5 to 10% higher.
[2] For calendar years 1993, 1994, 1995.

between the US and the CEC and provided the basis for the agricultural sector of the Uruguay Round. The most important provisions of the Uruguay agreement reached in December 1993 are as follows:

1   *Market access* Taking 1986–88 as the base year, border protection measures, such as variable import levies, were to be converted into tariffs, whose simple mathematical average over all commodities was to be reduced by 36 per cent over six years, with a minimum reduction of 15 per cent for each tariff. For the EC the tariff was to be the difference between the world f.o.b. market price and the intervention price plus 10 per cent and any monthly increments. Should the EC import price fall by more that 10 per cent of the 1986–88 import price (defined in ECU), a variable element might be added to the tariff, thus providing a 'special safeguard' for EC producers.

    In order to allow for a minimum access for imports, tariff quotas were to be introduced, with tariffs of 32 per cent of the basic tariff for imports amounting to 3 per cent of the EC market at the start and 5 per cent at the end of six years for wheat, meat, skimmed-milk powder, butter, cheese and eggs. Existing EC import arrangements such as those for New Zealand butter and sheep meat were to be tariffied (CEC 1994: 73).

    However, the EC has been accused of 'dirty' tariffication; the argument of Anderson, quoting Josling, is that the EC's claimed tariff equivalent's for 1986–88 of between 150 and 170 per cent for non-rice grains, 290 per cent for milled rice, and 220 to 340 per cent for dairy products, beef and sugar, are far higher than the actual tariff equivalents of the time (Anderson 1995).

2   *Internal support* With 1986–88 as a basis global internal support, the aggregate measure of support (AMS), was to be reduced by 20 per cent with credit given for reductions since 1986. Direct CAP aids, such as the compensatory payments under the MacSharry arrangements of 1992, based on fixed areas, animal numbers and yields, and therefore providing no incentive to increased production, were not included in this commitment. They were in the 'green box'.

3   *Export subsidies* With 1986–90 as a base, direct export subsidy expenditures were to be reduced, product by product, by 36 per cent over six years, and the volumes of subsidized exports by 21 per cent over the same period. These commitments excluded food aid.

4   *Rebalancing* If EC imports of non-grain feed ingredients were to increase to a level which threatened CAP reform, the EC and US agreed to consult each other over a solution.

5   *Peace clause* Internal support measures and export subsidies were to be considered exempt from action under GATT Article 16.

6   *Oilseeds* From a base area of 5,128,000 hectares of oilseeds in 1995–96 the EC agreed to a set-aside rate of not less that 10 per cent a year.

The choice of periods and ability to claim 'credit' for reductions in support since 1986, and the use of the ECU rather than the dollar, meant that this agreement provided little restraint to the EU. The tariffication of the variable import levies will just mean that EC market prices fluctuate with world prices, albeit at a much higher level, unless world prices fall drastically and then the safeguard measures will come into play (CEC 1994: 70–74).

Fruit and vegetables

This regime was not included in the MacSharry reforms. The NCC still complains forcefully about the implications of the CAP mechanism for keeping up prices, the effect of which falls most heavily on poorer consumers who already find it difficult to afford fresh fruit and vegetables and hence maintain nutritional standards. A high proportion of fruit is withdrawn from the market, most of which is destroyed or denatured, and this accounts for a third of expenditure in this sector. Furthermore, this is not only inferior fruit or vegetables. In 1986/87 almost half of all lemons and 60 per cent of nectarines, and in 1992/93 a quarter of all peaches were withdrawn. The level of import duties is still very high; in the 1980s the support price for tomatoes was 270 per cent of the world market price, and for lemons it was double. The average 'tax' on imported tomatoes was equivalent to 48p a pound (NCC 1995) – no wonder they were so expensive! However, in July 1996 the EU Ministers agreed to reform the fruit and vegetable sector by cutting production subsidies to no more than 4 per cent of value, rising to 4.5 per cent in 1999. This, it was stated, would avoid the widespread destruction of surplus fruit and vegetables of recent years (Buckley 1996).

Bananas are covered by separate quota provisions on imports which are designed to provide the ACP countries with some protection in the domestic market of the EU. Their quota has been reduced to 26 per cent of the total market (Southey 1996a).

Tobacco

Under the CAP the EU subsidizes the growing of tobacco by ECU 1 billion a year, which represents five times the value of the crop. The country most heavily dependent on it is Greece. At the same time, the EU is helping finance anti-smoking campaigns to the extent of ECU 15 million (£12m). This is a clear anomaly, but the Commission and Ministers appear politically unable to stop subsidizing production (Southey 1996c).

RECENT DEVELOPMENTS

The effect of the MacSharry reforms and the implementation of the Uruguay Round appears to have been some reduction in PSEs and CSEs, see the

OECD provisional estimates in Figure 9.24. The nominal tariff equivalent paid by consumers over all agricultural products fell from 80 per cent in 1986–88 to 60 per cent in 1994 for the EU(12) and then to an estimated 50 per cent in 1995 for the EU(15). The assistance to producers remained higher at 90 per cent (OECD 1996: 29). The Council of Ministers agreed to freeze basic farm prices for 1996–97 (Buckley 1996).

A temporary diversion was caused by a rise in the world price of wheat in 1993. This rose above the intervention price and continued to rise because drought in North America, Australia, and South Africa meant that they found it difficult to increase supplies. The EU's set-aside was maintained but at a lower rate of 12 per cent in 1994/95, which was reduced to 10 per cent in 1995/96 and then to 5 per cent for 1996/97 and 1997/98 (Hargreaves 1996d; Buckley 1997b). The EU stopped subsidizing exports of wheat in July 1995. By then, the market price of wheat was greater at 187 ECU/tonne than the original 1992 'target' price of 155 (green) ECU/tonne, and thus there was no justification for the compensation farmers were receiving under the MacSharry reforms (*Agra Europe* 1996a). It has now been calculated that over the four years 1993/94–1996/97 the EU overcompensated cereal farmers by ECU 8.5bn (£5.9bn) for price falls that never occurred. Yet in spite of this massive overpayment the agricultural commissioner Franz Fischler is

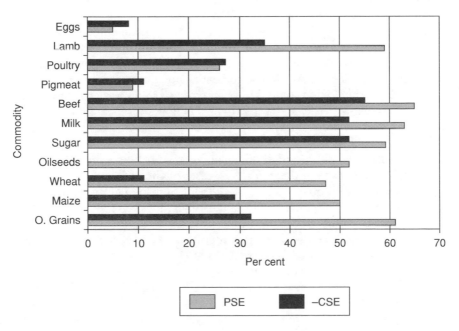

Figure 9.24 EU provisional consumer subsidy equivalents (CSEs) and producer subsidy equivalents (PSEs), 1995

still having great difficulty in persuading the European Parliament and Ministers to accept a reduction in arable aid and payments for set aside (Buckley 1997a).

The world price of wheat was so high that for the first time since 1974 the EU in December 1995 imposed a tax on exports, of ECU 25 (£20.85) per tonne. By April 1996 the tax was holding EU wheat prices $55 below world levels of around $240 per tonne (Hargreaves and Chote 1996). The effect of the export tax and set-aside was to reduce EU supplies of wheat to the world market and thus raise the world price even further. But then, during 1996, the price of wheat started to fall, and the EU stopped taxing exports and at the end of that year resumed their subsidization of them, much to the displeasure of the US, which threatened to do likewise (Hargreaves 1996c).

The lower intervention prices and thus market prices for grain are expected to work to reduce the price of feedstuffs. This, in turn, should reduce the CSEs and consumer prices for eggs, poultry and pig meat, which are so dependent on them.

British agricultural output is fluctuating and at constant 1990 prices was 8 per cent lower in 1995 than in 1992. CAP intervention expenditure in Britain fell by 62 per cent between 1991/92 and 1994/95. However, compensation, in the form of direct payments and the newly introduced system of set-aside, quadrupled, with the result that CAP expenditure in Britain increased from £1.6 billion to £2.2 billion over the period.

The UK Minister for Agriculture Douglas Hogg, in his message to the National Farmers Union at the beginning of 1996, commented on how well cereal farmers had done, with an increase in real net farm incomes of 245 per cent from the average for 1989–92 to 1995 because of good weather, the high world prices of cereals, and the devaluation of sterling that increased the EU payments for set-aside. However, pig and poultry farmers, dependent on cereals for feed and without production subsidies, had not done nearly as well, with an increase in net real income of only 60 per cent (Richardson 1996a).

The whole picture changed dramatically in March 1996 with the UK government's announcement that ten recent cases of Creuzfeldt-Jacob disease in young people were probably the result of them eating beef infected with BSE (bovine spongiform encephalopathy) in the 1980s. This was followed by a total ban on British exports of beef and products containing it by the CEC. This ban covered exports not only to other members of the EU, but also to third countries. The legal basis for the latter is not clear. In order to have the ban removed a mass slaughtering of cattle over the age of 30 months is being carried out and it may be extended. The incidence of BSE is now falling in the UK. There has, however, been a sharp decline in sales of beef and its price throughout the EU. The response of the CEC was to give EU beef farmers extra aid amounting to ECU 500m (£390m). There were also proposals for cutting the number of calves by 1 million. The European Agriculture

Guidance and Guarantee Fund (EAGGF) was permitted to raise the quantity that could be stockpiled in 1996 by another 150,000 tonnes of beef over and above the 400,000 tonnes of beef that were acquired in the first seven months of the crisis (Southey 1996b). As *Agra Europe* put it:

> The European Union's Council of agriculture ministers this week managed to help their beef producers to subsidies from a non-existent budget resource, agreed measures which did nothing to alleviate the coming chronic beef surplus and avoided taking any measures which will provide any long-term solution to the beef market problem . . . In 1995, EU-15 beef production totalled just over 8mt; with consumption estimated at 7.65mt and import commitments of 460 000t this meant an export surplus of 795t. Although this level of exports could be subsidised within the 1995–96 GATT export limits, it would only just have been allowed under the limit . . . agreed for 2000 . . . Now, however, consumption can be expected to decline by 15 per cent to 20 per cent on the 1995 level, while in all probability production – bolstered by too much intervention and producer compensation – will remain undiminished . . . The Union faces the prospect of an exportable surplus of beef in excess of domestic consumption of 2.7mt . . . The prospect is therefore in view of an intervention stockpile in excess of 5mt by the end of the decade.
>
> (*Agra Europe* 1996b)

The fear of a collapse in the market was so overwhelming that no one seemed to ask whether there was any sense in stockpiling a product that consumers manifestly did not want and were not likely to want in the future. The UK government has provided additional funds to eradicate BSE, announcing in the 1996 budget, 'About £3.3 billion has been set aside to protect the public and restore the market in British beef' (Hogg 1996).

Although the cause of BSE and its transmission are not firmly established it is thought that it originated in changes in the 1980s in the procedure for making meat and bonemeal which was used for cattle feed. The change in the temperature used for rendering allowed scrapie, a sheep disease similar to BSE, to pass into cattle feed through infected sheep tissue. In 1988 the government banned the use of slaughterhouse waste and rendered-down sheep in cattle feed and ordered the slaughter of all livestock infected or believed to be infected with BSE (Hargreaves 1996b). But its inspection scheme did not appear initially to have been very thorough. In addition, there is no clear labelling on the packages of feedstuffs, so that, as farmers have complained, they do not know what is inside them.

The basic question remains: Why should herbivores have been fed meat? This, as has been noted previously, is partly because the price of cereals was kept so artificially high under the CAP that it became cheaper to use as a substitute feedstuff a mixture of low-grade material and high-protein soya bean and fishmeal. Soya bean had become very expensive towards the end of the 1970s and early 1980s and fishmeal gives a flavour to milk, so meat became an alternative source.

In March 1996 the government also decided to ban the use of animal protein – that is, meat and bonemeal – in feed for pigs and poultry. This was in a situation in which there already appeared to be a worldwide shortage of soya beans and fishmeal. Consumers were transferring their purchase away from beef towards pigs and poultry. This, it was anticipated, would increase the demand for cereals in so far as wheat and barley make up more than 40 per cent of pigs' diets and 60 per cent of broiler chickens' compared with 7 per cent for dairy cows (Maitland 1996). However, as already mentioned, later in 1996 the price of cereals started to fall.

The BSE crisis has starkly demonstrated how far the CAP has put producer interests above those of consumers. Even as late as 1996 a German veterinarian, Oscar Riedinger, accused the EU's Scientific Veterinary Committee of:

> committing 'enormous errors' and of having gone against 'all microbiological practice'. Experts on the committee knew that feed made from mammalian meat and bonemeal should have been heated to 140 degrees centigrade when they met to discuss rules for the treatment of animal waste in 1990, but only agreed standards of 133 degrees for twenty minutes.
>
> (*Agra Europe* 1996c)

The UK's MAFF has been no better. It was very tardy in putting enough research effort into identifying the causes of BSE, while the government dealt with the problem as though it was a public relations exercise. Indeed, the average shopper is likely to place more trust in the inspection system of a large retailer than in the government. At this point in time (January 1998), Britain is forbidden from exporting beef, but imports it from other Member States whose slaughtering requirements are much less stringent than in the UK (they do not require the removal of the spinal cord).

GENERAL CONCLUSIONS

Health and nutrition objectives have been largely ignored by British agricultural policy and by the CAP. Recently, most effort by the CEC, politicians, academics and the agricultural lobbies has been devoted to trying to reduce expenditure on the CAP while not adversely affecting any farming sector. The inherent confusion at the centre of the CAP – namely, that it is based on the concept of a small family farm – is ignored. Such farmers were regarded as a stable section of society and the family farm as 'the essential foundation of agriculture in Western Europe' (CEC 1994: 63). Yet price support was regarded as the means of providing them with assistance notwithstanding that, by its very nature, it always gives more to the larger producer. The economic aspects of the situation are hardly taken into account.

For instance, in the first place there was a considerable variation in size of farm even before the expansion of the EC; the larger the output of the farm, the greater the benefit from any price support system. So at present 80 per cent of the benefits of the system go to 20 per cent of the farmers (CEC 1994: 69), that is, the larger farmers benefit much more than the smaller ones.

Secondly, the return that factors of production gain from protection is in inverse relation to their elasticity (Corden 1971). Labour is generally in very elastic supply, as has been shown by its massive exit since the early 1960s. Land is the most inelastic of the factors of production and the benefits of price support, whether due to minimum import prices and support buying or to production quotas as for milk, are capitalized in the value of land. Ironically and incorrectly, the increase in the price of land has been used as an argument for further protection.

Thirdly, in a situation in which the quantity of land available is fixed and the employment of labour is falling, the expansion in output has been achieved by technological improvements in breeds and inputs and the greater application of manufactured inputs such as fertilizers, pesticides and weed-icides. The heavy application of such chemicals at a higher rate than anywhere else in the world has contributed to the pollution of land and water. Furthermore, the set-aside programme, by reducing the use of the fixed factor, is likely to make matters worse. Not only are farmers 'being paid to grow ragwort in East Anglia', as an acquaintance put it, but the intensity of chemical application is not likely to be diminished on the remaining areas. The environmental objective of reducing the intensity of cultivation is recognized by the CEC, but is supported financially to a minis-cule extent compared with the price support schemes, which have the opposite effect.

Fourthly, there is the question of comparative advantage. The French have been the most insistent supporters of the CAP and the high prices that have been built into it because they regard themselves as having a compar-ative advantage in agriculture. Their expanse of fertile agricultural land is their 'green gold'. This is indubitably so, and British farmers have some-times commented on the vast potential of French agriculture were farmers to devote as much effort to the condition of the soil as the British do. However, within the confines of the EC the French would have been better able to exploit their advantage if agricultural prices had been kept down. Setting them at a high rate, as in 1967, and then raising them, encouraged an expansion in output in other areas, in particular the commercialized sectors of the new entrants, Britain and Denmark, with the result that the EC moved into surplus in an increasing number of products. Maintaining high prices for cereals, so that it was cheaper to import substitutes and oilseeds for fodder under low tariffs, increased the economic cost of the distortion. In particular, in Britain cereal output mainly of wheat, increased, but the use of cereals for feed declined fairly steadily, and Britain became a net exporter.

Fifthly, with respect to income distribution, a massive transfer is now taking place from consumers and taxpayers to farmers, accounting for about 60 per cent of EC expenditure and representing on average £12,500 per agricultural worker per year. The transfer is very inefficient in so far as farmers receive only ECU 100 out of every ECU 170 spent by consumers and taxpayers. But there is also the question of why agriculture should be singled out for such favourable treatment. Farm households are not on average worse off than the population at large. Furthermore, the burden of support with high prices for consumers falls most heavily on families with low incomes and with children, which spend a high proportion of their income on food.

Sixthly, the CAP also involves transfers between countries, generally from those with relatively small agricultural sectors to those with large ones, and not generally from high-income to low-income countries, with Germany and Britain bearing the chief cost. This transfer across foreign exchanges inevitably affects exchange rates. Furthermore, in so far as most EC countries are endeavouring to join a single currency this will mean that it is superimposed on a very distorted price structure. Thus Britain, a net contributor, and Ireland, a net recipient, would find the rate of exchange at which they entered lower and higher respectivley as compared with a situation in which agricultural protection was, for instance, at the same level as manufacturing, say, 6 per cent.

But above all there is still no common market in agricultural products. Prices vary, partly due to the CAP institutional framework. Even the free movement of goods has been disrupted by the BSE crisis.

If a common currency is adopted this may reduce the degree of price variation between the Member States who participate in it. But for Britain on the outside, the variation in her exchange rate with EMU members of the EU may add to the agricultural price instability engendered by the world market.

Finally, the CAP has now developed into a system of Byzantine complexity. The Council of Ministers seems unable to make a decision to reduce payments to farmers, even though the latter's numbers have been falling consistently and therefore the per capita payments expenditure on them has increased. The institution of the MacSharry reforms, with direct compensation payments to farmers, has increased CAP expenditure, not reduced it. The complexity is such that there is very little informed discussion about policy by either economists or the public at large.

The measures to restrict output directly rather than reduce price are inherently inefficient. They do not allow countries with the greatest comparative advantage to expand their output at the cost of others. Many farmers object to set-aside, that is, being paid to produce nothing. If such transfers are to be made, is this the most efficient way of making them? Indeed, why should agricultural producers enjoy such transfers rather than anyone else? If the objective is to maintain rural settlements, are there not better ways of doing so? At present, in many EU countries the total disposable income of agricultural households is greater than that of all households, but this appears to be increasingly due to their non-agricultural employment or pensions.

In addition, there are the other problems associated with the collection and distribution of a vast amount of money, namely, the cost of the bureaucracy, corruption, and fraud.

NOTES

1 Variously described as the threshold or sluice-gate price.
2 Unfortunately, the government ceased publishing these figures after 1989.
3 Farmers, partners, directors and workers.
4 Less 10 per cent to allow for administration.

REFERENCES

Statistics

CEC (various issues) *The Agricultural Situation in the Community*, annual publication, Brussels, CEC.

CSO (various issues) *Annual Abstract of Statistics*, London: HMSO.

Eurostat (various issues) *Yearbook of Agricultural Statistics*, Brussels: European Community.

Ministry of Agriculture, Fisheries and Food (MAFF) (various issues) *Agriculture in the United Kingdom*, London: HMSO.

OECD APMT (various issues) *Agricultural Policies, Markets, and Trade in OECD Countries*, annual publication, Paris: OECD.

WTO (previously GATT) (various issues) *International Trade*, annual publication, Geneva: World Trade Organization.

OTHER

Agra Europe (1996a) 'Panorama from Brussels – Variable Compensation', 5 July, P/2.

—— (1996b) 'Panorama from Brussels', 1 November, P/1–P/2.

—— (1996c) 'Feed expert attacks EU vets over bonemeal rules', 8 November, E/7.

Anderson, K. (1995) 'Impacts of new agreements on advanced economies', in G.H. Peters and D.D. Hedley (eds), *Agricultural Competitiveness: Market Forces and Policy Choice*, Dartmouth: IAAE.

Buckley, N. (1996) 'Farm ministers reach surprise reforms accord', *Financial Times*, 25 July.

——— (1997a) 'Cereal farmers given too much aid, says report', *Financial Times*, 10 June.

——— (1997b) 'EU set-aside rate held at 5%', *Financial Times*, 11 July.

Bureau of Agricultural Economics (1985) *Agricultural Policies in the European Community*, Policy Monograph no. 2, Canberra: Australian Government Publishing Service.

CEC (1994) *EC Agricultural Policy for the 21st Century*, European Economy No. 4, Brussels: CEC.

Corden, W.M. (1971) *The Theory of Protection*, Oxford: Oxford University Press.

CSO (1980) Annual Abstract of Statistics, London: HMSO.

Fennell, R. (1979) *The Common Agricultural Policy of the European Community: Its Institutional and Administrative Organisation*, Granada: Allanheld, Osmun.

Hargreaves, D. (1996a) 'Brussels expected to resist British dairy quota plan', *Financial Times*, 14 February.

——— (1996b) 'A farmer's nightmare: the crisis for UK producers over links between mad cow disease and human illness', *Financial Times*, 22 March.

——— (1996c) 'EU increases subsidies on wheat exports', *Financial Times*, 8 November.

——— (1996d) 'Fertilizer use threatened by cereal price reform', *Financial Times*, 19 December.

Hargreaves, D. and Chote, R. (1996) 'No bitter harvest forecast', *Financial Times*, 27–28 April.

Hogg, D. (1996) quoted in 'Budget 1996 – BSE fight gets extra £792m', *Financial Times*, 27 November.

Maitland, A. (1996) 'Industry faces rise in costs of protein', *Financial Times*, 26 March.

Moore, L. (1988) 'Agricultural protection in Britain and its economy-wide effects', *World Economy*, **11** (2).

NCC (1988) *Consumers and the Common Agricultural Policy*, London: National Consumer Council.

——— (1995) *Agricultural policy in the European Union*, London: National Consumer Council.

OECD (1987, 1995, 1996) *National Policies and Agricultural Trade*, annual publication, Paris: OECD.

Rayner, A.J., Ingersent, K.A. and Hine, R.C. (1993) in A.J. Rayner and D. Colman (eds), *Current Issues in Agricultural Economics*, London: Macmillan.

Richardson, D. (1996a) 'Subsidy cuts threaten agricultural unity – reliance on real markets will mean every farmer becoming his neighbour's competitor', *Financial Times*, 13 February.

——— (1996b) 'Small farms with room for improvement – the EU is considering plans to protect traditional farms from commercial reality', *Financial Times*, 27 February.

Rome Treaty (1957) Treaty establishing the EEC, trans. S. Nelson (ed.) (1993) *The Convoluted Treaties*, vol. 2, Oxford: Nelson & Pollard.

Southey, C. (1995) 'No farm reform, no EU enlargement', *Financial Times*, 24 November.

——— (1996a) 'EU alters banana import regime', *Financial Times*, 7 March.

——— (1996b) 'Beef aid package clears way for wider measures', *Financial Times*, 31 October.

——— (1996c) 'Europe Commission rejects cut in tobacco aid – hopes for drive against smoking lose out to plea for continued subsidy to small farmers', *Financial Times*, 14 November.

Tangermann, S. (1992) Eurostat (1992) *Agricultural Price Trends in the EC*, Brussels: EC.

Urry, M. (1997) 'Farmers furious at compensation cuts', *Financial Times*, 28/29 June.

WTO (1995) *International Trade*, Geneva: World Trade Organization.

10 Trade and production of motor vehicles[1]

Let us now turn to the production and trade in motor vehicles, which are regarded by economists as a classic case of an imperfectly competitive industry with differentiated products. Design and costs of production are both elements in a firm's competitive position. Each is producing models which are distinct from those of other firms but which could be substituted for them. Most economic analysis is devoted to passenger cars, although the category of motor vehicles includes commercial vehicles (CVs) that is vans, trucks, and buses and parts.

The UK industry that emerged after the Second World War had the same structure as in the 1930s. Austin, Morris, Standard, Rootes, and Singer were the largest British firms, although all were relatively small by international standards. They produced cars alongside some very well-established US firms: Ford established in 1911, General Motors since 1926 through its acquisition of Vauxhall, and later Chrysler, which purchased Rootes in 1964. There were also a number of luxury and specialist car producers such as Jaguar, Rolls-Royce and Bentley, and BSA, which produced Daimler and Lanchester. Thus the output of car producers in the UK was across the range from utility-type vehicles to mid-price cars and luxury cars. The largest five firms also produced CVs. In addition, there were a number of small specialist lorry producers. The percentage of motor vehicles supplied by each firm in 1947 is shown in Table 10.1.

Between 1945 and 1975, mergers and amalgamations in the industry proceeded apace (see Table 10.2). This was partly because firms operating in the UK were not large enough to exploit economies of scale and thus lower their costs of production. The minimum efficient scale of firm in 1947 was regarded as between 100 and 150 thousand units a year, whereas the largest firm, Morris, only produced 60 thousand units (Foreman-Peck et al. 1995: 98). The first big merger was Austin with Morris in 1952, to form the British Motor Corporation (BMC); unfortunately rationalization was not properly carried out and they continued to operate as different firms.

Each producer was responsible for the distinctive models it assembled and sold but was heavily reliant on the purchase of components from outside; in 1954 these accounted for around 75 per cent of the cost of a

Table 10.1 British motor vehicle production by firms, 1947
(estimated percentages by volume)

	Cars and taxis	Commercial vehicles
The 'Big Six'		
Nuffield	20.9	13.6
Ford	15.4	22.9
Austin	19.2	14.3
Vauxhall	11.2	20.3
Rootes	10.9	7.9
Standard	13.2	
Specialist car producers		
Rover	2.7	
Singer	2.1	
BSA[1]	0.6	
Jaguar	1.6	
Armstrong-Siddeley	0.8	
Rolls-Royce and Bentley	0.3	
Alvis	0.3	
Others	0.8	
Heavy vehicle builders		
Jowett		4.3
Leyland		2.2
AEC (ACV)		2.9
Albion		1.3
Dennis		0.9
Thornycroft		1.0
Scammell		0.7
Guy		2.4
Others		5.3
Total	100.0	100.0

Source: J. Foreman-Peck, S. Bowden and A. McKinlay (1995) The British Motor Industry, Manchester: Manchester University Press, p. 99.

Note: [1]Includes Daimler and Lanchester.

volume-produced car. Of the US firms, Vauxhall had a higher degree of vertical integration than Ford (Dunnett 1980: 19). In the 1960s, BMC and Ford purchased over 70 per cent and 50 per cent respectively of the value of their vehicles from outside (Foreman-Peck *et al.* 1995: 110).

Indeed, it has been argued that this diversity of output was only possible because of the well-developed component industry that included several large firms – Pressed Steel (bodies), Joseph Lucas (electrics), GKN (automotive driveline systems), and Dunlop (wheels, tyres and rubber products) – more able to exploit their own economies of scale. It was also assisted by the high level of protection.

The minimum efficient scale of plant increased during the 1950s and 1960s. It varied according to the operation carried out. A diagram of the operations is given in Figure 10.1 and the minimum efficient scale estimates

Table 10.2 Mergers in the British motor vehicle industry, 1945–68

	1945	Standard and Triumph
	1952	Austin and Nuffield (BMC)
	1955	Rootes and Singer
	1960	Jaguar and Daimler
	1961	Leyland and Standard-Triumph
	1966	BMC and Jaguar group
		Leyland and Rover
	1968	Leyland and BMH[1] (BLMC)
Commercial vehicles		
	1951	Leyland acquire Albion Motors
	1955	Leyland and Scammell Lorries
	1963	Leyland and the bus manufacturers ACV
	1967	Leyland and Rover, Alvis
		Aveling Barford
Components		
	1953	BMC acquire Fisher and Ludlow
	1953	Ford acquire Briggs Motor Bodies
	1965	BMC acquire Pressed Steel

Source: J. Foreman-Peck, S. Bowden and A. McKinlay (1995) The British Motor Industry, Manchester: Manchester University Press, p. 111.

Note: [1]BMC changed its name to BMH in 1967.

in the early 1970s are shown in Table 10.3. At that time the greatest economies appeared to be associated with the stamping of bodies and the casting of engines. They were not in assembly, where the initial integration took place. However, in 1965 BMC took over Pressed Steel and became self-sufficient in car body production, before combining with the Jaguar group in 1966 to form British Motor Holdings (BMH). The Labour governments of the 1960s made great efforts to rationalize the British industry. Under the auspices of the Industrial Reorganization Committee (IRC) BMH merged with Leyland Motors in 1968, which involved the body-building capacities of Pressed Steel, Fisher and Ludlow, Morris Bodies, Nuffield Bodies and Mulliners all being brought under the British Leyland Motor Corporation (BLMC) umbrella. It was hoped that Donald Stokes of Leyland would improve the management of BMH and that this would enable greater utilization of economies of scale in production and in R&D and marketing, as well as rationalization of designs. BLMC, now called Rover, thus became the British 'champion'.

In 1972 BLMC had a maximum car production capacity on a two-shift basis of 1,145,000, but it actually produced 916,240 units. This was considerably less than its other major competitors in Europe. Furthermore, it produced a wide range of models, though it changed them infrequently. The Morris Minor was 23 years old when it was discontinued in 1971. The Mini lasted more than 35 years. Both were very popular, but

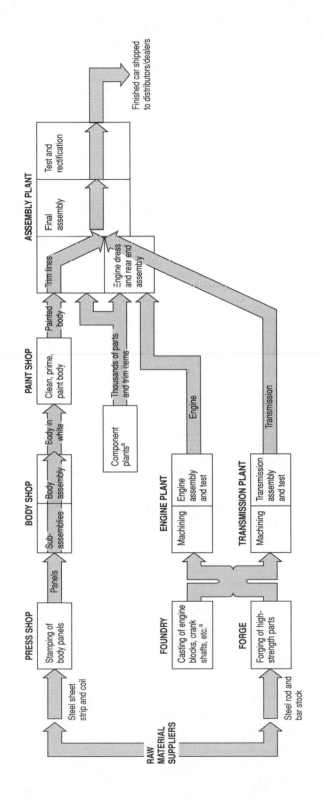

Figure 10.1 The automobile production system
Source: Central Policy Review Staff (1975) *The Future of the British Car Industry*, London: HMSO. Crown copyright. This figure is reproduced with the permission of the controller Her Majesty's Stationery Office.

[a] Internal and outside sources of supply.

Table 10.3   Minimum efficient scale per activity in the car industry (1,000 units per annum)

Activity	Pratten 1971	Rhys 1972	White 1971	Owen 1975	Rhys 1989
Casting of engine blocks	1,000	200	small	2,000	1,000
Casting of other parts					100–750
Power-train machining and assembly					600
Axle making and assembly					500
Pressing of various panels					1,000–2,000
Painting					250
Final assembly	300	200	200		250
Advertising					1,000
Finance					2,000–5,000
Research and development					5,000

Sources: G. Rhys (1989) 'Small car firms will they survive', *Long Range Planning*, vol. 22/5, No. 117, p. 25.
Quoted in J. Foreman-Peck *et al.* (1995) *The British Motor Industry*, Manchester: MUP.
C.F. Pratten (1976) *Economies of Scale in Manufacturing Industry*, Occasional Paper no. 47, Department of Applied Economics, Cambridge University.
G. Rhys (1972) *The Motor Industry*, London: Butterworth.
L.J. White (1971) *The Automobile Industry Since 1945*, Cambridge, Mass.: Harvard University Press.
N. Owen (1983) *Economies of Scale, Competitiveness, and Trade Patterns within the European Community*, Oxford: OUP, table 4.12.

were sold at such low prices that the Mini was near to making a loss. Notwithstanding the mergers, the production of cars by BLMC continued to decline (Foreman-Peck *et al.* 1995).

The problem most frequently encountered in production was that of labour unrest. This appears to have been due to the interaction of poor management and trade union activity, which found a fertile ground for disruption in the boredom and insecurity of the workforce. The strikes also tended to increase the larger the plant. The maintenance and improvement of quality was difficult. The managerial problems of BLMC proved so overwhelming that in 1974 it became bankrupt with the strain of reorganization, and this led the government to nationalize it in 1975.

GROWTH OF PRODUCTION AND EXPORTS

Government requirements during and immediately after the war were the main determinants of output in that period. The steady increase in output of passenger cars after 1931 was succeeded by drastic cuts during the war. This was then followed by a very rapid expansion (see Figure 10.2), with the number of passenger cars produced increasing from 219 thousand in 1946 to almost 2 million in 1964. The initial expansion of both production and exports was the result of government policy, which designated the car industry as an export earner and allocated steel to firms according to their exports. Thus to begin with most UK output was sent abroad. British exports of cars continued to increase, with fluctuations, until 1969 (see Figure 10.2).

The output of CVs had been kept up during the war for military purposes. Once the war ended, production increased rapidly to nearly half a million in the 1960s and then declined after 1970 (see Figure 10.3). Britain's exports also increased rapidly to around 144,000 in 1950 and then appeared to fluctuate. But after 1977 these exports started to decline.

This alteration in Britain's trading position was because of the changes in level of protection, the re-emergence of France and Germany as her competitors, and the UK's entry into first, EFTA and then the EC, aspects which we shall now discuss.

PROTECTION IN EUROPE

In the postwar period the UK tariffs were the original McKenna duties imposed in 1915 to save shipping space, that is, 33⅓ per cent on cars, commercial vehicles and parts with a Commonwealth preference rate of 22⅔ per cent for cars and parts. Thus the effective rate of protection in assembly was not greater than the nominal rate, and there was no particular incentive to import parts. The nominal rates of protection were then reduced

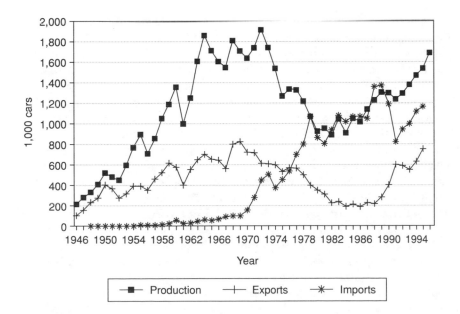

Figure 10.2 UK car production and trade, 1946–96

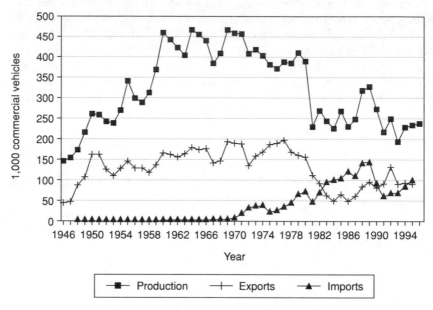

Figure 10.3 UK commercial vehicle production and trade, 1946–96

by the GATT rounds of tariff negotiations. After 1956 those on cars and commercial vehicles were reduced to 30 per cent, and in 1960 those for parts such as tyres, engines, and electrical equipment ranged from 15 per cent to 39 per cent. From 1968 onwards they were in line with the EC rates.

Before the formation of the EC the tariffs of the six ranged from 17 per cent for Germany to 45 per cent for Italy. The common external tariff (CET) of the EC to which they then moved was an average. By July 1968 when the CET became effective it was 22 per cent for assembled cars and 14 per cent for components. By 1972 the Kennedy Round reduced these to 11 per cent and 7 per cent respectively, with the duty on commercial vehicles remaining at 22 per cent. In 1991 the average EC common external tariff was 9.5 per cent. The only change resulting from the Uruguay Round is that by the year 2000 the duty on light CVs will be reduced to 10 per cent and that on parts and components will be reduced by a third. (PEP 1950: 77; White 1971; Jones 1981: 104; Maxcy 1981: 96, 66; Moore 1985: 49; GATT 1991, 1: 216; WTO 1995, 2: 32, 44).

In the 1970s Japan emerged as the lowest-cost and most efficient producer of small and medium-sized cars. The EC Member States endeavoured to reinforce protection of their industries by imposing VERs on imports of cars and CVs from Japan. In the UK the Society of Motor Manufacturers and Traders (SMMT) negotiated an agreement with the equivalent organization

Table 10.4   Non–tariff restrictions on imports
of cars and commercial vehicles (CVs) into EC
countries from Japan before 1993

Country	Restriction
France	3% market share.
Italy	2,500[1] cars; 750 light CVs since 1986.
Spain	1,000[1] cars; 200 CVs.
UK	11% market share.

Source: GATT (1991) *Trade Policy Review: The
European Communities 1991*, vol. 1, p. 216.

Note: [1]Direct imports.

in Japan to limit Japanese imports to 11 per cent of the British car and CV
market. France negotiated a VER of 3 per cent, while in Italy and Spain
the VERs were even more restrictive, see Table 10.4 (GATT 1991, vol. 1).

TRADE

In considering UK trade we will look at two aspects of the markets she has
been facing that interact with each other. First, during the period since the
Second World War the protection of her domestic market and her access
to foreign markets have been affected by the preferential trade schemes to
which she has belonged and the slow reduction of tariffs under GATT negotiations. These, as described above, have sometimes had a differential effect
on the products of the motor vehicle industry, which includes parts and
CVs as well as cars.

Second, that the market for cars is an example of imperfect competition
with product differentiation. Consumers can distinguish the products of each
firm, and firms compete as much in the provision of new models as by
price. In the model used by Smith and Venables (1991) each firm is regarded
as producing in its home country, and in selling abroad it is 'invading' the
territory of another. It reduces prices in its export market partly by reducing
the monopoly power of the firms already there. Consumption increases. As
the firm expands its output it can exploit further its economies of scale and
thus costs also fall. This is an attractive picture of consumers benefiting
without producers losing as a result of international trade.

Applying this theory to the situation in the immediate postwar period,
the question is why the very large US firms General Motors (GM), Ford,
and Chrysler did not export from the US to the rapidly growing European
market. The answer is that, in the first place, there was a dollar shortage
and the US therefore allowed the European countries to discriminate
against US goods in their foreign exchange allocation and by the maintenance of high tariffs on imports. Moreover, US cars were too large

for Europe, particularly European cities. Instead, these US firms invested in Europe to produce models more adapted to the terrain.

With regard to the UK, her production in the prewar period was directed to the home market and less than 10 per cent of production was exported. This was attributed by Dunnett (1980) not only to the high cost of production but also to the model design which was encouraged by the UK form of engine taxation and was unsuited to foreign markets. In spite of Commonwealth preference, US cars outsold British ones in the Commonwealth (ibid. 18).

In the immediate postwar period, Britain was the only European country with the productive facilities to increase output appreciably. Incentives in the form of foreign exchange allocations were provided for exports, and, in the late 1940s, up to two-thirds of production was exported; but as these incentives were later removed this proportion fell to around a third by the late 1960s. Her exports were of luxury and mid-price range cars, indeed her producers of luxury cars – Rolls-Royce, Aston Martin, and Jaguar – were heavily dependent on exports, particularly to the US market. In the 1940s and 1950s, Britain was the largest exporter of cars in the world. By the 1960s she also exported a greater number of commercial vehicles than any other country.

Why, after having achieved the foremost position in the world market for both passenger cars and commercial vehicles did Britain subsequently lose this position? This has been the subject of numerous enquiries and books. Let us first consider the changes in trading policy which throw some light on this central conundrum.

Exports from Britain still entered Commonwealth countries at preferential rates of duty, but a number of these countries, including India and Australia, raised their tariffs in order to foster their own production. Developing countries often imposed tight restrictions on imports of passenger cars in order to save foreign exchange. In general, commercial vehicles were regarded as investment goods and were not restricted so severely.

The British industry (indigenous firms and foreign subsidiaries) also faced increased competition on the world market from the renascent French and German industries, and then, in the 1970s, from Japan. Furthermore, these European and Japanese industries also posed more of a threat on her home market as her mfn tariff was negotiated down by successive GATT rounds of tariff reductions. Then in 1959 Britain entered EFTA. The Swedes were the only other car and CV producers in EFTA, and so, although Britain's imports of both passenger cars (mainly Volvos) and trucks increased, this represented a small proportion of the market (see Figure 10.4).

The most radical change occurred with the UK entry to the EC. With the removal of tariffs her producers came face to face with the other major firms operating in Europe and they rapidly expanded their share of the UK market, as has been described in Chapter 7 and illustrated in Figure 10.4. The success of Volkswagen (Germany) had been based on the 'people's car' of 1934, the Beetle, which was being produced with modifications until the

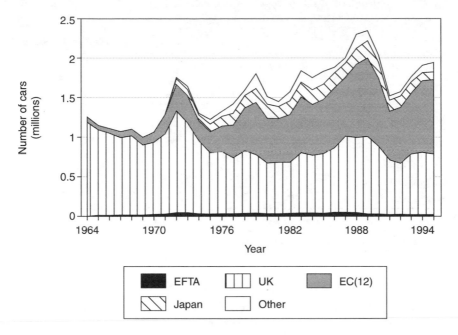

Figure 10.4 Supply to the UK car market: Domestic production and imports, 1964–95

1970s. As Volkswagen also had the largest output, 1.6 million cars in 1977, it was in the best position to exploit economies of scale. The other Continental volume producers, Peugeot–Citroen and Renault of France, and Fiat of Italy, covered the whole product range. These four all produced more than a million cars per annum. But the output of British Leyland, predecessor to Austin Rover, was only 740,000 even though it had a greater range of models – by the late 1970s, for instance, it was producing nine saloon cars. There were also the specialist producers, Daimler-Benz and BMW of Germany, and Alfa-Romeo of Italy. Alongside these were the subsidiaries of the US multinationals Ford, GM, and Chrysler, established before the Second World War, who were only in the volume sector of the market. They pursued profits and thus kept a tight control on costs and employed value engineering and short replacement cycles. In 1978 Peugeot–Citroen acquired Chrysler Europe and thus became the largest producer in Europe (Owen 1983). Fiat then took over Alfa-Romeo.

The structure of the European industry in 1986 is shown in Table 10.5. In spite of the removal of tariffs, most of the European 'champions' remained heavily dependent on their domestic markets, particularly Austin Rover, for which it accounted for 73 per cent, and Fiat/Alfa, 67 per cent.

Table 10.5 Structure of the European automobile market in 1986

	Sales in Western Europe			Exports to non-Community countries	
	× 1,000	On the national market (%)	Share of Community market	× 1,000	As % of sales in the Community
Volkswagen/Audi/Seat	1,687	53	14.6	378	22.4
Fiat/Alfa	1,625	67	14.1	16	1.0
Ford	1,352	33[1]	11.7	35[1]	2.6
Peugeot/Citroën	1,318	49	11.4	146	11.1
GM	1,260	45[2]	10.9	22[2]	1.7
Renault	1,225	57	10.6	110	9.0
Austin Rover	408	73	3.5	11	2.7

Source: CEC (1988) 'The economics of 1992' (The Emerson Report), *European Economy*, **35**, March.

Note: [1]Ford Werke only; [2]Opel only.

Removal of internal barriers to EC trade

The CEC's policy has been to remove obstacles to the functioning of the internal market. As described previously in Chapter 4, this led it to try and harmonize the legal requirements imposed by Member States for motor vehicles. 'Fifty-nine Community directives, relating to technical aspects such as emission controls and noise, were approved between 1970 and 1980' (Owen 1983: 42). The harmonization of technical requirements for passenger cars was completed in 1992 and became mandatory in 1996. If a car conforms to these requirements it can be sold in any Member State.

The CEC also tried to improve competition at the distribution end. At present, it is limited by the way retail outlets are tied to certain manufacturers. This is inconsistent with the requirement that practices should be prohibited which may affect trade between Member States and which have as their object or effect the prevention, restriction or distortion of competition within the EC. But this exclusion may be declared inapplicable if the practice improves the production or distribution of goods, or promotes technical or economic progress, while allowing consumers a fair share of resulting benefit. This is termed 'block exemption'.

Motor vehicle dealers have argued that cars qualify for block exemption; because motor vehicles are expensive, technically complex and require expert maintenance and repair, it is necessary to maintain a network of qualified dealers who can stock parts and have the technical knowledge, expertise and equipment necessary to specialize in particular brands of vehicles. In 1985 a regulation was introduced allowing 'block exemption' for ten years, and this was renewed in 1995 with qualifications for another ten years. In 1996 independent car dealers won their case in the European Court of Justice (ECJ) to buy vehicles in the cheapest EU market for resale in their own countries (Tucker 1996).

The variation in the list price of the same or corresponding motor vehicle is taken by the CEC as an indication of the degree to which impediments to trade between Member States still exist. Prices should not differ by more that 12 per cent over a period of less than a year, nor by more than 18 per cent between Member States.

The CEC has also endeavoured to restrict the amount of assistance that governments give to their national 'champions'. No government subsidies are permitted for direct costs, only for investment or rationalization. The Commission has several times intervened to prevent governments assisting car producers, the French government with Renault, the British government with Austin Rover. More recently, it insisted that if SEAT were to receive state aid of £237m, Volkswagen, its owner, had to agree to reduce its capacity by 30 per cent (Tucker and White 1995). It will be interesting to see whether it allows the British government to subsidize investment as requested by Ford for its Halewood plant (Simonian 1996a).

With the introduction of the SEM the national VERs on imports from Japan were no longer valid or enforceable. Any restraint had to be at an EC level. Under an agreement between the EC and Japan in July 1991, these national quotas were phased out and replaced by an overall quota of 1.23 million units of cars and light commercial vehicles and trucks (up to 5 tonnes) in 1999, calculated on the basis of a forecast 15.1 million vehicle market for the EC as a whole. All restraints are due to be removed by 2000. During the transitional period, EC and Japanese officials will meet twice a year to monitor the past and forecast future level of imports both in total and to each restricted market, in relation to the size of the market as a whole. There are to be 'no restrictions on Japanese investment or on the free circulation of its products in the Community', that is, on motor vehicles produced by Japanese 'transplants' (see *Financial Times* 5 August 1991; also Mattoo and Mavroidis 1995). Until recently the quota was not filled, but in 1997 exports to the EU from producers in Japan increased, partly to offset weak domestic demand (Nakamoto 1998).

Britain's experience of trade after entry into the EC in 1973

It was expected that the removal of trade barriers between Member States would lead to greater competition and the demise of the weaker firms. In particular, the French and German firms expected to oust Austin Rover (previously British Leyland) when Britain entered the EC in 1973.

Intra-EC trade increased faster than production. The competitive position of the major producing countries was largely a reflection of their relative unit costs, as can be seen in Table 10.6. The relative fall in French unit costs, particularly from 1965 to 1970, and the rise in German costs may be due to the realignment of their currencies, with the franc being devalued and the Deutschmark being revalued. By 1975 the unit costs of all three countries were below those of Britain. France had the lowest costs and was in the strongest competitive position, with trade surpluses with the other countries, while Germany increased her surplus with Britain and Italy's deficit turned into a surplus. In the event, British imports increased rapidly; at the same time, British producers lost one-third of their domestic market and gained very little increase in exports to France, Germany and Italy (Owen 1983).

The later development of labour costs from 1980 to 1989 were described in a report of the Economist Intelligence Unit (Pemberton 1991); a summary is given in Table 10.7. The labour cost to the employer consists of the wage the employee receives plus any additional payments made for pensions and social security contributions. In the UK these additional payments are called the employer's national insurance contribution, and amounted to 27 per cent of the total labour cost. In the other EC countries they amounted to 40 per cent or more of the total labour cost. In Britain the total wage cost per hour worked by the employee in 1980 was below that of the other countries, apart from Spain; by 1989 it was below all of them. Her wages were higher than those of Spain, France and Italy, but her additional costs were lower. Furthermore, her additional costs did not increase as fast as her wage costs between 1980 and 1989, whereas for the other European countries they increased faster.

The information on costs is scattered. However, it appears that in the 1970s Britain's unit costs were high compared with those of her competitors, and, as a result, imports from them increased very fast and British exports stagnated. Then, in the 1980s, her relative labour cost position improved relative to that of her competitors, largely due to her lower additional costs.

The effect on trade can be measured either in terms of the number of vehicles or in terms of value. Britain's trading position in terms of value for

Table 10.6 Comparative unit costs of car manufacture, 1955–77

	France	Germany	Italy
1955	160	77	n/a
1960	105	65	n/a
1965	91	70	99
1970	79	87	102
1975	89	93	91
1977	82	98	108

Source: N. Owen (1983) *Economies of Scale Competitiveness and Trade Patterns Within the European Community*, Oxford: OUP.

Note: Britain = 100 in each year.

Table 10.7 The cost of employing labour in the automobile industry in 1980 and 1989 (DM per hour)

Country	1980 Total	1980 Wages	1989 Total	1989 Wages	% change 1980–89 Total	% change 1980–89 Wages
UK	14.95	10.95	23.95	17.56	50.20	60.37
France	19.66	10.98	24.31	12.92	23.65	17.67
West Germany	26.91	15.96	39.69	22.97	47.49	43.92
Italy	17.15	8.1	30.84	14.06	70.83	73.58
Belgium	28.14	15.98	33.57	17.9	19.30	12.02
Spain	12.63	9.15	24.85	14.69	96.75	60.55
USA	24.83	17.89	35.53	26.71	43.09	49.3
Japan	14.5	11.33	34.8	26.77	140.00	136.28

Source: M. Pemberton (1991) *Europe's Motor Industry after 1992*, London: EIU.

the major categories comprising motor vehicles can be seen for 1973, when she had just joined the EC, and 1995 in Table 10.8. In 1973, total exports at £1,569 million were twice as large as total imports of £765 million. Exports of 'parts including tyres' was the most important item, accounting for 45 per cent of the total, and was much larger than exports of cars and CVs. Her surpluses were in CVs and 'parts including tyres', as she had a deficit in 'cars and taxis'. Her deficit in the last category was greatest with the other eight members of the EC, from whom her imports were almost three times the value of her exports. Her deficit with them was in terms of units as well as value.

By 1995 her exports of 'cars and taxis' were as great in value terms as that of 'parts' (see Table 10.8). She had moved into overall deficit, with exports of £15,370 million equivalent to three-quarters of imports. She had a deficit in all the major categories with the other fourteen members of the EU, except in agricultural tractors. The author is reluctant to use the values for the two tables to compare the fortunes of the different sectors because not only has there been a very high rate of inflation, but also there have been considerable changes in parts as electronic equipment becomes more important.

It is better to consider the development of trade in terms of units (see Figures 10.2 and 10.3). As shown in Figure 10.2, British exports of cars declined after 1969; the turnround in the late 1980s is due to inward investment, which will be described later. Britain's exports of commercial vehicles continued to increase until 1977, but then declined, see Figure 10.3; in the mid-1980s they started to increase again. On the other hand, imports of cars and CVs increased rapidly after 1969 due to liberalization and then entry into the EC, as described previously. The supply of home-produced cars and imports to the UK market from 1964 to 1995 is shown in Figure 10.4. Imports from the EC(12) have accounted for an ever-increasing proportion. In 1970, only 15 per cent of the purchase of new cars in the UK were imports; those

Table 10.8 UK trade in motor vehicles in 1973 and 1995 (£m)

	Exports 1973				Imports 1973			
	Total	EC(8)	EFTA	USA	Total	EC(8)	EFTA	USA
Cars and taxis	373	110	36	78	437	306	45	2
CVs	214	41	18	2	54	29	22	1
Parts (inc. tyres)	703	220	112	95	225	154	18	33
Industrial trucks and tractors	58	13	21	0	18	9	3	4
Caravans and trailers	30	20	4	0	1	1	0	0
Agricultural tractors	156	20	25	8	10	4	0	3
Total	1,569	440	206	190	765	510	91	48

	Exports 1995			Imports 1995		
	Total	EC(14)	USA	Total	EC(14)	USA
Cars and taxis	6,705	4,685	828	9,745	8,249	162
CVs	702	477	13	1,669	1,532	3
Parts (inc. tyres)	6,183	4,533	465	8,539	6,518	298
Industrial trucks and tractors	765	353	138	467	352	33
Caravans and trailers	195	55	10	156	132	15
Agricultural tractors	805	366	150	290	240	32
Total	15,370	10,641	1,612	20,897	17,039	548

Source: SMMT (1974) *Motor Industry of Great Britain 1974*, London, (1996) *Motor Industry of Great Britain 1996, World Automotive Statistics*, London.

from France, Germany, and Italy accounted for 10 per cent, and from EFTA 1.4 per cent. By 1978 the proportion supplied by France, Germany, and Italy, had risen to 23 per cent, and that of Japan had risen to 11 per cent, restricted by the agreement already mentioned. By 1982 the number of cars imported exceeded the number produced; UK production accounted for 42 per cent of registrations of new cars in the domestic market, France, Germany and Italy for 29 per cent and Japan for 11 per cent. By 1995 France, Germany, and Italy, supplied 31 per cent, the EU(12) as a whole supplied 48 per cent, and Japan supplied 5 per cent of the British domestic market.

INVESTMENT

Since the 1960s the UK's production and exports have partly been the result of inward direct investment. The government has always tried to control the location of new investment. Immediately after the Second World War this was done with the aid of Industrial Development Certificates, which restricted the expansion of car plants on existing sites and prohibited new plants in the South East or West Midlands. Regional development assistance was also provided to induce firms to areas of high unemployment. As a result, new factories were established in Merseyside, Clydeside, Swansea and Edinburgh. In particular, in the 1960s in Merseyside Ford was induced to establish a new plant at Halewood, GM at Ellesmere Port, and Triumph, later part of BL, at Speke. But it was difficult to maintain quality, labour relations were poor, and the factories were dogged by strikes. Speke was forced to cease production in 1978 (Wagstyl and Peel 1997). Furthermore, this policy is regarded as responsible for increasing the transport costs of firms and preventing them exploiting economies of scale (Foreman-Peck *et al.* 1995).

The next inflow of inward direct investment occurred after the decline in UK production and the massive increase in imports that occurred with Britain's entry to the EC.

Imports from Japan had increased, but as detailed above their entry into the EC was restricted by VERs. Japanese firms began to respond in the 1980s by investing in production facilities in the EC, particularly Britain. Rather than set up in the traditional areas of volume car production, which had acquired a reputation for being strike prone, they invested in greenfield sites. Nissan was first, with an investment in Sunderland that began production in 1986 with a capacity of 50,000 cars per annum. Honda acted in co-operation with Rover but also established production in Swindon, which came on stream in 1989. Toyota established a plant in Derbyshire that came into production in 1993.

The French regarded this establishment of Japanese 'transplant' factories in Britain with dislike and suspicion. Peugeot's chairman has described them as a 'Japanese aircraft carrier' off the coast of Europe (see *Independent* 4 January 1993). At first, France threatened to include imports from Nissan's UK plant within their overall Japanese quota unless it had an EC content of 80 per cent. However, this would have been inconsistent with the EC definition whereby 'origin is assigned to the country where a product has been wholly obtained or where it has undergone its '"*last substantial working or processing*"' (GATT 1991, 1: 118–19). Eventually, the EC Commission persuaded France to accept these cars as being of British origin, and, in any case, the local content very soon reached 80 per cent.

The reason for the concern is that assembly itself accounts for only about 10 per cent of the value of a car. Thus it might just have led to an increase in imports of components from Japan. However, the extent of this trade has been affected by the just-in-time (JIT) methods introduced by the Japanese. These require the component suppliers to be able to deliver their products within a certain time to the final producers. As a result, although the establishment of Japanese production in the UK initially led to increased imports of components, this tailed off as more components came to be purchased from domestic suppliers – and, in some cases, the Japanese component manufacturers also invested in production facilities within the UK.

Nissan steadily expanded the output of its subsidiary in Sunderland. In 1997 it announced further investment of £215 million alongside its existing plant, which will involve an extra direct employment of 800 with another 2,700 in the components industry. This will bring its total investment to nearly £1.5 billion and, it hopes, an output of 350,000 cars in 2000. Honda is now expanding its production at its Swindon plant from 100,000 to 150,000 by the end of 1998. Toyota is investing to produce a second model at its plant in Derbyshire which will lift its capacity from the 117,000 cars produced in 1996 to 200,000. The additional production from Japanese subsidiaries is intended not only for the British domestic market but also for export to the rest of Europe (Griffiths 1997b).

Ford has now decided to locate the production of Jaguar at Halewood in Merseyside with government assistance. It is still investing in Southampton, just as GM is in its plants at Ellesmere Port and Luton, and BMW is in Rover. Thus, although Britain's volume car production is entirely in the hands of foreign companies at the moment, their record of investment appears better than it was under indigenous ownership. The attraction of Britain as a location is low wage costs and the flexibility of the labour force, a dramatic change from the 1960s and 1970s (Griffiths 1997b, Simonian 1997b, Wagstyl and Peel 1997).

Having declined after entry into the EC, Britain's car production increased to around 1.7 million in 1996. This can be seen from Figure 10.5, which looks at the UK output of different firms since 1968 in terms of their present grouping. As mentioned previously, the British production of all the major firms declined from 1968 to 1980. BLMC was worst affected and Ford least, even though its total output was less than that of BLMC (Foreman-Peck *et al.* 1995: 129). But like the other US firms it was producing far fewer models. The US multinationals appeared less overwhelmed by the difficult labour market in which they were operating.

The major revival has come in the late 1980s with the establishment of plants by Nissan and Toyota, and recently, Honda. In 1995 Rover (taken over by BMW in 1994) accounted for 31 per cent, Ford 18 per cent, and GM 14 per cent of British production. Japanese subsidiaries accounted for a fifth of UK production. There was a great deal of difference between the firms in their export orientation (see Table 10.9). Ford produced almost solely for the domestic market. GM exported 43 per cent of its production, but as can be seen from Table 10.10, it also imported 52 per cent of its requirements for home sales. Rover sent most (69 per cent) of its Land Rovers abroad, but was dependent on the home market for 57 per cent of sales of its other cars. The Japanese subsidiaries were the most export-orientated, with between 70 per cent and 76 per cent of their output going abroad.

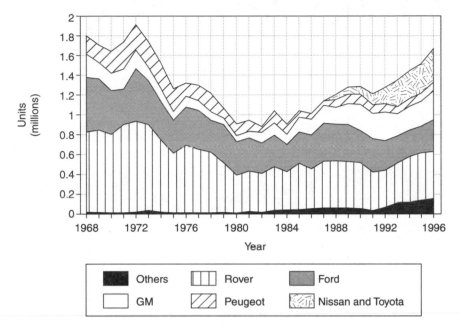

Figure 10.5 UK car production by firm, 1968–96

EC INDUSTRIAL POLICY

Apart from the application of EC policy as laid down by the treaties, the CEC is more directly concerned with the motor vehicles industry. As reported by GATT, it 'considers the motor vehicle industry as a strategically important sector, with a vital impact on upstream and downstream activities. The industry accounts for 8 per cent of manufacturing employment and 9 per cent of industrial value added'. (GATT 1991, 1: 215.) In 1994 it accounted for 11 per cent of EC(12) exports and 9 per cent of its imports. Of the vehicle exports, 66 per cent were intra-EC, another 10 per cent went to other countries in Western Europe and 24 per cent went to the rest of the world.

The CEC regarded the car industry as the manufacturing industry likely to benefit most from the creation of the Single European Market (SEM) because this would provide it with opportunities to further exploit economies of scale. It provided figures showing the minimum efficient technical scale (METS) for car production was 200 per cent of UK production, and 20 per cent of EC production, with the cost gradient at half of METS being 6–9 (CEC 1988: 186). However, it also produced figures showing that the potential economies of scale depended on the stage of manufacture. The CEC calculated that the SEM would strengthen the EC car industry so as to reduce imports from outside and increase exports.

Table 10.9 UK production of cars in 1996 and 1995, and allocation to the export and home markets in 1995

| Manufacturer | 1996 production | 1995 production | | Numbers of cars and percentages | | | | % of total car exports in 1995 |
| | | | | 1995 for exports | | 1995 for home market | | |
		Total	%	Total	%	Total	%	
Total Rover Group	473,217	473,951	31	228,147	48	245,804	52	31
Austin–Rover	376,323	374,418	24	159,324	43	215,094	57	21
Land Rover	96,894	99,533	6	68,823	69	30,710	31	9
Ford	328,028	273,896	18	37,457	14	236,439	86	5
GM Vauxhall	268,228	231,196	15	99,919	43	131,277	57	13
Nissan	231,627	215,346	14	161,216	75	54,130	25	22
Honda	105,810	91,084	6	63,487	70	27,597	30	9
Toyota	116,973	88,440	6	67,401	76	21,039	24	9
Peugeot/Talbot	85,108	78,379	5	27,030	34	51,349	66	4
Jaguar/Daimler	38,590	41,023	3	32,726	80	8,297	20	4
Rolls-Royce	1,706	1,427		920	64	507	36	0
Total	1,686,134	1,532,084	100	744,611	49	787,473	51	100

Source: SMMT (1996) Motor Industry of Great Britain 1996, World Automotive Statistics, London; 1996 production supplied by SMMT directly.

This kind of calculation can be criticized on a number of counts. Most of the data used relating to economies of scale were drawn from the 1960s (Pratten 1988) and the greater use of computers, particularly in changing from one specification to another, have changed these considerably. The METS now appears to be declining. However, the cost of developing a new model are still very high, which is why Rover had to resort to the assistance of Honda.

The EC Commission's anticipation of the benefits that European car producers would derive from the SEM appears to have been fundamentally misconceived. US subsidiaries operating in the EC were treated like domestic firms. But multinationals could benefit from the removal of barriers to intra-EC trade not only by expanding their existing plants, but also by locating production in the lowest cost source within the EC, which is what they proceeded to do. In the 1960s the US multinationals were attracted to Belgium, and then, in the 1970s, to Spain, which, at that time, was not yet a member of the EC but was expected to join.

Exports of cars by France and Germany peaked in 1992 and by Italy in 1990. Britain's exports have increased and in 1995, at 746,000 were three-and-a-half times as large as in 1988. A major contributing factor to this was the increase in exports by Nissan, Honda, and Toyota. In 1995 these three firms accounted for 40 per cent of British cars allocated for export (see the last column of Table 10.9). Exports by the Rover group have increased since 1988 and now represent 31 per cent of the total. Exports by Ford and GM–Vauxhall have fluctuated a great deal and in 1995 represented 5 per cent and 13 per cent of the total. Thus there is no evidence of the indigenous producers benefiting from the SEM by expansion in their country of origin, least of all by increasing exports.

But regrouping and rationalization has continued, with units that were at one time in BLMC passing from one firm to another. Jaguar was privatized in 1984 and acquired by Ford in 1989. Leyland, a producer of lorries, was sold to DAF, which in turn was taken over by the US firm Paccar in 1996 (Griffiths 1996). LDV, a producer of vans, which emerged from the collapsed DAF group in 1993, is being partially sold to Daewoo, a Korean company, in exchange for investment of £200m and access to Daewoo's engineering and product skills to develop a new generation of vans (Simonian 1998).

German firms have been relocating production away from Germany, where wages and social costs are regarded as too high and the labour force too inflexible. Volkswagen took over one of Spain's largest vehicle assembly plants, SEAT, as the manufacturing base for its small car, the Polo. Eastern Europe may soon become another such area of development; Volkswagen's acquisition of a stake in Skoda, in the Czech Republic, is just the beginning of this trend.

In 1994 BMW, a German manufacturer of luxury cars, deciding that its future lay in globalization, purchased Rover in order to complement its range with Rover's front-wheel-drive small cars, including the Mini, and also the four-wheel-drive Land Rover. BMW produced about the same number of cars, half a million a year, but it was much more profitable. Before the takeover, Rover was investing about £200 million a year, 3 per cent of its sales revenue, which contrasts with BMW's rate of investment of 7 per cent. After the takeover, BMW raised the level of investment in Rover to £600 million a year. On top of its purchase price of £1 billion (£800 million paid to British Aerospace for its 80 per cent shareholding, and £200 million paid to Honda for the remaining 20 per cent), it claims to have invested £2 billion in Rover, about the same amount as the goverment provided over the thirteen years it was nationalized between 1975 and 1988. The proportion Rover exported has been raised from around 30 per cent to nearer the BMW average of 54 per cent of sales (Hasselkus 1997).

A variation in the story was provided by the takeover of the British firm Lotus by Proton of Malaysia in 1996 to buy into its skill and technology. Lotus not only produced sports cars, but also acted as a design and engineering consultant to other car firms.

There have also been rationalization and mergers of firms producing parts, the most significant of which has been the recent merger of Lucas with the US firm Varity in 1996.

The production of multinationals has become organized on a global basis, with the sourcing of components (e.g. for the Ford Fiesta and the Ford Escort) taking place throughout Western Europe (Dicken 1992). The major multinationals operating in Europe are Ford, GM, Volkswagen, and now BMW, Nissan, Toyota, and Honda. The UK no longer has an indigenous mass producer of cars and thus is dependent on the multinationals plus her producers of speciality or luxury cars such as Rolls-Royce. Vickers is now offering Rolls-Royce for sale.

Imports have increased rapidly and in 1997 they accounted for 66 per cent of new car registrations (see Table 10.10) (Griffiths 1998). The Ford group had 19 per cent, GM 14 per cent, BMW 13 per cent and the Peugeot group 11 per cent. The top three best-selling models on the British market were Ford's Fiesta, Escort and Mondeo.

There is also a considerable degree of intra-firm trading by the multinationals (see Table 10.11). The UK registration of new cars identifies the country of production. This is compared with the exports to that country of UK-produced cars (see the last column in Table 10.11). GM appears to engage in the greatest degree of intra-firm trade; it exports 44 per cent of its British output and then imports 150 per cent of this mainly from the rest of the EU to supply the British market. You would expect this in so far as individual plants within the EU specialize in particular models, but perhaps not the high degree of variation between the different multinationals.

The problem the CEC has to face is that of surplus capacity in Europe. Productive capacity for cars is 15½ to 16 million, whereas actual output is around 13 million. The congestion and pollution caused by the use of passenger cars means that governments are not likely to favour an

Table 10.10 UK new car registrations in 1997

	New car registrations 1997	Share (%) 1997	Production 1996
Ford group	405,860	18.7	
Ford	396,353	18.3	328,028
Jaguar	9,507	0.4	38,590
General Motors[1]	311,238	14.3	297,739
Vauxhall	294,550	13.6	268,228
Saab[1]	16,688	0.8	
BMW group	280,986	12.9	
BMW	63,724	2.9	
Rover[2]	217,262	10.0	473,217
Peugeot group	246,999	11.4	
Peugeot	167,472	7.7	85,108
Citroen	79,527	3.7	
Volkswagen group	187,794	8.7	
Volkswagen	119,767	5.5	
Audi	35,524	1.6	
SEAT	16,753	0.8	
Skoda[3]	15,750	0.7	
Renault	159,235	7.3	
Nissan	96,172	4.4	231,627
Toyota	72,465	3.3	116,973
Fiat group	94,224	4.3	
Fiat	88,328	4.1	
Alfa Romeo	5,896	0.3	
Volvo	40,485	1.9	
Mercedes–Benz	42,530	2.0	
Honda	55,612	2.6	105,810
Mazda	31,293	1.4	
Total	2,170,725	100.0	1,686,134
UK produced	733,189	33.8	
Imports	1,437,536	66.2	
Japanese makes	309,299	14.2	
Korean makes	53,927	2.5	

Sources: SMMT figures direct; J. Griffiths (1998) 'Imports dominate growing car market', *Financial Times*, 8 January.

Notes:
[1] GM holds 50% of Saab and has management control.
[2] Includes Range/Rover Discovery.
[3] VW holds 70% of Skoda and has management control.

expansion in the car 'park'; the incentive schemes they have offered have been for replacing old 'bangers' with new cars. The EU market is therefore becoming a replacement one.[2]

With respect to exports in terms of units, Britain has increased her exports of cars, largely to the rest of the EU, but France and Germany are not so

Table 10.11 Intra-firm trade of multinationals producing cars in the UK in 1995

	New UK registrations	UK production	Exports by destination
Ford			
UK	249,110	273,896	
Germany	27,118		11
Belgium	118,101		900
Spain	6,435		3
Portugal	3,382		1
USA	6,576		
Total Ford	410,722		37,457
GM Vauxhall Opel			
UK	140,000	231,196	
Germany	42,315		39,656
Belgium	27,594		2,811
Spain	79,316		2,875
Finland	3,504		1,369
Japan	1,402		1,199
Total GM	294,131		100,584
Nissan			
UK	65,194	215,346	
Japan	20,692		969
Spain	6,086		14,087
Total Nissan	91,972		161,693
Toyota			
UK	22,302	88,440	
Japan	31,872		
USA	210		
Total Toyota	54,384		67,410
Honda			
UK	20,520	91,084	
Japan	16,178		22
USA	9,074		
Total Honda	45,772		3,847

Source: SMMT (1996) *World Automotive Statistics*, London: SMMT, tables 14, 56, and 2.

successful and those from Italy are declining, although these trends may have been reversed by the rise in the value of sterling in relation to the Deutschmark in 1997. Exports of CVs show no clear growth. Exports of automotive products in terms of dollars by the EU(12) to the rest of the world fluctuated, but there is no clear sign of an expansion from 1990–94.

CONCLUSION

The argument of the CEC that the SEM would lead to indigenous producers being able to exploit economies of scale in their home base and increase their exports appears fallacious. Multinationals have taken advantage of it to relocate production to the cheapest source. The multinationals may be German, French, American or Japanese. They have been attracted to the UK because of her relatively low labour costs and the flexibility of her labour force. Britain's car industry is entirely foreign owned apart from a few producers of specialities. UK production is increasing, however, while Italian production is falling and that of France and Germany shows no clear trend.

The argument here is that this very high degree of regionalization in production and trade is a result of the operations of multinationals unencumbered by tariff barriers within the free trade area of the EC and EFTA. However, it is also the result of the restrictions imposed on the entry of imports from Japan. It will be interesting to see whether this trade pattern is maintained when the restrictions are removed in the year 2000, and also how successful developing countries such as South Korea and Malaysia are in increasing their exports to the EC.

NOTES

1   Statistics in the text and for the tables and graphs have been obtained from the Society of Motor Manufacturers and Traders (SMMT) annual publication *Motor Industry of Great Britain World Automotive Statistics* for various years with some recent data supplied directly.
2   Indeed, because of congestion there has been a rapid expansion in sales of motorcycles and mopeds as substitutes.

REFERENCES

CEC (1988) 'The economics of 1992', (The Emerson Report), *European Economy*, **35**, March.
Dicken, P. (1992) *Global Shift*, 2nd edn, London: Paul Chapman.
Dunnett, P.J.S. (1980)*The Decline of the British Motor Industry: The Effects of Government Policy, 1945–79*, London: Croom Helm.
Foreman-Peck, J., Bowden, S. and McKinlay, A. (1995) *The British Motor Industry*, Manchester: Manchester University Press.
GATT (1991) *Trade Policy Review: The European Communities 1991*, 2 vols, Geneva: GATT.
Griffiths, J. (1996) 'Survey – world commercial vehicles: market momentum is finally slowing down', *Financial Times*, 10 December.
—— (1997a) 'Exports drive increase in car production', *Financial Times*, 8 January.
—— (1997b) 'Back on track for a bumper year', *Financial Times*, 6 March.
—— (1998) 'Imports dominate growing car market', *Financial Times*, 8 January.
Hasselkus, W. (1997) 'The strategic development of Rover', Maurice Lubbock Lecture, Said Business School, Oxford University.
Jones, D.T. (1981) *Maturity and Crisis in the European Car Industry: Structural Change and*

Public Policy, Sussex European Paper No. 8, Sussex European Research Centre, Brighton: University of Sussex.

Mattoo, A. and Mavroidis, P.C. (1995) 'The EC–Japan consensus on cars: interaction between trade and competition policy', *The World Economy*, **18** (3).

Maxcy, G. (1981) *The Multinational Motor Industry*, London: Croom Helm.

Moore, L. (1985) *The Growth and Structure of International Trade Since the Second World War*, Brighton: Harvester Wheatsheaf.

Münchau, W. (1996) 'German carmakers warn on jobs', *Financial Times*, 1 February.

Nakamoto, M. (1998) 'Japanese carmakers renew their European offensive', *Financial Times*, 15 January.

OECD (1983) *Long-Term Outlook for the World Automobile Industry*, Paris: OECD.

Owen, N. (1983) *Economies of Scale, Competitiveness and Trade Patterns within the European Community*, Oxford: Oxford University Press.

Pemberton, M. (1991) *Europe's Motor Industry after 1992*, London: Economist Intelligence Unit.

PEP (1950) *Motor Vehicles*, PEP Engineering Reports No. 11, London: Political and Economic Planning, 77.

Pratten, C. (1988) 'A survey of the economies of scale', Study No. 17 in Commission of the European Communities, *Costs of non-Europe: Basic Findings*, vol. 2, *Studies on the Economics of Integration*, Brussels: CEC

Simonian, H. (1995) 'Hard road to higher sales', *Financial Times*, 15 December.

—— (1996a) 'Going global is nothing new', *Financial Times*, *World Motor Industry*, suppl. p. IV, 5 March.

—— (1996b) 'Parts and the big story', *Financial Times*, *Automotive Components*, suppl. p. II, 21 May.

—— (1997a) 'Past reputation helps seal fate of Halewood', *Financial Times*, 17 January.

—— (1997b) 'Competitive pressures have forced two luxury carmakers to move into the minicar market', *Financial Times*, 17 March.

—— (1998) 'LDV–Daewoo deal set for go-ahead this month', *Financial Times*, 17/18 January.

Smith, A. and Venables, A.J. (1991) 'Economic integration and market access', *European Economic Review*, **35**.

Tucker, E. (1996) 'Private car dealers win cross-border sales ruling', *Financial Times*, 16 February.

Tucker, E. and White, D. (1995) 'Seat agrees to cut capacity by 30 per cent', *Financial Times*, 5 October.

Wagstyl, S. and Peel, M. (1997) 'Where are 1,300 people to get jobs?', *Financial Times*, 17 January.

White, L.J. (1971) *The Automobile Industry since 1945*, Cambridge, Mass.: Harvard University Press.

WTO (1995) *Trade Policy Review: European Union*, 2 vols, Geneva: World Trade Organization.

11 Textiles and clothing

In the 1940s and 1950s Britain's textile industry was still in its long retreat from the dominant export position it had held in the nineteenth century and up to the First World War. The wool industry maintained its position as a net exporter, but the cotton industry was fighting a strong rearguard action to protect its home market from the invasion of imports. One of the reasons for acceding to Commonwealth preference with the Ottawa agreements of 1932 was that Britain had hoped to retain its position as an exporter of manufactures to the Commonwealth against competition from Japan. But in the 1950s this system began to go into reverse; imports of cotton textiles from India, Pakistan and Hong Kong increased rapidly under the preferential rate of zero. In 1958 imports of cotton cloth into Britain became greater than exports (Briscoe 1971).

The British textile problem had arisen because of the industrialization of developing countries. Their wage costs were very much lower, and textiles, and to an even greater degree clothing, were labour-intensive industries. Their investment in new machinery meant that in many cases it was more up to date than Britain's. Although the value of the British machinery had been written off and thus did not represent a cost, the old machinery was slower and more apt to develop faults. Furthermore, by working their plant for long hours, developing countries spread the cost of their investment over many units.[1] Lower productivity was not sufficient to offset their cost advantages.

The response of the government was to introduce the Cotton Industry Act of 1959 which provided subsidies for the scrapping of old carding and spinning machines and looms, and also a 25 per cent subsidy on investment in new machines. In addition, the government negotiated in 1959 'voluntary' export restraint agreements with India, Hong Kong, and Pakistan, by which imports from those countries were limited to 175, 164 and 38 million square yards of cotton cloth respectively.

This did not stem the flow of imports. Other countries rushed in to seize their opportunity. The quotas were extended to other developing countries as they in turn expanded their exports to Britain. However, when she joined EFTA in 1959, the UK agreed to remove all restraints on imports of manufactures from other member countries. This led to a rapid increase in imports of textiles, particularly from Portugal and Austria, which she tried to control by means of an 'understanding'. This expansion was regarded as one of the greatest sources of trade creation by the EFTA Secretariat (EFTA 1969). With the restriction on imports from developing countries, this appears to be more of a trade diversion from them to EFTA countries (Moore 1985).

Imports of other products such as cotton yarn increased. More significantly, the restrictions in quantity encouraged the developing countries to increase the unit value of their exports by processing cotton cloth further into clothing. There was a rapid increase in imports of cotton clothing into the UK, with Hong Kong supplying 62 per cent of the value of woven cotton clothing and 73 per cent of knitted clothing in 1963 (Cotton Board 1965). The British government introduced limits on different categories of goods, which the industry hoped would reduce the total.

Thus within ten years there was a complete volte-face in regard to cotton textile imports. Free entry for Commonwealth products was replaced, for those taking advantage of it, by a quota system, the most rigid system of protection. As each attempt to block a particular source encouraged another, the quota system was gradually extended to cover almost all developing and semi-industrialized countries. Global quotas for cotton textiles then encouraged the imports of cloths made of man-made fibres.

The US and other European countries were facing, to a lesser degree, a similar situation and applying similar remedies. In an endeavour to halt this proliferation of quotas GATT introduced, in 1961, a Short Term Arrangement and then, in 1962, a Long Term Arrangement (LTA) for cotton textiles. The LTA permitted the bilateral negotiation of quotas but stated that they should not be less than the actual imports of the previous year and were normally to be increased by 5 per cent a year. Although the LTA violated the main principle of non-discrimination, GATT hoped that its provisions would restrict unbridled protectionism. Under the LTA the EC agreed to increase its very low import quotas by 88 per cent, a development dourly dismissed by a Lancashire millowner as '88 per cent of nowt is nowt'. Britain signed the LTA but was only willing to allow a 1 per cent per annum increase in her import quotas, arguing that she was importing more Asian textiles per head and in proportion to expenditure on clothing than any other country. The British cotton industry was very anxious that other countries should liberalize their imports, hoping that this would reduce the pressure on the British market.

UK textiles manufacturers were in favour of entry into the EC because they thought they would obtain a greater degree of protection from developing countries, although their poor competitive position was shown by a report *Cotton and Allied Textiles*, produced by the Textile Council in 1969. British wages were lower than in the EC, but manufacturers had less modern machinery and productivity was lower, so that yarn production costs in the EC and Austria were 85–90 per cent and in Portugal and the Far East 75–80 per cent of those in the UK in 1969. In weaving, British manufacturers were undercut by a number of EC firms, and costs in Hong Kong, India, Pakistan, and Japan were around 30 per cent lower. Nonetheless, the report stated:

(a) We expect the industry to be internationally competitive by the mid-1970s.

(b) At that point we expect it to be viable subject only to protection against goods imported at prices unrelated to costs, either because of Government subsidies or incentives or dumping;

the UK participating in any international schemes there may be for the regulation of international trade in textile goods.

(c) We therefore envisage a dismantling of the quota arrangements and their replacement by a duty against imports from the Commonwealth of cotton yarn, piecegoods and made-up items, supported by effective measures to provide safequards referred to in (b) above.

(Textile Council 1969: 129)

This was the most thorough survey carried out for any industry prior to entry to the EC. The conclusions, however, do not seem to follow from the findings. They were based on the cotton industry carrying out a much greater level of investment than planned and working the plant for longer, that is, a 'six or seven day operation' (ibid. 70).

The textile manufacturers have always presented their case as if they had a common cause with the clothing producers. This is incorrect; protection in the textile industry raises the price of cloth, the input into the clothing industry. Man-made fibre producers and textile manufacturers were anxious to restrict imports of clothing in order to retain one of the main outlets for their products. They lose market share not only from imports of fabric directly but also from the fabric incorporated into imported clothing.

THE MULTI-FIBRE ARRANGEMENT (MFA)

Developing countries had increased their export earnings, in spite of the LTA, by increasing their exports of items with higher value added such as clothing. They had also increased their exports of textiles with less than 50 per cent cotton, which were not covered by the LTA. The US responded in 1971 by negotiating quotas on imports of man-made fibre textiles and clothing. Once more, GATT endeavoured to control their proliferation, in this case by agreeing to extend the LTA to include most fibres. The Arrangement Regarding International Trade in Textiles – the Multi-Fibre Arrangement (MFA) – came into operation in 1974.

The MFA embraced textiles and clothing of most textile fibres (excluding hard fibres and initially ramie and silk). Bilateral quota agreements were negotiable under it, but were to be expanded by 6 per cent a year. The MFA was subsequently renewed three times, with new versions coming into operation in 1978, 1982, and 1986, and was then extended further in 1991. In 1986 the scope of the Agreement was expanded to cover goods made from silk blends and vegetable fibres.

The EC negotiated quotas in terms of weight of textile yarn and fabric and pieces of most items of clothing, in contrast to the US which negotiated quotas in terms of square yardage. The grouping of products to which the quotas are applied differs between industrialized countries, and has varied over time; in 1984 the EC had 114 categories. Some flexibility was introduced into this system by a 'swing provision' whereby an exporting country could transfer a quota between product categories in the same year, a provision by which up to 10 per cent of the unused portion of its previous year's quota could be 'carried over', and a 'carry forward' provision by which it could utilize up to 5 per cent of the following year's quota.

The EC had to negotiate overall quotas and then to distribute them by agreement between Member States – 'burden sharing' as it was called! With the delay in obtaining statistics and difficulty in negotiating with both Member States and exporters, the EC first reached a bilateral agreement in 1975. Meanwhile, imports into the EC increased by 41 per cent over two years in comparison with a 3 per cent increase for imports into the US. This led the EC to adopt a much more restrictive approach in the next round of negotiations.

The CEC divided products according to 'sensitivity'. The most sensitive products were those in which the developing countries had achieved the highest degree of penetration in the EC market. Group 1 included the most sensitive products, cotton yarn, cotton fabric, fabrics of synthetic fibres, T-shirts, pullovers, trousers including jeans, blouses, and shirts. For each of these categories the growth rate of import quotas was limited to 1–2 per cent per annum. Group 2 included other sensitive products whose market penetration exceeded 20 per cent for the Community as a whole, and for which import quotas were allowed to increase by 4 per cent per annum. The growth rates for Group 3, other textile products, Group 4, other clothing, and Group 5, articles for technical use were set in relation to the degree of market penetration by imports.

The 'burden sharing' was supposed to be arranged so that the EC countries with the lowest level of MFA imports took the greatest proportion of the increase in quotas. Thus, under the formula, Germany with 25.5 per cent and the UK with 21.0 per cent accounted for nearly half the EC total. France had 16.5 per cent, Italy 13.5 per cent, Benelux 9.5 per cent, Spain 7.5 per cent, Denmark 2.7 per cent, Portugal and Greece 1.5 per cent each, and Ireland 0.8 per cent (Silberston 1989: 3).

The number of items covered by quota varied with the individual bilateral arrangements. As a second line of defence, there was also a 'basket mechanism' whereby new restrictions were introduced on imports of a product from a particular country if they were increasing above a certain rate, the relevant rate being lower the more 'sensitive' the product.

When the EC was negotiating for the renewal of the MFA in 1978, under the guise of helping the least developed countries the EC was relatively more 'generous' with its quotas to countries with relatively little productive capacity but *reduced* its quotas for imports from Hong Kong and Taiwan. Again, when the MFA was renewed in 1982, quotas on imports from Hong Kong, South Korea, Macao, and Taiwan were *reduced*.

However, at the same time, the EC concluded a whole series of preferential trade agreements with Mediterranean countries and African Caribbean and Pacific (ACP) countries which had signed the Lomé Agreement under which manufactures from these countries were allowed into the EC market freely.

In addition, there were special provisions for 'outward processing traffic' (OPT). This has generally involved continental EC countries contracting out their more labour-intensive processes to Eastern Europe or what was Yugoslavia. When an EC country exports textiles or clothing to another country for reimportation after further processing, the only tariff imposed is on the value added.

> The EC restrictions [on OPT] are:
>
> (i)   only producers based in Europe can use OPT quotas (buyers are therefore excluded);
>
> (ii)   OPT must be used for the same products which are produced at home (i.e. textile firms cannot do OPT for clothing products); and
>
> (iii)   the fabric used must be produced in Europe.
>
> Individual EC member states define the amount of OPT processing that each firm can carry out . . . [In] Italy each firm can only produce 30% of its sales in OPT, and the authorisation is granted only if the firm's unions agree to the redeployment . . .
>
> In . . . Germany until 1st January 1992 each firm could produce 30% of its sales in OPT in each country in which it had established off-shore production. (Thus each firm could produce 100% of its sales in OPT, as long as production in each country did not exceed 30% of the firm's sales). Since 1992, OPT is no longer linked to the sales of German firms.
>
> (Navaretti *et al.* 1995: 128–9)

In 1989, OPT accounted for 12 per cent of EC imports of clothing (GATT 1991, 1: 193).

This account does not cover all the EC provisions relating to trade in textiles and clothing but it demonstrates its main features, namely, that they involved:

1 A hierarchy of discrimination, in ascending order of restraints:
   (a) barrier-free access for members of the EC and EFTA;
   (b) ACP countries' free access;
   (c) preferential access for Mediterranean countries;
   (d) outward processing provisions;
   (e) tariffs on imports from other industrialized countries; and
   (f) MFA developing countries face VERs and this system has been
        extended to Taiwan; if they are eligible for the GSP, they will face
        no tariffs up to a certain quantitative limit (tariff quota) (CEC 1993:
        65–6).

2 A categorization of imports and grouping according to 'sensitivity'.

This system was to dominate British trade in textiles and clothing after she
entered the EC.

COMPARATIVE INDUSTRIAL STRUCTURE

Before considering the changes that have occurred since Britain joined
the EC and thus became a party to the MFA, let us first consider the
industrial structure of the textile and clothing industries in the main EC
countries.

The British cotton industry, which also spins man-made staple fibres
and weaves man-made and mixture cloths, was, as stated previously, in a
long-term decline. Over the 1960s there were a large number of mergers.
These encompassed horizontal and vertical integration which extended
from the textiles industry to the clothing industry. Much of the takeover
activity was financed or backed by the two large man-made fibre producers,
Courtaulds and ICI, who were anxious to retain the outlet for their products. Courtaulds took over firms directly and ICI financed Viyella
International. Thus by 1968 four firms, Courtaulds, Viyella International,
English Sewing Cotton, and Carrington & Dewhurst, controlled 47 per cent
of the industry's output in spinning (excluding waste spinning), 33 per cent
of its weaving, 20 per cent of its bleaching, 62 per cent of its dyeing and
61 per cent of printing. They also had knitting capacity and manufactured
some clothing (Briscoe 1971). The wool industry did not appear as concentrated, although there was a high degree of vertical integration in the woollen
sector. Production was fluctuating in a slow decline. Less information is
available on the clothing industry although the output appeared to have
increased.

However, the contraction in employment was very clear; in 1950 nearly
a million people were employed in textiles and half a million in clothing in
Great Britain, but by 1969 this had declined to 651,000 in textiles and
390,000 in clothing (ibid. 1971).

Another important feature was the structure of the retail trade. The share of independents in the sale of clothing had fallen from 53 per cent in 1950 to 35 per cent in 1967; this was also their share in the sale of household textiles. Multiples and mail order were becoming increasingly important. Concentration had increased so that the fifteen largest retailers accounted for 40 per cent of the sales of clothing and household textiles. The biggest was Marks & Spencer with 10 per cent (by 1989 this had risen to 16 per cent) and then Great Universal Stores with 4 per cent. These large retailers had the advantage of being able to cut out the wholesalers, whose margin accounted for 13 per cent of the price of the final product (Textile Council 1969). Competition between these retailers was largely on price, but Marks & Spencer has always placed great emphasis on quality. These large retailers were in a very strong bargaining position with respect to both domestic producers and foreign exporters. Marks & Spencer pursued a policy of buying British domestically produced garments, but this involved very tight quality control and some producers resented their degree of dependence on its orders. The author remembers in the mid-1960s a manufacturer of knitted cardigans complaining that Marks & Spencer had taken over their innovation in the fashioning of pockets – their differentiating feature – and that because they were devoting so much of their productive capacity to supplying Marks & Spencer (under its brand name) they were afraid of losing their other customers.

This situation should be compared with that of the two major producers of clothing in the EC – Germany and Italy – whose retail sector was very much less concentrated, with independents accounting for 50–60 per cent of their market. When the MFA was introduced, imports, particularly from LDCs, accounted for a much smaller proportion of their markets.

Another aspect of clothing and furnishing fabrics is the importance of differentiation. In clothing, this is regarded as fashion and in France and Italy was thought of as being determined by the couture houses who designed new garments for the very wealthy. However, in Britain, design had been identified in the 1950s and 1960s as being a weakness in production and great efforts had been made in educational and training courses to remedy this. There was an explosion in British design and fashion, largely directed at the younger generation. The author remembers a manager at Montague Burton's large clothing plant at Leeds expressing profound relief that the Beatles wore suits. Many well-established British manufacturers of high-quality garments were very slow to adapt to any fashion changes, but the street scene was vibrant. Exports more than doubled between 1961–63 and 1967–68 (Briscoe 1971). Another development was the increasing use of casual clothes such as jeans, track suits, and T-shirts; this was partly the Americanization of fashion, which arrived earlier in Britain than in the rest of the EC. In many cases it also represented the increasing use of circular knitted fabric.

Thus the clothing industries in the three countries were pointing in different directions. It has been argued by Steedman and Wagner that in

Britain the result of the domination of the market by large retailers meant a concentration by the industry on long runs of standardized products; in women's outerwear, a run of 15,000 garments is quoted (Steedman and Wagner 1989: 41). Garment manufacturers had difficulty in producing smaller runs of the higher-quality items because there was a shortage of machinists with sufficient skill to make them or to make a rapid transition from one style to another. Hence British manufacturers tended to be in direct competition with imports from low-wage countries. Britain imported low-priced garments and exported higher-priced ones, but the latter were not as expensive as German exports.

The West German industry responded to this competition from low-wage countries by abandoning the production of the cheaper items; by 1987, imports of clothing constituted 60 per cent of retail sales. The government was reluctant to protect and subsidize it. The German clothing industry pursued a policy of concentrating on high-quality production, which it found possible because of its superior system of training and greater investment. In women's outerwear the typical length of run was 150–300 garments. The manufacturers made great use of OPT provisions for their more labour-intensive operations, generally in Poland or Yugoslavia (Steedman and Wagner 1989). The value of West German clothing exports has been greater than that of Britain since 1973 and was increasing faster in the 1980s (Moore 1991).

Italy was an even larger exporter. Her clothing industry also went up market, aiming for a high degree of variety. But its production was organized in a very decentralized fashion, with the retailer or manufacturer transferring production to small subcontractors while keeping control over finance and marketing. This enabled them to avoid the heavy social security contributions and tax.

In both Italy and Germany, per capita expenditure on clothing was very much higher than in Britain. In each case the fortunes of the clothing industry were important to the textile industry as it was its major customer. The hosiery industry represented a halfway house in so far as knitting was generally combined with garment making; knitted fabrics are more difficult to handle than woven ones because they are less dimensionally stable.

ENTRY INTO THE EC

As stated in Chapter 4, entry into the EC meant that Britain abandoned Commonwealth preference and placed the common external tariff (CET) on imports from non-member countries who were not members of any of the association agreements such as that of the ACP and EFTA. Therefore, her major suppliers in Asia faced a tariff although this was waived for limited quantities of goods for countries that had signed MFA agreements with the EC and were entitled to the generalized system of preference (GSP). There are other constraints, as Bangladesh discovered when in 1997 she faced the withdrawal of 7,000 licences issued under the GSP for exports of T-shirts to the EU because they were made with non-Bangladeshi yarn (Wolffe 1997).

In addition, in so far as the quotas under the MFA were set for individual categories of goods and extended to cover those of man-made fibres, it represented a much greater degree of restriction on her traditional developing country suppliers than existed before.

Thus under the MFA the EC placed the most stringent barriers on imports from the cheapest sources. As can be seen from Table 11.1, wage and labour costs were very much lower in developing countries than in industrial countries. Information is only available for textiles in 1980 and Britain's costs per operator hour appeared about the middle of the EC range, with those of Greece and Portugal very much lower. However, costs in Asian developing countries appeared lower still, except for Hong Kong. By 1991 the average cost per operator hour in textiles was higher in Hong Kong, South Korea, Taiwan, and Thailand than in Portugal, but still well below that of the larger EC countries. Mill operation was greater, indicating a more efficient use of capital. The missing information is on productivity; but in Hong Kong, South Korea and Taiwan it appears comparable to that in the fully industrialized countries, and in other developing countries it may be lower but no so much lower that it outweighs their advantage in low wages.

Labour costs are even more important for clothing where they account for 80 per cent of the cost of assembly (Silberston 1989: 65). As can be seen from Table 11.1, labour costs per hour were higher in Hong Kong, South Korea and Taiwan than in Portugal, but those of the other Asian countries and the listed Latin American ones were much lower. Silberston's data for the manufacture of cotton shirts (see Table 11.2) show that South Korea and Hong Kong had lower costs that Portugal, followed by Britain, and with West Germany the most expensive.

To summarize diverse sources of information, even allowing for differences in productivity and quality all the evidence showed that the developing countries' costs of production in textiles and clothing were lower than those of the EC countries. Portugal's wages were lower than those of the three most advanced developing countries, but her total costs of production did not appear to be lower (Silberston 1984, 1989; Moore 1991). The question, then, is the degree to which the MFA has led to trade diversion with quotas, as described in Chapter 3.

Quotas are only *effective* in so far as they reduce imports below the level they would be in their absence. Clearly, this is somewhat difficult to ascertain. But this is regarded as occurring when either (a) there is a high degree of quota utilization, or (b) producers are willing to pay for the right to export, that is, there is a premium on the quota. This will vary from year to year according to how fashionable or 'hot' the product is.

Some idea of the restrictiveness of the quotas can be obtained from Table 11.3, which shows the utilization of quotas at 98 per cent and over in

Table 11.1   Cost comparisons in the textile and clothing industry (US$)

Country	Textiles Average cost per operator hour 1980 Total	1991 Total	1991 Direct wages	Mill operation 1991 Hours/year	Clothing Labour cost 1991 per hour
European Union					
UK	5.75	10.2	8.14	6438	7.99
East Germany		9.1	6.57	4000	
West Germany	10.16	17.0	11.00	6334	14.81
France	7.91	12.6	7.17	7008	12.41
Netherlands	11.68	18.1	10.55	6558	14.95
Italy	9.12	17.3	8.51	6841	13.50
Ireland	5.13	8.8	6.92	6574	7.50
Belgium	11.82	17.4	9.08	6966	12.57
Denmark	9.12	18.3	14.96	6523	15.91
Greece	3.49	5.7	4.05	6159	4.26
Portugal	1.68	3.2	2.10	6147	2.65
Spain	4.90	7.7	4.74	7550	7.11
Asia					
Hong Kong*	1.91	3.4	2.92	8104	3.39
South Korea*	0.78	3.6	2.61	8406	2.75
Taiwan*	1.26	5.0	3.78	8513	3.74
India*	0.60	0.6	0.38	8304	0.25
Indonesia*		0.3	0.21	8496	0.18
Malaysia*		1.0	0.59	7128	0.62
Pakistan*	0.34	0.4	0.24	7600	0.24
Philippines*		0.7	0.52	7776	0.46
Sri Lanka*		0.4	0.34	8288	0.39
Thailand*	0.33	5.0	3.78	8513	0.59
China*		0.3	0.25	6885	0.24
Japan	4.35	16.4	9.40	6587	7.44
US	6.37	10.3	8.05	7373	6.77
Turkey	0.95				
Latin America					
Brazil*		1.5	0.96	7599	0.76
Mexico	3.10	2.8	1.52	7092	1.17
Argentina*	3.33	2.4	1.49	7261	1.81
Peru*		1.3	0.94	7054	0.88
Uruguay	0.89	2.1	1.25	6804	1.59
Venezuela		1.7	1.11	7225	1.38

Source: Werner International.

Note: *EU restricts imports from them under the MFA or equivalent arrangements (see M. Majmudar (1996) 'Trade liberalisation in clothing', *Development Policy Review*, March.

Table 11.2 Cost of cotton shirt production (DM per piece)

	UK	West Germany	Portugal	South Korea	Hong Kong
Raw material	9.34	9.19	8.53	7.48	7.78
Direct and indirect labour	3.21	4.36	1.43	1.05	0.80
Depreciation	0.40	0.35	0.30	0.26	0.22
Other manufacturing expenses	1.02	1.27	1.08	0.70	0.78
Total manufacturing cost	13.97	15.17	11.34	9.49	9.58

Source: Z.A. Silberston (1989) *The Future of the Multi-Fibre Arrangement*, London: HMSO, p. 65.

1986. This is an extremely high rate which, in practice, it is difficult to achieve. Nonetheless, as can be seen, it was achieved by at least one of the four Far Eastern producers – Hong Kong, South Korea, Taiwan, and Macao – for many products, and also by other countries in Asia and Eastern Europe. The first eight 'sensitive' products appeared to be the ones for which the largest number of countries are up against the restraints. Silberston also showed the very high levels of quota utilization by the main quota holders for the eight 'sensitive' products between 1983 and 1988 (Silberston 1989: 131).

Quota premia are more difficult to obtain. Hamilton (1988) estimated that the average quota premium for textile and clothing exports to the EC was 14 per cent during 1980–84. Silberston (1989) calculated that in 1988 these premia amounted to up to 26 per cent of the export price for shirts for the EC market. But the quota premia for exports from Pakistan appear much higher, varying between 50 per cent of the export price of clothing and cloth to 80 per cent for knitwear (Chaudhry and Hamid 1988). Hong Kong is the only country which has systematically auctioned its quotas. Some information on them is given in Table 11.4.

However, apart from these indications of the direct effects of quotas there is also the effect on trade. In spite of restriction by MFA quotas import penetration in the clothing industry increased from 25 per cent of the value of consumption in 1978 to 39 per cent in 1988. Silberston has illustrated the effect of successive MFAs on the pattern of imports (see Table 11.5). Trade diversion is indicated by the increase in the proportion supplied by the EC to 40 per cent (although some of it appears to be at the expense of EFTA countries), and the decline in the proportion supplied by developing countries. In particular, the proportion supplied by Hong Kong, which was the most restricted, declined from 31 per cent under the MFA 1974–77 to 20 per cent in 1987. But the proportion supplied by the other LDCs increased from 21 per cent to 29 per cent over the same period.

This represented another form of trade diversion from the countries who found themselves most restricted by their quotas, particularly Hong Kong,

Table 11.3 Effective limitation on imports into Britain due to VERs – utilization of quotas 98% and greater in 1986

Category description		Four Far Eastern producers[1]	Others
1	Cotton yarn not for retail sale		Turkey, Egypt, Peru
2	Woven cotton fabrics	H.K., S. Korea, Taiwan	Turkey, Thailand, Peru, USSR, GDR
3	Woven synthetic fabrics	Taiwan, S. Korea	Portugal, Brazil, China
4	Knitted shirts etc.	H.K., S. Korea, Taiwan, Macao	Thailand, India, Pakistan, Philippines, China, Czech.
5	Knitted sweaters	H.K., S. Korea, Taiwan, Macao	Portugal, Thailand, China, Romania, Philippines, Poland, Turkey, Pakistan, Bulgaria
6	Woven trousers and men's shorts	H.K., Macao	Portugal, Cyprus, China, Thailand, Hungary
7	Woven/knitted blouses	H.K., Macao	Cyprus
8	Men's woven shirts	H.K., S. Korea	Portugal, China, Romania, Yugoslavia, Thailand
9	Cotton terry towelling		China, Czech.
10	Knitted gloves	Taiwan	
12	Knitted socks, stockings	S. Korea, Taiwan	Thailand
13	Knitted underpants	S. Korea, H.K.	Turkey
14A	Men's woven coated coats	Taiwan	
14B	Men's woven coats		Hungary, Poland, GDR
15A	Women's woven coated coats	S. Korea	
15	Women's coats	H.K.	Czech.
16	Men's woven suits	H.K., Taiwan, Macao	Thailand, Hungary, GDR
17	Men's woven jackets		Hungary, GDR
18	Men's other woven underwear	Taiwan	China, Czech.
19	Woven handkerchiefs		China, Czech.
20	Woven bedlinen		Portugal, Spain, Romania
21	Parkas, anoraks, windcheaters	H.K., S. Korea	Thailand, China
22	Spun synthetic yarn	S. Korea	Spain, Romania, Thailand
24	Knitted pyjamas/ nightgowns	H.K., Taiwan	Romania, Thailand
26	Woven/knitted dresses	Taiwan, Macao	China, Poland
27	Woven/knitted skirts	H.K., Macao	China
28	Knitted trousers	H.K., S. Korea, Taiwan	
29	Women's woven suits	H.K., Taiwan	

Source: Department of Trade and Industry.

Note: [1]Hong Kong (H.K.), S. Korea, Taiwan, Macao.

Table 11.4 Hong Kong quota premia on clothing exports to the UK in 1983 and 1988

Category		Hong Kong $ per garment				Percentage quota premium	
		Export price		Quota premium			
		1983 c.i.f.	*1988*	*1983*	*1988*	*1983 (5)/(3) %*	*1988 (6)/(4) %*
(1)	*(2)*	*(3)*	*(4)*	*(5)*	*(6)*	*(7)*	*(8)*
4	Knitted and T-shirts	17.49	17.12	2.42	3.00	13.8	17.5
5	Sweaters	33.11	71.51	3.17	14.99	9.6	21.0
6	Woven trousers	37.62	50.31	5.58	5.06	14.9	10.0
7	Blouses	28.93	52.71	2.92	3.58	10.3	6.8
8	Men's woven shirts	22.33	43.67	3.33	11.49	14.8	26.3
26	Dresses	49.17		0.83		1.8	
27	Skirts	35.53	61.94	2.08	9.88	5.9	16.0
28	Knitted trousers	25.74		3.75		14.5	

Sources: Z.A. Silberston (1984) *The Multi-Fibre Arrangement and the UK Economy*, London: HMSO, p. 30, (1989) *The Future of the Multi-Fibre Arrangement*, London: HMSO, p. 57.

Table 11.5 Shares of UK import market for clothing[1] (by value)

	MFA I 1974–1977 average (%)	MFA II 1978–1982 average (%)	MFA III 1983–1986 average (%)	MFA IV 1987 (%)	1994
EC (10)	26	29	35	33 ⎱	27
EC entrants[2]	5	5	6	7 ⎰	
EFTA	8	6	5	4	s & s2
Other OECD[3]	6	7	7	4	
All OECD	45	47	53	48	
Hong Kong	31	25	22	20	
Other LDCs	21	25	22	29	
All LDCs	52	50	44	49	
CPE[4]	3	3	3	3	
Total	100	100	100	100	

Sources: Z.A. Silberston (1989) *The Future of the Multi-Fibre Arrangement*, London: HMSO, p. 26; WTO (1996) *International Trade 1995*, Geneva: WTO.

Notes:
[1]SITC Division 84; [2]Spain and Portugal; [3]Including Israel; [4]Centrally planned economies.
s & sSweden and Switzerland

to other developing countries. Asian countries, for instance, regarded themselves as having gained from this. The EC has also agreed to be more 'generous' with its quotas for the poorest countries; Bangladesh, for instance, does not face any quotas. This process has been assisted by the movement of businessmen from Hong Kong and other quota-restricted countries to set up clothing firms in Singapore, Macao, Thailand, Malaysia, Sri Lanka, and

Mauritius (Silberston 1984: 23). It has also been assisted by the concentration of retailing activities in the UK, with the large retailers taking over many of the design functions and thus being in a position to search Asia for cheap venues for production; Marks & Spencer has also been willing to provide technical assistance. The overall effect has been the reduction in the proportion of clothing imports supplied by Hong Kong.

The effect of EC entry and the MFA on the British textile and clothing industries

For textiles the changes in the absolute quantities of production, consumption and trade in textiles from 1973 to 1988 are shown in Table 11.6. It is clear that the British textiles producers did not benefit from entry in so far as their production – that is, of cotton, man-made fibre and wool yarns, woven cotton, man-made and wool cloth, and knitted fabric – declined at each stage of manufacture. Production declined more than consumption because of the increase in net imports (imports – exports). Almost all the increase in imports came from EC countries. The only appreciable increase in imports from MFA countries was 174 million square metres of man-made fibre cloth. Imports of woven cotton fabric from MFA countries actually declined.

Only the consumption of man-made fabric increased. In terms of total fabric consumption this appears to have been offset by the decline in consumption of other fabrics. Adding up the fabric items in column three

Table 11.6 UK changes in production, consumption, imports and exports of textiles, 1973–88

MFA category	1973–88 quantity change in				Increase in quantity of imports from		
	Produc-tion	Consump-tion	Exports	Imports	EC(8)[1]	EC(11)	MFA countries
Cotton yarn mkg	−71.7	−12.1	−10.0	49.6	19.1	28.6	2.7
Spun mmf[2] yarns mkg	−66.2	−27.0	−3.5	35.7	18.3		3.9
Wool yarns mkg	−58.3	−44.1	−4.4	9.8	7.4		0.3
Woven cotton fabric msq metres	−271.0	−97.0	−8.0	182.0	131.9		−41.8
Woven mmf[2] msq metres	−261.0	178.0	67.0	506.0	250.7	255.3	174.3
Wool fabrics msq metres	−86.0	−51.0	−22.0	13.0	11.7	11.7	
Knitted fabrics mkg	−44.0	−31.0	−6.0	7.0	4.0	4.0	0.3

Source: Data from Z.A. Silberston (1984) *The Multi-Fibre Arrangement and the UK Economy*, London: (1989):HMSO, *The Future of the Multi-Fibre Arrangement*, London: HMSO.

Notes: [1]EC(8) Denmark excluded from 1973 for all except wool yarns; [2]mmf = man-made fibres.

of Table 11.6, between 1973 and 1988 the changes in consumption were (178 man-made fibre minus 97 cotton minus 51 wool) million square metres minus 31 mkg knitted fabric. This is negative assuming that an average square metre of knitted fabric weighs considerably less than one kilogram. The reduction in the consumption of fabric is due to the increasing net imports of clothing.

Figure 11.1 shows that clothing output has tended to fluctuate. The output of hosiery, which has tended to decline, is also shown. But there has been a steady increase in consumption, that is, expenditure in real terms on clothing. This is partly due to a fall in the real price of clothing, that is, the price index for clothing and footwear rose more slowly than the retail price index. This, in turn, appeared to be due to the increase in the relative amount of imports, which are lower priced than home production, and also, Silberston suggested, to reductions in the margins of wholesalers and retailers (Silberston 1989). In 1994 imports had reached 58 per cent of home demand; 27 per cent of these imports came from other EU countries and 52 per cent from Asia. Asian producers therefore accounted for 30 per cent of British consumption. On the other hand, 41 per cent of the sales of UK producers were for export, with 77 per cent of them going to other Western European countries (WTO 1995b; CSO 1996).

An additional consumer expenditure was on household textiles such as sheets, towels, and furnishing fabrics (see Figure 11.2). Expenditure on these in real terms started to increase rapidly after the mid-1980s. Textile production

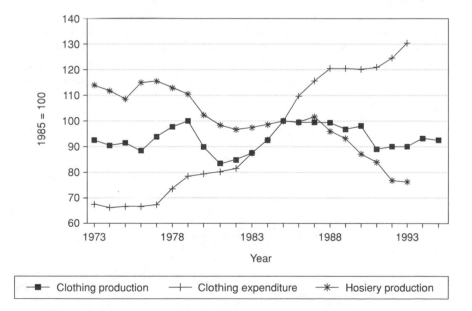

Figure 11.1 Clothing production and expenditure, 1973–95

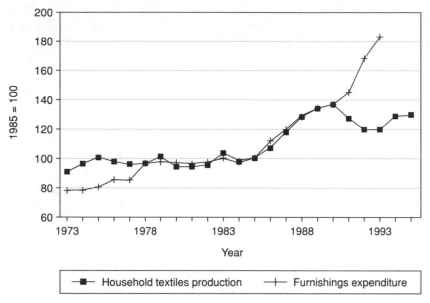

Figure 11.2 Soft furnishings production and expenditure, 1973–95

of these 'made-ups' has fluctuated, but recently has not increased as fast as expenditure. These are more difficult to identify in international trade.

The output of the textile industries from 1973 to 1995 with hosiery included again is shown in Figure 11.3. There was a sharp decline in production of yarn, cloth and carpets between 1973 and 1981. This was partly due to a decline in consumption, and also, for cotton and spun man-made fibre yarn, to a more than doubling in the quantity of imports. Then production appeared to stabilize until the late 1980s, after which the production of cotton yarn continued its sharp decline. Entry to the EC may have enabled UK manufacturers to gain greater protection against developing countries, but they also faced greater competition from other EC manufacturers. In 1994 the import penetration ratio for textiles was 44 per cent; on the other hand, 32 per cent of textile sales were for export. More than two-thirds of this trade was with other Western European countries.

Costs and benefits for the UK economy

Economists and consumer groups have been concerned with the cost of the MFA to the final consumer, in keeping prices of clothing and household goods above what they would otherwise have been, in comparison with any benefits that arose from maintaining employment in the industry. The MFA was such a complicated edifice, restricting trade at three different

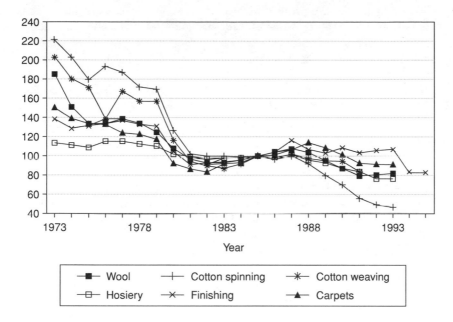

Figure 11.3 Textile production, 1973–95

levels of manufacturing – that is, of yarn, cloth, and clothing – that its effect on prices is difficult to calculate. But Silberston in his report of 1984 estimated that its removal would lead to an average fall in import prices of 11 per cent. He then assumed that the present distributive margin of 100 per cent would not fall proportionally, so that there would a 5 per cent reduction in prices. He retained this assumption in his 1989 report. The value of retail sales of clothing and household textiles in 1988 he took as £17bn in 1988. A 5 per cent reduction in this amounts to £860m and allowing for an increase in consumption due to the lower price leads to his calculation that the gain in consumer surplus at 1988 prices would be £870m. Then, by adding price saving in intermediate products he made this up to £980 million. Most of the reduction in employment in the UK textile and clothing industries was due to an increase in productivity. The effect of the liberalization of the MFA would be greater the greater the elasticity of supply of the industries considered. Silberston's highest estimate was a loss of 33,000 jobs in the UK industries, which means that the cost of retaining the MFA worked out at £29,700 per worker per year, compared with average annual earnings in 1988 of £8,500 in textiles and £7,650 in clothing. 'Every job saved therefore costs the consumer three or four times as much as each textile and clothing worker earns' (Silberston 1989: 122). The MFA was therefore a grossly inefficient form of redistribution from consumers to workers.

Thus in Britain MFA protection has not maintained the output of the textile industry; the picture is one of trade diversion towards other EC member countries. This has also occurred in clothing. Moreover, there appears to have been some trade diversion from Hong Kong, the most heavily restricted country, to other LDCs.

The EC also funded some research into labour-saving technology so that the EC clothing industry could compete better with low-wage countries. This was under BRITE (Basic Research in Industrial Technologies in Europe) which is:

> 'aimed entirely at process technologies, not product development'. In the first phase of this programme in 1985, machine-makers in the clothing industry received financial support to the extent of 50 million DM for developing 'new manufacturing techniques for non-stable material'. The largest project in this area [was] the collaboration between German sewing-machine maker Pfaff with the British robot producer GEC and the British textiles group Courtaulds. The aim [was] to innovate robotic technology that [would] successfully automate the labour-intensive sewing operations.
>
> (Mitter 1992: 4).

In general, the use of automation and dedicated machines is only economically feasible for long runs of production. They have been used in Britain on men's shirts. Some German shirt manufacturers were reported as having used them in the 1970s but then abandoned them in the 1980s as they moved to small batches of high-fashion men's shirts and ladies blouses (Steedman and Wagner 1989). GATT disapproved of this endeavour to obliterate the comparative advantage of LDCs.

When the SEM came into effect in 1993, individual country quotas were supposedly replaced by EU quotas. But only in 1995 were UK national import licences replaced by EC ones, so that products now coming in under quota can circulate freely throughout the EU.[2]

PRESENT TRADE ARRANGEMENTS

The EU uses four instruments to restrict and monitor trade:
1   With respect to monitoring for those countries not facing quotas there is a system of surveillance so that importers have to obtain export licences in their applications for import licences.
2   Certificates of origin are required for all countries except Turkey (Majmudar 1996: 42–3). However, consumers are not provided with this information and therefore cannot benefit from it. These are just administrative barriers to trade.

3   There are tariffs which are relatively high compared with other manufactures, that is, 0–25 per cent for non-preferential sources of supply. Tariffs on textiles and clothing are also to be reduced.

4   It is the MFA quotas, however, which represent the greatest restriction on trade. The EC has, in 1996, 163 product categories.[3] These products are then placed into groups, IB, IIB, or IIIB, for clothing according to their 'sensitivity', or level of import penetration. The most sensitive clothing products, that is, those in Group IB are, with the category number given in brackets, T-shirts (4), pullovers (5), trousers (6), blouses (7), and shirts (8). The EU quotas for individual exporting countries in 1996 are shown in Table 11.7. For the dominant supplying countries (Hong Kong, South Korea, Taiwan, and China), product categories are also classified by fibre blends, with separate quantity restraints sometimes being applied to each type. There are some separate quotas for children's clothing and, in addition, five children's garments can be substituted for three adult ones. Some flexibility also remains in the system with 'swing', 'carried over', and 'carry forward provisions' (Majmudar 1996).

In addition, the special provisions for 'outward processing traffic' (OPT) have been reinforced by the European Agreements discussed below.

Under the WTO Agreement on Textiles and Clothing negotiated as part of the Uruguay Round, these MFA quotas are due to be gradually phased out from 1 January 1995 and eliminated by 2005. This is to be carried out in three stages based on the quantity of imports in 1990. An importing country can choose the categories to be integrated subject to the proviso that they must be selected from each of the following groups:

●   tops and yarns;
●   fabrics;
●   made-up textile products; and
●   clothing.

Liberalization takes the form of the complete removal of quotas on the one hand, and an acceleration in the rate of expansion of the remaining quotas on the other. Let us call the previously negotiated growth rate of products still covered by quotas G. The timetable comprises:

●   **Stage 1**   Beginning on 1 January 1995, 16 per cent of textiles and clothing trade in volume terms came under normal world trade rules, and the quotas of the remaining products are to increase by 16 per cent a year for the next three successive years, that is, by (G x 1.16) per cent per annum.

●   **Stage 2**   Beginning on 1 January 1998, an additional 17 per cent of trade must be completely liberalized and the remaining quotas must be increasing by 25 per cent in each of the next four successive years, that is, by (G × 1.16 × 1.25) per cent per annum.

- **Stage 3**   Beginning on 1 January 2002, an additional 18 per cent of 1990 trade must be completely liberalized. Remaining quotas must be increased at a rate at least 27 per cent higher than under stage 2 in each of the following three years, that is, by (G × 1.16 × 1.25 × 1.27) per cent per annum.
- **Stage 4**   End of transition – beginning on 1 January 2005, all quotas abolished (Khanna 1994).

Under the Textiles and Clothing Protocol of the Europe Agreements with the Central and Eastern European countries (CEECs), Bulgaria, the Czech Republic, Hungary, Poland, Romania and Slovakia:

For textiles and clothing import duties on CEEC output will be abolished over six years and those on outward processing trade – whereby CEEC producers receive materials from an EC firm, process them and return

Table 11.7   EU quotas for clothing imports in Group IB in 1996 (1,000 pieces)

Country	T-shirts Cat.(4)	Pullovers Cat.(5)	Trousers Cat.(6)	Blouses Cat.(7)	Shirts Cat.(8)
Belarus	671	570	298	400	297
Brazil	36,792		3,827		
Bulgaria		5,185	2,500	1,909	5,662
China	75,243	23,586	24,787	11,888	16,705
Czech Republic	8,106	4,362	4,392	1,740	5,641
Hong Kong	45,793	35,729	63,015	36,861	53,767
			(6a) 52,898		
Hungary	12,252	6,341	4,984	2,898	3,416
India	55,221	29,000	7,343	57,268	41,048
Indonesia	36,332	28,538	10,351	7,624	11,995
Macao	13,257	12,383	13,355	5,204	7,288
Malaysia	11,911	5,530	7,006	30,374	7,275
Pakistan	23,757	6,281	25,596	15,390	5,027
Philippines	19,044	9,114	7,935	5,042	6,061
Poland	25,199	9,395	6,848		4,820
Romania	29,568	19,212	8,919	2,332	11,404
Russia	2,505	1,588	2,788	785	2,392
Singapore	21,606	12,273	12,483	10,583	7,173
Slovak Republic	3,497	3,767	3,396	1,309	3,668
South Korea	14,721	33,869	5,729	9,639	31,808
Sri Lanka			7,379	11,429	9,346
Taiwan	10,701	20,876	5,450	3,353	8,879
Thailand	29,956	21,132	7,616	7,129	4,396
Ukraine	1,500	1,200	1,100	500	800
Vietnam	4,345	1,680	2,749	140	8,339

Source: Data supplied by CEC Directorate-General 1, 10 June 1996.

them to the same firm – immediately. Quantitative restrictions will be removed in not less than five years and not more than half the time agreed in the Uruguay Round for the abolition of the MFA.

(Winters and Wang 1994: 35)

This means that in comparison with the MFA developing countries the CEEC countries receive preferential treatment. EU textile and clothing imports from the latter are reported as having risen threefold in the last five years. Nonetheless, in only two out of the eighty-nine categories covered by quotas are the CEECs anywhere near filling them. Indeed, the CEC is considering scrapping them to save on paperwork. The OPT provisions are the most important. In 1993 they accounted for 10 per cent of extra-EU's imports of clothing, with Germany importing 60 per cent of it. In Germany in 1995, 72 per cent of her textile exports to Eastern Europe and 86 per cent of her clothing imports back were part of this traffic (WTO 1995a, 1: 101; Luesby 1997).

In respect to the phasing out of the MFA the industrialized countries are dragging their feet; the US, the EU and Canada have started with products not currently subject to import restraints (which at the moment account for a third of imports). The EU has not so far issued its future plan for liberalization. At the moment the EU restrains more products, and generally restricts the growth of these quotas from the dominant suppliers (i.e. Taiwan, China, and Hong Kong) to 0–2 per cent per annum, whereas it is more liberal with respect to its imports of clothing from Thailand, the Philippines, and some from India, allowing quotas to grow by 6–7 per cent. Bangladesh faces no quotas.

In September 1996 there was a fierce reaction by British textile producers to the proposal of the CEC, at the behest of Eurocoton, the trade body, to impose anti-dumping duties of between 3 per cent and 36 per cent on imports of undyed cotton fabric from India, Pakistan, Indonesia, China, Taiwan and Egypt, who were said to be undercutting German, French and Italian weavers by between 28–36 per cent. Little cotton fabric is now produced in Europe – just over a fifth of the amount imported. The UK producers dye, print and finish the fabric, most of which goes into home furnishings, and are very anxious that their costs should not be raised as they are already facing increasing competition from imports, as can be seen from Figure 11.2. Egypt and India in particular are investing in finishing capacity (Luesby 1996). Provisional duties were imposed for six months in 1996, but they had to be scrapped when the Council of Ministers did not agree to them in May 1997; their decision was queried by the French President Chirac. There was uproar when, a few months later, the European Commission moved to open a *third* investigation into the dumping of unbleached cotton from six Asian countries. Textile importers, wholesalers, the Europewide consumer organization Beuc, and some MEPs began to combine to oppose it (Buckley 1997).

The EU is also endeavouring to use the inducement of greater access to its market as a lever to open markets for its own exports (Majmudar 1996). The EU clothing *firms* are also beginning to show interest in further liberalization. The larger ones often supply their more inexpensive brands from producing units, which they may not own, in Asia. They may supply the design and the material according to the location. But since some of the fastest growing markets are in Asia, they now appear to be willing to locate clothing production in a developing country provided that they gain in return some access for their up-market products into that country.

But the leading textile and clothing exporters, including India, Pakistan, Indonesia, Thailand, Malaysia, Philippines, Argentina and Brazil, have not agreed to a trade liberalization pact that would include the removal of their trade barriers as a quid pro quo for the EU reducing quotas on sensitive products (Southey 1996). Why should they accede to conditions being attached to the implementation of a WTO international agreement that has already been ratified!

In Britain, plans for relocation in response to the phasing out of the MFA (and maybe the introduction of a minimum wage) are already being put into operation. The unions say that British industry rates are based on a guaranteed minimum of around £3 an hour, which is generally raised to £4 with productivity pay. This compares with the 62p an hour earned by Moroccan clothing workers. They fear a loss of 50,000 jobs in the textile and footwear industry by the end of the decade. Coats Viyella is planning to close twelve UK factories and double its non-UK production to 40 per cent. Courtaulds is planning to increase overseas production from 20 per cent to 30 per cent, Claremonts from 15 per cent to 20 per cent, and Dewhirsts from 25 per cent to 50 per cent (Halsall 1996).

However, the informal sector of the clothing industry, consisting of small firms farming out work to individual homeworkers, appears to be thriving. It is used to supply the retailers with high-fashion relatively low-priced garments. Work is seasonal and, during peak periods, needed very quickly. It is estimated that in London alone there are 30,000 to 40,000 homeworkers, largely Asian women from Pakistan and Bangladesh, dependent on such work because of family responsibilities and lack of knowledge of English (Bowman 1992). These workers are not generally included in the official statistics.

CONCLUSION

Britain began erecting a protective system of quotas on imports when her cotton textile producers found they could no longer compete with those from India, Pakistan, and Hong Kong. This was extended over time, and then, as an EC Member State, she automatically became party to the MFA. The EC negotiated a quota system of Byzantine complexity to restrict imports from developing countries. Trade diversion occurred as Britain's imports from the rest of the EC increased. The UK's output of most textile products continued to fall. The cost of the MFA to Britain in terms of lost consumer surplus is three to four times the benefits derived from employing extra workers. Thus it is from an economic point of view very inefficient. It is also very regressive in so far as common items of clothing are the most severely restricted.

The only advantage British firms have in the production of clothing with respect to imports from the low-waged LDCs is in their rapid response to changing requirements. With the larger firms this appears to be dependent on their use of EPOS. With the small firms and subcontractors it depends on their flexibility and use of homeworkers.

NOTES

1   John Bowen has told me that at least one company (Coats) exported fully depreciated second-hand machinery from the UK to India, thus further lowering costs in the latter.
2   DTI Notice to Importers 2490; Imports of Restricted Textiles – 1996 Arrangements.
3   But the textile agreement includes products which were not included in the original MFA agreement; thus the importing countries have been able to water down the initial stages of liberalization by proffering products which had not been restricted.

REFERENCES

Bowman, S. (1992) 'New openings for women in the UK: design and craft for computer-aided retailing', in S. Mitter (ed.) *Computer-aided Manufacturing and Women's Employment*, London: Springer-Verlag.

Briscoe, L. (1971) *The Textile and Clothing Industries of the United Kingdom*, Manchester: Manchester University Press.

Buckley, N. (1997) 'Commission faces fight on cotton "dumping"', *Financial Times*, 2 December.

Choudhry and Hamid (1988) 'Foreign trade barriers and export-led growth', in Asia Development Bank, *Bangladesh Today*. Manila: ADB.

CEC (1993) 'The European Community as a world trade partner', *European Economy*, **52**.

Cotton Board (1965) *Quarterly Statistical Review*, Manchester: Cotton Board.

CSO (1996) *Annual Abstract of Statistics*, London: Central Statistical Office, table 12.2.

DTI (n.d.) *Bulletin of Textile and Clothing Statistics*, Department of Trade and Industry, London: HMSO.

EFTA (1969) *The Effects of EFTA on the Economies of Member States*, Geneva: EFTA.

GATT (1991) *Trade Policy Review: European Communities*, Geneva: GATT.

Halsall, M. (1996) '50,000 jobs in textiles could go overseas', *Guardian*, 13 September.

Hamilton, C.B. (1988) in E.R. Baldwin, C.B. Hamilton and A. Sapir (eds) *Issues in US–EC Trade Relations*, Chicago: University of Chicago Press.

Khanna, S.R. (1994) 'The new GATT Agreement: implications for the world's textile and clothing industries', *Textile Outlook International*, March.

Luesby, J. (1996) 'Textile makers warn on anti-dumping move', *Financial Times*, 17 September.

—— (1997) 'EU may scrap redundant clothing and fabric quotas', *Financial Times*, 9 May.

Majmudar, M. (1996) 'The MFA phase-out and EU clothing sourcing: forecasts to 2005', *Textile Outlook International*, March.

Mandelbaum, J. (1992) 'Competitiveness of the Mexican textile chain', *Textile Outlook International*, November.

Mitter, S. (ed.) (1992) with assistance from Anneke van Luijken, *Computer-aided Manufacturing and Women's Employment: The Clothing Industry in four EC Countries*, for Directorate-General Employment, Social Affairs and Education of the European Communities, June 1990, London: Springer-Verlag.

Moore, L. (1985) *The Growth and Structure of International Trade Since the Second World War*, Brighton: Harvester Wheatsheaf.

—— (1991) 'International trade in textiles and clothing', in *Journal of the Textile Institute*, **82** (2).

—— (1994) 'Protection and competition in the US market for textiles and clothing', *Journal of the Textile Institute*, **85** (2).

Navaretti, G.B., Faina, R. and Silberston, A. (1995) *Beyond the Multi-Fibre Arrangement: Third World Competition and Restructuring Europe's Textile Industry*, Paris: OECD.

NCC (1990) 'Textiles and clothes', Working Paper No. 2, International Trade and the Consumer series. London: National Consumer Council.

Silberston, Z.A. (1984) *The Multi-Fibre Arrangement and the UK Economy*, London: HMSO.

—— (1989) *The Future of the Multi-Fibre Arrangement: Implications for the UK Economy*, London: HMSO.

Southey, C. (1996) 'EU's call for textile deal goes unheeded', *Financial Times*, 13 September.

Steedman, H. and Wagner, K. (1989) 'Productivity, machinery and skills: clothing manufacture in Britain and Germany', *National Institute Economic Review*, May.

Textile Council (1969) *Cotton and Allied Textiles*, Manchester: Textile Council.

Textile Statistics Bureau (formerly the Cotton Board) *Quarterly Statistical Review*.

Winters, L.A. and Wang, Z.K. (1994) *Eastern Europe's International Trade*, Manchester: Manchester University Press.

Wolffe, R. (1997) 'Bangladesh warns on textile jobs', *Financial Times*, 12 September.

WTO (1995a) *Trade Policy Review: European Union*, 2 vols, Geneva: World Trade Organization.

—— (1995b) *International Trade Trends and Statistics*, Geneva: World Trade Organization.

12 High-technology industries and research and development

In the nineteenth century and first half of the twentieth century, British inventions were often the work of individuals working in relative isolation. But in the 1930s, research was becoming professionalized and was increasingly carried out in specialized departments of large firms.

Research institutes had been established by UK governments to address problems of general interest: for instance, the National Physical Laboratory, the Road Research Laboratory, the Building Institute, and there are also some agricultural institutes of very long standing, such as Rotherham. In manufacturing there were also research institutes for jute, and cotton, but in many cases they were partly financed by the industry itself. (Furthermore, the very large firms that emerged, for instance in the textile industry, were reluctant to support independent research institutes.)

The Second World War changed all this. In anticipation of the war the governments of Britain and Germany increased their research efforts. The importance of advanced technology in modern warfare became all too obvious, with the Battle of Britain largely won because of the invention of radar, then the terror of the V1/V2 rockets raining down on London, and finally the dropping of two atomic bombs on Japan to bring the Allies ultimate victory. Airpower was so important that by the end of the Second World War the British aircraft industry had become very powerful and was in the vanguard of technological development, ahead of the US in jet propulsion (Muller 1995). Until the 1960s it was armament-based, part of the British government's direct involvement in research and development.

DEFENCE AND ARMAMENTS

In 1960–61, 80 per cent of UK expenditure on research and development (R&D) was for military, space and nuclear projects, compared with 89 per cent of that in the US and 70 per cent in France (OECD 1971). Some of the R&D carried out in the 1950s and 1960s was eventually utilized for civil purposes. But the primary objective was the production of armaments and to improve defence capabilities. The proportion devoted to defence declined over time as individual military prowess became less important for Western governments with their co-operation in NATO. Nonetheless, the military component remains important for the US, UK, and France, the three Western countries which are also important exporters of armaments.

The ending of the cold war in 1990 led to a reduction in military expenditure on R&D and armaments. The US industry consolidated itself round three large vertically integrated groups, Boeing, Lockheed Martin and Raytheon, with sales in 1996 of more than $90bn (£56bn). But in Europe, rationalization of the defence industries has proceeded very slowly; eight European companies competing in the same market had a combined turnover of less than $60bn. Some firms have been reluctant to relinquish sectors which in the past have been highly lucrative. France has found it difficult to accept that the most efficient organization would be one in which her firms would not have a controlling interest. Thus the French government found it difficult to privatize Thomson–CSF, a defence electronics group in which it held 58 per cent. GEC of the UK was encouraged to make a bid which would lead to a rationalization of its Marconi defence arm with Thomson–CSF and might have meant that Europe retained a competitive defence electronics industry. But this was then rejected by the French government on the grounds of national security. Eventually, it chose as a partner for Thomson–CSF, Alcatel Alsthom, adding the satellite business of Aerospatiale and Dassault's electronics interests, described as a French–French solution (Gray and Buchan 1997; Nicoll 1997b).

The armaments industry thus consists of a number of firms both sides of the Atlantic competing fiercely for a shrinking number of defence orders. National governments decide on their level of defence expenditure and choice of weapons, but an additional element in the decision is the reluctance of countries to share their defence technology. For instance, when the UK purchased Advanced Medium-Range Air-to-Air Missiles (Amraams) from the US it had difficulty in finding out how they worked. The US has sometimes also placed limitations on the re-export of her technology; for instance, she would not allow Sweden to re-export its Grippen fighters with Amraam to Finland, although she allowed eighteen US jets with the missile to be exported there instead. As a result, Europe no longer wishes to be entirely dependent on the US for its missile technology, and future purchases are likely to be more directed at European firms. However, the US has a huge technological lead and it would require £900m to develop the Future Medium-Range Air-to-Air Missile (Fmraam) proposed by the UK Ministry of Defence (MoD). At the moment the MoD is awarding the competing teams, led by BAe and Hughes of the US, the expert in the field, £5m for research on their proposals for an Fmraam (Gray 1996a, 1997a, 1997b).

In addition, the amount of work a country receives in collaborative projects for producing aircraft depends on the order the government places for the planes. Germany, Britain, Italy and Spain have co-operated in the production of a Eurofighter. But the general contraction in defence expenditure entailed a reduction in orders. In particular, Germany said in 1992 that it wanted to cut the number of aircraft it would purchase from 250 to 140. However, the division of work according to intergovernmental agreement depended on orders and this would have resulted in Germany's share of the work carried out by Daimler-Benz Aerospace (Dasa) falling to 23 per cent and it would have lost managerial control. Eventually, the German order was raised to 180, allowing Dasa to retain the 30 per cent of the work it felt it needed. The UK's share has been raised to 38 per cent. The production investment required for the project is £4.5bn (Gray 1996a) and, in total, is anticipated to be £42bn (Atkins 1997).

Thus the location of production and trade in defence products are often the result of government policy and defence expenditure rather than any cost advantage. Furthermore, permission for exports is generally required, and the government is inevitably drawn in to such sales, as there is national anger and political furore when weapons and aircraft supplied by Britain are later used against her or her allies. Some people intensely dislike the sale of arms and Britain's apparent dependence on them. UK firms also have to comply with the COCOM[1] restrictions by which members of NATO agreed not to supply high-technology products to Russia and Eastern European countries. Since the end of the cold war these restraints have been relaxed.

Armaments and defence products are not usually identified in the trade statistics, so it is difficult to know their magnitude or the proportion of world trade accounted for by the individual countries. However, Samuel Brittan stated that in 1993 total UK defence exports, including indirect sales, came to £3.4bn. Most of the sales were to the Middle East and Africa but 25 per cent were to NATO allies and other European countries. Arms exports employed about 80,000 people. They amounted to 0.5 per cent of GDP or 1.5 per cent of exports including invisibles (Brittan 1996).

The International Institute of Strategic Studies reports that after declining for seven years to 1994, international trade in arms, measured at constant 1995 prices, increased in 1995 to $36.9bn and then again in 1996 to $39.9bn. This was in spite of the decline in defence expenditure in Europe. The Middle East and North Africa accounted for the largest share of imports at 39.5 per cent in 1996, followed by East Asia with 23 per cent. The leading exporter was the US with around 42 per cent of the total, but the proportion supplied by the UK and France had increased to 22 per cent and 14 per cent respectively in 1996. In 1995, the UK supplied $7.4bn, and in 1996, $8.8bn at 1995 prices (Nicoll 1997a).

In spite of the defence orientation of so much of R&D expenditure in the immediate postwar period, economists have tended to consider it as one of the determinants of (civilian) trade in high-tech products.

GAPS IN TECHNOLOGY

A dynamic economic theory such as that of 'technological gaps' is required to explain the effect of a country's R&D expenditure on her trade. A strong performance by a firm, industry or country in originating innovations is assumed to be reflected in a strong competitive position in world markets for product groups with rapid rates of innovation. The implicit assumption is generally that this innovation takes the form of new products.

Indeed, US industrial economists surveying the changes in production, trade and investment in manufactures taking place in the US in the 1950s and 1960s regarded the investment by firms in the development of new products as part of a competitive strategy. According to the 'technological gap theory', a firm could export such products just because it was the innovator, even though it was not the cheapest producer. However, in the longer run, the firm might find it cheaper to supply a foreign market by transferring its know-how to manufacture there. This could be done by licensing foreign producers, or, more frequently, by direct investment in the foreign country. In the very long run, when information on the new technology had been disseminated throughout the world, the new product would be in the nature of a 'commodity' and would be produced in the cheapest location. The account of how the nature of production changes over time is called the theory of the product cycle.

The goods a country exports are affected by time lags. First, there is the lag between the initial commercial production in the innovating country and sales in the importing country, which is termed the demand lag. Secondly, there is the lag between production in the innovator and the importing country, which is called the imitation lag. Exports are regarded as a function of the difference between them. The returns to the innovating firm are in the nature of monopoly profits.

Vernon's (1996) explanation for the US being the source of most innovations was that high wages encouraged the substitution of capital for labour in the provision of consumer durables, and also in the process of production and therefore in investment goods. Also, consumers with high incomes were more willing to try out new products.[2]

An OECD research committee was set up to investigate the degree to which gaps in technology explained trade between member countries. A distinction was drawn between an 'invention' – that is, the idea for an improved product or process – and an 'innovation', which occurs when, for the first time, a firm sells a new or better product or production process with resulting commercial success. It compiled a list of what it regarded as the 110 major innovations in manufacturing occurring between 1945 and 1966. The US was responsible for most of them, with US firms accounting for 60 per cent; European firms accounted for 38 per cent, of which UK firms were responsible for 14 per cent and German firms for 11 per cent (OECD 1970: 185). Thus at that time Britain was the second largest innovating country.

RESEARCH AND DEVELOPMENT IN BRITAIN

Britain's comparative record in R&D

However, because an identification of innovations is a very time-consuming business, most of the comparative analysis is in terms of inputs, that is, expenditure or employment on R&D. An implicit assumption is therefore made that there is a high correlation between inputs and outputs. Expenditure can be considered in absolute terms – that is, the total research effort of the country – or alternatively, in relation to income or GDP, which shows the research orientation of the country. R&D is also sometimes analysed according to who finances it, and where it takes place, in the business sector, government institutions, universities, or independently.[3] However considered, the US dominates the picture.

In 1963–64, expenditure on R&D as a proportion of GDP was greatest in the US with 3.4 per cent and the UK with 2.3 per cent, followed by France with 1.9 per cent (OECD 1971). By 1992 the proportions of the top two had declined, whereas those of Japan, France, and Germany had risen, as can be seen from Table 12.1.

Some figure on the *levels* of expenditure can be seen in Table 12.2. In 1963–64, Britain's expenditure on R&D in total and in industry, later categorized as the business enterprise sector, was about a tenth of that in the US and greater than that of Japan and of any other European country. Sixty-four per cent of R&D in both the UK and US was carried out in the industrial sector, but there was a considerable difference in financing: in the UK a third of industrial expenditure was financed by the government, whereas in the US it was

Table 12.1 Comparative gross domestic expenditure on R&D (GERD) in relation to GDP and the OECD total and relative employment of researchers of the major participating countries

	GERD/GDP (%)		Share of GERD (%)	Share of researchers (%)
	1981	1992	1991	1989
US	2.4	2.7	42.6	42.9
Canada	1.2	1.5	2.2	2.8
Japan	2.1	2.8	19.2	20.7
France	2.0	2.4	7.1	5.4
Germany	2.4	2.5	10.1	8.0
Italy	0.9	1.4	3.7	6.0
UK	2.4	2.1	5.4	3.4
EC	1.7	1.9	30.6	27.6
OECD	2.0		100.0	100.0

Source: OECD (1994) *Science and Technology Policy: Review and Outlook*, Paris: OECD

Table 12.2   Relative expenditure on R&D 1963–64 to 1994 (£bn)[1]

Countries	Total R&D			Business enterprise sector R&D			
	1963–4[a]	*1988[b]*	*1994[b]*	*1963–4[c]*	*1975[d]*	*1988[b]*	*1994[b]*
US	7.52	77.8	108.0	4.82	10.87	55.7	76.5
Japan	0.38	28.0	44.0[2]	0.21	2.55	20.3	31.3[2]
Germany	0.51	16.0	23.2	0.33	2.65	11.6	15.3
France	0.59	11.1	17.1	0.26	1.64	6.6	10.5
UK	0.77	10.2	14.6	0.49	1.33	6.9	9.5
Italy	0.10	5.6	8.2[3]	0.07	0.45	3.3	4.7[3]
Canada	0.15	3.6	5.6		0.31	2.0	3.1[3]

Sources:
[a]   OECD (1970) *Gaps in Technology: Analytical Report*, Paris: OECD.
[b]   P. Jones (1996) 'Research and experimental development (R&D) statistics', *Economic Trends*, **514**, August.
[c]   OECD (1967) *The Overall Level and Structure of R&D Efforts in OECD Member Countries*, Paris: OECD.
[d]   OECD (1979) *Trends in Industrial R&D in Selected OECD Member Countries 1967–1975*, Paris: OECD.

Notes:
[1]   Exchange rates $/£ taken for 1963–64 at 0.357 and for 1975 at 0.450. For 1988 and 1994 purchasing power parity exchange rates of the OECD used.
[2]   1993.
[3]   Provisional.

much higher at 57 per cent. In France, government financing was also high at 30 per cent, but the proportion was much lower in Japan and Germany at 6 per cent and 7 per cent respectively (OECD 1968).

Skilled labour cost less in Britain and Japan than in the US in 1963–64, and therefore the divergence in terms of manpower was relatively less. British R&D input in terms of manpower was 29 per cent and her research scientists and engineers were equivalent to 23 per cent of the number employed in the US, still well above that of any other European country. But employment in Japan was greater still (OECD 1968).

After 1969, expenditure on R&D increased much faster in Japan, Germany and France than it did in the US and Britain. In Britain, gross expenditure on R&D (GERD) and workers employed on it actually declined in the early 1970s (OECD/DSTI 1976). The result can be seen in Table 12.2. The increase over time is exaggerated by inflation. But divergences in price levels between countries in 1988 and 1994 have been corrected by using purchasing power parity exchange rates. The figures show that by 1994 Japanese total real expenditure on R&D was three times that of Britain, while Germany's was 59 per cent and France's 17 per cent greater (see Table 12.2). But the greatest total expenditure was still that of the US at $108bn; of which 71 per cent was carried out in the Business Enterprise Sector, with similar proportions allocated to this sector in the other countries, except for France where the public sector was of relatively greater importance.

The comparable recent situation in relation to the OECD as a whole can be seen from Table 12.1. In 1989 the US employed 43 per cent of researchers in the OECD, and Japan employed a fifth (see Table 12.2). Britain employed only 3.4 per cent, a proportion which was considerably lower than her major European competitors. This was a reflection of her relatively low proportion, 5.4 per cent, of OECD R&D expenditure, which was partly due to the relatively small proportion of her GDP, 2.1 per cent, that she devoted to it. The proportion of GDP devoted to R&D was, in 1992, greater in Japan at 2.8 per cent than it was in the US, but both countries had higher ratios than the major European countries.

Information on changes in the *real levels* of UK R&D expenditure since the 1960s is patchy. Figure 12.1 shows the slight dip in R&D performed in the business sector (BERD) in the early 1970s, after which it rose with fluctuations; it increased by 29 per cent between 1966 and 1981, and then by another 32 per cent to 1990, which has been the peak of activity (Jones 1996: 18, 30).

Total employment in BERD has declined since 1981 from 195,000 to 161,000 in 1994, see Table 12.3. The decline has been of support staff, not scientists and engineers. Most of the recent decline between 1989 and 1994 appears to have been of personnel occupied in defence.

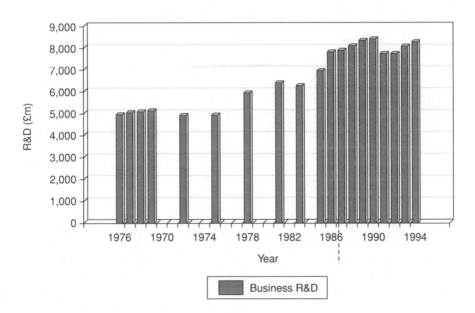

Figure 12.1 UK Business enterprise R&D, 1966–94[1]

Source: P. Jones (1996) 'Research and experimental development (R&D) statistics 1994', *Economic Trends*, **514**, August.

Note: [1]1990 = 100.

Table 12.3   Personnel engaged on R&D
within business enterprises in the UK, 1981,
1989 and 1994 (full-time equivalents
thousands)

	1981	1989	1994
Total	195	176	161
Scientists and Engineers			
Total	77	85	85
Civil		66	71
Defence		19	14
Technicians, laboratory assistants and draughtsmen			
Total	66	46	41
Civil		37	35
Defence		9	6
Administrative, clerical, industrial and other staff			
Total	52	45	35
Civil		36	30
Defence		9	6

Source: P. Jones (1996) 'Research and experimental development (R&D) statistics 1994',
Economic Trends, **514**, August, table 13.

This may well be associated with the greatest change, which has been in
the role of government finance, see Figure 12.2. UK government expenditure on R&D in real terms reached a peak in 1980–81, since when it has
tended to decline. The chief changes have been in expenditure on military
R&D. In real terms this dropped after 1966–67 and then began to rise after
1970–71 to a peak of £2,966 million in 1980–81 (£1,628m in current prices).
Since then it has tended to fall, so that in 1994–95 it was 80 per cent of
the 1966–67 level. Almost all the real reduction in government finance of
R&D since 1980–81 has been of military expenditure.

The government's finance of civil R&D, see Figure 12.2, has not risen
above the level reached in the early 1970s, and in the early 1990s was below
it. There has been no increase with national income. This has been due
partly to the government's perception that, although the UK's record of
innovation was in the past second only to that of the US, relatively few
of these innovations had been taken up by British firms and converted into
commercial success. The innovators have generally attributed this to the
lack of imagination and emphasis on short-term profits of these firms. A
number of innovations – jump jets and hovercraft, for example – were later
taken on by foreign firms. Sometimes the product was reinvented, such as
microwaves, first discovered in the 1930s. However, contrary to all logic,
the Conservative government that took office in 1979 attributed this to a
lack of commercial orientation by the innovators. In order to provide this
and reduce public expenditure the government introduced the policy of
expecting a higher and higher proportion of research to be financed by the
private sector.

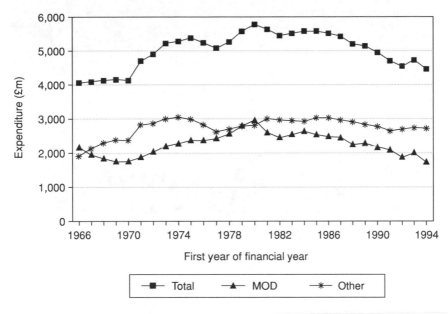

Figure 12.2 Government R&D finance, 1966 to 1994–95[1]. Real terms (1990–91 = 100) £million

Source: P. Jones (1996) 'Research and experimental development (R&D) statistics 1994',
         Economic Trends, **514,** August.

Thus university researchers with fewer and fewer supporting staff have had to spend a considerable proportion of their time filling in applications for money. Not surprisingly, their research record has deteriorated. Furthermore, their perspectives have had to be limited by those of the firms from whom they obtain their money whose interests have generally been short term. Only the pharmaceutical industry, whose top management have qualifications in chemistry and whose thinking has to be long term because of the amount and period of testing required of new drugs, and because of the importance of patents, has maintained its position with respect to innovation.

Government finance now accounts for a smaller and smaller proportion of R&D carried out in the business sector. In 1981 the UK government financed 30 per cent of the R&D of business enterprises[4] but by 1990 this had fallen to 17 per cent, and by 1994 to 12 per cent (see Figure 12.3). This was partially balanced by an increase in foreign financing to 16 per cent: 'Funds from abroad include those from overseas parent companies, contracts for R&D projects, support for R&D provided through the EU schemes and international collaborative projects typically for aerospace or defence projects.' (Jones 1996: 16 and table 12).

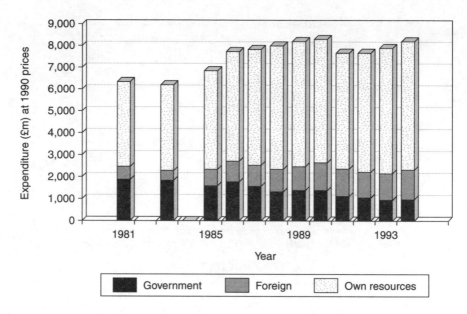

Figure 12.3 Finance of business R&D, 1982–94[1] Real terms (1990–91 = 100)
£million

Source: P. Jones (1996) 'Research and experimental development (R&D) statistics 1994',
Economic Trends, **514**, August.

The distribution of R&D in Britain

Britain's gross (domestic) expenditure on R&D (GERD) in 1994 was £14.6 billion, which was 2.19 per cent of GDP. It can be viewed either from the point of view of the sector in which the R&D is carried out, or in terms of the sector providing the funds. The position in 1994 is shown in Figure 12.4.

Let us begin with the *sphere of activity*. Higher education accounts for 17.55 per cent, and government 13.8 per cent. Two-thirds of the R&D is carried out in the business sector, which was extended in 1986 to include the UK Atomic Energy Authority, transferred from the government. The business sector itself finances only 72 per cent of this. Taking the *finance* for all sectors of R&D, around a half is provided by business, a third by the government, and 13 per cent comes from abroad (see Figure 12.4).

In 1994, of the 12 per cent finance the government provided for the business sector, 67 per cent was for military purposes. Or to put it the other way round, half the defence R&D carried out in the business sector in 1994 was financed by the government. The reduction between 1989 and 1994 in defence R&D performed by the business sector of £556m at 1990 prices was equivalent to the reduction in MOD expenditure over the corresponding six financial years (Jones 1996: tables 5, 11, and 12). The 'peace dividend'

Sectors carrying out the work

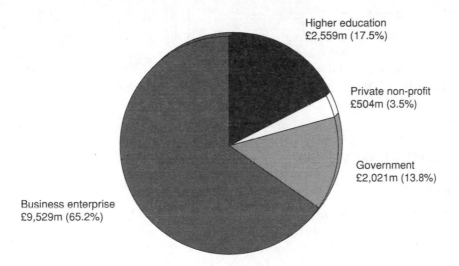

Higher education
£2,559m (17.5%)

Private non-profit
£504m (3.5%)

Government
£2,021m (13.8%)

Business enterprise
£9,529m (65.2%)

Sectors providing the funds

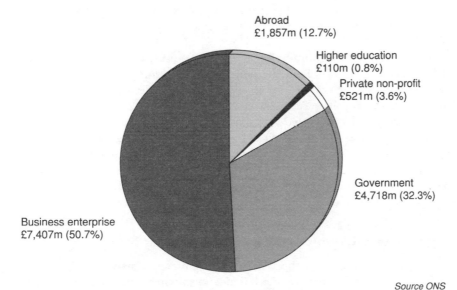

Abroad
£1,857m (12.7%)

Higher education
£110m (0.8%)

Private non-profit
£521m (3.6%)

Government
£4,718m (32.3%)

Business enterprise
£7,407m (50.7%)

Source ONS

Figure 12.4 Gross expenditure on R&D (GERD) by sectors in the UK, 1994
Source: *Economic Trends* (1996), **514**, August, p. 15.

from the reduction in defence R&D was equivalent to £10 per annum per head of the population at 1990 prices.

Assessment

UK expenditure on R&D has not increased as fast as in Japan or the other major industrial countries. But as initially a high proportion of this was defence related and this is where most of the reduction has occurred, it may not have a corresponding effect on trade in civilian products. BERD was generally increasing until the late 1980s.

MEASURING OUTPUT

Patents

The above measures of R&D are all of inputs. There have been efforts to measure the output of a country in a less onerous way than by identifying each individual innovation. One of these is by the patents taken out. This is not a complete measure in so far as some innovations cannot be patented. For instance, it is difficult to patent mixtures; thus, of the man-made fibres, the acrylics, which were mixtures, were not patented, whereas nylon and polyester were. Furthermore, sometimes firms do not take out patents because to do so involves specifying the product or process precisely, which enables other firms to follow suit, with slight alterations in order to avoid paying royalties.

Nonetheless, although imperfect, the CEC and OECD have summed the patents taken out by individual countries, distinguishing between the application made by the country for its own market, for external markets, and for the US market. The situation in 1988 (see Table 12.4), was dominated by the US, which accounted for 51 per cent of patent applications in her own economy and abroad. Next comes Japan with 20 per cent of external applications, then West Germany with 8.5 per cent, Britain with 4 per cent and France with 3.3 per cent. In their domestic economies the relative importance of foreign patent application varies; West Germany has the lowest with 63 per cent (CEC 1993: table 80).

Balance of payments receipts and payments

Another measure used is the receipts and payments made for the use of technology and the effect on the balance of payments (see Table 12.5). In 1990 half the total, a massive $16.5 billion receipts, were to the US, and she was the only large developed country with a positive balance. Britain, whose receipts were $2 billion, greater than those of France but less than those of Germany, had a small negative balance of $85 million.

Table 12.4 1988 Patent applications within countries, and patent applications taken out by them abroad, and their share of patent applications in the US. Growth rates given for 1984–88

Country	Patent applications in country			External patent application		
	Total	Growth (%)	% foreign	Total	Growth (%)	% of US applications
Belgium	33,867	39.9	97.5	6,003	34.1	0.4
Denmark	11,080	38.5	89.2	7,639	102.8	0.4
Federal Republic of Germany	84,306	13.5	63.2	128,026	40.7	8.5
Greece	13,764	294.4	97.3	212	34.2	0.0
Spain	26,251	145.3	93.0	2,722	32.4	0.2
France	66,095	24.1	81.2	53,150	45.6	3.3
Ireland	3,901	15.7	81.4	939	78.5	0.1
Italy	52,939	47.8	61.7	25,271	64.6	1.4
Netherlands	40,115	55.0	93.6	20,433	46.6	1.1
Portugal	2,464	33.0	97.8	105	1,212.5	0.0
UK	79,916	21.2	75.2	54,926	54.2	4.0
USA	146,904	28.4	48.8	200,842	35.9	51.2
Japan	345,239	20.4	10.6	101,192	60.0	20.2

Source: CEC (1993) 'The European Community as a World Trade Partner, *European Economy*, **52**, table 80.

Table 12.5 Technology balance of payments in major OECD countries in 1990

	$ million			Ratio	
	Receipts (x)	Payments (m)	Balance (x − m)	m/x	m/BERD[1]
USA	16,470	3,133	13,337	0.19	0.030
Japan	2,344	2,569	−225	1.10	0.040
UK	1,970	2,055	−85	1.04	0.164
Belgium	1,879	2,505	−626	1.33	1.061
France	1,896	2,507	−611	1.32	0.144
Germany	4,999	5,701	−702	1.14	0.185
EC Total	12,677	17,579	−4,902	1.39	0.280
Total OECD	32,885	25,073	7,812	0.76	0.110

Source: OECD (1994) *Science and Technology Policy: Review and Outlook*, Paris: OECD, table 11.35.

Note: [1]BERD = Business enterprise R&D.

Thus British expenditure on R&D appears to have fallen in real terms. However, viewing the competition as between countries, in terms of patents and international expenditure on technology she appears to hold second position in Europe, that is, behind Germany.

INNOVATION BY INDUSTRY

The importance of innovation varies for different industries. The OECD defined 'science based' or 'research intensive' industries as those 'based not on a once-for-all dose of technology, but for which a continuous stream of

Table 12.6   Intensity of R&D expenditure in the OECD area[1]. R & D expenditure ÷ output by industry

1970		*Inten-sities*	*1980*		*Inten-sities*
High			*High*		
1	Aerospace	25.6	1	Aerospace	22.7
2	Office machines, computers	13.4	2	Office machines, computers	17.5
3	Electronics and components	8.4	3	Electronic and components	10.4
4	Drugs	6.4	4	Drugs	8.7
5	Instruments	4.5	5	Instruments	4.8
6	Electrical machinery	4.5	6	Electrical machinery	4.4
	Average	10.4		Average	11.4
Medium			*Medium*		
7	Chemicals	3.0	7	Chemicals	2.7
8	Automobiles	2.5	8	Automobiles	2.3
9	Other manufacturing industry	1.6	9	Other manufacturing industry	1.8
10	Petroleum refineries	1.2	10	Non-electrical machinery	1.6
11	Non-electrical machinery	1.1	11	Rubber, plastics	1.2
12	Rubber, plastics	1.1	12	Non-ferrous metals	1.0
	Average	1.7		Average	1.7
Low			*Low*		
13	Non-ferrous metals	0.8	13	Stone, clay, glass	0.9
14	Stone, clay, glass	0.7	14	Food, beverages, tobacco	0.8
15	Shipbuilding	0.7	15	Shipbuilding	0.6
16	Ferrous metals	0.5	16	Petrol refineries	0.6
17	Fabricated metal products	0.3	17	Ferrous metals	0.6
18	Wood, cork, furniture	0.2	18	Fabricated metal products	0.4
19	Food, beverages, tobacco	0.2	19	Paper, printing	0.3
20	Textiles, footwear, leather	0.2	20	Wood, cork, furniture	0.3
21	Paper, printing	0.1	21	Textiles, footwear, leather	0.2
	Average	0.4		Average	0.5

Source: OECD (1970) *Gaps in Technology: Analytical Report* (1980), *Technical Change and Economic Policy*, Paris: OECD.

Note: [1]Weighting of the eleven main countries.

new products and processes is necessary in order to keep in the market' (OECD 1970: 123, 135). These are generally classified as those with the highest proportion of R&D expenditure to output (that is, value added by the industry) and are called the high-technology industries. The group of industries regarded as high-tech has remained the same over the period; as can be seen from Table 12.6, they include aerospace, office machines and computers, electronics products, drugs, instruments and electrical machinery. In 1970 and 1980 their average expenditure on R&D was equal to more than 4 per cent of their output. Other chemicals and automobiles are regarded as medium-technology industries, and textiles and footwear as low-technology industries.

However if we look at more recent statistics for the five main countries, see Table 12.7, we can see that their relative R&D expenditure in these industries varies considerably. Comparing Britain's research effort of 1987–89 with that for 1976–78 and other countries, a decline for aircraft is apparent and, to a lesser degree, for computers. She showed an increase in research intensity for communications equipment, pharmaceuticals, instruments, electrical machinery, motor vehicles and industrial chemicals. In particular, in 1987–89 she had the highest research intensity of all of the countries for pharmaceuticals, and a relatively high one for communications equipment.

We can look at the changes in Britain over time, but unfortunately, not for the same business categories (see Figure 12.5). The greatest increases in R&D between 1981 and 1994 have been in chemicals and services, with some increases in transport equipment, mechanical engineering and other manufacturing. There has been a decline in R&D in aerospace.

How far can a country's R&D input be related to its trading position? The conclusion of the OECD study was that, although a country's expenditure on R&D appeared to be the main factor determining the country's position in exports of high-tech goods, it did not explain the growth in trade. Some countries such as Canada and Italy showed a very rapid growth in exports of high-tech products even though their expenditure on R&D was relatively low. In other words, the difference between their demand and imitation lag was very small.

What can be said about Britain and her trade in high-tech products? Let us begin with aircraft. In 1994 she was a small net exporter of aircraft to other EC countries and to the rest of the world, but between 1980–90 she appears to have lost 6 per cent of her market share (OECD 1994). However, information is limited, and the situation is blurred because so many aerospace projects are co-operative efforts between countries – as with Airbus – and defence-related data is restricted.

The position with respect to trade in the other categories of high-tech products is shown in Table 12.8. It is clear from the first column that in 1994 Britain only had an export surplus in chemicals, including pharmaceuticals, and instruments. In chemicals and the subgroup pharmaceuticals she had net exports with all the areas shown except for Western Europe

Table 12.7 R&D intensity ratios for high- and medium-technology industries. Business enterprise R&D expenditure/value added of sector, as a percentage

	US		Japan		Germany		France		UK	
	1976–8	*1987–9*	*1976–8*	*1987–9*	*1976–8*	*1987–9*	*1976–8*	*1987–9*	*1976–8*	*1987–9*
High-technology										
Aircraft	18.7	21.4	5.9	7.6	30.1	22.6	14.1	15.2	14.9	9.7
Computers	15.4	16.1	3.5	6.5	7.3	8.8	13.0	10.8[2]	11.5	7.9
Communications equipment	7.9	14.3	3.6	5.3	6.6	10.7	10.3	11.8[2]	8.3	11.6
Pharmaceuticals	7.8	10.6	5.5	8.0	8.0	9.8	5.6	8.2	8.3	13.2
Instruments	5.6	5.1	2.6	6.3	2.2	3.1	2.2	2.6	1.6	3.1
Electrical machinery	5.4	1.5	2.9	4.4	3.2	3.6	1.8	2.1[2]	2.4	3.7
Medium technology										
Motor vehicles	2.8	4.5	1.8	2.7	2.0	3.2	2.2	2.8	1.4	2.5
Industrial chemicals	2.0	2.7	2.3	4.4	3.2	4.2	2.1	3.1	1.7	2.6
Other manufactures	1.3	1.1	0.8	1.3	0.1	0.7	0.4	0.4	1.5	1.2
Non-electrical equipment	1.1	1.3	1.7	2.5	1.8	2.9	0.6	1.0[2]	0.8	0.9
Rubber, plastics	1.3	0.8	1.2	1.5	0.5	1.1	1.8	1.7	0.3	0.4

Source: OECD (1994) *Science and Technology Policy: Review and Outlook*, Paris: OECD, table 11.32.

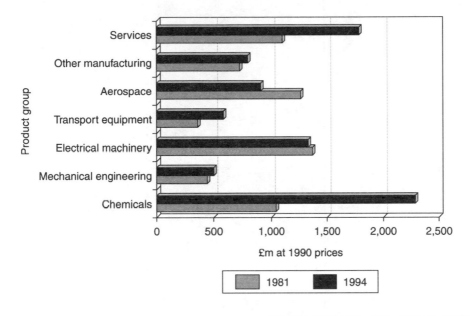

Figure 12.5 UK business R&D in 1981 and 1994

excluding the EC (i.e. Switzerland). In instruments she had net exports to all the groups shown apart from North America. Between 1980 and 1990 in chemicals and pharmaceuticals she appeared to be maintaining her market share, but in instruments was slowly losing it (OECD 1994).

In the other high-tech products she had surpluses with the EC and Eastern Europe and deficits with North America and Asia and Oceania. A high proportion of these imports come from the newly industrializing countries of Asia.

The position in her domestic market and her export ratios are not as easy to show as might be expected because of the amount of intra-industry trade. For instance, the value of Britain's exports of office machinery and computers is greater, at 123 per cent, than the value of her domestic production, see Table 12.9, column 2; this is only possible because exports contain imported components. Thus exports are related not only to domestic production, column 3, but also to domestic production plus imports, column 4. The ratio for all products is 30 per cent or over. Similarly, imports are related not only to domestic consumption, column 5, but also to domestic consumption plus exports, column 6. Imports account for 30 per cent or more of the latter. The degree of intra-industry trade appears particularly high for the first two categories, which consist of electronic equipment.

The British trading position is also affected by the policy of the EU towards R&D and trade, which will now be discussed.

Table 12.8 UK balance of trade in high-tech products in 1994 by area

Division SITC3	Commodity	Balance (£ million)						
		Total	EC	W. Europe (excl. EC)	E. Europe	North America	Middle East and North Africa	Asia and Oceania
5	Chemicals	4,314	244	−68	172	780	820	1,439
54	Pharmaceutical	1,701	415	−207	124	354	304	456
75	Office machines and computers	−1,126	814	766	211	−1,256	113	−2,007
76	Telecommunications, etc.	−226	1,455	−6	193	−466	112	−1,611
77	Electrical machinery	−744	812	371	29	−983	325	−1,709
87	Instruments	717	474	58	53	−249	220	132

Source: Government Statistical Service (1996) *Business Monitor MA20, Overseas Trade Statistics of the United Kingdom with the World,* 1994.

Table 12.9 Import penetration and export sales ratios for high-tech industries, 1994

(1)	(2) SIC Division	(3) X/P (%)	(4) X/(P+M) (%)	(5) M/C (%)	(6) M/(C+X) (%)	(7) X − M ($m)
Office machinery and computers	30	123	51	120	58	−1.48
Radio, TV and computer equipment	32	93	48	93	48	
Chemicals	24	51	36	47	30	6.57
Instruments	33	69	41	67	39	−1.88
Electrical machinery nec.	31	47	30	50	34	

Source: CSO (1996) *Annual Abstract of Statistics*, table 12.2; WTO (1995b) *International Trade Trends and Statistics*, Geneva: WTO.

Notes:
[1]Standard Industrial Classification Division.
X = exports; P = sales home producers; M = imports; $C = P + M − X$.

EU POLICY

The larger industrial countries have now come to regard their production and exports of high-technology products as matters of national prestige. They expect to be at the frontiers of technology. Governments therefore scrutinize their national levels of R&D expenditure with care. In Europe these national aspirations appear to have been elevated to the EU level.

This reluctance of governments to leave these industries to market forces can be rationalized. The traditional argument is one of 'market failure', that the social returns from R&D expenditure may be greater than the private returns. As a result, less research may be undertaken than is socially optimal. However, it does not appear to be the main motive underlying British or EU research projects.

The EU, and France in particular, dislikes being dependent on the US and Japan for basic technology, especially in electronics. An additional concern of all European governments it to maintain their highly skilled sectors. The knowledge and problem-solving skills of highly trained workers must be kept up to date, it is argued, and this is only possible by intimate contact with production. Furthermore, these skills are also required for adaptation and absorption of the new technology. Some of the EU countries fear that the reduction of trade barriers at an international level will lead to them importing more of the high-tech products from the US and Asia, so that Europe will be pushed into the production of lower-tech goods and may become a low-skill, low-income environment.

In formulating industrial policies, one of the assumptions of the CEC, particularly Delors, was that much of the advantage of the US lay in being able to exploit economies of scale because of her large home market. Thus it was hoped that the Single European Act (SEA) of 1986 by removing non-tariff barriers to trade would enable EC firms to further exploit economies of scale, in particular those that arise from the spreading of R&D expenditure over more units of output. The assumptions underlying this theory have already been disputed in an earlier chapter.

The SEA also added Title VI Research and Technological Development to the treaty which specified formally:

> The Community's aim shall be to strengthen the scientific and techno-logical base of Europe's industry and to encourage it to become more competitive at international level.
>
> (European Communities 1988)

It then went on to advocate co-operative research projects the like of which were already taking place. But the desire to protect the high-technology sector has also permeated the commercial policy of the EU. This, in turn, has attracted inflows of direct investment, which we shall later discuss.

Subsidization of research

The EC has sought to strengthen its position in these industries by the direct subsidization of research. It has, in particular, encouraged inter-EC Member States research projects. In order to avoid conflicts with EC competition policy, which forbids collaboration at the stage of developing products for an immediate market, this had to be 'pre-competitive research' (Stubbs and Saviotti 1994).

The major high-tech areas are covered, but not always in the same way. There is also some divergence in the way they are organized. For instance, the European Research Co-ordination Agency (EUREKA) was an inter-govermental initiative set up in 1985 at the suggestion of François Mitterand as a response to the 'star wars' Strategic Defence Initiative (SDI) of the US. It has no funds of its own and national governments can contribute as much or as little as they like. It involves collaboration between research organizations of at least two Member States, and is concerned with 'downstream' or near market research. Its most important projects have been the Joint European Submicron Silicon Initiative (JESSI) on semiconductors, and its high-definition television (HDTV) programme, which will be discussed later (Peterson 1996).

The other EU research programmes are directly under the control of the CEC. As can be seen from Table 12.10, there are a number of biotech-nology projects but they do not receive nearly as much funding as the electronic projects. The European Strategic Programme of Research in Information Technology (ESPRIT) was launched in 1984–88 with a budget of ECU 750m. Its objective was pre-competitive research in microelectronics,

Table 12.10   The main EC programmes for promoting new technologies

Name	Dates	Budget cost[1] (ECUm)	Main objective
ESPRIT European Strategic Programme for R&D in Information Technology	I 1984–88 II 1988–92 III 1992–94	750 1,600 1,350	To promote European capabilities and competitiveness in IT technologies, primarily microelectronics systems development
RACE R&D in Advanced Communication Technologies for Europe	Definition phase 1985–87 RACE I 1990–94 RACE II 1992–94	21 460 489	To establish European competence in broadband communications by developing the equipment, standards and technology necessary for an Integrated Broadband Communications (IBC) system
TELEMATICS	1990–94	380	Development of telematic systems in areas such as transport, health and public administration
BRITE/EURAM Basic Research in Industrial Technologies in Advanced Materials for Europe	BRITE I 1985–88 EURAM I 1986–88 BRITE/EURAM I 1989–92 BRITE/EURAM II	100 450 660	Support for industrial R&D which upgrades technological/materials base of production
BAP Biotechnology Action Programme	1985–89	75	Support for infrastructure development in biotechnology with particular emphasis on research and training
BRIDGE Biotechnological Research for Innovation Development and Growth in Europe	1989–93	100	As for BAP, but emphasis on larger, more comprehensive projects in areas such as advanced cell culture, molecular modelling, etc.
BIOTECH	1992–96	164	Orientated towards basic research and safety assessment and seen as complementary to BRIDGE

Source: M. Sharp and K. Pavitt (1993) 'Technology policy in the 1990s: old trends and new realities', *Journal of Common Market Studies*, **31** (2), June.

Note: [1]The figures given as budget cost exclude any industrial contribution for the ESPRIT and other programmes which are shared-cost programmes. Actual expenditures under the programmes are therefore approximately twice the amount of the budget cost given.

advanced information-processing and software technology, as well as applications in computer-integrated manufacturing and office systems. Half the costs of the projects that are launched are paid by the CEC. The funding was doubled to ECU 1600m for ESPRIT II from the 1988–92 budget. The principal areas for research were microelectronics, IT processing systems, and applications technologies. Firms and universities were involved and UK firms took part in 129 projects. ESPRIT III, with a funding of ECU 1350m from 1990–94, was concerned with microelectronics, advanced business and home systems peripherals, high-performance computing and networking, technology for software-intensive systems, computer-integrated manufacturing and engineering, and open microprocessor systems (Stubbs and Saviotti 1994).

The R&D in Advanced Communications Technologies for Europe (RACE) projects were to establish European competence in broadband communications by developing the equipment, standards and technology necessary for an Integrated Broadband Communications (IBC) system.

There has been some disagreement as to how important and effective these collaborative research policies have been. The problem is that inter-country projects tend to be expensive in relation to output. Sometimes each country is suspicious about the degree to which it is benefiting, though academics generally welcome the exchange of ideas.

Furthermore, the subsidization of research, if it appears to be successful in improving the trade balance, may result in complaints by competitor countries to the WTO. However, as this research is 'pre-competitive', this should not occur.

A report to the EU Council of Ministers in February 1996 has warned of a 'disturbing' competitiveness gap between Europe's IT industry and that of the US and Japan. Europe is way behind in adopting the Internet; the US has four times the number of households online. The proportion of households in Europe with a PC is only half the US level of 40 per cent (Denton 1997). This may be partly the result of the trade policy the EU is pursuing.

EU TRADE POLICY

The CEC has been concerned by the overall trade balance of the EU in high-technology manufactures, and, in particular, that the ratio of EU exports of high-tech products to imports from third countries was declining, from a slight overall surplus of 1.1 in 1982 to a deficit of 0.8 in 1991. This decline was particularly marked in relation to trade with the most competitive developing countries (MC15), with whom it fell rapidly in the early 1980s and ended up at 0.7 in 1991, see Table 12.11 (CEC 1993: 214).

In addition, as can be seen from Table 12.5, in 1990 all the larger countries of the EU had negative balances for technology transfer; the US is the

Table 12.11 Community trade in high-tech products: Export/import ratio by selected trade partners, 1982–90

Partner	1982	1984	1986	1987	1988	1989	1990	1991
Extra-EC	1.1	1.0	1.0	0.9	0.8	0.8	0.8	0.8
USA	0.4	0.5	0.6	0.6	0.5	0.5	0.5	0.5
Japan	0.2	0.1	0.1	0.1	0.1	0.1	0.1	0.1
EFTA	1.2	1.2	1.2	1.1	1.1	1.1	1.1	0.9
MC15[1]	2.0	1.2	1.2	0.9	0.7	0.8	0.8	0.7

Source: CEC (1993) 'The European community as a world trade partner' *European Economy*, **52**, table 92.

Note: [1]MC15 is the most competitive developing countries. The group comprises Argentina, Brazil, Hong Kong, India, Indonesia, Israel, Macau, Malaysia, Mexico, Philippines, Singapore, South Korea, Taiwan, Thailand, and the former Yugoslavia.

only large country with a positive balance. This suggested that the international position of the EU in high-technology products was not strong and was deteriorating.

In trade policy the EU has shown least concern with respect to pharmaceuticals, in which Europe traditionally has had a strong position as a net exporter and for which import penetration is only 10 per cent. As already mentioned under the Uruguay Round, the EU has agreed to abolish import tariffs on pharmaceuticals.

Aircraft

A number of EC countries became worried that they were almost totally dependent on two large US firms, Boeing and McDonnell-Douglas, for the supply of commercial aircraft. In 1966 France and Germany, later joined by the UK and Spain, established a consortium consisting of one firm from each country to develop a wide-bodied jet, called the Airbus. The four governments contributed a considerable amount towards the estimated $2 billion development costs, Germany alone contributing almost DM 11 billion between the mid-1960s and 1989. This has been a continuing source of conflict with the US. The importance of the project can be gauged from the fact that it accounted for about half the EC output of aircraft (GATT 1991: vol. 1). In July 1992 the US and EC agreed to limit government financial support to their aviation industry; production and marketing subsidies are outlawed and aid for development is to be no more than 33 per cent (*Financial Times (FT)* 24 February 1993). At present Aérospatiale (France) and Dasa (Germany) each own 37.9 per cent of Airbus, BAe (UK) owns 20 per cent and Casa (Spain) 4.2 per cent. It is a *Groupement d'Intérêt Economique*, which means that it does not make profits or losses on its own account; they all accrue to the four partners. Negotiations are now proceeding to make it into a profit-making company in order to reduce its costs; this should take place by the start of 1999. This may also entail a readjustment of production (Skapinker 1997a, 1997b, 1997c).

Electronics

The CEC has appeared most concerned about EU firms being at the leading edge of technology with respect to the electrical and electronics industry. Most government assistance to this industry in Britain and France, as in the US, went initially for defence purposes. This was not permitted in Germany and Japan and, as a result, their firms appear to have developed a more commercial orientation. Japan purchased the right to use US innovations and was very adept at developing them for consumer products.

In the 1980s Japan became the leading producer of 'active' electronic components, that is, semiconductors, integrated circuits and microprocessors. In 1989 she accounted for 42 per cent of the total world production, with the US accounting for 26 per cent and Europe only 12 per cent. Of the European total, West Germany accounted for 31 per cent, France 19 per cent and the UK 16 per cent (Dicken 1992: 311). Recently, the US appears to have reclaimed its position as the largest producer (*FT* 12 December 1992). As far as can be ascertained, the EC is a net importer of most types of electronic products.

The consumer electronics industry is relatively fragmented, with only Sony and Matsushita of Japan commanding more than 10 per cent of the global market. Of EU companies, Philips (Netherlands) has 9 per cent and Thomson (France) 6 per cent (Rawsthorn 1997).

EC has encouraged European mergers

The EC Commission encouraged the co-operation and amalgamation of European firms: for example, Olivetti taking over Sinclair Acorn; Siemens purchasing Plessey from GEC. It hoped that this would lead to the EC being able to withstand competition from the US and Japan with European ownership rather than as a subsidiary of a Japanese or US firm such as emerged with Fujitsui's purchase of 80 per cent of ICL.

The CEC likes alliances and mergers of EU firms, such as GEC and Siemens with respect to Plessey. However, each is a large cautious firm, with large cash balances (in 1995 GEC had a cashpile of £2.9bn (Wighton 1995: 5) and no good record of innovation).

The natural tendency of firms has been to seek alliances outside the EU with US and Japanese firms, such as the recent agreement between IBM (US), Motorola (US), Siemens (Germany) and Toshiba (Japan) to produce high-powered memory chips – a gigabit dynamic random access memory (D-Ram).

Standards

The Single European Market (SEM) was meant to involve the final abolition of all standards that interfered with intra-EC trade. Thus it was meant
to promote competition between EC firms which would lead to them being
able to exploit their economies of scale by their spreading of R&D. The
CEC seems to have thought of this in terms of strengthening the position
of EC firms, but the foreign multinationals derived just as much benefit.

In the Tokyo Round the EC agreed not to use its establishment of
standards as a form of protection for its domestic industry. Nonetheless,
at the 1986 meeting of the International Radio Consultative Committee
(CCIR) it refused to agree to a Japanese–US standard for a high-definition
television system (HDTV) because it wanted to insulate the European
market from competition from US and Japanese producers. The EC adopted
a rival 1,250-line system and proposed an evolutionary MAC system,
claiming that this would minimize the transition costs for EC consumers –
although EC consumer organizations complained that they had not been
consulted. After the EC taxpayer had invested ECU 625m (£516m) on
research and development, with additional funds by Philips (Netherlands)
and Thomson (France), Britain blocked any further expenditure, which
it said would serve no good purpose. Then, at the beginning of 1993
Philips announced that, although it had carried out the development
work, it would not produce any HDTVs because there were no programmes
to transmit on it. Meanwhile, the Japanese had begun broadcasting eight
hours a day on their HDTV system and US firms had developed a
digital technology which appeared likely to sweep the board (*FT* 17
November 1992; 9 and 12 February 1993). At the beginning of 1993 the
programme was cancelled and the incoming EC Commissioner, Martin
Bangemann, said that the EC would have to adopt the US standard (*FT*
19 February 1993).

Digital television is now being broadcast in France and Germany but the
standards battle has not been concluded. The 'driver' in this area is the
arrival of satellites capable of carrying hundreds of channels. The terrestrial
broadcasters are endeavouring to compete with this. The emphasis seems
to be on increasing the number of channels rather than the resolution of
the picture, and there is a trade-off between them.[5]

The US has been establishing standards for digital TV and these should
be consistent with TV reception in a PC, but they do not include those for
a video format. It is anticipated that it will be about five years before the
US broadcasters begin digital transmissions (Kehoe 1996). However,
proposals have been put forward in Britain for terrestial transmission of
digital television before then.

The newest consumer electronic products are the digital video discs
(DVDs). After a battle between Sony and Philips and the rest of the industry
over technical specifications, partly due to the royalties involved, a disc

dominated by Toshiba technology was accepted. The regulations for it are less concerned with protecting the producers of discs than protecting the software of films downloaded on to them. This is to be done by a system of regional codes, or 'flags', that are built into the discs and will mean that they cannot be played in any other region (Parkes 1997). It appears that this is a gross impediment to trade, and it is not clear why governments and the CEC are willing to agree to such a system to protect the marketing plans of the large film corporations.

Tariff protection

The French wanted to increase the protection of what they claim are 'infant' or rather 'sunrise' industries. Britain and Germany did not, because, in many cases, protection of the producers of intermediates raised the costs of other consuming firms. It also raises the price of investment as well as consumer goods.

The EU has had a relatively high CET of 14 per cent on integrated circuits, radios, television receivers, and video recorders. Telecommunication devices had a tariff of 7.5 per cent and computer equipment 3.5 per cent. The tariff on most silicon chips was 7 per cent but as high as 14 per cent on others. There have been a series of cases where the EU has been criticized for reclassifying a production into a higher tariff category. Britain has reclassified personal computers that can be used as televisions as consumer electronic products with a tariff of 14 per cent (Williams 1996). With such easily transportable products these decisions have implications for the location of production and direct investment.

Japan is the major supplier of standard micro chips. But most IT firms in the EU are in favour of liberalization, arguing that it is a global industry and tariffs prevent production being carried out at minimum cost. Siemens of Germany, one of the largest EU firms, was campaigning against tariffs on semiconductors, even though it has invested heavily in chip production (Taylor 1997).

Eventually, the EU responded to a WTO proposal advocated by the US to scrap all tariffs on information technology products, including computers, semiconductors and software by the year 2000 (Dunne 1995). In March 1997 the EU agreed to the Information Technology Agreement (ITA), which covered the following:

1   computers (including accessories and components);
2   telecoms equipment (including fax machines, modems, pagers, etc.);
3   semiconductors;
4   semiconductor manufacturing equipment;
5   software (e.g. diskettes and CD-Roms); and
6   scientific instruments.

The tariffs will be cut in four equal stages, beginning in July 1997 and then on 1 January each year until 2000. However, the EU has agreed to scrap its semiconductor tariffs a year early, with half the reduction coming this July. In return, the EU will be admitted to the industry's Semiconductor Council created by the US and Japan last year (Williams 1997).

Most IT firms are strongly in favour of this agreement, hoping that it will help maintain growth in this $600bn trade, and in particular, assist their entry into developing country markets.

Non-tariff barriers to trade

In the 1980s many EU Member States had imposed VERs on electronic goods imported from Japan. Faced with these limitations, the Japanese firms began to invest in other parts of Southeast Asia to supply the EC market. The EC then extended the VERs to include these countries as well. But these had to be phased out with the introduction of the SEM in 1993 and now the CEC claims there are none (WTO 1995a, 1: 57).

These electrical consumer products were not at the leading edge of technology. Indeed, many of them are produced in developing countries with very little R&D expenditure. However, the argument appeared to be that the EC firms must be profitable in these consumer goods in order to remain in the high-technology sector of the industry. There are now only two EU producers of consumer electronic products left, Philips (Netherlands) and Thomson Multimedia (France). The latter is still in the state sector and its proposed sale to Daewoo (Korea) has been cancelled (Buchan *et al.* 1996). Its losses are financed by the defence sector Thomson–CSF of the same group.

Since Fujitsu took over ICL (UK) in the 1980s there has been no European firm producing mainframe computers (Dicken 1992). ICL continues to design and manufacture its mainframe computers in Britain but is pulling out of its loss-making personal computer business (Cane 1996; Taylor 1996).

There were few European producers in the personal computer (PC) market. Groupe Bull (France) sold its loss-making Zenith Data Systems to Packard Bell (US) in 1996 (Jack 1996). Olivetti, Europe's last mass producer of PCs, was making a loss and has sold its shares in Acorn, the Cambridge-based PC company (Hill 1996; Simkins 1996; Denton 1997). Germany's Escom filed for bankruptcy. Most of the remaining firms are basically assemblers of imported components (Nairn 1997).

Anti-dumping duties

In the 1980s the EC started using anti-dumping procedures as a form of protective policy. The situation for electronic goods at the end of April 1996 is shown in Table 12.12. The countries shown have producers on whose exports to the EU anti-dumping duties are imposed, or who have agreed

Table 12.12 Definitive anti-dumping duties and undertakings in force on 30 April 1996

Product	Country	Duty or range (%)	Date of expiry
Audio tapes	Japan	25.5–15.2	5 May 1996
	South Korea	9.2–0	
Car radios	South Korea	34.4–3.4	8 August 1997
Colour TVs (small)	South Korea	19.6–10.4	In force until
	China	15.3–7.5	outcome of
	Hong Kong	4.8–2.1	review on 20 July 1996
Colour TVs (all sizes)	Malaysia	23.4–7.5	1 April 2000
	Singapore	23.6–0	1 April 2000
	Thailand	29.8–3	1 April 2000
Colour TVs (large)	South Korea	17.9–0	In force until
	China	25.6	outcome of review
Electronic weighing scales	South Korea	26.7–9.3	22 October 1998
	Singapore	31–15.4	22 October 1998
	Japan	31.6–15.3	28 April 1998
Floppy discs	China	39.4–35.6	21 October 1998
	Japan	40.9–6.1	21 October 1998
	Taiwan	32.7–19.8	21 October 1998
	Hong Kong	27.4–6.7	10 September 1999
	South Korea	8.1	10 September 1999
	Malaysia	46.4–12.8	13 April 2001
	Mexico	44–0	13 April 1996
	USA	44–0	13 April 1996
Large aluminium electrolytic capacitors	Japan	75–11.6	4 December 1997
	South Korea	70.6	18 June 1999
	Taiwan	75.8–10.7	18 June 1999
TV broadcast cameras	Japan	96.8–52.7	30 April 1999
Microwave ovens	China	20.8	4 January 2001
	Malaysia	31.7	4 January 2001
	Thailand	31.8–20.3	4 January 2001
	South Korea	32.8–4.8	4 January 2001
Video cassettes and cassette reels	South Korea	3.8–1.9	In force until
	Hong Kong	21.9–0	outcome of review
	China	ECU 2.22–0.92	on 25 October 1996
Photocopiers	Japan	20–10	11 October 1997

Source: Information supplied by the Department of Trade and Industry, UK.

to supply products at a certain minimum price. They may be different for producers within the same country.

After an anti-dumping investigation, in 1990 the EC Commission negotiated a minimum import price with eleven Japanese semiconductor producers of dynamic random access memory (D-Rams) chips; an anti-dumping duty of 60 per cent was imposed on exporters who did not participate in the undertaking (GATT, 1991, 1: 214). The EC also imposed a provisional anti-dumping duty of 10.1 per cent on imports of memory chips from South Korea as it began an investigation into dumping (*FT* 18 September 1992). This has buttressed the position of European electronic firms already established in Europe (often to supply the defence industries), and induced US and Japanese firms to establish subsidiaries. In 1988 five of the ten leading semiconductor firms in Europe were American. In addition, there was IBM (US) which produces its own semiconductors and which for a long time has dominated the world market in mainframe computers.

These anti-dumping duties were suspended in 1995 because D-Ram prices were rising. They then began to fall and the situation was reviewed again early in 1997, whereupon the CEC decided to reintroduce minimum import prices for imports of computer memory chips from Japanese and South Korean manufacturers. They have about 80 per cent of the $5bn EU market for D-Rams. The CEC said that the minimum price would be based on current manufacturing costs plus a 'single digit' profit margin. Siemens approved of the move, but US manufacturers with EU subsidiaries said that the manufacture of products such as personal computers in Europe would no longer be viable (Buckley *et al.* 1997). The move appeared quite inconsistent with the EU's signing of the Information Technology Agreement a few weeks later. By the end of 1997 the CEC had lifted the anti-dumping duties on South Korean D-Rams after the manufacturers had reached an industry-to-industry accord on data collection. A similar agreement may be reached with Japan (Buckley 1997b).

In May 1994 the EU imposed anti-dumping duties of as much as 96.8 per cent on imports of broadcasting cameras made by five Japanese electronics companies as a response to complaints by Philips (Netherlands) and Thomson (France). The Japanese market share had risen from 52 per cent in 1989 to 70 per cent in 1992. The duties on cameras from the individual firms were 62.6 per cent on Sony, 82.9 per cent on Ikegami Tsushinki, 52.7 per cent on Denshi and 96.8 per cent on Matsushita and JVC, which the Commission said did not co-operate in its investigation, see Table 12.12.

In September 1995 the European Commission reimposed anti-dumping duties of 20 per cent on Japanese photocopiers, see Table 12.12, and extended them to larger models, arguing that the Japanese companies concerned – Canon Copier, Ricoh, Matsushita, Minolta, Konica, Sharp, and Toshiba – were continuing to dump their products at artificially low prices on the European market to the detriment of the European photocopying industry. This was in response to complainants Rank Xerox, Oce Nederalan and Olivetti-Canon for whom the duties provide a breathing space. Duties were initially imposed in 1987 and since then *imports* of Japanese photocopiers have fallen sharply. But their market share has increased as the Japanese companies have moved production to inside the EU (*FT* 15 September 1995: 5, 18 September 1995: 3).

In 1995 the CEC imposed provisional anti-dumping duties on microwave ovens from China, South Korea, Thailand and Malaysia, see

Table 12.12, after investigating complaints from the domestic industry that 'dumped' imports had increased from 2.17m units accounting for 30.4 per cent of the market in 1989 to 3.05m units accounting for 42 per cent of the market and that the EU industry had suffered substantial injury as a result (Foreign Staff, 11.7.95).

The latest request for an anti-dumping duty comes from Philips (Netherlands), complaining that personal fax machines (weighing less than 5 kg) are being dumped by Japan, China, South Korea, Malaysia, Singapore, Taiwan, and Thailand. The Japanese manufacturers contesting the case say that imports from Japan have decreased in recent years in both unit and value terms, and that leading EU producers such as Philips and France's Sagem have increased sales and production (Buckley 1997a).

Anti-dumping duties are also very high for large aluminium electrolytic capacitors. The highest anti-dumping duty on floppy discs is for Malaysia, and then for Mexico and the US at 44 per cent, with some exceptions, see Table 12.12.

There has been strong criticism of the EC for introducing these measures. The GATT's anti-dumping provision was meant to prevent a firm selling in a particular market below its price in other markets, or below the cost of production, as a temporary competitive strategy to bankrupt competitors, after which prices would be raised again. It was not meant to be used to exclude external competitors whose long-term costs were lower. The EC's method of calculation and its use of statistics have been severely criticized. The anti-dumping duties imposed have often been very high and have varied greatly between firms exporting from the same country. The lowest cost and most efficient firms appear to have been the most penalized. Sometimes, in order to avoid their imposition, the Japanese firms have agreed not to sell below a certain price.

These non-tariff barriers have similar effects to a tariff in raising the price of the products on the EC market. The National Consumer Council of the UK calculated that the annual cost to EC consumers of anti-dumping duties on video cassette recorders ECU 272.5 million (1989), on compact disc players ECU 146.1 million (1989), on video cassettes ECU 48 million (1987), on dot matrix printers ECU 512.6 million (1988), on electronic typewriters was ECU 104.5 million (1987), and on photocopiers ECU 339.5 million (1988) (quoted in GATT 1991, 1: 213).

Direct investment

The high prices in the EC protected market have encouraged investment, though not necessarily by European firms. Colour television production in the UK was ceded first to the European firms Philips (Netherlands) and Thomson (France)[6] and then to inward investing Japanese firms. Now virtually all colour televisions and video recorders produced in Britain are made by foreign firms (Eltis and Fraser 1992). Britain's 'big six' manufacturers are Toshiba, Sony, Hitachi, Matsushita and Mitsubishi of Japan, and Samsung of South Korea, which together account for three-quarters of TV production in Britain. Other companies with plants in the UK are Sanyo of Japan, Tatung of Taiwan, and the LG Group of South Korea. Asian manufacturers have spent £1bn since 1990 on expanding their productive capacity in Britain. In 1996 UK output of TV sets was 6.2m and two-thirds of them were exported. She is the leading producer in the EU, accounting for 35 per cent of its total output (Marsh 1997).

The EC is very concerned that such inward investment should not be of 'screw driver' firms, mere assemblers of imported components. In order to prevent this the EC has sometimes tried to impose duties on the imported components. In many cases it has treated the foreign subsidiary more harshly than its indigenous firm, which may be importing a relatively higher proportion of its components.

But Britain has benefited not only from direct investment in products using silicon chips, but now also from investment in the production of semiconductors themselves. This production is capital- rather than labour-intensive, with a plant costing $1bn or more, but it also requires clean air, copious water supplies, an adequate labour force, and reliable utilities (Kehoe and Taylor 1995: 17). Scotland is the most popular location as it is well provided with these facilities, and 'Silicon Glen' provides 35 per cent of personal computers with one in ten of the microchips made in Europe. But other peripheral areas of the UK have also gained. Furthermore, there are many plans to expand output (see Table 12.13), with a £2.4bn plan by Hyundai in Fife, a £1.1bn chip plant being built by Siemens in North Tyneside, and a £1.2bn plant by LG Semicon in South Wales. But in 1996 the supply of standard 16-megabit dynamic random access memory (D-Ram) chips increased far faster than demand, leading to a 70 per cent fall in their price (Burton 1996). This has led these producers to delay bringing on their new production, and some, such as Fujitsu, are proposing to leapfrog to producing the most advanced memory chips, 64-MBSDRAMS (Cane and Tighe 1996).

This expansion of production has led to fears of a shortage of skilled labour. In response to this the government co-operated with US and Japanese firms to set up a National Microelectronics Institute for training purposes in Scotland (Buxton and Wagstyl 1996). The US-owned Applied Materials, the world's largest supplier of wafer-processing equipment, is also to establish a £12m European Technical Centre in North Tyneside to train up to 300 graduates a year to be employed as equipment engineers in the semiconductor sector (Tighe 1996).

Thus Britain's electronic industry is largely the result of foreign direct investment – output is about twice the level in the early 1970s. Electronic products account for more than 40 per cent of Scotland's exports (Buxton 1995a: 21). In 1994 the UK was the fourth largest exporter of office machines and telecom equipment, with 5.9 per cent of the world market. Thus she was the largest European exporter. She was the fifth largest importer and

Table 12.13   1996 plans to build or extend electronics plants in the UK

Firm	Investment	Area
Semiconductors		
Fujitsu (Japan)[1]	£816m	Durham
LG Semicon (South Korea)[1]	£1.2bn	South Wales
Siemens (Germany)[1]	£1.1bn	Tyneside
Hyundai (South Korea)[3]	£2.4bn	Fife
QPL (South Korea)[5]	£230m	South Wales
Circuit boards		
Interconnection Systems (UK)[2]	£120m	Tyneside
Kohdensha (Japanese)[4]	£6.5m	Fife
Computor monitors		
Shinho Electronic Telecomm. (South Korea)[4]	£8.2m	Fife

Sources:
[1] S. Wagstyl, J. Burton and W. Munchau (1996) 'Chip giants to gamble on recovery', *Financial Times*, 17 July.
[2] C. Tighe (1996) 'Tyneside wins tussle for £120m electronics plant', *Financial Times*, 20 June.
[3] J. Buxton (1996) 'Scotland searches soul over chip jobs', *Financial Times*, 2/3 November.
[4] J. Burton and J. Buxton (1996) 'Koreans to invest £8m in Scotland', *Financial Times*, 30 May.
[5] A. Cane and C. Tighe (1996) 'Fujitsu delays semiconductor plan', *Financial Times*, 2/3 March.

her net balance was –$1.48bn. The only large developed country with posi-
tive net exports is Japan.

The importance of foreign-owned companies just reflects the position in
UK manufacturing as a whole (UK's stock of foreign investment has risen
from £52bn in 1986 to £131bn in 1994); the UK has 40 per cent of the
stock of US and Japanese investment in the enlarged EU. Foreign-owned
companies provide 18 per cent of the UK's manufacturing jobs, 24 per cent
of its net output, 32 per cent of manufacturing investment, and about 40
per cent of its manufactured exports (Buxton 1995b: 4). But it is unlikely
that this is what the EU Commission means by a strong industry.

CONCLUSION

Britain's expenditure on R&D as a percentage of GDP has declined since
the 1960s. In comparison with her major competitors her outlay has fallen
not only in relation to GDP, but also in total because her income has
been growing more slowly. The greatest reduction has been that in defence
R&D financed by the government and therefore the impact on civilian R&D
is less.

Her receipts from the exports of technology are less than half those of
Germany, the major earner in the EU, but her deficit in such trade is lower.

In her trade in high-technology goods she only had overall surpluses in chemicals, including pharmaceuticals and instruments.

The CEC has been particularly concerned with the EU's performance in IT industries and has endeavoured to buttress the position of the EU electronics firms. Tariffs were relatively high, but under the Information Technology Agreement they are due to be abolished by 2000. The CEC, however, has also imposed a large number of anti-dumping duties. It is this contingent protection plus the natural resources available that has induced Japanese and South Korean firms to invest in electronics production in the UK. As a result, the British electronics industry is largely foreign owned. She is a large exporter of office and telecommunications equipment, although overall she has a net deficit. The cost of this protectionist policy is borne by consumers in the form of the higher price of equipment. As a result, the ownership of home computers and access to the Internet is considerably lower than in the US.

NOTES

1 Coordinating Committee for Multilateral Export Controls, a voluntary group of most NATO nations.
2 Chris Gannon, having worked in the telecommunications industry, states that it is not a matter of incomes: 'In my field in the USA people are much more willing to be the first customer and to benefit from new technology. In the UK people always ask who tried the system first and there is a strong propensity to wait "until the bugs are ironed out".'
3 That is, charity research institutes.
4 This includes services.
5 Information supplied by Chris Gannon.
6 Ferguson was acquired by Thomson in 1987.

REFERENCES

Atkins, R. (1997) 'Eurofighter set for lift off as Germany gives the go-ahead', *Financial Times*, 27 November.
Brittan, S. (1996) 'Bad excuses for arms sales', *Financial Times*, 19 February.
Buchan, D., Gowers, A. and Peel, Q. (1996) 'France may split Thomson in sell-off', *Financial Times*, 9 December.
Buckley, N. (1997a) 'Brussels probes fax dumping', *Financial Times*, 4 February.
—— (1997b) 'Anti-dumping duties lifted on Korean D-Rams', *Financial Times*, 1 December.
Buckley, N., Kehoe, L. and Taylor, P. (1997) 'EU chip decision puzzles industry', *Financial Times*, 12 March.
Burton, J. (1996) 'LG Semicon shares fall in first full day's trading', *Financial Times*, 12 November.
Buxton, J. (1995a) 'New monarchs of the glen', *Financial Times*, 15 November.

—— (1995b) 'London is voted the best city again', *Financial Times*, 24 October.

Buxton, J. and Wagstyl, S. (1996) 'Scots win semiconductor institute', *Financial Times*, 21 June.

Cane, A. (1996) 'ICL strengthens Microsoft lies: US company steps closer to domination of operating software', *Financial Times*, 11 December.

Cane, A. and Tighe, C. (1996) 'Fujitsu delays semiconductor plan', *Financial Times*, 2/3 March.

CEC (1993) 'The European Community as a World Trade Partner', *European Economy*, **52**.

Denton, N. (1996) 'Oftel eases way for digital TV', *Financial Times*, 20 December.

—— (1997) 'Drive to plug the gap', *Financial Times*, 3 February.

Dicken, P. (1992) *Global Shift*, 2nd edn, London: Paul Chapman.

Dunne, N. (1995) 'US and EU to discuss ending IT tariffs', *Financial Times*, 1 December.

Eltis, W. and Fraser, D. (1992) 'The contribution of Japanese industrial success to Britain and to Europe', *National Westminster Bank Quarterly Review*.

European Communities (1988) *Single European Act*, Cm3720, London: HMSO.

Gannon, P. (1997) *Trojan Horses and National Champions*, London: Apt-Amatic Books.

GATT (1991) *Trade Policy Review: The European Communities 1991*, 2 vols, vol. 1, Geneva: GATT.

Gray, B. (1995) 'Eurofighter deal may end deadlock', *Financial Times*, 18–19 November.

—— (1996a) 'Project pulls out of spin', *Financial Times*, 30 August.

—— (1996b) 'UK puts faith in Europeans', *Financial Times*, 30 August.

—— (1997a) 'Dogfight to arm the Eurofighter', *Financial Times*, 17 February.

—— (1997b) 'MoD may delay Eurofighter missile contract', *Financial Times*, 17 February.

—— (1997c) 'Courtship rebuffed', *Financial Times*, 5/6 April.

Gray, B. and Buchan, D. (1997) 'France bars GEC from making bid for Thomson', *Financial Times*, 5/6 April.

Hill, A. (1996) 'Olivetti promises finance details in early October', *Financial Times*, 19 September.

Jack, A. (1996) 'Bull optimistic despite first-half loss', *Financial Times*, 30 July.

Jones, P. (1996) 'Research and experimental development (R&D) statistics 1994', *Economic Trends*, **514**, August.

Kehoe, L. (1996) 'Battle for the eyeballs', *Financial Times*, 28 November.

Kehoe, L. and Taylor, P. (1995) 'The chips are down as the stakes rise', *Financial Times*, 3 August.

Marsh, P. (1997) 'Sharp rise planned in TV set output', *Financial Times*, 14 April.

Muller, P. (1995) 'Aerospace companies and the state in Europe', in J. Hayward (ed.), *Industrial Enterprise and European Integration*, Oxford: Oxford University Press.

Nairn, G. (1997) 'Pulling the PC plug', *Financial Times*, suppl. *New Year Review*, 8 January.

Nicoll, A. (1997a) 'World arms sales growth put at 8 per cent', *Financial Times*, 15 October.

—— (1997b) 'Why Europe defence groups agree on need to consolidate', *Financial Times*, 16 October.

OECD (1968) *Statistical Tables and Notes: A Study of Resources Devoted to R&D in OECD Member Countries in 1963/64*, Paris: OECD.

—— (1970) *Gaps in Technology: Analytical Report*, Paris: OECD.

—— (1971) *The Conditions for Success in Technological Innovation*, Paris: OECD.

—— (1979) *Trends in Industrial R&D in Selected OECD Member Countries 1967–1975*, Paris: OECD.

—— (1994) *Science and Technology Policy: Review and Outlook*, Paris:OECD.

OECD/DSTI (1976) *Science Resources/Newsletter*, Science Resources Unit No.1, Paris: OECD, September.

Parkes, C. (1997) 'Brussels in digital video disc standards talks', *Financial Times*, 13 January.

Peterson, J. (1996) 'Research and development policy', in H. Kassim and A. Menon (eds), *The European Union and National Industrial Policy*, London: Routledge, ch. 6.

Rawsthorn, A. (1997) 'TV revolution "will fuel sales" ', *Financial Times*, 4 February.

Ridding, J. (1995) 'Contender powers up for semiconductor wars', *Financial Times*, 18 October.

Simkins, J. (1996) 'De Benedetti warns of "crisis" at Olivetti', *Financial Times*, 29 November.

Skapinker, M. (1997a) 'Airbus partners face hard decisions', *Financial Times*, 6 January.

—— (1997b) 'Overdue departure', *Financial Times*, 14 January.

—— (1997c) 'Airbus owners agree consortium's future', *Financial Times*, 15 October.

Stubbs, P. and Saviotti, P. (1994) 'Science and Technology Policy', in M. Artis and N. Lee (eds), *The Economics of the European Union*, Oxford: Oxford University Press.

Taylor, P. (1996) 'ICL to pull out of personal computers after £188m loss', *Financial Times*, 9/10 March.

—— (1997) 'Warm welcome from industry', *Financial Times*, 27 March.

Tighe, C. (1996) 'Centre to deal with skills crisis in chip industry', *Financial Times*, 4 November.

Vernon, R. (1966) 'International investment and international trade in the product cycle', *Quarterly Journal of Economics*, **80**, 190–207.

Wighton, D. (1995) 'A record that was easy to break', *Financial Times*, 8/9 July.

Williams, F. (1995) 'WTO chief tries to avoid confrontation', *Financial Times*, 14 December.

—— (1996) 'US attacks EU tariffs on computers', *Financial Times*, 23 May.

—— (1997) 'IT accord to scrap tariffs by year 2000', *Financial Times*, 27 March.

WTO (1995a) *Trade Policy Review: European Union*, 2 vols, Geneva: World Trade Organization.

—— (1995b) *International Trade Trends and Statistics*, Geneva: World Trade Organization.

13 Trade in services: Liberalization and growth

Services are distinguished from goods by their lack of tangibility, which means that they cannot be stored. The production and consumption of services must occur at the same time and, it used to be said, in the same place. But with the advent of telecommunications, telephone calls and the transmission of data, pictures and sound can take place over vast distances almost simultaneously. So the definition has to be qualified and it now encompasses items whose consumption and production generally take place at the same time and which are not tangible. They have therefore been regarded as more difficult to trade than manufactures. Of course, some services are associated with trade in goods such as shipping, air transport, and insurance. Indeed, one of the arguments for liberalizing trade in telecommunications is that they are the means by which merchandise trade is organized.

However, it must be remembered that from the point of view of a country such as the UK the use of a ship to export a car to the US or import a machine tool from there only appears in the balance of payments if the payment for its use is made to foreign residents. If the ship is owned by a company resident in Britain, wherever it may go, the payment for its use by a firm resident in Britain is a transaction between residents of the same country, and therefore does not enter the country's balance of payments.

Apart from the provision of services in conjunction with trade in goods, and also tourism, the service sector was previously regarded as a producer of non-tradeables. But the technological developments in telecommunications and electronics have radically changed this. Furthermore, as the EC Member States became increasingly dependent on the service sector the barriers to supplying them across national boundaries began to appear as serious impediments to competition and efficiency. These are not tariffs but national regulations and public procurement. The Single European Act (SEA) was designed to remove the remaining non-tariff barriers to intra-EC trade. It was negotiated and passed when the service sector in the rest of the EC – that is, banks, airlines, railways, telephones and broadcasting – were largely government controlled.

This must be seen in the larger context of the liberalization and competition introduced into airline and telecommunication services by the US, and the programme of privatization and liberalization introduced by the Thatcher government in the UK. The reduction in prices that followed these reforms eventually induced the CEC to persuade EU countries to follow suit. This meant dismantling the state control of these industries in most EU countries and breaking up monopolies.

By the time the Single European Market (SEM) was established on 1 January 1993, privatization was well under way. This became far more important for trade than the opening up of public procurement tenders to all EC firms.

Another EC policy that will affect trade in services is the provision in the Treaty of European Union signed at Maastricht in 1993 for 'Trans-European Networks', described in Chapter 4.

THE GROWTH OF UK TRADE IN SERVICES

Having outlined developments at the European level, let us now consider Britain's position. The importance of liberalization to her should not be underestimated. The UK is now predominately a service economy, with two-thirds of her output and three-quarters of employment accounted for by services.

In respect of trade, the Government's Office for National Statistics emphasizes the difficulty in identifying which residents receive or render a service when there are so many intermediaries providing them.[1] It distinguishes six main categories of traded service:

1   general government;
2   sea transport;
3   civil aviation;
4   travel, which includes leisure travel (i.e. tourism, and business travel);
5   financial and allied institution services; and
6   other business services.

Recent developments in the volume of trade – that is, with the removal of the effect of changes in the price level – of these different categories is shown in Figures 13.1, transport and 13.2, financial and business services. Figure 13.1 shows that the volume of exports of shipping services more than halved between 1974 and 1984 and imports also fell. Exports of aviation services were increasing, with fluctuations, and so also were imports. The same was true of travel.

Figure 13.2 shows the wide fluctuation in exports of financial services, with the major peak in 1986 and 1987. There are no volume figures for earlier years. Indeed, the concept of volume is rather difficult in this case in so far as much of the return to the financial sector consists of the difference in the price at which financial assets are bought and sold, and this depends much more on the instability of the market in these assets than any services provided by the finance houses.

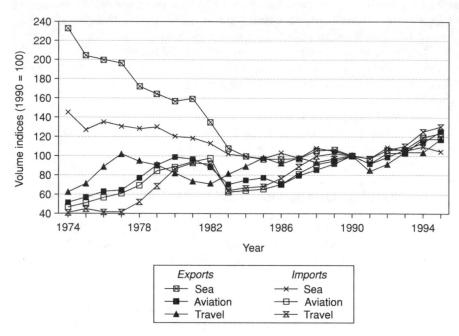

Figure 13.1 Volume of trade in services, 1974–95. Exports and Imports 1990 = 100

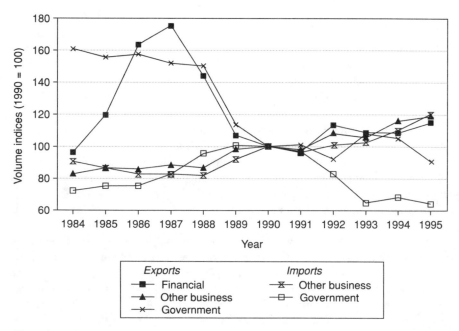

Figure 13.2 Financial business services, 1984–95. Exports and Imports 1990 = 100

The category of other business services is a heterogeneous collection of individual consultancy services, computer and telecommunication services etc., royalties and educational services. Individual consultancy appears to have been declining, except that for management and economic consultants, and for accountants. But the exports of most of the others has been increasing rapidly. The value of royalites received tripled between 1985 and 1995, but so did the payments for them.

Exports of government services fell from 1984 to 1990, but then just fluctuated. Imports rose somewhat in real terms between 1984 and 1990 and then fell.

The balance of trade in the different sectors is shown in Figure 13.3. The increasing deficit in travel is outweighed by the much larger surplus in finance, which is also increasing in financial terms.

Britain's trade in services with the different continents, the EU, and her most significant trading partners is shown in Table 13.1. With all continents except Europe she had a surplus. She had a deficit with the rest of the EU, the most important contributors being France £1bn and Spain £2.5bn. Her most important individual trading partner was the US, with whom she had a surplus of £2bn.

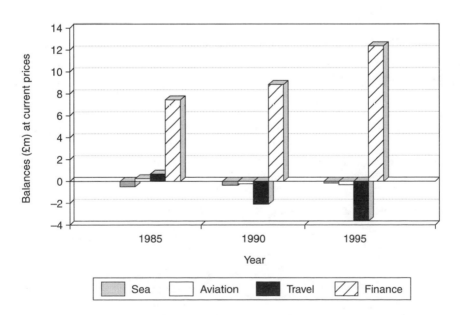

Figure 13.3 Service sector balances, 1985, 1990, 1995. £million current prices

Table 13.1 Geographical distribution of trade in services in 1995 (£m)

	Credits	Debits	Balance
Europe	19,416	21,625	−2,209
Africa	1,979	1,287	692
America	12,197	9,574	2,623
Asia	10,261	5,151	5,110
Australasia and Oceania	1,583	939	644
International organizations	108	—	108
Unallocated	−290	536	−826
World total	45,254	39,112	6,142
EU total	15,666	17,958	−2,292
Germany	3,891	3,253	638
France	2,528	3,709	−1,181
Italy	1,489	1,133	356
Netherlands	1,590	1,536	54
Belgium and Luxembourg	1,258	985	273
Ireland	1,484	976	508
Greece	439	1,049	−610
Spain	929	3,413	−2,484
USA	10,072	7,941	2,131
Japan	2,494	883	1,611
Australia	1,272	728	544
Saudi Arabia	1,645	328	1,317

Source: D. Townsend (1966) 'Geographical breakdown of the balance of payments current account', *Economic Trends*, **516**, October.

TRADE LIBERALIZATION

To what degree is recent liberalization likely to affect the UK's pattern of trade and how are British firms responding? To answer this it is necessary to consider the various types of liberalization.

Harmonization, the policy the EC had long pursued with respect to goods, took on an added significance with the advent of electronics, when it became impossible to interconnect computers or telephones without some agreement on standards. So let us consider standards first.

Standards

For *telecommunications and computing* the setting of standards is a global problem and is therefore negotiated through the International Organization for Standardization (ISO). There is also a similar organization, EAN International, for agreements on bar codes (Gooding 1995). Not only cost minimization but also the necessity of having mutually compatible standards for interconnection to take place is driving the process forward.

However, as described in Chapter 12, the EU has had far more problems, some of which have been self-inflicted, in setting standards for high-definition television.

In June 1997 the EU entered into agreement with the US and Canada for the mutual recognition of inspection, testing and certification of information technology and telecommunications equipment, production of pharmaceuticals, medical devices and leisure marine craft. This allows for industries to have their products tested for both EU and North American standards in one country – a mutual recognition of testing rather than of standards. It could save telecoms and information technology businesses $1.37bn a year (Thoenes 1997).

Standards for *air traffic*, also an international problem, are negotiated by the International Civil Aviation Organization (ICAO), an intergovernmental organization affiliated to the UN. It has developed technical standards for the industry, but they are not binding. Its members signed the 'Chicago Convention' of 1944 which affirmed that each country has absolute sovereignty over the airspace above its territory. Each government developed protective barriers around its own national aviation market and organized its own airspace and air-traffic control. As a result, in Western Europe there were 54 control centres, 31 technical systems, and 70 different computer languages involved in the management of air traffic (Kassim 1996: 107).

The EU has also encountered problems due to incompatible standards in instituting its master plan for a high-speed rail network. Initially, high-speed trains only operated within a Member State. But the opening of the Channel Tunnel meant that the Eurostar locomotive, which runs from London to Paris and Brussels, had to be built to run on four different types of power supply and three signalling systems in order to be able to go through the different Member States. As a result, each locomotive was very expensive, costing £24m. In addition, Britain's loading gauge – the diameter of tunnels and the positioning of her rail platforms – is too small to accommodate continental European rolling stock (Batchelor 1995).

The CEC has also been pressing for other types of harmonization, for instance in managing traffic flows. Lack of standardization not only raises the cost of equipment, but also means that a system sometimes cannot be operated at all.

Single European Act (SEA) 1986 instituting the Single European Market (SEM) on 1 January 1993

The situation before the SEA and the changes it brought about will now be discussed in order to show how much more liberalized the EU markets in which UK firms are operating have become.

Financial services

The national regulations with respect to financial services were aimed primarily at prudential or safety objectives, but tended to limit entry as a side effect. In each EC country there was freedom of establishment for foreign banks, but under conditions which differed between countries (CEC 1988). Apart from the UK, all branches of foreign banks were required to maintain their own minimum endowment capital, the definition of which varied from Member State to Member State. The number of branches a foreign bank could open in a Member State was also often limited.

The most important change was introduced by the Second Banking Directive (89/646/EEC) by which a 'green passport' for banks and financial firms, which were authorized in a Member State to operate and set up branches, was extended to any other without further authorization. No endowment capital was required. Thus was introduced the concept of the 'home country', that is, the EU Member State that has granted authorization, which then becomes responsible for supervising the bank's activities wherever it may operate. The Directive also allowed for reciprocal access to the SEM for banks from non-member countries (Molyneux 1996).

These principles of mutual recognition and home country control were also introduced for firms operating in the securities market. However, Molyneux has argued that there are still impediments in the workings of the market in the form of derogations that can be used by Member States in the light of the 'general good'. Secondly, there are tax obstacles, when tax on, for instance, interest and dividends that is removed at source may be remitted to a national but not a non-national of a Member State (ibid.).

Restrictions on international payments on the current account had been removed throughout Western Europe in 1958. In Britain, restrictions on capital account payments were removed by the Conservative government in 1979, and then, beginning with West Germany and the Netherlands, they were removed for the other EC countries.

Road transport

The SEA also included provisions for a common transport policy. This involved the removal of all quantitative restrictions by 1992, such as the limit to the number of permits issued to hauliers to move goods between Member States, and the prohibition of 'cabotage'. 'Cabotage' is the transportation of goods or people within a Member State by a haulier that is not a resident of it. Its prohibition involves losses in efficiency associated with the movement of empty vehicles. For road haulage these were estimated by Ernst and Whinney to cost the EC ECU 1.2bn, of which 20 per cent might be due to regulatory restrictions (CEC 1988: 96). Liberalization has consisted of increasing the number of vehicle permits for inter-Member State haulage, and extending cabotage, so that by July 1998 qualified EU carriers in one Member State will be allowed to undertake domestic road haulage in another, while carrying out inter-Member State haulage. Regulation 2454/92 also provided for a limited amount of cabotage to be practised by international coach operators (Lee 1997).

Air transport

In air transport each Member State had a flag-carrying airline, which it generally owned and was willing to subsidize. International scheduled air services were organized by bilateral agreements between the governments concerned, who decided how many airlines would operate a route and which they would be. Generally, each government nominated only one airline, its 'flag carrier', on a route. Secondly, each government would specify in each agreement which points in its country would be served by the airline of the other country. Thirdly, the governments decided how capacity was to be shared between the two countries, generally on a 50–50 basis. Fourthly, the designated airlines had to agree on fares for each route in line with the rates determined by the International Air Transport Association (IATA). This had to be approved by both governments before the service could be brought into operation (Kassim 1996).

With respect to domestic services the government of a country had complete control over market access, the degree of competition on individual routes, and the level of air fares. Even in respect to charter flights, which, according to the 'Chicago Convention', only required authorization from the country of destination, most governments imposed severe restrictions on entrants.

It was therefore a completely cartellized system with government sanction. The only access an airline had to the market of another Member State was by the bilateral agreement between its own and the other government. In 1987 only 5 per cent of European routes had multiple designation, that is, more than one airline per Member State per route. The fifth freedom – the freedom for a carrier to carry commercial traffic between two foreign states on a route to or from the home state – was effectively prohibited. Full cabotage was not allowed (CEC 1988: 97; Kassim 1996). It was estimated that costs were 20 per cent higher than in North America and that an increase in competition would allow a reduction in fares of 15–20 per cent (CEC 1998: 98).

The US then decided to break away from this cartellized system in 1978. The UK and the Netherlands also signed a liberal bilateral agreement in 1984, which allowed several airlines on a route. Indeed, relative to the other EC countries they pursued relatively liberal policies. The UK had the greatest number of independent airlines in Europe and the strongest consumer lobby. It pioneered low-cost travel assisted by a liberal charter policy. It was the only European country to have an independent civil aviation authority (Kassim 1996).

The UK's flag carrier was British Airways (BA). The Thatcher government had started the process of privatizing BA in 1981. In 1984 the government set out in a White Paper the four objectives of its airline policy, as follows:

(i)   to encourage a sound and competitive multi-airline industry;
(ii) to promote competition in all markets both internationally and domestically;
(iii) to ensure adequate safeguards against anticompetitive behaviour by airlines;
(iv) to privatize BA.

(Vickers and Yarrow 1988: 349)

BA was privatized in 1987 and, in the same year, took over British Caledonian, one of its chief competitors.

By 1995 BA was the most important international airline, carrying 25 million passengers a year. If domestic flights are combined with international ones it is the ninth largest in the world, with 32 million passengers (Rice and Tucker 1997). Its competitive position was strengthened by its landing rights; in 1996 it held 38 per cent of the take-off and landing slots at the main London airport, Heathrow, which is the most valued airport (Skapinker 1996a).

BA's position with respect to the US was governed by the Bermuda II agreement signed in 1977, which lays down details of which airlines can fly between specified US and UK cities, the number of flights they can operate, and, in some cases, the types of aircraft they can use.

The CEC was initially handicapped in its efforts to formulate an EC airline policy by uncertainty as to whether it could apply competition policy in that area. But in the mid-1980s the European Court ruled in the *Nouvelle Frontières* case that the competition rules did apply to the air transport sector. The CEC then drew up in succession three air transport liberalization packages. The first package came into effect in 1987; it allowed any number of airlines to compete on routes within the EC, thus overriding the insistence of some Member States that their flag carriers be guaranteed 50 per cent of their market; the ratio was to be reduced gradually to 40 per cent. The 'fifth freedom' was permitted for 30 per cent of the traffic. The second package extended the provisions of the first; in particular, the 'fifth freedom' was permitted for 50 per cent of the market.

The third package, which was agreed in 1992 and which came into force on 1 January 1993, expanded the market access of Member States; it permitted multidesignation on all routes and the fifth freedom without quota restraint, and since 1 April 1997 full cabotage has also been allowed. Thus an airline of one Member State can compete on the domestic routes of another Member State. These rights have also been extended to the European Economic Area, that is, Norway, Iceland and Liechtenstein in addition to the EU. However, EU Member States are still allowed to deny access to very congested airports and to allocate traffic on a non-discriminatory basis between airports in the same airport system. Airlines are now free to set their own fares, with some safeguards against excessively low or high rates. Capacity restrictions have been removed. Most importantly, the third package introduced an EC-wide licensing system with a Communitywide airworthiness certificate and Community ownership and control criteria, which allowed any carrier that satified them to operate services anywhere in the EU (Bray 1996; Kassim 1996; Skapinker 1997c).

The CEC has acted circumspectly in relation to the granting of state aid, as this area is very politically sensitive. It has continued to allow governments to subsidize Air France, Iberia of Spain, Olympic Airways of Greece and Aer Lingus of Ireland, but it is scrutinizing state aid more carefully. In 1997 it agreed to aid of £955m to Alitalia for restructuring, on condition that it sold its 35 per cent stake in Malev the Hungarian airline and disposed of its holdings in various regional airports; the Italian government also agreed not to give Alitalia preference in the allocation of traffic rights (Tucker 1997a). New airlines are unwilling to enter markets to compete against subsidized carriers, so this is restricting the benefits of liberalization. An additional constraint cited by Mr Ornstein of Virgin Express is that of obtaining slots at airports such as Frankfurt, Madrid, Barcelona, Milan and Brussels. Many of these shortages are regarded as artificial (Skapinker 1997c).

Rail transport

Air transport has been affected by the improvement in railways, particularly the opening of the Channel Tunnel in 1994. The EU drew up in 1990 a master plan for the development of high-speed rail involving a tenfold increase in the 2,900 km of track capable of running high-speed trains. This would link most of the major cities of Europe by 2010. EU airlines are so worried at the possibility of losing customers that they have been lobbying the CEC to limit rail subsidies. In view of the large subsidies the airlines have received in the past the CEC has been unsympathetic and has told them that they will have to learn to compete (Skapinker and Batchelor 1995).

Telecommunications and computing

The other major area of services is telecommunications and computing. The rapid and continuing technological advances they exhibited meant that the CEC was being forced to develop a policy for them alongside the institution of the SEM.

THE EC'S TELECOMMUNICATIONS POLICY

The initial form of co-operation between European countries was the European Conference for Post and Telecommunication (CEPT), set up by a diplomatic conference in 1959. It was the domain of the post, telephone and telegraph administrations (PTTs), and dealt with tariffs (i.e. charges) and after the mid-1970s, the technical standards necessary for interconnecting telecommunications networks. The telecommunications sector was exempt from the Public Procurement Directive to governments to open their tenders to European manufacturers. The PTTs were regarded as vital to the national interest and their purchase of equipment was a national affair (Schneider *et al.* 1994).

The EC's policy in this area was in response to what was perceived as a failure to keep up with the US and Japan in the information technology industry. Its first intervention was with ESPRIT in 1979. The Directorate-General III (DGIII) responsible for the SEM then endeavoured to harmonize requirements for telematic equipment, but was opposed by the British, French and Germans, particularly with respect to videotext. The DGIII was concerned with computer networks. The PTTs were not co-operative.

The US, however, then deregulated and liberalized its telecommunications market, followed, in 1984, by the UK, which started privatizing British Telecom and licensed Mercury as a competitor, which entered the market in 1986. It also established Oftel as an independent regulator. One of the reasons for the Conservative government engaging in this privatization, apart from any ideological ones, was that the industry was anticipated to require vast funds for investment and the government was anxious to keep down its PSBR. However, BT has never had any difficulty in raising money on the open market; in 1997 it raised $1.5bn with a five-year bond issue (Lapper 1997).

The effects of these privatizations were twofold. First, it demonstrated the importance of the large firms. After the US courts forced AT&T in 1983 to split from its local services companies, the 'Baby Bells', it formed joint ventures with Philips and Olivetti to enter the European markets. At the same time, IBM diversified into telecomunications by investing in MCI. The EC industrial policy makers became afraid that US multinationals, with their hegemony in information technology, would conquer Europe's communications market.

Secondly, the US began to put pressure on the EC to open its telecommunications market. The CEC began to take a more active stance in order to improve EC competitiveness, engaging users as well as producers in discussions. Between 1984 and 1992 the Council and CEC passed 40 major decisions pertaining to telecommunications. In 1987 the CEC put forward a Green Paper the provisions of which aimed at deregulation and increased competition, although the network infrastructure and basic services were to remain under the exclusive control of the national PTTs. It also asked for a separation of the PTTs' regulatory functions from their operational ones (Schneider *et al.* 1994).

In 1993 the Council of Ministers adopted Resolution C93/231/01, which provided for the liberalization of public telephony services by 1 January 1998.[1]

Meanwhile in the UK in 1991 the Oftel regulator abolished the duopoly of BT and Mercury by permitting licences of any new network provided that it was not an international one. The government decided that BT would not be allowed to compete directly with cable companies in the transmission of broadcast entertainment until 2001. But the cable companies transmitting broadcast entertainment (i.e. TV and radio) were allowed to carry telephony. In 1997, three of these companies – Nynex, Bell Cablemedia, and Videotron – merged with Mercury to form C&W Communications, representing about 70 per cent of all UK cable customers and with more than 500,000 telecoms subscribers, 600,000 television customers and potential access to 6 million homes. The second largest cable company, Telewest, then attached itself to the national fibre-optics network of BRT, the former British Rail telecoms operator owned by Racal (Price 1997). In 1996 the UK introduced 'number portability', that is, the customer's right to retain the same phone number when changing operators (Cane 1997d). Finally, in 1997 the UK regulator permitted competition in international services, with fifty companies awarded licences to compete with BT and Cable & Wireless Communications. It is hoped that the UK might become the hub for international traffic (Cane 1998).

The UK system goes some way to achieving the final objective of the CEC, which is an information superhighway throughout the EU, described as follows:

> a fully digital, broadband, fibre-optic network which can carry a wide range of services such as the combination of voice, video, and data known as 'multimedia' ... The key to its success lies in its flexibility and its ability to integrate previously independent technologies such as telephony, television and computers.
>
> (Curwen 1995: 337)

Full liberalization of the $200bn EU telecommunications market was instituted at the beginning of 1998. Only three Member States – Greece, Ireland and Portugal – have been allowed a period of grace before exposing themselves to unfettered competition. The others face possible legal action by the CEC if they do not comply with its market-opening rules.

The German market is the largest in the EU and is regarded as the most lucrative. Deutsche Telekom, partially privatized in 1996 but still majority owned by the government, has been preparing to lose its monopoly of public voice-telephony services. In the past six years it invested DM 150bn mainly in digitalizing its networks and building a modern fibre-optics system across

Eastern Germany. It still retains considerable monopoly power, although it is legally obliged to negotiate terms for interconnecting its rivals to its network. It is facing fierce competition. Chief of its competitors is o.tel.o, a new company owned by Veba and RWE, two large energy and industrial conglomerates, which have invested DM 7bn (£2.6bn) in it. Cable & Wireless pulled out of this alliance when it realized how much investment was needed. Other competitors are Viag Interkom, which is 50 per cent owned by Viag and 50 per cent by BT, and Mannesmann, which has joined with Deutsche Bahn to build an alternative network along the railway operator's tracks. Deutsche Telekom objected to the low prices for 'interconnection' between its network and those of its rivals set by the German regulator. Deutsche Telekom thinks the charges should include some return for its investment programme. In addition, o.tel.o has complained to the German regulator about the high 'routing charge', a one-off of £29, imposed by Deutsche Telekom. High interconnection charges are likely to continue to be a cause for complaint and legal action throughout the EU. European companies and the CEC wonder if a Euro-regulator might not be more effective than the present national regulators, such as Oftel, in fighting the former telecommunication monopolies (Atkins 1997b; Cane 1997d, 1997e; Tucker 1997b; Fisher 1998).

The German mobile telecommunications market has been liberalized since 1990. The largest mobile operator is majority owned by Mannesmann, two are owned by Deutsche Telekom, and a fifth owned by Viag Interkom is due to enter soon.

Thus BT is participating in the German market, the largest in the EU, in its alliance with Viag. The German firms are far too strongly entrenched for British firms to compete in other ways. In France, BT is a partner with Compagnie Générale des Eaux in Cegetel, which is likely to be the chief competitor to France Telecom. In Ireland it has established a subsidiary in partnership with the Electricity Board. This is part of its global strategy of forming alliances which will be discussed later.

Broadcasting

The conflicts over the standards for HDTV have been discussed in the previous chapter. With respect to broadcasting television there was a great deal of confusion. The Member States initially had complete control over transmission due to their ability to allocate a limited number of frequencies. It was public service-orientated. In Britain there was the public sector BBC financed by the TV licence and ITV financed by advertising, and both had to comply with certain social requirements. A similar situation existed in France.

Government policies were confused because they were pursuing contradictory policies. Fraser describes Margaret Thatcher's policy in Britain towards the BBC and ITV as follows:

> Her heroic, deregulatory approach to broadcasting policy . . . came into
> conflict with her personal desire to maintain political control over the
> broadcasting system, even over the content of television programmes.
>
> (Fraser 1996: 209)

The same conflict between the desire for deregulation and control was a
feature in France. In addition, there was the anxiety of the subsidized producers of programmes that they would be swamped by imports from the
US.

The CEC's competence with respect to the sector was established by
the European Court of Justice ruling in 1974 that a television programme
was a 'service' as defined by the Treaty of Rome and had a 'transnational'
character. This meant that the French endeavour to restrict the amount
of imports from the US, which in any case was opposed by other
Member States, was difficult to pursue. The CEC introduced a Directive
in 1986 called 'Television without Frontiers' which imposed two restraints
on television networks: first, that there should be a minimum of 60 per
cent of European programmes broadcast, and secondly, that they should
spend at least 10 per cent of their programming budgets on purchases
from independent producers. The UK opposed the Directive, insisting on
maintaining national control over broadcasting even though, according to
Fraser, there was by a 'gentleman's agreement', dating from the 1950s, on
an 86 per cent quota for British programmes on the BBC–ITV duopoly
(Fraser 1996). The CEC's requirements were later watered down. But, in
any case, government control of broadcasting was being undermined by
satellite television and the increased use of cables. The CEC also tried to
limit concentration among broadcasters. In general, though, the CEC has
been ineffectual in this area and it does not appear to have affected trade
(ibid.).

INTERNATIONAL AGREEMENTS

Uruguay Round

The liberalization of the service sector within the EC provided some impetus
towards the adoption of the provisions with respect to services in the Uruguay
Round. Those supplied in the exercise of government authority were
excluded. The negotiations were with respect to trade in commercial services
between members of GATT, with the EU negotiating as one entity. They
comprised the supply of a service:

(a) from the territory of one member into the territory of any other member;
(b) in the territory of one member to the service consumer of any other
    member;

(c)　by a service supplier of one member, through commercial presence in the territory of any other member;

(d)　by a service supplier of one member, through presence of natural persons of a member in the territory of any other member.

The General Agreement on Trade in Services (GATS) was negotiated as a separate treaty. Each member was to accord mfn treatment to the services or service supplier of any other member. Further liberalization was then negotiated on the basis of a schedule of services put forward by each member. Foreign suppliers could be accorded national treatment (i.e. no discrimination between national and foreign suppliers) and market access (i.e. freedom of entry and exit). Progressive liberalization was to be achieved over a period of five years.

In respect to broadcasting, the US demanded that American audio-visual products should not be limited by quota and that the 'Television without Frontiers' Directive should not apply to new technologies. They wanted 'market access' and 'national treatment' for the audio-visual sector, which would have put an end to European subsidies. Under great pressure from France the EU took a derogation – that is, an exemption – with respect to broadcasting services.

Negotiations were still continuing on many of the packages when the body of the GATS agreement was signed in 1994. The following Telecoms Agreement reached in 1997 is one of the most important.

WTO Telecoms Agreement

In February 1997, under the aegis of the World Trade Organization, sixty-eight countries, including the EU, accounting for more than 90 per cent of world telecoms revenues, signed a Telecoms Agreement. The countries agreed to open their markets to foreign competition, allow overseas companies to buy stakes in domestic operators, and abide by common rules on fair competition in the telecoms sector. The world's biggest markets, which include the US, the most developed members of the EU,[2] and Japan, will be liberalized by 1 January 1998 when the agreement comes into effect. It covers all forms of basic telecommunication services including voice telephony, data and fax transmissions, and satellite and radio communications (Williams and Cane 1997).

It is estimated that competition will cut the cost of international calls by more than 80 per cent and the Institute for International Economics calculated that it could cut telecoms bills by up to $1,000bn, equivalent to 4 per cent of world GDP. It will assist the development of the global information highway and boost foreign investment in modernizing and expanding the telecoms network in developing countries (Williams 1997a). 'Mr Ian Taylor, the UK science and technology minister, said the deal should usher in explosive growth in turnover and investment worldwide, "The market is already worth $600bn annually and is growing at 10 per cent a year. Some analysts are predicting an extra £20bn worth of telecoms business for the UK alone over the next 10 to 15 years" ' (Williams and Cane 1997).

WTO Financial Services Agreement

In December 1997 agreement was at last reached on introducing international competition into trade in services, in a multilateral framework subject to legally binding fair-trade rules and WTO disciplines. In total, 102 countries agreed to open up their banking, insurance, and securities markets in varying degrees to foreign competition. Many of these are developing countries which have resisted foreign participation in their markets until now. However, the recent turmoil in the Asian currency markets, which revealed how primitive and inefficient many of the financial systems in East Asian countries were, has persuaded them to join in order to restore stability and investor confidence. Developing countries in Asia and Latin America have agreed with the US and EU to lower barriers to foreign suppliers of financial services, not only in cross-border trade, but also in other ways such as by the establishment of local branches or subsidiaries. This agreement covers 95 per cent of the worlds multitrillion dollar financial services market, involving $18,000bn in global securities assets, $38,000bn in international bank lending, and about $2,500bn in worldwide insurance premiums. It will come into effect in March 1999 (Jonquières 1997; Williams 1997b).

FOREIGN DIRECT INVESTMENT

International alliances and FDI

Thus British firms are facing markets in other EU countries which are gradually opening up. Now, with the WTO Telecoms and Financial Services Agreements, markets in the rest of the world will also be liberalized. In so far as firms in the UK have been operating in a domestic market which has already been liberalized they might be expected to benefit from their experience. But in order to exploit this advantage they often need presence in these markets, because, in the nature of services, production and consumption must occur at the same time and often in the same place. Their approach to this varies, as will be described.

British firms have established presence in several different ways. First, by franchising: for instance, in 1996 BA reached an agreement with British Mediterranean Airways, a UK-based carrier, whereby it would fly to Beirut, Amman and Damascus. It now has nine franchisees (see Table 13.2 for the previous ones). These are independent airlines with aircraft painted in BA colours and staff wearing BA uniforms, and these arrangements provided it with £50m revenue in 1995 (Skapinker 1996b).

Table 13.2 British Airways (BA) stakeholding and alliances in 1995

Shareholdings (%)	Alliances	Other operations
British Asia Airways (100)	Cityflyer Express[1]	Merger with British Caledonian
Brymon European (100)	Brymon European[1]	
BA Regional (100)	Loganair[1]	Merger with Dan-Air
TAT (49.9)	TAT[1]	
Deutsche BA (49)	Deutsche BA[1]	
GB Airways (31)	GB Airways[1]	
Air Russia (25)	Maersk Air[1]	
US Air (24.6)	US Air[2,3,4]	
Quantas (21)	Quantas[5]	
	Manx Airlines[1]	
	American Airlines[2a]	

Source: H. Kassim (1996) 'Air transport', in H. Kassim and A. Menon, *The European Union and National Industrial Policy*, London: Routledge; M. Skapinker (1996a) 'A day for eating words', *Financial Times*, 12 June.

Notes:
[1]   franchising; [2] code sharing; [3] joint sales/marketing agreement; [4] frequent flyer programme; [5] joint operations.
[a]   1996.

BA has also concluded a series of alliances, as can be seen in Table 13.2. Generally, BA has taken an equity share in its partner: for instance, initially almost half of Deutsche BA and TAT. Together these lost £68m in 1996. Now BA has taken full ownership of TAT and bought a majority share in Air Liberté, an independent French airline. BA has set up these alliances in order to take advantage of the complete liberalization of EU aviation, permitting cabotage, that came into effect on 1 April 1997. Consultants advised BA to drop routes in which it was not one of the largest carriers and accounted for less than 40 per cent of the flights. In Germany it is therefore concentrating on domestic routes, and its presence on these routes has already led to a reduction in the fares of Lufthansa, its chief competitor. BA is regarded as an efficient airline and its present inability to make profits in these markets is discouraging independent airlines such as British Midland and Virgin Express from entering (Skapinker 1997c, 1997d).

BA has also concluded alliances with US airlines, as have many of the European companies. It has a 24.6 per cent stake in US Air and in 1996 it concluded an agreement with American Airlines for code sharing. The competition problems involved with the latter have already been discussed.

BA is competing with other groupings, the biggest of which is the Star Alliance, which consists of Lufthansa of Germany, United Airlines of the US, Scandinavian Airlines System, Thai Airways, Air Canada, and Varig of Brazil. For economy passengers it is competing with some recently established low-cost airlines, such as Ryanair and EasyJet. BA is now itself planning to set up a new low-cost, no-food-or-frills airline 'Operation Blue Sky', based at Stansted, to begin operation in 1998. The existing small low-cost airlines regard it as a plan to knock them out of the market and are afraid that Blue Sky will be cross-subsidized by BA's traditional routes; they are planning to appeal to the EU's competition Directorate (Gresser 1997; Nicoll and Gresser 1997; Skapinker 1997e).

In *telecommunications*, BT has for more than three years been constructing a web of stakes and alliances – forty-four partnerships and distributorships for Concert Communications its previous alliance with MCI (US), which had 6 per cent of the $670bn global telecoms market. In 1997 Telefonica of Spain, which has a foothold in South America, joined it. BT has a 75 per cent stake in Concert. In 1994 it acquired a 20 per cent stake in MCI and then in March 1997 it made a $20bn (£12.4bn) bid in cash and shares for the rest of MCI (Burns and Cane 1997; Cane 1997a). However, in the summer of 1997 MCI warned that its future profitability would be harmed by the difficulties it was having in breaking into North America's liberalizing local markets. BT thereupon forced MCI to accept a 15 per cent reduction in the buying price, to the pleasure of BT shareholders. But this led to two other bids: first, by an aggressive US Telecom company, World-Com, a $30bn all-shares one; and second, by GTE, the largest US local telephone operator, a $28bn all-cash offer. World-Com then raised its bid to $37bn in terms of its own shares to which MCI agreed. MCI paid BT a penalty of $450m and an additional $15m for breaking the merger agreement. World-Com agreed to pay BT $7bn in cash rather than shares for its 20 per cent of MCI. Thus BT emerges with a $3bn net profit from its investment in MCI. It will buy the 25 per cent of Concert held by MCI and will undoubtedly be looking for other alliances (Cane 1997c).

Concert is now competing on the world market with Global One – a joint venture between Deutsche Telekom, France Telecom and Sprint, the US long-distance operator – and WorldPartners – a co-operative partnership led by AT&T, the largest US carrier, and Unisource, an alliance of smaller European operators. These three global carriers – Concert, Global One and World Partners – face some independent large operators such as NTT of Japan, and Cable & Wireless, and some small ones (Cane 1997b). (It might be noted that both BT & Cable & Wireless were once nationalized UK companies.)

These webs of alliances in aviation and telecommunications have been fairly recently established. They are partly an aspect of the provision of services. The British firms BA and BT in their aggressive approach are utilizing their knowledge of competitive markets. But the spread of alliances is also the result of governments endeavouring to increase competition in their domestic market, which entails the restriction of the larger providers. Unable to expand at home, firms expand their activities abroad.

The UK financial sector has recently had several examples of straightforward takeovers by firms from other EU Member States. For instance, Morgan Grenfell was acquired by the Deutsche Bank, Kleinwort Benson by the

Dresdner Bank, and Barings by ING of the Netherlands. This appears to be the case of an investor with a non-specific factor, capital in the form of cash, endeavouring to gain control of some specific factor, namely, financial expertise. The problem with these types of specific skills is that they are incorporated in people who may require large financial incentives to stay with the firm. Presumably the investor hopes that these skills can be taught to other people.

FDI in services

For some time now services have accounted for a significant proportion of foreign direct investment. This is measured either in terms of the stock at any particular time, or in terms of flows, that is, the addition to a stock over a period of time. Taking the three largest investors in the mid-1980s, the percentage of its FDI stock held abroad in services by the US was 43 per cent, by the UK was 35 per cent, and by Japan was 57 per cent. The equivalent percentage flows were 53 per cent for the US, 38 per cent for the UK, and 62 per cent for Japan (UN 1989: 10–12). In 1989, 47 per cent of the flow of Japanese investment in the EC was in finance and insurance, and 12 per cent in commerce (Balasubramanyam and Greenaway 1992). Britain was the destination of 40 per cent of the investment by the US and Japan in the EC, but it is not clear whether it conformed to the average distribution for the EC as a whole.

Table 13.3   Foreign direct investment flows in services for US, UK, and Japan (£bn)

	Average inward flows p.a.		Average outward flows p.a.	
	1975–80	*1981–85*	*1975–80*	*1981–85*
United States				
Total	7.6	17.6	15.6	9.1
Developed ME			11.7	6.2
Developing ME			3.9	2.9
United Kingdom				
Total	2.8	2.7	4.7	7.9
Developed ME			3.8	6.3
Developing ME			1.0	1.7
Japan				
Total	0.3	0.7	4.0	9.4
Developed ME			1.8	5.1
Developing ME			2.2	4.3

Source: UN (1989) *Foreign Direct Investment and Transnational Corporations in Services*, New York: UN.

Notes:
Average UK exchange rate 1975–80 taken as 2.023 $/£ and for 1981–85 taken as 1.585 $/£ as calculated from CSO (1990) *Monthly Review of External Trade Statistics. Annual Supplement*, No. 11, F1.
ME = Market economies.

The inward and outward flows of direct investment in services by the three major investors – US, UK, and Japan – are shown in Table 13.3. Generally, the outward flow was in other developed market economies. In the 1980s the flow *into* the US was almost twice as great as her outflow. For the UK, outflows have always been greater then inflows.

The position for the UK in 1995 is shown in Table 13.4. Columns 2–6 show the *stock* of investment in the different categories of services that the UK holds abroad. Columns 7–11 show the average outward *flows* of investment in these different services. The negative flows to North America in distribution and transport represent disinvestment. But it is much more difficult to explain the negative stock values in transport in North America (the ONS sticks by its figures), which must surely include airlines. Either it represents a downgrading of the value of assets, with a contribution possibly of changes in exchange rates, or it represents a peculiar form of financing. Whichever it is, £1.8bn is a very large amount of negative equity.

MONOPOLY AND MERGER POLICY

Where does the demarcation occur between international co-operation to provide a better service and a cartel to restrict or pre-empt entry by other firms? That is difficult to determine, and initially, the CEC did not appear equipped to examine the subject; in particular, its powers with respect to mergers appeared limited. The CEC has examined some of the mergers in the industry under Article 86, the abuse of dominant position, under which it gave qualified approval to BA's takeover of British Caledonian in 1988. In 1990 this was replaced by the Merger Regulation. The CEC's authority with respect to mergers has become important, as the effect of the deregulation of the industry has been to encourage amalgamation, with the larger firms swallowing the smaller ones and engaging in alliances with other large or medium-sized ones.

However, there is some disagreement about the competence of the CEC with respect to alliances between the airlines of EU Member States and those of third countries. A number of transatlantic alliances have already been formed (see Table 13.5). The first three have been implicitly approved by the EU, even though the first, the KLM–Northwest Airlines, has 59 per cent of the take-off and landing slots at Amsterdam airport, and the second, the Lufthansa–United Airlines of the US–Scandinavian Airlines System (SAS) group, have 63 per cent of the slots at both Frankfurt and Copenhagen airports. All three have been granted anti-trust immunity in the US (Skapinker 1997b).

But considerable objections have been raised to the alliance of BA and American Airlines (AA). Although together they would hold only 39 per cent of take-off and landing slots at Heathrow, they control 60 per cent of flights between the UK and US, 70 per cent of traffic between London and

Table 13.4 Outward direct investment in services by UK companies overseas (£m)

Region	Stock by industrial activity of overseas affiliates at end of 1995					Flow by industrial activity of overseas affiliates 1992–95 average				
	Distribution	Transport	Financial services	Other services	Total services	Distribution	Transport	Financial services	Other services	Total services
EU	5,306	1,070	12,096	9,693	28,165	1,053	220	1,898	910	4,081
Germany	848	449	637	838	2,772	88	138	144	67	436
France	1,691	−249	3,138	1,662	6,242	193	−56	56	281	474
Netherlands	1,799	865	5,296	3,913	11,873	608	134	1,057	248	2,047
Rest of Western Europe	241	5	268	1,241	1,755	−13	46	62	31	127
North America	2,851	−1,749	9,801	13,774	24,677	−177	−429	721	1,757	1,873
Canada	158	65	1,124	1,391	2,738	−7	−37	−5	14	−34
USA	2,694	−1,814	8,677	12,384	21,941	−170	−392	729	1,743	1,911
Other developed countries	1,179	365	2,807	3,973	8,324	142	131	355	475	1,102
Australia	155	342	1,104	3,102	4,703	51	101	152	419	722
Japan	832	26	107	214	1,179	52	26	−3	7	81
New Zealand	21	3	948	61	1,033	10	1	126	2	139
South Africa	171	−5	647	596	1,409	29	4	81	48	161
Rest of world	1,039	1,974	5,770	4,134	12,917	142	369	529	210	1,250
Hong Kong	361	288	487	2,317	3,453					
Bermuda	32	38	2,893	782	3,745					
World total	10,616	1,664	30,742	32,815	75,837	1,147	336	3,559	3,383	8,426
Commonwealth	1,028	1,508	7,906	8,324	18,766	119	261	674	581	1,636
Developing countries	968	1,969	5,765	4,104	12,806	126	359	537	208	1,230

Source: ONS MA4 1995 Economy: Overseas Direct Investment.

Table 13.5   Airline Atlantic alliances

Alliances	Date	Airport slots (%)
Allowed antitrust immunity in US		
KLM–Northwest airlines	1992	59% Amsterdam
Lufthansa–SAS–United Airlines	1996	63% Frankfurt
		63% Copenhagen
Swissair–Sabena–Austrian Airlines–Delta	1996	
Facing EU objections		
British Airways–American Airlines	1996	39% Heathrow

Source: M. Skapinker (1997b) 'BA rivals point to Heathrow's strengths', *Financial Times*, 15 January.

New York, 90 per cent between London and Chicago, and all flights between London and Dallas (Skapinker 1996a). The British government has decided not to refer it to the Monopolies and Mergers Commission provided that the alliance gives up 168 take-off and landing slots a week at Heathrow to be made available for transatlantic flights operated by other airlines; 98 of these must be on a permanent basis. Mr Van Miert, EU Competition Commissioner, threatened to take the UK to the European Court of Justice if it approved the alliance. But the UK government has argued that although the CEC had a right to look at the deal, the UK alone could make a decision to exempt it from European competition rules. At the other side of the Atlantic the US government has said it will only grant the two airlines anti-trust immunity if the UK and US sign an 'open skies' agreement, which entails the removal of government control over which airline is allowed to fly where. The UK government appears willing to agree to this (Rice and Tucker 1997).

The Competition Directorate has now said, in a preliminary report in July 1997, that BA should cede 350 take-off and landing slots at London's Heathrow airport. The CEC also wants a reduction in the frequency of its flights on certain transatlantic routes, and, in particular, that BA and AA should halve the frequency of flights between Heathrow, Chicago, Miami, Boston and Philadelphia. 'We don't care if BA and AA increase the size of the planes they use on those routes so that they are carrying the same number of people as before', said an official. 'Our real concern is the number of flight frequencies.' The Transport Directorate, headed by Neil Kinnock, seemed surprised, but an official from it said that BA and AA would only have to cede slots and frequencies when a competitor demanded it. 'We don't want to penalize the consumer', he said! (Tucker and Wagstyl 1997).

CONCLUSION

Two-thirds of Britain's income is at present derived from services and her positive balance in this sector outweighs roughly half the negative balance in merchandise trade.

The response of British firms to the liberalization of the aviation and telecommunications markets has been to construct a web of alliances. They anticipate benefiting from the franchise fees and the investment stakes they possess. Prices in these markets are also falling. However, the object of liberalization of the EU markets pressed by the CEC was to increase competition, and the formation of these large alliances may eventually have the reverse effect. The Competition Directorate now appears to be taking a much more stringent line than it did in the past with respect to the effect of large mergers on competition, and it will be interesting to see the effect of this.

NOTES

1   'For example, a UK broker may earn commission on arranging the charter of a Norwegian ship for the carriage of goods between an American parent company and its French subsidiary. Payment for the charter plus the broker's commission may be made to the broker in London through a British subsidiary, with consequential settlements over inter-company accounts and between the broker and the shipping company. In such cases, the financial flows will bear a very imperfect relationship to the underlying services' (ONS (1996) 'Geographical analysis of the current account of the balance of payments', *Economic Trends*, **510**, April, p. 16).
2   There are delays for EU member Spain (December 1998), Ireland (2000), and Portugal and Greece (2003).

REFERENCES

Atkins, R. (1997) 'Exchange of hostilities', *Financial Times*, 2 April.
—— (1997) 'Defensive giant limbers up', *Financial Times*, 19 December.
Balasubramanyam, V.N. and Greenaway, D. (1992) 'Economic integration and foreign direct investment: Japanese investment in the EC', *Journal of Common Market Studies*, **30** (2).
Batchelor, C. (1995) 'Difficulties with diversity', *Financial Times Survey – International Standards*, 13 October.
Baxter, A. (1995) 'Deadlines draw closer', *Financial Times Survey – International Standards*, 13 October.
Bray, R. (1996) 'Chocks away in the EU', *Financial Times – Aerospace*, suppl., 30 August.
Burns, T. and Cane, A. (1997) 'BT and Telefonica plan strategy link-up', *Financial Times*, 19 March.
Cane, A. (1997a) 'BT pieces together a global jigsaw', *Financial Times*, 18 March.
—— (1997b) 'Everybody is talking: alliances are being welded and broken almost

daily as global telecommunications groups jostle for position', *Financial Times*, 27 March.

—— (1997c) 'Dial M for merger', *Financial Times*, 15/16 November.

—— (1997d) 'EU telecoms shake-up heralds a bloody war', *Financial Times*, 19 December.

—— (1997e) 'Long-distance visionary', *Financial Times*, 19 December.

—— (1998) 'Ring in the new', *Financial Times*, 2 January.

CEC (1988) 'The economics of 1992' (The Emerson Report), *European Economy*, **35**, March.

Curwen, P. (1995) 'Telecommunications policy in the European Union: developing the information superhighway', *Journal of Common Market Studies*, **33** (3).

Fisher, A. (1998) 'German clash as telecom market opens', *Financial Times*, 2 January.

Fraser, M.W. (1996) 'Television', in H. Kassim and A. Menon (eds), *The European Union and National Policy*, London: Routledge, ch. 11.

Gooding, C. (1995) 'Standardise and deliver', *Financial Times Survey – International Standards*, 13 October.

Gresser, C. (1997) 'Rivals fear clouds behind Blue Sky', *Financial Times*, 18 November.

Jonquières, G. de (1997) 'Happy end to a cliff hanger', *Financial Times*, 15 December.

Kassim, H. (1996) 'Air transport' in H. Kassim and A. Menon (eds), *The European Union and National Policy*, London: Routledge, ch. 7.

Kassim, H. and Menon, A. (eds) (1996) *The European Union and National Industrial Policy*, London: Routledge.

Lapper, R. (1997) 'BT adds $500m to five-year issue', *Financial Times*, 18 April.

Lee, N. (1997) 'Transport policy', in M. Artis and N. Lee (eds), *Economics of the European Union*, Oxford: Oxford University Press.

Molyneux, P. (1996) 'Banking and financial services', in H. Kassim and A. Menon (eds), *The European Union and National Policy*, London: Routledge, ch. 13.

Nicoll, A. and Gresser, C. (1997) 'BA sets up no-frills airline', *Financial Times*, 18 November.

ONS (1996) 'Geographical analysis of the current account of the balance of payments', *Economic Trends*, **510**, April, 16.

Price, C. (1997) 'Key battle is for callers', *Financial Times – Telecoms*, suppl., 19 March.

Rice, R. and Tucker, E. (1997) 'UK defiant on transatlantic alliance', *Financial Times*, 15 January.

Schneider, V., Dang-Nguyen, G. and Werle, R. (1994) 'Corporate actor networks in european policy-making: harmonizing telecommunications policy', *JCMS*, **32** (4).

Skapinker, M. (1996a) 'A day for eating words', *Financial Times*, 12 June.

—— (1996b) 'Smooth take-off for shake-up', *Financial Times*, 19 September.

—— (1997a) 'Alliance is biggest issue', *Financial Times*, 7 January.

—— (1997b) 'BA rivals point to Heathrow's strengths', *Financial Times*, 15 January.

—— (1997c) 'Freedom to go a little crazy', *Financial Times*, 11 March.

—— (1997d) 'Pathfinder's prospects', *Financial Times*, 29/30 March.

—— (1997e) 'BA's turbulent ride', *Financial Times*, 8/9 November.

Skapinker, M. and Batchelor, C. (1995) 'In the path of a speeding train', *Financial Times*, 3 September.

Thoenes, S. (1997) 'Pacts set to boost transatlantic trade', *Financial Times*, 14/15 June.

Tucker, E. (1997a) 'Brussels to clear Alitalia aid', *Financial Times*, 11 July.
—— (1997b) 'Euro-regulator spectre hovers backstage', *Financial Times*, 19 December.
Tucker, E. and Wagstyl, S. (1997) 'Brussels sets airline hurdle high', *Financial Times*, 28 July.
UN (1989) *Foreign Direct Investment and Transnational Corporations in Services*, New York: United Nations.
Vickers, J. and Yarrow, G. (1988) *Privatization: An Economic Analysis*, Cambridge, Mass.: MIT Press.
Williams, F. (1997a) 'US, EU vie for credit on telecoms', *Financial Times*, 17 February.
—— (1997b) 'New rules for a trillion-dollar game', *Financial Times*, 15 December.
Williams, F. and Cane, A. (1997) 'World telecoms pact set to slash cost of calls', *Financial Times*, 17 February.

14 Regional policy and taxation

In this chapter we shall consider some of the other dimensions of the British economy and their interaction with EU policy. We shall begin by considering the problem of regional disparities and the policies of both the UK government and the EU towards them. Then we shall move on to consider tax policies.

A divergence in prosperity between areas is apparent to anyone who travels round the UK. To those seeking work it is even more obvious. The question was, and is, should the UK government intervene to reduce the disparities, and, if so, how? Does intervention improve or worsen economic efficiency? Once Britain became a member of the EC the question then was whether Britain's assistance to her poorer regions distorted competition at the EC level. Also, should regional policy and objectives be decided by Member States or at the EC level?

REGIONAL POLICY OF THE UK

The contrasting fortunes of Britain's slow-growing northern regions, with high unemployment, and the faster-growing southern regions have long been officially recognized. The first attempt at alleviation was in 1928 with the Industrial Transference Board, which was set up to subsidize the movement of labour out of areas of industrial decline.

In contrast to this, the policy after the Second World War was directed at taking jobs to the workers, particularly in the areas with declining industries – coal, shipbuilding, textiles, and later, steel – in which unemployment was high. This was because of the fear that relocation would add to congestion, especially in the South East. In 1946 the Labour government passed the New Towns Act, and in 1947 the Town and Country Planning Act, which introduced the Green Belt and land-use controls. A system of Industrial Development ment Certificates (IDCs) remained from the Second World War. Because of general full employment these certificates were not used in the 1950s, but then in the 1960s one in five applications to locate in the South East or West Midlands were refused (Gudgin 1995: 53). Thus, as described in previous chapters, Ford and GM were induced to set up their new plants in Merseyside, while new steel strip mills were built both in Scotland *and* in Wales, where one new mill would have been better able to exploit economies of scale.

A system of regional investment incentives and building grants was introduced for Development Areas (those with high levels of unemployment) by the Local Employment Acts of 1960 and 1963. Then from 1964–70 the Labour government introduced Regional Development Grants. Great importance was attached by Labour to the regional problem because it appeared that, with the demand management policies being pursued, full employment and excess demand in the South East were leading to the introduction of deflationary policies by the government despite the high levels of unemployment that might exist elsewhere in the country. Thus it was hoped that effective regional policies might even out levels of unemployment and alter the macroeconomic constraint, so that 'stop' policies did not have to be introduced so soon after economic growth was resumed.

By the late 1960s, Development Areas covered 40 per cent of the area of Great Britain plus Northern Ireland and over 20 per cent of the population. These grants remained until they were abolished in 1988. The Labour government also introduced a Regional Employment Premium (1967–77) which was a direct subsidy to employers for employing labour. These policies were very effective in inducing firms to move to the assisted areas, with 250,000 jobs moved into Development Areas between 1963 and 1971 and an additional 140,000 created by indigenous firms (ibid. 53–4).

However, the flaws in this approach became obvious when many of the plants which had moved to the assisted areas then closed after Britain's entry to the EC and the severe depression of 1979–82. With generalized unemployment there was less enthusiasm for regional policies. Spending on them declined by 30 per cent in real terms, partly due to the abolition of the Regional Employment Premium discussed below. Moreover, inner-city problems had begun to seem more serious than regional problems, and in 1977, Labour's Inner City Act provided for assistance to inner cities at the expense of regional aid (ibid. 55).

The Conservative government of 1979, pursuing free market principles, approached the regional problem in a different way. Areas eligible for assistance were reduced considerably and restricted to areas of high unemployment. Automatic capital grants were abolished and the focus was on increasing competitiveness rather than the subsidization of capital equipment. Expenditure on regional policy was, in 1995, only a quarter of the peak levels in the 1960s and 1970s (ibid. 57). However, the regional problem is no worse, partly because of the flows of inward investment described below. These may, in turn, be the result of greater flexibility in the labour market, which had the effect of lowering relative labour costs, particularly in Wales, Northern Ireland and Scotland (ibid. 58–9). This flexibility can be ascribed in part to the Conservative government's deregulation of the labour market and the decline in the strength of the trade unions.

The allocation of public spending

Apart from direct aid for industry, expenditure on schools, roads, and other services, is also included in the public expenditure in a region. The formula for the allocation of public funds was devised in 1978 by Joel Barnett, the Treasury chief secretary. It partly reflected the sparsity of population, the cost of building roads, the cost of rural education, and the higher incidence of certain diseases in Wales and Scotland, but the main consideration was the poorer state of their economies and relatively low per capita income. In spite of changes in relative prosperity, public spending per head is 23 per cent higher in Scotland, 16 per cent higher in Wales and 37 per cent higher in Northern Ireland than in England. The Scots have sometimes justified their high share by the North Sea oil revenues, which they regard as originating in Scotland. But these are less than the transfer they have received from the UK Treasury.

Towards the end of 1997 a row erupted about this allocation; the English regions complained of discrimination in comparison with Wales and Scotland. In particular, the chairman of the Northern Development Company, the investment agency for the North East, said that funds should be diverted to English regions such as the North, which was now the poorest region of the UK. In terms of unemployment and dependence of families on family credit or income support, the only area poorer was the subregion of Merseyside.

The allocation of such public money is therefore likely to come under much greater scrutiny, particularly with the establishment of the Scottish parliament and Welsh assembly. Furthermore, the Scottish parliament may acquire the right to a 'tartan' tax varying the basic rate of income tax by up to 3p (Buxton 1997b; Groom 1997; Groom and Buxton 1997b; Parker and Jones 1997; Parker *et al.* 1997).

The UK's regional problem

Let us now examine the disparities in employment and incomes. For the allocation of assistance the UK was divided up into standard regions. Graham Gudgin has shown their changes in employment between 1952 and 1993 (see Table 14.1). Employment in all regions was higher in 1966 than in 1952; for the UK as a whole it was 13 per cent higher. Since 1966 it has fallen in the West Midlands, Yorkshire and Humberside, the North West, and the North; the North West in particular has lost jobs at an average rate of 0.3 per cent per annum over forty years. Employment has remained roughly the same in Wales and Scotland and has increased and then declined in the East Midlands. The fastest rates of growth have been in East Anglia and the South West, with levels 59 per cent and 37 per cent above those in 1952. Employment in the South East appears to have increased to 1966 and then declined. However, this masks the decline

Table 14.1   Regional employment changes, 1952–93
(1952 = 100)

	1966	1979	1993
South East	119.3	118.6	115.1
East Anglia	118.2	141.5	159.2
South West	121.2	124.5	137.0
East Midlands	116.2	126.8	124.6
West Midlands	117.1	112.0	101.2
Yorkshire and Humberside	110.6	107.6	101.4
North West	103.2	97.2	86.1
North	108.6	103.7	92.7
Wales	110.0	112.3	107.8
Scotland	103.7	109.2	105.0
Northern Ireland	111.6	120.0	122.9
United Kingdom	113.3	113.0	108.8

Source: G. Gudgin (1995) 'Regional problems and policy in the UK', *Oxford Review of Economic Policy*, **11** (2).

Notes:
All figures are derived from Department of employment estimates adjusted for regional boundary changes etc. Figures include the self-employed, but prior to 1966 assume that the self-employed grew *pro rata* with employees in employment.

in employment in London of a quarter, whereas employment in the rest of the South East doubled (Gudgin 1995: 32–3).

One of the factors contributing to the disparity has been the changes in the fuel industry, with the drastic decline in the coal mining that has been so important to the East Midlands, Yorkshire and Humberside, Wales and the North. This is a long-term decline which speeded up in the 1980s (see Chapter 8).

The other major factor was the decline in manufacturing employment, which, it has been argued, was accelerated both by entry to the EC, and also by the policy of an overvalued pound pursued by the Conservative government between 1979 and 1981. The shift in regional employment from manufacturing to services between 1970 and 1995 is shown in Figure 14.1. As can be seen, in 1970 in the northern regions – the North, North West, Yorkshire (and Humberside), East Midlands, and West Midlands – manufacturing employment was initially as large or larger than employment in services. The other regions were more heavily dependent on services. By far the greatest concentration in the service sector was in the South East, which accounted for 40 per cent of employment in the region in 1970.

By 1995, manufacturing employment had contracted in all the regions. Those regions where the contraction was greatest – that is, more than 50 per cent – such as the South East, North West, West Midlands and Scotland, showed a considerable increase in service sector employment. But so did

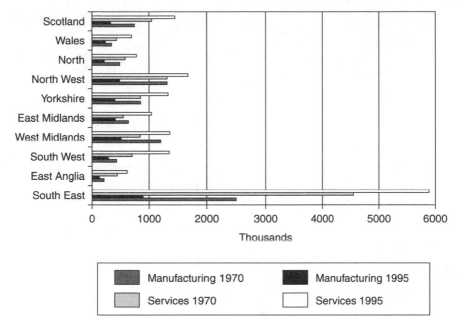

Figure 14.1 Manufacturing and service employment by region, June 1970 and 1995

the South West. The South East continued to account for by far the greatest service sector employment in the UK, but its proportion had slipped to 36 per cent.

Gudgin has argued that an important feature of the situation was the greater shift in manufacturing employment away from large cities, including London. Employment in manufacturing in towns and rural areas increased from 1960–71 and did not decline as fast as the national average thereafter. He also suggests that this is due to the change in factor proportions required by manufacturing industry. Industrial output is proportional to the area of factory floor space, but increased labour productivity means that fewer workers are required proportionally. It is very difficult to acquire additional land to expand in the large conurbations and it is expensive to increase the number of floors in a factory (Fothergill *et al.* 1985, quoted in Gudgin 1995). This is confirmed by a Business Strategies report which identified the key factors in job creation in the major cities from 1981 to 1995 as being the existence of a well-educated workforce and room for growth. Huddersfield was the most successful, while the least successful with their *loss* of jobs shown in brackets, were Glasgow (98,110), Manchester (109,993), Birmingham (123,251) and Liverpool (169,441) (Groom 1998).

Sectoral composition of regional GDP

How far does an increase in employment lead to an increase in GDP? Gudgin's figures ranked in descending order of GDP growth are shown in Tables 14.2. The fastest overall increase in GDP is in East Anglia, but this is mainly due to a rapid increase in employment; the growth of GDP per employee at 1.6 per cent per annum is only slightly above the average. The fastest increase in GDP per employee is in the East Midlands and Greater London, with entirely different rates of growth of overall GDP.

The contribution of different sectors to the GDP of the different regions in 1992 is shown in Table 14.3. Gudgin regards the private export sector as an important determinant of the sustainability of growth. It comprises the primary sector, the manufacturing sector, and the finance and business services sector, less a deduction for local consumption of them. This accounts for 31 per cent of GDP for the UK as a whole. It is highest in the East and West Midlands due to the high proportion of manufacturing in their GDP, and above the national average for Yorkshire, North West and the North for the same reason. It is also high in the South East due to its very large finance and business services sector, which accounts for 27.6 per cent of its GDP. The author regards these sectors as the most exposed to competitive pressure from the rest of the world and most affected by international commercial policy.

Table 14.2   Annual growth in real gross domestic product and productivity, 1971–92

	GDP	Employment	GDP per employee
Rural south and east			
South East (excl. London)	2.0	0.9	1.1
East Anglia	2.9	1.3	1.6
South West	2.3	0.8	1.6
East Midlands	2.3	0.4	1.9
Urban south and Midlands			
Greater London	0.9	−0.7	1.8
West Midlands	1.0	−0.4	1.5
North of England			
Yorkshire and Humberside	1.5	−0.1	1.6
North West	1.0	−0.5	1.5
North	1.3	−0.4	1.7
Wales	1.6	0.1	1.5
Scotland	1.6	0.2	1.4
Northern Ireland	1.7	0.4	1.3
United Kingdom (excl. continental shelf)	1.6	0.0	1.5

Source: G. Gudgin (1995) 'Regional problems and policy in the UK', *Oxford Review of Economic Policy*, **11** (2); CSO *Regional Accounts* (GDP); Department of Employment (Great Britain); Department of Economic Development (Northern Ireland).

Note: Employment includes the self-employed.

Government services are an important contributor to GDP in some areas; they are relatively lowest in the South East and by far the highest in Northern Ireland. The last column of Table 14.3 compares the distribution for the region with that for the UK as a whole; a positive figure indicates it is greater and vice versa. The figure is negative in the South East and positive in the North, Wales, Scotland and a positive 12 per cent for Northern Ireland. This represents the success of the government's policy of relocating its administration out of London towards the more deprived areas.

The distribution of R&D expenditure between regions is also revealing (see Table 14.4). Minute though it may appear in relation to regional GDP, it shows up the high-tech nodes. As can be seen, the two regions with the highest proportion of business and government R&D in total and in relation to GDP are the Eastern, which includes Cambridge, and the South East, excluding Greater London (GOR).[1] The contribution of the higher educational sector is small, 0.4 per cent for the UK, and fairly evenly distributed.

Table 14.3 Composition of regional economies, 1992 (% GDP)

	Primary	Manufac-turing	Finance and business services	Private sector export base	Government services	Excess/deficit in government services
South East	1.0	15.2	27.6	31.8	15.3	−1.4
East Anglia	5.5	21.4	14.7	29.6	16.6	−0.1
South West	3.7	18.9	16.5	27.1	19.9	2.2
East Midlands	5.1	27.6	12.0	32.7	15.4	−1.4
West Midlands	2.8	29.1	14.4	34.3	14.8	−1.9
Yorkshire and Humberside	4.8	25.4	13.6	31.8	16.5	−0.2
North West	2.1	27.1	14.7	31.9	15.6	−1.2
North	4.3	27.8	11.5	31.6	17.6	0.9
Wales	4.1	26.0	12.0	30.1	19.0	2.3
Scotland	3.3	20.8	15.9	28.0	19.7	3.0
Northern Ireland	4.7	19.2	12.0	23.9	28.5	11.8
United Kingdom	2.8	21.4	18.8	31.0	16.7	0.0

Source: G. Gudgin (1995) 'Regional problems and policy in the UK', *Oxford Review of Economic Policy*, **11** (2); CSO *Regional Accounts*, London: CSO.

Notes: Private sector economic base is calculated as sum of GDP in primary and manufacturing sectors plus GDP in financial and business services, less a deduction for local consumption of financial and business services. The latter is estimated at 12 percentage points in all regions, reflecting the minimum proportion across regions in this sector. Government services are Standard Industrial Classification (SIC) sectors public administration and defence, health, and education. Excess/deficit in government services is the difference between share of government services in regional GDP and its share in national GDP.

Table 14.4 Expenditure on research and development, 1995

| | R&D performed within: | | | | | |
| | Businesses | | Government | | Higher education institutions | |
	(£m)	RGDP (%)	(£m)[1]	RGDP (%)	(£m)	RGDP (%)
United Kingdom	9,379	1.3	2,076	0.3	2,695	0.4
North East	230	0.9	16	0.1	91	0.3
North West (GOR) & Merseyside	1,121	1.5	82	0.1	223	0.3
North West (GOR)	993	1.5	71	0.1	162	0.2
Merseyside	128	1.5	11	0.1	60	0.7
Yorkshire & the Humber	279	0.5	46	0.1	209	0.4
East Midlands	615	1.3	65	0.1	142	0.3
West Midlands	663	1.1	179	0.3	149	0.2
Eastern	2,024	3.0	261	0.4	195	0.3
London	881	0.9	281	0.3	669	0.7
South East (GOR)	2,301	2.2	674	0.7	404	0.4
South West	777	1.4	249	0.5	122	0.2
England	8,890	1.5	1,852	0.3	2,205	0.4
Wales	96	0.3	31	0.1	102	0.4
Scotland	332	0.6	175	0.3	336	0.6
Northern Ireland	61	0.4	18	0.1	52	0.3

Source: ONS (1997) *Regional Trends*, **32**, 160.

Note: [1]Figures include estimates of NHS and local authorities' R&D.

Unemployment and migration

How far is the divergence in the growth of employment inversely correlated with unemployment in the areas? Gudgin states:

> At the scale of individual counties, huge differences in employment change are reflected only in much smaller differences in unemployment ... Inter-regional migration flows are not sufficiently strong to equalize unemployment rates across regions, but they greatly diminish the disparities that might otherwise occur ... Since 1979, net migration of working-age people out of the regions in the northern half of the UK has been 422,000. Net migration into the three regions of southern England has been 448,300 ... except in Northern Ireland, almost all the regional differences in growth of working-age population are due to migration.
>
> (Gudgin 1995: 23–4)

Why does migration not completely obliterate the differences in unemployment rates in Britain, a single currency area? One reason is the difficulty of obtaining accommodation; rented accommodation is scarce and house prices in the South East are multiples of those in the North. Another reason is that many of the unemployed are unskilled or have skills appropriate to a declining industry and the demand for these workers is lowest.

The average unemployment rates in 1996 are shown in Table 14.5. The government figures of those claiming unemployment benefit are given in column 2, but because there is so much suspicion of these figures – the entitlements to benefit have been changed at least seventeen times – the International Labour Organization (ILO) figures of unemployment are placed alongside in column 3. They show a UK average unemployment of around 8 per cent, with noticeably higher levels in the North East, Merseyside and Northern Ireland. The most serious problems are regarded as being the high levels of unemployment in the major conurbations. The assisted urban areas – Strathclyde, Tyneside and Merseyside – are in the old assisted regions. But by 1996 there was much less divergence in unemployment between the regions themselves than there had been previously.

There is concern that many of the new jobs created are temporary or part time. As can be seen from Figure 14.2 (Royal Commission 1978; CSO 1996), in the UK as a whole there was a decline in male full-time

Table 14.5 UK regional unemployment and average weekly earnings, 1996

Region	Unemployment		Average weekly earnings		
	Claimant (%)	ILO (%)	Males (£)	Females (£)	All (£)
United Kingdom	7.5	8.2	390	282	350
North East	10.6	10.8	348	252	314
North West (GOR) & Merseyside	8.0	8.4	368	264	330
North West (GOR)	6.9	7.3	369	262	331
Merseyside	13.1	13.3	362	271	325
Yorkshire & Humberside	8.0	8.1	351	253	316
East Midlands	6.8	7.4	353	249	318
West Midlands	7.4	9.2	360	257	324
Eastern	6.1	6.2	382	280	346
London	8.9	11.3	514	365	454
South East (GOR)	5.4	6.0	413	293	367
South West	6.2	6.3	365	261	327
England	7.3	8.1	396	287	356
Wales	8.2	8.3	346	251	313
Scotland	7.9	8.7	364	262	325
Northern Ireland	10.9	9.7	337	257	306

Source: ONS (1997) *Regional Trends*, **32**.

Notes:
North West (GOR) = Cumbria, Cheshire, Greater Manchester, Lancashire.
South East (GOR) = Berkshire, Buckinghamshire, East Sussex, Hampshire, Isle of Wight, Kent, Oxfordshire, Surrey, West Sussex.
Eastern = Cambridgeshire, Norfolk, Suffolk, Bedfordshire, Essex, Hertfordshire.

employment but an increase in part-time jobs, whereas for females there was an increase in both full-time and part-time jobs. The full-time and part-time employment figures by region for June 1995 are shown in Table 14.6. The relative shift towards part-time work would not pose a problem if that is what employees wanted – indeed, it might be welcomed as providing flexibility for both the worker and employer. The complaints arise because part-time rates of pay are generally lower than full-time rates, and part-time workers often do not have the same entitlements to holidays or promotion as full-time workers.

The flexibility of the labour force, which is regarded as an attraction by inward investors into the UK, is also indicated by the degree not only of shift work reported by 16 per cent of males and 12 per cent of females, but also of Saturday working by 29 per cent of males and 22 per cent of females, and Sunday working by 14 per cent of males and 12 per cent of females. This is a feature for all regions, except that the proportion of shift, Saturday and Sunday work is relatively low for London. Average weekly hours of work for full-time employees are 44 for the UK, and there is not much variation by region (ONS 1997).

This situation may be affected by the Working Time Directive passed in November 1993. The CEC is already issuing a formal warning to the UK, and to France, Greece, Italy, Luxembourg and Portugal, for failing to implement it. Under this measure most employees would not be required to work more than 48 hours a week, could restrict the night work and shift work they carry out, and are also entitled to four weeks' annual paid leave. The CEC is proposing to extend these provisions to workers excluded

Table 14.6   UK employment by region in June 1995

	Male		Female	
	Full-time	*Part-time*	*Full-time*	*Part-time*
South East	3,145	435	2,017	1,520
London	1,468	186	1,016	523
South East – London	1,677	249	1,001	997
East Anglia	362	46	200	214
South West	745	110	442	464
West Midlands	932	97	507	440
East Midlands	696	85	380	368
Yorkshire	825	104	453	471
North West	1,040	114	598	531
North	496	62	273	258
Wales	441	52	251	235
Scotland	887	95	525	437
Northern Ireland	241	43	160	125
Total	9,811	1,241	5,824	4,997

Source: CSO (1996) *Labour Market Trends,* January.

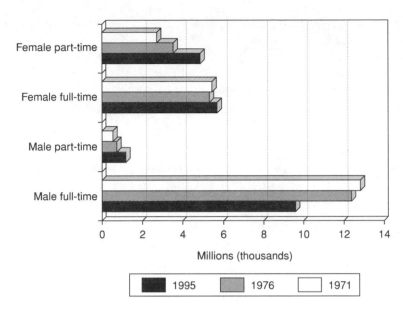

Figure 14.2 Full- and part-time employment in Great Britain, June 1971, 1976, 1995

from the original Directives, namely, transport and offshore workers, junior doctors and others (Taylor 1997b).

Now that the Labour government has opted in to the social provisions of the Maastricht Treaty Britain will also have to implement the December 1997 Directives, thus extending rights covering holidays, pensions and dismissal from full-time to part-time workers (Smith 1997). All workers will have equal access to pay, bonus, shift and other wage supplements (Taylor 1997a).

Wage levels began to diverge further in the 1980s (Gudgin 1995: 20). Figures 14.3 and 14.4 illustrate the wide variation in average weekly earnings for men and women between London and the rest of the country. Men and women in London on average earn 32 per cent and 29 per cent respectively more than the national average. The statistics are given in the last three columns of Table 14.6.

REGIONAL POLICY OF THE EC

How far has British regional policy been affected by the EC? Some provisions have been disallowed, such as the Regional Employment Premium, which, as it was a subsidy to employers for their direct cost of employing workers, was not consistent with the Treaty of Rome.

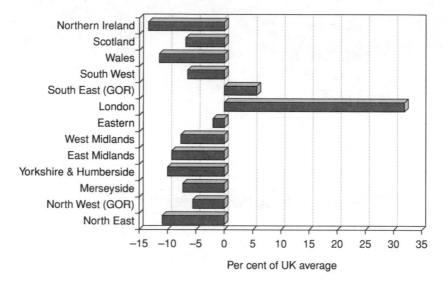

Figure 14.3 Male average earnings per region, 1996 (per cent of UK average)

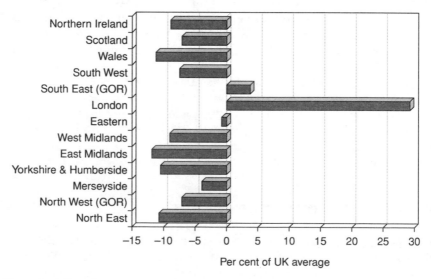

Figure 14.4 Female average earnings per region, 1996 (per cent of UK average)

Initially, EC assistance to the poorer regions was only through the European Investment Bank and the ECSC. In 1975 the European Regional Development Fund (ERDF) was founded, but only to buttress the existing regional policies of Member States. Declining industrial regions in Britain and France gained a considerable amount of its disbursements (Dignan 1995: 65). To a slight degree it compensated the UK for its contributions to the CAP.

The EC has been concerned with regional disparities which it describes as a lack of 'cohesion', because it fears that greater integration will lead to a widening of disparities between the core and periphery and this will pose a threat to further integration. It was anticipated that this would occur as a result of the institution of the Single European Market (SEM) and, even more likely, as the result of monetary union.

The EU distinguishes several different types of area entitled to assistance. First, there are Objective 1 regions in which GDP per head is below 75 per cent of the Community average. These are eligible for the greatest assistance. They have the highest rates of unemployment, largely due to a rapid growth in the labour supply. Objective 1 regions contain 17 per cent of EU employment but half its agricultural employment. Objective 2 includes older industrial regions in more prosperous Member States, and Objective 5b covers rural areas with relatively undiversified economies (Begg *et al.* 1995: 3–7).

The whole of Greece, Ireland, Portugal and much of Spain are classified as Objective 1 regions and eligible for maximum assistance, together with the Mezzogiorno in Southern Italy, the East German Länder, Northern Ireland, and, in 1994, Merseyside and the Highlands and Islands of Scotland.

Since the signing of the Maastricht Treaty the EU has increased its allocation of funds to increase 'cohesion and solidarity' within the EU and this has included a new 'cohesion fund' to provide additional aid to the four poorest countries, Spain, Greece, Portugal, and Ireland. Since 1989 the EU has tried to insist on *additionality*: that is, EU funding should add to, rather than substitute for, expenditure of Member States in their deprived areas. But although the UK allows local authorities a little more latitude than before, basically the EU's allocation of aid to it just offsets some of Britain's overall net contribution to the EU. The allocation of EU structural funds to the UK under the different headings is shown in Table 14.7. Converting the EU total allocation for 1996 in ECUs into sterling at ECU 1.229 to £1 gives an EU allocation of £1,035m, which is more then double the UK government allocation of £474m. However, Blake has argued that through the tax and transfer system the deprived regions gain far more (see Table 14.9). In 1991 there was a transfer of £13bn from the South East including London to the rest of the country. Northern Ireland, in particular, received £3.6bn equivalent to $2,255 per head (Blake 1995). Thus regionally deprived regions within the wealthier national economies gain far more from intra-country transfers than they do from EU aid. For instance, Northern Ireland

Table 14.7   Allocation of EU structural funds (ECUm)[1,2]

	Objective 1[3]			Objective 2[3]			Objective 5b[3]		
	1996	1997	1998	1996	1997	1998	1996	1997	1998
United Kingdom	376	402	436	749	784	810	147	149	149
North East	—	—	—	108	112	115	5	6	6
North West (GOR)									
& Merseyside	130	139	151	124	135	140	5	6	6
North West (GOR)	—	—	—	124	135	140	5	6	6
Merseyside	130	139	151	—	—	—	—	—	—
Yorkshire &									
the Humber	—	—	—	109	115	119	9	8	8
East Midlands	—	—	—	28	31	32	12	12	12
West Midlands	—	—	—	130	139	143	7	7	7
Eastern	—	—	—	—	—	—	11	11	11
London	—	—	—	26	31	32	—	—	—
South East (GOR)	—	—	—	5	5	6	—	—	—
South West	—	—	—	10	11	12	39	40	40
England	130	139	151	540	579	599	88	90	90
Wales	—	—	—	66	67	69	33	33	33
Scotland	50	53	57	143	138	142	26	26	26
Northern Ireland	196	210	228	—	—	—	—	—	—

Source: ONS (1997) *Regional Trends*, **32**.

Notes:
[1]   Only allocations resulting from the Commission's Single Programming Documents are shown. Allocations resulting from Community Initiatives, the value of which is about 8 per cent of the total Objective 1, 2 and 5b allocations, are not included because not all of these can be allocated to the Government Office Regions in the table.
[2]   At 1994 prices. The average exchange rate in 1996 was £1.00 = ECU 1.229.
[3]   See Technical notes.

benefits more from the fiscal transfer of the UK than Ireland does from the EU.

There is the question of whether decisions about regional allocation should be taken at the EU level, the national level or even lower. The first would involve decisions about fiscal transfers between countries being made at the EU level and would raise the question of sovereignty and the degree to which it represents taxation without representation. It would also represent a violation of 'horizontal equity', that is, 'similarly disadvantaged *persons* would not be treated equally because they would not all be located in Objective 1 regions' (Dignan 1995: 93). These problems are going to become even more acute if a monetary union comes into being.

The other question is the degree to which EU regional policy is effective. It is being recognized within the EU, just as within the UK, that the greatest degree of unemployment is among the unskilled, for whom demand is evaporating. Regional programmes are being adjusted to invest in human capital. However, high standards of education in a region do not necessarily improve

Table 14.8 The effect of general government taxation, transfers and expenditure on the regions in 1991

Region	Net receipts	
	Total (£bn)	Per head (£)
North	1.160	375
Yorkshire & Humberside	1.280	257
East Midlands	−0.747	−185
East Anglia	−0.233	−112
Greater London	−3.677	−534
Rest of South East	−9.326	−868
South West	1.222	259
West Midlands	−0.040	−8
North West	0.690	108
Wales	2.438	843
Scotland	3.051	598
Northern Ireland	3.611	2,255
United Kingdom	−1.962	−34

Source: N. Blake (1995) 'The regional implications of macroeconomic policy', *Oxford Review of Economic Policy*, **11** (2).

its position, because the SEM, by introducing the mutual recognition of professional qualifications, has made migration easier. For instance, it has been estimated 'that up to 30 per cent of newly qualified graduates from tertiary education in Ireland obtaining employment do so outside Ireland' (Begg 1995: 99).

The prospect of EU enlargement has entailed another rethink about the cost of regional transfers. The addition of the proposed ten members, all relatively poor countries, would increase the population of the EU by a third, from 370m to 500m, but it would increase the GDP by only 5 per cent. A prolonged argument about finance seems certain. In Agenda 2000 the Commissioner responsible for regional policy proposes to reduce the proportion of the EU population eligible for special assistance from 50 per cent to 35–40 per cent. The reform will be mainly applied to Objective 1. Most applicant countries will need at least fifteen years to reach the 75 per cent of average income of the EU, which is the point at which you are no longer eligible. Of the present recipients, Spain, Italy, Greece and Portugal are determined to keep their share of EU regional aid, but it is recognized that the improvements in Ireland's GDP per head mean that hers will gradually be phased out. The CEC would like a more efficient use of the 'cohesion funds' set up; it would like to curb programmes and target unemployment (Barber 1997). In December 1997 the EU's director-general of regional policy said that Northern Ireland, and the Highlands and Islands of Scotland are likely to lose their Objective 1 status in 2000–2006, but Merseyside will retain it and South Yorkshire may qualify for it (Groom 1997).

INWARD INVESTMENT

The financial aid that the UK government provides for investment in 'assisted' areas is open to all firms. However, foreign firms have always been more willing than British companies to go to the peripheral areas of the UK.

Of all the Member States, Britain has gained most inward foreign investment. In 1996 at £16bn it received 40 per cent of the inward direct investment reported by the EU members, but much took the form of mergers and acquisitions rather than greenfield investment. US companies continued to be the largest net direct investors in the UK adding £7bn to their holdings (Adams 1997; Jonquières 1997). In manufacturing it is the deprived areas that have gained relatively the most. One of the most notable beneficiaries has been Wales, which, with only 5 per cent of the population, has attracted 16 per cent of inward investment, amounting to £10bn of capital investment from 1,600 projects. The most recent has been the £1.7bn investment in a semiconductor and electronics plant being built on a greenfield site at Newport, South Wales, by LG of South Korea, which will employ 6,100 people. This was supported by state aid of £247m, much of which is being spent on training the local workforce (Wolffe 1997). About a quarter of Britain's manufacturing employees now work for non-UK companies: this is an increase from a fifth in 1990. Furthermore, these companies have assisted considerably in increasing productivity (Burton 1997; Buxton 1997a; Marsh 1997).

The UK government is concerned that the assisted areas might compete against each other in the provision of inducements for projects. Comparisons are made between the £30,000 per job that LG Electronics was awarded, which is to be investigated by the comptroller and auditor general, and the £16,000–£17,000 per job awarded to Siemens for its £1.1bn microchip plant near Newcastle (Jowit 1997; Wagstyl 1997a). There were proposals for a government code to try and prevent 'gazumping' (Groom and Buxton 1997a). However, the government has decided that the DTI will help adjudicate disputed cases but will not exercise a veto (Wighton 1997).

STATE AID TO INDUSTRY

The CEC is concerned about the competition between Member States for investment from third countries by means of deregulation or subsidies to the detriment of them all. The UK Department of Trade and Industry (DTI) claims that it pays out less than its EU rivals. It is difficult for the CEC to monitor the amount of state aid being given because it can take various forms such as the provision of roads, loan guarantees, and so on. Apart from the cost, the only internal restraining influence on EU government regional assistance is that already established companies may complain about unfair competition (Wagstyl 1997a).

Begg has described the attraction of Britain to foreign investors as 'the benefits of relatively lower labour costs and lack of regulation complemented by the English language' (Begg 1995). However, South Koreans often remark on how low land prices are in Wales in comparison with Seoul.

At the end of 1997 this benign picture was being undermined by the turmoil in the foreign exchange markets and the depreciation of most Asian currencies. The fall of 25 per cent in value of the Korean won against the dollar makes it more difficult for Korean firms to borrow on the international market and service their debts. Some doubt was being thrown on whether Hyundai would complete its proposed £3bn semiconductor plant in Scotland, particularly in view of the plunge in memory chip prices on the world market and the removal by the EU of its anti-dumping duties on D-Rams from Korea (Burton 1997; Buxton 1997a).

Margaret Beckett, Secretary of State of Trade and Industry for the new Labour government, has emphasized that she is concerned with promoting the UK as a base for R&D and high-technology products (Wagstyl 1997b). This is a role that Britain has performed for some time for certain specialities. In particular, Britain has a strong position in pharmaceuticals due to investment by indigenous companies, and foreign firms such as Astra, which in 1995 took over the R&D of Fisons, and Pfizer. Most of this has taken place in the South East, but there are also concentrations in the North West and Scotland. The UK has the biggest biotechnology sector in Europe (Green 1997).

CHANGES IN TAXATION

This book is not the place to go in depth into the intricacies of the UK tax and benefit system. But they must be mentioned because of their impact not only on income distribution, but also on the efficiency of the British economy.

In Britain in 1960, 10 per cent of personal income was paid as direct tax, largely through the pay-as-you-earn (PAYE) system (see Table 14.9), while 16 per cent was paid in the form of indirect taxes which included:

1   excise duties on petrol and alcohol, tobacco and cigarettes;
2   'rates', the tax paid to local authorities assessed on the value of property; and
3   purchase tax, which was levied at the wholesale stage on luxuries such as cosmetics and consumer durables.

Employees' and employers' National Insurance contributions amounted in total to only 4.4 per cent of personal incomes. This was because until October 1985 no National Insurance contributions were paid until an earnings floor had been reached; thereafter, employers paid 9 per cent and employees

Table 14.9 Ratio of direct and indirect taxes and social security payments to total personal income, 1960, 1970 and 1974

	1960				1970				1974			
	Direct taxes[1]	Social security[2]	Indirect taxes[3]	Taxes on consumption	Direct taxes[1]	Social security[2]	Indirect taxes[3]	Taxes on consumption	Direct taxes[1]	Social security[2]	Indirect taxes[3]	Taxes on consumption
UK	9.8	4.4	16.0	13.7	14.9	5.3	19.3	15.2	14.6	6.9	15.4	12.2
France	4.5	13.5	19.4	n.a.	4.6	14.5	17.6	n.a.	4.7	15.1	15.4	n.a.
West Germany	8.0	11.4	16.9	10.2	10.4	13.1	15.2	10.5	12.8	15.0	14.2	n.a.
US	12.0	5.0	11.2	n.a.	11.5	6.5	11.3	n.a	11.1	8.2	10.8	n.a.

Source: Royal Commission on the Distribution of Income and Wealth (Diamond Report) (1977) Report No. 5, *Third Report on the Standing Reference*, Cmnd. 6999, London: HMSO, table 54, pp. 119–20.

Notes:
1 Direct taxes and compulsory fees.
2 Contributions paid by employers and employees.
3 Overestimate because it includes all indirect taxes and all sectors.

10.45 per cent on the whole of an employee's pay up to a ceiling above which no further national insurance was payable.

By 1970 the relative amount of tax paid in each of these categories had risen. In particular, the amount paid in direct taxes had risen to 15 per cent, largely because the real tax thresholds at which income started being paid had fallen (Royal Commission 1978: table Q.1).

As the British government and tax authorities contemplated entry to the EC they came face to face with the very different tax regimes on the Continent. In France and Germany the direct taxes paid were lower and social security contributions were higher than in the UK.

There was a great deal of discussion in Britain about the high social security payments. Britain was gradually raising hers but in 1974 they were only half those of France and Germany, which had also been rising, see Table 14.9.

The EC had agreed, after expert appraisal by the Neumark Committee in 1962, to adopt a common system of sales tax, the value-added tax (VAT), to replace the variety of consumer taxes in the Member States:

> VAT is collected as a proportion of the value added (sales minus purchases which is equal to wages plus profits) at each stage of the production and distribution chain. Thus the tax accumulated when the final product is sold will be precisely equal to that collected with the same *ad valorem* rate ... When the output of a firm is used as input by another firm, the input tax is rebated ... VAT is a sales tax, and ... the final consumer pays [it].
>
> (Hitiris 1994: 115)

For internationally traded goods the EC decided to apply the destination principle to reassure the Member States that they would acquire the revenue from their indirect taxes. Thus the UK government gains the VAT on imported goods, and rebates it on those it exports. In April 1973 Britain moved over to this system of VAT. It was originally set at 10 per cent. Services like postage, education, health, finance and insurance were exempt; no VAT was imposed on them, but they could not reclaim it on inputs. There were also zero-rated goods such as food, fuel, construction, children's clothes, books and newspapers, and medical prescriptions. For these no VAT is charged on outputs and VAT on inputs is reclaimable (James and Nobes 1983). VAT is also not charged on businesses with turnover below a certain value; this lower limit is frequently changed.

Britain also had a highly developed social security system intended as a safety net for the old, the sick, and the unemployed, unable to fend for themselves. It provided benefits for those whose incomes fell below a poverty line. The number of claimant households has increased rapidly. In 1966 there were 2 million recipients of benefits on a weekly basis; by 1978 this had risen to 3 million, with almost 5 million dependent on supplementary

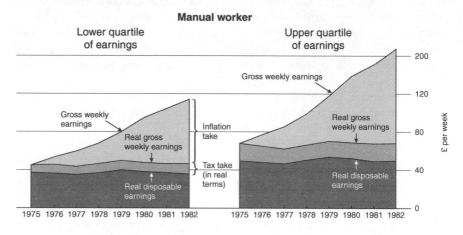

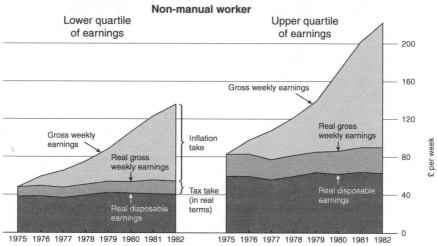

Figure 14.5 The effects of tax[1] and inflation on the real[2] disposable earnings[3] of men[4] in Great Britain 1975–82

Source: CSO (1984) *Social Trends*, **14**, p. 79.

Notes: [1]Income tax plus National Insurance contributions; [2]at April 1975 prices; [3]the husband's earnings plus family support (family support is the value of family allowance or child benefit, which replaced family allowance from April 1977); [4]based on a married man with two children under 11.

benefits. In the National Insurance Act of 1974 provision was made for the poverty line to be raised in accordance with the general level of prices or earnings (whichever was the more generous to the beneficiaries). In 1977 a tax allowance for children other than the first was replaced by a direct payment of child benefit for all children, paid to the mother (Royal Commission 1978: ch. 4). Unemployment benefit had been raised by the

Labour government of the 1960s in order to encourage firms not to hoard their excess workers. But then the question of the incentives to work arose – would a redundant worker accept a job at a lower rate of pay than he was getting in unemployment benefit? In order to ease the problem of those in work with low pay a system of family income supplements was introduced.

Entry to the EC resulted, as described previously, in UK manufacturers facing the full blast of competition from other EC producers in their own home market. Output and employment fell. The macroeconomic turmoil of the 1970s was associated with high and crratic inflation. In particular, fuel prices rose rapidly due to OPEC, and food prices due to the CAP. Workers were faced with a reduction in demand for their services just as their cost of living was rising. They were worse off in 1981 than they were in 1973 (Pauley 1982). As can be seen from Figure 14.5, over the period 1975 to 1982, although the nominal earnings of men, both manual and non-manual, rose, after allowing for inflation and tax their real disposable income did not. This applied to those both in the top and bottom quartile of earnings.

Benefits were upgraded roughly in line with inflation but not according to the consumption basket of the poorest people. It was in the late 1970s that the poverty trap emerged. This occurs when due to the overlap of the tax system (income tax plus employee's national insurance contributions) and the benefit system, a low-paid worker finds that he gets nothing from an extra pound of income that he earns, or indeed that because of his loss of benefits he is worse off.

This is illustrated for November 1977 in Figure 14.6. The gross weekly earnings of a married man with two children aged 4 and 6 are plotted on the abscissa. The returns he got from earning an extra £1 are shown on the ordinate. If a man kept it all – that is, was £1 better off – at all levels of income, the graph would be a horizontal line at £1. But even earning only £25 a week that was not possible; the loss of rent and rate rebates meant that he gained far less than that. He would not immediately lose family income supplement because it was awarded for a year. But in the long run, indicated by the dotted line, he would be losing that as well. If his earnings were high enough, around £35, for the loss of these benefits to be combined with the start of taxation, then he actually became worse off, as shown in the diagram by the shaded area. With gross earnings of £45 the situation improved somewhat, but then there were two severe negative dips: the first was the loss of free welfare milk, and the second occurred around £65 with the loss of free school meals and rate rebates.

The overall effect on income of this high effective marginal tax rate is shown in Figure 14.7. With gross earnings of £25, because of benefits disposable income was considerably higher, but there was very little increase in it with increases in gross earnings until all the benefits were lost. This is called the poverty trap. The more benefits are means tested the more

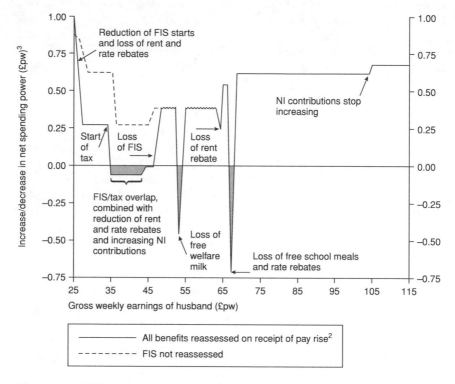

Figure 14.6   Differences in net spending power for a £1 increase in gross earnings: As at November 1977 for married couples with two children aged 4 and 6[1]

Source: DHSS; Royal Commission on the Distribution of Income and Wealth (Diamond Report) (1978), Report No. 6, *Lower Incomes*, Cmnd. 7175, London: HMSO, p. 83.

Notes:

[1]Figures 14.6 and 14.7 were drawn on the following assumptions: the family is a hypothetical one, consisting of a married couple with two children aged 4 and 6 living in typical (not GLC) accommodation; rent of £5.60 per week and rates of £2.20 per week are assumed; and it is also assumed that the gross income of the family is earned solely by the husband, who has work expenses of £2.00 per week.

[2]In practice, a family's benefits do not change immediately after a husband's pay rise. For example, the combined effect of the fact that Family Income Support (FIS) is awarded for 12 months at a time, and the annual upratings of the benefit, is that the level of FIS payable is likely to change little, if at all, provided that the earnings increase is about average. Some other benefits, such as free school meals, are similarly awarded on a 12-month basis.

[3]*Net spending power* is defined as gross weekly income *plus* benefits (family allowances, FIS, rent rebates, rates rebates, the value of free school meals and free welfare milk) *less* tax (income tax and national insurance contributions by the employee) *less* gross housing costs (rent and rates) *less* work expenses.

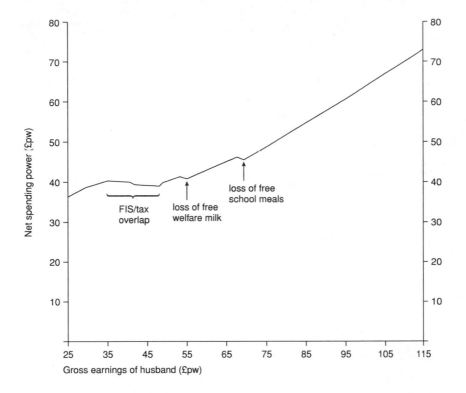

Figure 14.7 The relationship between net spending power and gross earnings of the husband: As at November 1977 for married couple with two children aged 4 and 6

Source: DHSS; Royal Commission on the Distribution of Income and Wealth (Diamond Report) (1978), Report No. 6, *Lower Incomes*, Cmnd. 7175, London: HMSO, p. 83.

Notes: See notes for Figure 14.6.

entrenched it becomes. Thus the poorest people in the community face the highest marginal rate of tax. They become locked into poverty. This is morally iniquitous. Nonetheless the poverty trap has remained in existence for the last twenty years.

Who gets caught in the poverty trap? The first necessary condition is that the wages the worker can earn must be low. Thus he generally has few skills and resides in an area of low wages such as in the Northern cities. Secondly, it depends on his family structure. The more children in the family, the more likely he is to fall into the trap, because the benefits paid out are partly dependent on the number and age of his children whereas the tax system now takes no account of them. Figure 14.8 shows how in 1983 the poverty trap, in terms of a married man being unable to increase

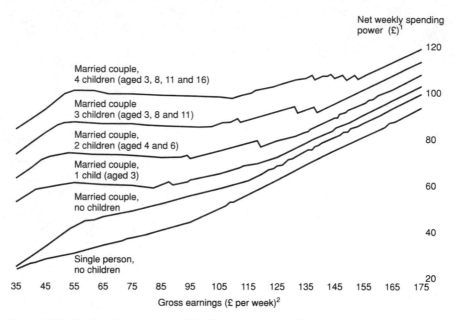

Figure 14.8 Poverty Trap April 1983. Net weekly spending power: By level of earnings[2] and type of family

Source: CSO (1984) *Social Trends* **14**, p. 80,

Notes: [1]Gross earnings less deduction for tax, National Insurance, rent, rates, and work expenses, plus receipts of all benefits which are applicable; [2] gross earnings from full-time work where head of household only is in employment.

his disposable income as his earnings rose, extended over a longer range of earnings the larger his family. The single parent family is also caught in the poverty trap for a wide range of earnings. The present situation is shown in Figure 14.9.

The Conservative government returned in 1979 endeavoured to reduce its social security bill that accounted for about a third of public expenditure (Pauley 1984). It cut some of the benefits and untied them from the price/earnings index, and removed the earnings-related element of unemployment benefit in 1980 (Dean 1983).

> Nonetheless by 1986 8.3 million people were living on supplementary benefit. They include[d] over two-thirds of the unemployed, over half of all single parent families, a quarter of pensioners and a substantial minority of the sick and disabled. Among them [were] two million school age children. All these people are dependent on roughly the same low equivalent income ... They are increasingly referred to as an underclass.
>
> (Bradshaw and Huby 1988)

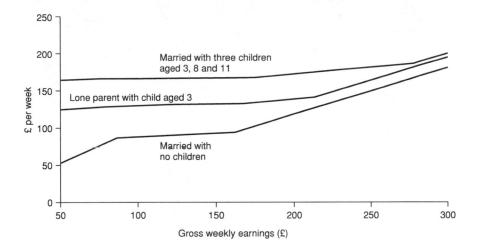

Figure 14.9 Poverty Trap July 1995. Net weekly spending power[1]: By gross weekly earnings[2] and type of family.

Source: CSO (1984) *Social Trends*, **26**, p. 104.

Notes: [1]Gross earnings less deduction for tax, National Insurance, rent, and council tax, plus receipts of all benefits which are applicable for a family paying average local authority rent; [2] gross earnings from full-time work where head of household only is in employment.

Particularly noticeable was the increase in the number of lone parents claiming supplementary benefit, which had increased far faster than the number of lone-parent families. By 1995 it had increased to over a million one-parent families on income support. Ten million people in total, about a sixth of the population, were living on income support, and this figure included three million children. The number of people receiving sickness and invalidity benefit had also increased very fast, to 2 million in 1995. In addition, there were rent rebates, rent allowances, and council tax benefits. There is an overlap of categories in so far as some people claim several benefits. There were also 10.5 million people receiving a state pension. Almost all of these pensions were contributory entitlements, as was the unemployment benefit received by 427,000 people. But the government regards them all as transfers to be paid out of tax revenue because the schemes are unfunded. All the governments of the 1980s and 1990s have been very anxious to reduce unemployment and the expense of the social security scheme. The Labour government under Tony Blair is very keen to get people off benefit and into work. It is going to reduce lone-parent benefits and is endeavouring to cut the number claiming disability benefits, which has increased from 2 million in 1982 to 6.5 million in 1997 (Buckby 1997).

Membership of the EU was only a contributory factor in so far as it affected National Insurance contributions. Where it has been important is in shifting the burden of taxation away from direct to indirect taxation by the institution of VAT. But in both cases the *rates* of tax are set by the governments of the Member States. The VAT was originally set in 1973 at a uniform rate of 10 per cent, but from 1977 to 1979 there were two rates, of 8 per cent and 12.5 per cent. Then it was raised under the Thatcher government in 1979 to 15 per cent and later by John Major to 17.5 per cent. Indirect taxes tend to be regressive, that is, the burden of them falls relatively more heavily on those with lower incomes. So to that extent the shift from direct to indirect taxation is regressive. High food prices associated with the CAP have also been a particular burden on poor people with large families, who often spend a quarter of their income on food.

These taxes also affect economic efficiency. The EC's system of taxation places high taxes on the *employment* of labour through the high National Insurance contributions rather than the actual income earned. When allowance is also made for the VAT placed on the good or service the divergence becomes even greater. Let us assume we have a large building firm carrying out repairs and therefore liable for VAT. The labour cost of an additional contract to be carried out is £100. The customer will pay this plus VAT, equal to £117.5. For simplicity let us take the National Insurance contributions for a worker with weekly earnings of more than £205 in 1995: the employer's contribution is 10 per cent and the employee's is 8 per cent. These deductions from £100 leave £84. If he was on the basic rate of tax at that time of 25 per cent he would be left with £61. So the return to the worker is only 52 per cent of the amount the customer pays. The worker, in turn, has to pay VAT on the goods and services he purchases. This divergence at the margin between the cost of providing a good or service and the price the customer pays for it, and therefore the value that he attributes to it, represents considerable economic inefficiency. Some inefficiency is almost inevitable with any proportionate income tax. The question is whether the shift towards indirect taxation makes it worse, and the degree to which it reduces output. The more inelastic the demand and supply schedules, the less indirect taxation will affect the level of output.

Economists have ceased to be interested in these microeconomic aspects of indirect taxation. They have been more concerned with replacement ratios, that is, the ratio of earnings in work to benefits that a worker is entitled to when unemployed, an in-or-out version of the poverty trap. In 1983 it was stated that the few who did receive more money out of work were heads of large households, unlike most of the unemployed (NIER 1983). The replacement ratios for unemployed workers without children in 1991 were considerably lower than in 1971 (Blöndal and Pearson 1995).

The econometric work on the subject has treated replacement ratios and poverty traps as problems of individual households. The effect of the geographical concentration of such households in urban areas is not considered. To the author, who has just spent twenty-five years in inner-city Manchester, it appears to be one of the explanations of the inner-city problems. The decline in external sources of earning such as work in manufacturing has left a large number of unskilled or semi-skilled workers with no alternative occupations. The erratic efforts by governments or charities to improve such an area by construction work may lift a certain number of people out of unemployment for a short period of time. But because they lose benefits so fast the total income of the area hardly increases, certainly not enough to encourage anyone else to set up business. In other words, the multiplier effect is near zero.

That is why investment in the assisted areas from outside the region, most of which has been foreign, is so important. It provides employment producing goods to be sold abroad or in other parts of Britain. In other words, it provides an export injection to the area which continues for a longer time. It is this kind of investment that has enabled Wales and Scotland and the North to reduce their unemployment. It has reduced the divergence between their level of unemployment and the UK average. In Scotland this has been assisted by the development of North Sea oil. Inward investment has not been an important factor in the North West, in particular Merseyside, and that is why there has been such a long period of declining employment.

One of the inducements to inward investment has been the increased flexibility of the labour force, which has allowed a greater divergence in wage levels. Average wages in the North, Wales and Scotland remain below the UK average. But inward direct investment (see Chapter 11 and Wolffe 1997), has often required training of the workforce, generally subsidized by the government, which has raised their skill and earnings.

CONCLUSION

Britain's system of taxation and benefits has led to a rapidly increasing number of people dependent on income support while, at the same time, locking single-parent families and large families of low-paid workers in the poverty trap. Governments have been trying to unravel the system generally by reducing the taxes and National Insurance contributions at low levels of income. But most of the aid provided by the wealthiest region, the South East, to the rest of the country is through the fiscal system.

The progress that has been made in reducing regional disparities has been in lowering the *relative* level of unemployment in the deprived areas. This appears to be the result of the Conservative government's liberalization of the labour market in the 1980s, which has been a factor inducing an inward flow of foreign investment. But it has also increased the divergence in earnings between the regions.

Specified flows of regional aid by the UK government have declined considerably and are about half those of the EU to the UK. Thus the DTI claims not to be undermining the 'level playing field' that the CEC has tried to establish for trade between Member States. The CEC has also tried to avoid competition between Member States in deregulation to attract inward investors. Nonetheless, Britain with the least regulated labour market has been the major EU recipient of investment from third countries.

NOTES

1   Government Office Region (GOR) of the South East comprises Berkshire, Buckinghamshire, East Sussex, Hampshire, Isle of Wight, Kent, Oxfordshire, Surrey, and West Sussex (ONS 1997).

REFERENCES

Adams, R. (1997) 'Direct overseas investment hits £16bn', *Financial Times*, 17 December.
Barber, L. (1997) 'EU braced for enlargement war', *Financial Times*, 14 July.
Begg, I. (1995) 'Factor mobility and regional disparities in the European Union', *Oxford Review of Economic Policy*, **11** (2).
Begg, I., Gudgin, G. and Morris, D. (1995) 'Regional policy in the European Union', *Oxford Review of Economic Policy*, **11** (2).
Blake, N. (1995) 'The regional implications of macroeconomic policy', *Oxford Review of Economic Policy*, **11** (2).
Blöndal, S. and Pearson, M. (1995) 'Unemployment and other non-employment benefits', *Oxford Review of Economic Policy*, **11** (1).
Bradshaw, J. and Huby, M. (1988) 'Trends in dependence on supplementary benefits', paper given to the Institute for Fiscal Studies Conference on the *Economics of Social Security*, 15 April.
Buckby, S. (1997) 'Tough love makes for hard choices', *Financial Times*, 17 December.
Burton, J. (1997) 'Hyundai chip plant delay "makes sense"', *Financial Times*, 28 November.
Buxton, J. (1997a) 'Scotland anxious about project's future', *Financial Times*, 28 November.
—— (1997b) 'Revenue sets up register to levy possible tartan tax', *Financial Times*, 19 December.
CSO (1996) *Labour Market Trends*, January.
Dean, M. (1983) 'How to cheapen a quality of life', *Guardian*, 11 March.
Dignan, A. (1995) 'Regional disparities and regional policy in the European Union', *Oxford Review of Economic Policy*, **11** (1).
Fothergill, S., Kitson, M., and Monk, S. (1985) *Urban Industrial Change*, DOE and DTI Inner Cities Research Programme 1.1, London: HMSO.

Green, D. (1997) 'A favourite tonic for foreign companies', *Financial Times*, 24 July.

Groom, B. (1997) 'The Disunited Kingdom', *Financial Times*, 1 December.

—— 1998) 'Room to spread helps create job opportunities', *Financial Times*, 8 January.

—— (1997) 'Regions may face thin time on smaller slice of the EU pie', *Financial Times*, 1 December.

Groom, B. and Buxton, J. (1997a) 'Refereeing the regions in fight for investment', *Financial Times*, 22 October.

—— (1997b) 'Call for public spending shake-up', *Financial Times*, 14 November.

—— (1998) 'Room to spread helps create job opportunities', *Financial Times*, 8 January.

Gudgin, G. (1995) 'Regional problems and policy in the UK', *Oxford Review of Economic Policy*, **11** (2).

Hitiris, T. (1994) *European Community Economics*, London: Harvester Wheatsheaf.

James, S. and Nobes, C. (1983) *The Economics of Taxation*, Oxford: Philip Allan.

Jonquières, G. de (1997) 'Britain doubles share of EU inward investment', *Financial Times*, 14 July.

Jowit, J. (1997) 'Watchdog to investigate £247m grant for LG', *Financial Times*, 11 December.

Marsh, P. (1997) 'An international blend of ideas', *Financial Times*, 21 July.

NIER (1983) 'Few are better off out of work', *Financial Times*, 24 February.

ONS (1997) *Regional Trends*, No. 32 and previous issues, Office of National Statistics.

Parker, G. and Jones, S. (1997) 'Barnett hits at Treasury explanation of formula', *Financial Times*, 4 November.

Pauley, R. (1982) 'Workers worse off than in 1973', *Financial Times*, 29 November.

—— (1984) 'Caught in the traps of a welfare jungle', *Financial Times*, 18 October.

Royal Commission on the Distribution of Income and Wealth (Diamond Report) (1978) Report No.6, *Lower Incomes*, Cmnd. 7175, London: HMSO.

Smith, M. (1997) 'Brussels plans to extend curb on hours', *Financial Times*, 16 December.

Taylor, R. (1997a) 'Part-time staff poised to secure a fairer future', *Financial Times*, 15 December.

—— (1997b) 'Brussels to warn Britain on working hours rules', *Financial Times*, 16 December.

Wagstyl, S. (1997a) 'Granting and groaning', *Financial Times*, 24 July.

—— (1997b) 'Screwdriver assembly out, science in', *Financial Times*, 24 July.

Wighton, D. (1997) 'Climbdown on inward investment', *Financial Times*, 27 November.

Wolffe, R. (1997) 'Setting the pace for the rest of Europe', *Financial Times*, 10 July.

15 Conclusion

During the postwar period Britain has undergone a dramatic change from being a highly industrialized country to one in which the service sector accounts for three-quarters of employment and two-thirds of output. De-industrialization – that is, a decline in the proportion of employment in the manufacturing sector – had started in the late 1960s, but it was accelerated by Britain's entry to the EC. After entry, her output of manufactures *fell* because imports from the other EC Member States ousted her home-produced goods from her own market. Her increase in exports to the other Member States was not sufficient to compensate for this and, in any case, some of these extra exports appear to have been diverted from the rest of the world. So far from participating in a rapidly growing market her rate of growth fell; indeed, it became negative from 1979–81.

This was partly because of the macroeconomic difficulties that developed countries had in adjusting to the quadrupling of the oil price from 1973–74 and then its doubling from 1978–80. Inflation rose erratically and the rate of growth in the EC fell. Britain, who was developing her own supplies of oil, should not have been as badly affected, but the appreciation of the pound aggravated her worsening competitive position with respect to manufacturing. This shrinkage of the industrial base with the development of a natural resource is called the 'Dutch' disease.

So the contraction of manufacturing output is ascribed both to competition from other EC countries and to the development of North Sea oil. However, the very high levels of unemployment that accompanied it showed that neither macroeconomic policies nor the labour market were working efficiently.

Margaret Thatcher, leading the Conservative government that took over in 1979, severely reduced employment in the loss-making steel and coal industries and introduced legislation restricting the activities of trade unions. She was determined to reduce the role of the government in the economy and proceeded with a programme of privatization of nationalized industries. This was in contrast to the CEC which was pursuing a policy of intervention and tried to deal with the crisis in the EC steel industry with production quotas and VERs on imports from third countries.

Britain as a member of the EC was also party to other schemes for protecting the EC's declining manufacturing industries, such as the vast and intricate Multi-Fibre Arrangement. She also had VERs on imports of motor vehicles from Japan, as did most of the other EU producers. With the SEM these were replaced by an EU quota.

The CEC and its Member States had aspirations to be at the forefront of technological development, particularly with respect to 'electronics'. The Member States subsidized their computing firms and the CEC subsidized on a 50/50 basis a series of intra-EC research programmes. A series of anti-dumping duties were placed on electronic products imported from Asia. However, US firms increased their dominance, and the Japanese their output of microprocessors. The EU is still a net importer of office and telecommunications equipment.

Ironically, these non-tariff barriers on cars and electronic products induced an inflow of foreign investment, a high proportion of which came to Britain, attracted partly by the flexibility of the labour force and the use of English. As a result there has been an increase in UK output from these two industries, electronics and cars, which are almost entirely foreign owned.

The CEC has gradually abandoned its policy of intervention and followed the British example of deregulation and privatization. This is already leading to greater competition and lower prices in the EU service sector, most noticeably in telecommunications and airlines.

Meanwhile, in Britain the privatization and the break-up of the public utilities led to a reduction in costs and employment and provided a bonus for shareholders. The separate firms were not allowed to reamalgamate. As a result, their only scope for expansion has been into another industry or abroad. The takeovers that have occurred in the formerly nationalized industries have often been by foreign firms. In the service industries, which are dependent on networking, large alliances have been formed. This development does not appear to have been anticipated. At the moment there are several alliances in most of the service industries and they appear to be competitive. But there is the potential for cartel-type activity.

Until the Merger Regulation of 1990 the EU had very little control over such developments. Now the Competition Commissioner has entered into the fray, arguing with both the US and the UK competition authorities about recent proposals. Whereas the greater exploitation of economies of scale was regarded as one of the benefits of the SEM, now that it is being exercised on a global scale the CEC has become very worried by it. However, this will be a problem of developing countries as much as developed ones as these alliances in telecommunications and airlines are extended to them. Some international agreement on competition policy seems essential.

The scandal of the EU is still the CAP, which has raised the price of food well above world prices for most of the period and has accounted for two-thirds or more of EC expenditure, even though the number of people employed in agriculture has been steadily declining. The only modification has been to reduce the payment made per unit of output. It still remains a subsidy to one particular section of the population, which is very inefficient in so far as consumers pay far more than farmers receive and what is received tends to be capitalized in the value of land. It is also very inequitable in so far as the burden falls most heavily on the poorest people, who spend a quarter of their income on food, whereas the benefits go mostly to the largest farmers. Britain is still a net contributor to the EC because of the CAP.

The economic aspects of Britain's membership of the EC have been the concern of this book. But to the original members of the EC, economic integration was a means of transcending the aggressive and divisive nationalism of Member States. Economic institutions were established for political ends, the ultimate being the creation of a Federal State of Europe. Britain joined because she was afraid of being left out of the decision making, but she has never wholeheartedly supported the aims of full integration. This is often ascribed by commentators to the 'delusions of grandeur' acquired from ruling an empire. Such accusations ignore Britain's geographical and economic location, as a medium-sized, densely populated economy on the edge of Europe. In 1996 the EU accounted for 57 per cent of her exports and 55 per cent of her imports of *merchandise*. But it accounted for only 35 per cent of her exports and 47 per cent of her imports of *services*, and services account for most of her employment and output. Or to take the total current account, the EU accounts for about half the UK's credits and debits. Furthermore, she is the second largest foreign direct investor and much of this investment is located in the US; she also has workers distributed round the globe. The UK may be interested in exchange rate stability but this is as much with the rest of the world as with the EU.

The major question now is whether she should join the EMU. This is yet another step in the direction of achieving political integration by economic means. Indeed, some think it will only work effectively if there *is* political integration. But in view of the lack of British enthusiasm for the political objective the economic costs and benefits must be carefully considered. Here it should be said that although most EU Member States fulfil the Maastricht monetary requirements for joining the EMU they have failed badly with respect to the other macroeconomic objective of maintaining full employment. Britain's 6 per cent unemployment is about half that in France and Germany and considerably lower than the EC average.

Should this influence Britain's decision? It should certainly affect her assessment of the forecast costs and benefits. The obvious benefit is the saving in transaction costs of converting from one currency to another, but this pales into insignificance besides the other considerations. Proponents claim that there will be efficiency gains, as the common currency will make costs and prices transparent and lead to production gravitating towards the cheapest location. This is already happening, even in the absence of a common currency. The problem is that in some countries, such as Germany, employment in manufacturing is falling without it increasing in other industries and the common currency will prevent governments of such Member States adjusting their economies by altering their exchange rates, or their relative tax rates. Keynesian-type government deficits are also ruled out by the Maastricht requirements. Thus monetary union may make full employment more difficult to attain.

On the other hand, if European unemployment is a microeconomic problem it may be possible to correct it by reducing high levels of social security payments and deregulating the labour market. But this type of adjustment should be undertaken *before* forming a monetary union, not afterwards, so that the correct exchange rates can be established. The danger of going into the EMU in the present circumstances is that the recent levels of unemployment may continue or worsen, and this may lead to serious social unrest. Meanwhile, governments of the participating countries will have given up their main measures for controlling unemployment. Britain is occupying a ringside seat waiting to see whether EMU works or not before joining. Yet even this may be uncomfortable if sterling appreciates, because the money markets assume, as they appear to be doing, that the euro will be a relatively soft currency.

What impact has the EU had on the rest of the world and what will be the effect of EMU? The cost anticipated from the economic theory of customs unions is that of trade diversion. However, this has arisen not so much from the common external tariff as from the CAP and the use of VERs and anti-dumping duties. The removal of barriers to trade between Member States has been of benefit not only to them, but also to third country exporters and firms operating in the EU. All firms have benefited from the greater opportunity to exploit economics of scale as a result of harmonization and standardization.

The most severely distorting measure has been the CAP, which has kept EU domestic prices generally well above world prices, and has undermined the world market in sugar and distorted it in grains and oilseeds. Present measures to reduce surpluses do not involve an equivalent reduction in cost. The financial transfers between countries have largely been the result of the CAP. Germany has been the chief contributor, followed by Britain.

The benefits to the rest of the world appear largely to be the result of the dynamism incorporated into the EU process of removing barriers to trade. This applies particularly to services, for which the EU's measures of liberalization appeared as a pilot project for the Uruguay negotiation of GATS.

Now while on the one hand EU integration is being deepened by the EMU, there is also a queue of aspiring entrants which, if admitted, would broaden it. All new members must accept and adhere to the *acquis communautaire*. Why does the EU appear such a desirable club? Partly for the same reasons that induced Britain to join – the opportunity to compete on equal terms with Member States in a large growing market, and participation in EU decision making. Thus Austria, Finland, and Sweden were quite readily accepted as small countries that were likely to be net contributors to the budget. However, many of the others desire entry at least in part because they expect to benefit from EU transfers. The Eastern European countries are likely to be admitted, although this will require considerable adjustment to the CAP in order to avoid a massive increase in expenditure. Already the costs to the regional funds are being calculated. The EU is reluctant to admit Turkey because of human rights abuses, but also because it is a large country of 60 million people, of which a high proportion, 40 per cent, are engaged in agriculture.

As the EU enlarges it gets nearer to Russia and the Middle East, and in this situation, its casual diplomacy of concluding preferential trade agreements will no longer be appropriate. Indeed, those agreements so far concluded with the ACP countries and most Mediterranean countries may appear provocative to others which have to trade under less favourable terms; these include Russia, and the large countries of Asia, which have the potential to be the EU's best customers, particularly for investment goods and chemicals. The EU, in its signing of the Information Technology Agreement (ITA) and the WTO Telecoms Agreement in 1997, has recognized the benefits that may be derived from globalization, even though some Member States have found it difficult to put the latter into effect.

The US had hoped that under the EU's second pillar of integration – that is, its common foreign and security policy – it would pursue a more active foreign policy. But Member States have tended to act independently; EU policy requiring agreement of all fifteen has been difficult to achieve.

The incoming Labour government, anxious to adopt a pro-EU stance, has said that in principle it would expect to join EMU after the next general election. William Hague, the new leader of the Conservative party, opposes doing so. Meanwhile, there is increasing social unrest among the unemployed in both France and Germany. The politicians in both countries seem unable to adopt any effective course of action, but, nonetheless, cling to their aspirations for further European integration and the installation of EMU. What will happen next? This economist is not prepared to forecast.

Index

acid rain 182
Acorn 116, 309
acquis communautaire 79, 90, 375
ACV (bus manufacturers) 236
Adams, R. 358
Adelman, M.A. 145
Adler, F.M. 135
advanced gas-cooled reactors (AGRs) 151, 160
Advanced Medium-Range Air-to-Air Missiles (Amraams) 284
AEC (ACU) 235
AEG 114
Aer Lingus 327
Aerospatiale 284, 305
African, Caribbean and Pacific (ACP) countries 83–4, 207, 224, 263–4, 266, 376
Agenda 2000 proposals 98, 357
aggregate measurements of support (AMS), 87, 223
Agra Europe 197, 225, 227, 228
Agreement with Associated Territories 68, 71
Agricultural Act (1947) 65, 188
agricultural unit of account (AUA) 195, 196, 201
agriculture 13–14, 34, 42, 87, 373–4; Britain's entry to EC and 69–72, 74–6; exports *see* exports; output 10, 11–12, 23–7; prices 68–9, 188–98, 201–4, 207, 211, 216, 218, 220–2, 225, 229–30; production (effect of CAP) 188–231; protection 64–6; *see also* Common Agricultural Policy

Agriculture in the United Kingdom (MAFF) 198
aid 7, 91; EU Industrial Policy 105–7, 111; Marshall Plan 8, 64; state (to industry) 358–9; *see also* subsidies
Aim (mini-programme) 114
Air Canada 334
Air France 327
Air Liberté 334
air traffic (standards) 323
air transport (in SEM) 325–7
Airbus 104–5, 305
aircraft industry (EU trade policy) 104–5, 283, 284–5, 305–6
airlines 333–5, 337, 339–40, 373
Albion Motors 235, 236
Alcatel Alsthom 284
Alfa-Romeo 243, 244, 255
Alitalia 327
alliances (international) 333–6, 339, 340, 373
Alvis 235, 236
American Airlines 104–5, 334, 337, 339
Andean Pact 84
Anderson, K. 223
Anglo-Iranian Oil Company 149
anti-dumping duties 41, 58, 81–2, 89, 91, 111, 279, 309–12, 359, 373, 375
Apple 116
Applied Materials 313
Area Boards (gas) 151, 159
Area Boards (electricity) 151, 159
area distribution (UK trade) 126
armaments and defence 283–5
Armstrong-Siddeley 235
Association Agreements 68, 71
Aston Martin 242

Astra 359
asymmetric shock 93, 99
AT&T 328, 335,
Atkins, R. 285, 330
Audi 244, 255
Austin 234, 235–6
Austin Rover 243, 244, 245, 252
Austrian Airlines 339
autarchy 31, 37
Aveling Barford 236
average cost curve 51, 53, 54
average cost pricing 53, 56, 57, 154
Aylen, Jonathan 107

'Baby Bells' 328
BAe 284, 305
Bailey, R. 151
balance of payments 28, 93; preferential
    trading areas 125, 130, 135; receipts
    and payments (research and
    development) 294–6; UK's comparative
    position 5–9, 15; UK's trade policy 63,
    73–5, 76
balance of trade 127–9, 135, 141, 297,
    300, 321
balancing item 7
Balassa, B. 126
Balasubramanyam, V.N. 138, 336
Baldwin, Robert E. 57
Baltic republics 83
Bangemann, Martin 116, 307
Bangemann Group report (1994) 116
Bank of England 7, 15, 16, 21, 70, 95,
    179
Barber, L. 100, 357
Bardacke, E. 85
Barham, J. 83
Barings 336
Barnett, Donald 109–10
Barnett, Joel 345
'basic balance' 8–9, 15
Basic Research in Industrial Technologies
    in Europe (BRITE) 276, 303
basket mechanism 262–3
Batchelor, C. 323, 327
Baxter, A. 80
BBC 350–1
Beckett, Margaret 359
beef 78, 204, 210–11, 222, 226, 227–8

Begg, I. 355, 357, 359
Bell Cablemedia 329
Bentley 234, 235
Bermuda II agreement 326
Bertrand assumption 55
Beuc (consumer organization) 279
Bill of Accession 76
Biotechnological Research for Innovation,
    Development and Growth in Europe
    (BRIDGE) 303
Biotechnology Action Programme (BAP)
    303
biotechnology projects 302, 303, 359
Bladen-Hovell, R. 94–5
Blair, Tony 100, 367
Blair House Agreement 222–4
Blake, N. 355, 357
'block exemption' 244
Blondal, S. 368
BMW 243, 250, 253–4, 255
Boeing 104, 284, 305
Boulton, L. 183
Bowden, S. 235–6
Bradshaw, J. 366
Bray, R. 327
Brescia 111
Bretton Woods system 8–9, 94, 195
Briggs Motor Bodies 236
Briscoe, L. 259, 264, 265
Britain: agriculture (effect of CAP)
    188–231; comparative position 5–27;
    current account balances 139–42;
    economic trends 1–3; energy sector
    144–85; EU entry 69–77, 130–4, 188;
    high-technology industries 283–315;
    motor vehicles (trade/production)
    234–57; regional policy 343–53, 354,
    369–70; services sector 318–40;
    taxation 345, 357, 359–69; textiles and
    clothing industry 259–81; trade (impact
    of EFTA) 70–1, 75, 77, 82, 124–8, 131;
    trade development (impact of
    preferential trading areas) 119–42;
    trade policy 63–91
British Aerospace 254
British Airways (BA) 104, 326, 333–5,
    337, 339
British Caledonian 326, 327
British Coal 147, 161, 162, 182

British Energy 160, 163
British Gas 154, 156–8, 169, 181,
British Gas Corporation (BGC) 151, 152, 154
British Leyland 243, 245, 249
British Leyland Motor Corporation (BLMC) 236, 238, 250, 253
British Mediterranean Airways 333
British Midland 334
British Motor Corporation (BMC) 234, 235–6
British Motor Holdings (BMH) 236
British National Oil Corporation (BNOC) 152, 156
British Petroleum (BP) 149, 152, 181
British Rail 172, 329
British Steel 109, 110, 111
British Telecom 328, 329, 330, 335
Britoil 156
Brittan, Leon 114
Brittan, Samuel 285
broadcasting (EC policy) 330–1
Brown, C.J.F. 25
Brown, Gordon 95, 183
Brown Book 152, 158, 159, 162, 163, 166, 176
BRT 329
Brussels Agreement (1988) 221
BSA 234, 235
BSE crisis 78, 204, 211, 226, 227–8
Buchan, D. 284, 309
Buckby, S. 368
Buckley N. 181, 224, 225–6, 279, 311–12
budget deficits 96, 97, 98, 125
budget limitation (CAP reform) 220–1
'budget stabilizer' mechanisms 221
Building Institute 283
Bull 113, 114, 115, 116, 309
Bundesbank 95, 98
'burden sharing' 262
Bureau of Agricultural Economics 204, 207
Burns, T. 335
Burton, J. 313, 314, 358, 359
business enterprise sector R&D (BERD) 288–90, 293–5
Business Strategies report 347
butter (effect of CAP) 212–15
Buxton, J. 313–14, 345, 358, 359

Cable and Wireless Communications 329, 330, 355
cabotage 324–5, 326, 334
CAE 113
Cane, A. 309, 313, 314, 329–30, 332–3, 335
Canon Copier 311
capital 29, 68; human 19, 20–1, 34; labour ratios 34; physical 19, 34; stock 20–1
capital account 5, 7, 9, 95, 135, 136–8
Capital Liberalization Directive (1988) 94
car industry 81, 137; production 234–41, 248–57; trade 234, 241–8
carbon taxes 182–3
Carrington and Dewhurst 264
cartels 58, 102, 325
Casa (of Spain) 305
'Cassis de Dijon' principle 79–80
CBI 135
CE Electric 162
Central and Eastern European States (CEECs) 82–3, 111, 221, 278–9
Central Electricity Generating Board (CEGB) 149, 150, 151, 155–6, 159, 161
Central Policy Review Staff 237
Centrica 158–9
cereals/cereal regime 189, 190, 201–6, 217, 222, 225–6, 229–30
certificates of origin 276
CGE 114
Channel Tunnel 323, 327
Chaudhry and Hamid 269
cheese (effect of CAP) 212–15
Chernobyl accident 182
'Chicago Convention' 323, 325
child benefit 362
Chirac, Jacques 279
Chote, R. 100, 226
Chrysler 137, 234, 241, 243
Churchill, Winston S. 148
Citroen 243, 244, 255
Claremonts 280
Clark, B. 105
clothing and textiles industry 87, 259–81
co-responsibility levies 207, 211, 221
Coal Act (1938) 149
Coal Act (1990) 151
coal industry 148, 182; Conservative

policy 156, 161–2, 372; consumption 3,
24–5, 145–6, 161–2, 164–5, 168–71,
173; costs 153, 155, 156, 177; ECSC
67, 77–8, 85, 90, 106–7, 110, 146, 355;
nationalization 149–51; prices/ pricing
146, 147, 153, 161–2, 177, 183;
privatization 161–3, 176, 183;
production (government protection)
163–4; production decline 174–6, 346,
372; subsidies 106, 146, 165–6, 176
Coal Industry Act (1985) 151
Coats Viyella 280
Cohesion Fund 96, 355, 357
commercial vehicles (CVs) 234, 239,
240–1, 242, 247, 256
Commission of the European Community
(CEC) 77–9, 83, 90, 99, 370, 372–3;
Agenda 2000 proposals 98, 357;
Emerson Report 54–5, 56–7, 108, 244;
policies affecting trade 102–17; regional
policy 352, 357–8
Committee of Permanent Representatives
(COREPER) 77
commodity categories (UK trade changes
since 1970) 126–30
commodity regimes, CAP (effect on
Britain) 201–16
Common Agricultural Policy 28, 41, 83,
91, 94, 128, 355, 376; effect on UK
agriculture 188–231; food prices 363,
368, 373–4, 375; origin/development
68–9; pressures for reform 217–24;
recent developments 224–8; UK
accession to 3, 16, 23–4, 71–6, 134;
UK reservations 69–70
Common External Tariff (CET) 16, 44,
46, 47–8, 51, 75, 82–3, 87, 91, 127,
138, 240, 266, 308, 375
common foreign and security policy
(CFSP) 90, 376
Common Sugar Policy 207
Commonwealth Preference Scheme 3, 63,
66–7, 70, 71, 75, 207, 239, 242, 259
Commonwealth Sugar Agreement 207
community indifference curves 30–2
Compagnie Générale des Eaux in Cegetel
330
Compagnier Internationale
d'Informatique (CII) 113

comparative advantage 3, 27, 28–9, 30,
32–5, 38
comparative industry structure
(textiles/clothing) 264–6
comparative position (Britain) 5–27
comparative research and development
record 287–92
competition: imperfect 28, 54–6, 57,
60–1; perfect 28, 29, 30, 33, 35; policy
(EU) 102–5, 111
Competition Directorate 105, 114, 339,
340
computing industry 112–17, 322–3,
327
Concert Communications 335
Conoco 158, 182
Conservative government 17, 21, 112,
138, 290, 330–1; energy policy 150–1,
156–62, 172, 183, 372; privatization
programme 1, 16, 109, 183, 328;
regional policy 344, 369–70; taxation
policy 366, 368
construction industry 22, 23
consumer price 55
consumer subsidy equivalent 40, 220,
224–5, 226
consumer surplus 38–40, 45, 48, 53–4, 75,
134, 275, 281
consumers 30, 44–5; pressure for CAP
reform 217–18
consumption 35–6, 44, 47; of coal 3,
24–5, 145–6, 161–2, 164–5, 168–71,
173; community indifference curve
30–2; effect of CAP on 188–231; of
energy 24–5, 144–5, 148, 162,
168–74, 184–5; of textiles 272–4,
275
Continental Airline 104–5
Continental Shelf Convention 152
contingent protection 58, 82, 89, 91
conversion rates (under CAP) 195–7
Cooper, C.A. 45–6
Coordinating Committee for Multilateral
Export Controls (COCOM) 285
copyright protection 88
Corden, W.M. 42, 51, 229
Corn Laws (abolition) 34, 65, 70
corporation tax (CT) 166
Corzine, R. 157–8, 182

costs: agriculture 189; car industry 245–7, 250; energy sector 144, 145, 153–4, 155–6, 176–7; marginal 30, 46, 51, 55, 144, 153–4; reduction effect 53, 54; steelmaking 109–10, 111; textile/clothing 259, 267–9; in trade theory 28–30, 51, 53–7; of transport 145, 147, 249; *see also* opportunity cost
Cotton and Allied Textiles (Textile Council) 260–1
Cotton Board 260
Cotton Industry Act (1959) 259
cotton textiles 66–7, 121, 259–81
Council of Auditors 78
Council of Ministers 69, 77–8, 115, 196, 215, 221, 225, 230, 279, 304, 329
countervailing duties 82, 111
Cournot assumption 55
Courtaulds 264, 276, 280
Crafts, N.F.R. 15, 19–21
Creuzfeldt-Jacob disease 226
cross-subsidization (energy sector) 153, 158
CSO 65, 120, 130, 193, 198–9, 273, 301, 336, 348–9, 351–2, 362, 366–7
current account 5, 7, 9, 22, 28, 95, 136–8; balances (UK) 139–42
Curwen, P. 329
customs union 28, 44–9, 51–4, 56–8, 63–4, 67, 83, 93, 133, 375

Daewoo 253, 309
DAF 253
Daimler 234, 236, 252
Daimler Benz 243
Daimler Benz Aerospace (DASA) 285, 305
Dassault 284
Davignon Plan 107
de-industrialization 2, 25–6, 106, 372
de Gaulle, Charles 71
Dean, M. 366
defence and armaments 283–5
deflation 96, 98, 344
Delors, Jacques 78, 105, 301
Delta (mini-programme) 114
Delta Airline 104–5, 339

demand: elasticities of 40, 50, 55, 59–60, 126; lag 286, 297; schedule 40–3, 45, 47, 49
demand management 9–10, 16, 344
democracy problem 98
Dempsey, J. 182
Denison, E.F. 147
Dennis 235
Denshi 311
Denton, N. 304, 309
Department of the Environment 169
deregulation policies 331, 373, 375
Deutsche BA 334
Deutsche Bahn 330
Deutsche Bank 335
Deutsche Telekom 329, 330, 335
Deutschmark 22, 94, 95, 96, 195, 197, 245
devaluation 94; sterling 8, 9–10, 15, 21–2, 23, 95, 226
developing countries 58; EU preferential agreement with 83–5
Development Areas 344
'development index' 84
Dewhirsts 280
Diamond Report (1978) 351, 360–1, 364–5
Dicken, P. 254, 306, 309
Digest of United Kingdom Energy Statistics (DUKES) 148, 150, 151, 152, 164, 168, 173–4, 178–9, 182
digital technology 307–8
Dignan, A. 355, 356
direct investment (high-technology industries) 312–14
direct taxes 359–60, 368
Directorate-General III (DGIII) 328
Directorate-General XIII (DGXIII) 116
Directorates General 78
dirigisme 105, 112, 113
'dirty float' 15
discrimination (in theory of trade) 28–61
'dollar shortage' 7, 8, 15
domestic fuel consumption 169–70
Dresdner Bank 336
Drive (mini-programme) 114
DTI 162, 168, 173–9 *passim* 270, 310, 358, 370
Dunlop 235

Dunne, N. 308
Dunnett, P.J.S. 235, 242
Dunning, J.H. 137
'Dutch disease' 34, 372

EAGGF 226–7
EAN International 322–3
Eastern Group 182
EasyJet 334
Econfin 100
economic growth (OECD's analysis)
    10–22
economic integration: European 67–71,
    90; moves towards monetary 93–100
economic and monetary union (EMU)
    95–100, 197, 230, 374–6
economic rent 50, 81, 144–5, 146, 153,
    166, 176, 177
economic structure (changes in) 22–7
Economic Trends Annual Supplement 168
economies of scale 343, 373, 375; high
    technology industries 302, 307; motor
    vehicles 234–6, 241, 249, 251, 256;
    steel industry 106, 111; in theory of
    trade 29, 51–8
Economist Intelligence Unit 246
Eden, R. 153
effective protection 43, 64
efficiency gain 38, 39, 45, 47, 54
Ekostahl 110
elasticities: of demand 40, 50, 55, 59–60,
    126; of supply 43, 44, 46, 60
electrical equipment (standardization) 80
Electricité de France (EdF), 180
electricity industry 22–3, 148;
    Conservative policy 159–61;
    consumption 25, 168–71, 173–4; costs
    155–6; generation 161–2, 164–5, 175;
    legislation 151, 159; liberalization of
    180–1; nationalization 149, 151, 181;
    net effective cost 155, 156;
    prices/pricing 154–6, 159–61, 180–1,
    183; privatization 159–60, 161;
    production of 163–4
electronics (EU trade policy) 306, 373
Elf 158
Eltis, W. 312
Emerson Report (1988) 54–5, 56–7, 108,
    244

employment: full 9, 15, 29, 30, 34, 133,
    343, 344, 374; full-time 351–3; part-
    time 351–3; Regional Employment
    Premium 344, 353; regional problems
    345–7; trends 10–11, 12–14, 25–6; *see
    also* labour; underemployment;
    unemployment
Enders, A. 83
Energy Report, The 175, 176–7
energy sector: consumption 24–5, 144–5,
    148, 162, 168–74, 184–5; effect on UK
    economy 174–82; exports 123, 124,
    144, 146, 178–9; imports 123, 124,
    144, 146, 178–9; nationalizations
    149–52; output 24–5; pollution 182–3;
    pricing policies 144–7, 149–50, 153–6;
    privatization 156–63, 176, 183; UK
    policies 148–74, 372; UK trade 178–80
English Sewing Cotton 264
Enterprise Oil 156
Environmental Protection Agency 182
equity problem 98
Escom 309
EURAM 303
Eurocoton 279
Eurofighter 285
Europe Agreements 83, 277, 278
European Airbus 104–5, 305
European Atomic Energy Community
    (Euratom) 67, 77, 90
European Central Bank (ECB) 95,
    97–8
European Coal and Steel Community
    (ECSC) 67, 77–8, 85, 90, 106, 107,
    110, 146, 355
European Community: Commission *see*
    Commission of the European
    Community (CEC); industrial policy
    (motor vehicles) 251–6; institutional
    structure 77–9; liberalization of intra-
    EC trade 79–82, 85–9; regional policy
    353, 355–7
European Confederation for Post and
    Telecommunications (CEPT) 328
European Council 77
European Court of Justice 77, 78, 79, 85,
    244, 326, 331, 339
European Currency Unit (ECU) 94,
    196–7

European Economic Community (EEC) 67–71, 103; anticipated economic cost of entry 72–6

European Free Trade Area (EFTA) 3, 44; effect on UK trade 70–1, 75, 77, 82, 124–8, 131, 141–2; motor vehicles 239, 242, 248, 257; textiles and clothing 259–60, 264, 266, 269, 271

European integration: common foreign and security policy 90, 376; EMU 95–100, 197, 230, 374–6; institutions/origins 67–71, 90; monetary (moves towards) 93–100; political 67, 374

European Investment Bank 355

European Monetary System (EMS) 94–5, 196

European Parliament 77–8, 79, 226, 279

European Regional Development Fund (ERDF) 355

European Research Co-ordination Agency (EUREKA) 302

European Strategic Programme for Research and Development in Information Technology (ESPRIT) 113–14, 115, 116, 302–4, 328

European Union (EU): enlargement of 82–5; motor vehicle industry 239–41, 245–8; moves towards monetary integration 93–100; policies affecting trade 102–17; research and development policy 301–4; trade policy (high-technology products) 304–14; UK's entry 69–77, 130–4, 188; UK's entry (motor vehicles) 245–8; UK's entry (textiles/clothing) 266–76

Eurostar (locomotive) 323

Eurostat 194

EuroX countries 100

Exchange Rate Mechanism (ERM) 22, 23, 94–5, 99

exchange rates 54, 230, 288, 375; under CAP 195–7; fixed 8–9, 15, 68, 94, 141, 195–6; green 195, 196–7; monetary integration 93–5, 99–100; UK's comparative position 7–9, 15–17, 21–3

excise duties 96

exports 2–3, 87–8; distribution of (UK) 119–22; energy sector 94, 123, 124, 144, 146, 178–9; food/agriculture 188,

191, 205–8, 210–11, 214–16, 219, 223, 226; motor vehicles 238–48, 252–3, 255–6; research and development 297, 299, 301, 304–5, 314–15; services sector 319–21; steel 108, 111; textiles and clothing 259–62, 269–73; in trade theory 35–7, 39, 60; UK (comparative position) 7, 9, 21; UK (trade policy) 64–7, 70–1, 76; UK trade 125–35 *passim*; VERs *see* voluntary export restraints (VERs)

factor endowment 33–4

factors of production 33–5, 42, 43, agriculture 42, 217; free movement of 68

family income, tax and 359–67

Family Income Supplement 363, 364–5

Federal State of Europe 374

Federal Trade Commission 104

Fennell, R. 192, 196

FEOGA 205

fertilizers 217, 218

Fiat 243, 244, 255

financial services 319, 320, 324, 333, 335–6

Financial Services Agreement (WTO) 333

financial transfers (on EEC membership) 75

fines system (EU policy) 104

fiscal policy 9, 10, 97

Fischler, Franz 225–6

Fisher, A. 330

fishing industry (output) 23–4

Fisher and Ludlow 236

Fisons 359

fixed exchange rates 8–9, 15, 68, 94, 141, 195–6

flag-carrying airlines 325, 326

food and agriculture *see* agriculture

Ford 137, 234, 235, 241, 243, 244, 245, 249, 250–3, 254–6, 343

foreign aid 7

foreign direct investment 7, 16, 58, 373; impact on UK trade 135–42; in services 333–7, 338

foreign exchange *see* exchange rates

Foreman-Peck, J. 234–6, 238, 249, 250

forestry (output) 23–4

fossil fuel energy equivalent (FFEE) 148, 164, 173

fossil fuels 144, 148, 182; pricing policy 153–4; *see also* coal; gas; oil

Fothergill, S. 347

France (computing and telecommunications) 113–14, 330, 335

France Telecom 330, 335

Fraser, M. W. 330–1

free movement of factors 68

free trade 28, 31, 34, 36–7, 58, 83

free trade area 44–8, 57, 63–4, 93; *see also* European Free Trade Area (EFTA) North American Free Trade Area (NAFTA)

fruit and vegetables (CAP reform) 224

fuels *see* energy sector

Fujitsu 114, 306, 309, 313, 314

full-time employment 351–3

full employment 9, 15, 29, 30, 34, 133, 343, 344, 374

Future Medium-Range Air-to-Air Missiles (Fmraams) 284

Gannon, P. 112, 113, 114–15, 116, 117

gas industry 22–3, 175, 181–2; Conservative policy 156–9; consumption 24–5, 168–70, 173–4; costs 145, 154, 176–7; legislation 151, 157–8; levy 166–7; liquified natural (LNG) 146, 150; nationalization 149, 151–2; natural (North Sea) 24–5, 34, 123, 148, 151–2, 154, 156–8, 163–5, 169, 176, 183; prices/pricing 145–7, 152, 154, 157–8, 161, 176–7; privatization 156–9, 161

Gaul, J. 105

Gaz de France 182

Gazprom 181

GDP 1–2, 133–4; Britain's comparative position 5–6, 17–19, 22–3, 25; effects of monetary integration 96–9; regional (sectoral composition) 348–9

GEC 114, 276, 284, 306

General Agreement on Tariffs and Trade (GATT) 42, 47, 63, 70, 81–2, 121, 145; Article XXIV 44, 64; effect of CAP 208, 219–24, 227; high-technology industries 305, 310, 312; Kennedy Round 240; motor vehicles 240–2, 249, 251; textiles and clothing 260–1, 263, 276–7, 279; Tokyo Round 80, 307; Uruguay Round 58, 64, 85–9, 219–24 *passim*, 240, 277, 279, 305, 331–2, 375

General Agreement on Trade in Services (GATS) 88–9, 332, 375

General Electric 113

general equilibrium analysis 30–2, 59; of tariffs 35–7

General Motors 234, 241, 243, 244, 249, 250–3, 254–6, 343

generalized system of preference (GSP) 71, 83–5, 264, 266–7

Germany 97, 105–6; clothing industry 265–6; computing and telecommunications industry 112; Deutschmark 22, 94–6, 195, 197, 245

GKN 235

Glais, M. 67, 107

Global One 335

Gooding, C. 322

goods (current account balance) 141–2

government: debt 96, 97, 98, 136; deficit 96, 97, 98, 125, 136, 138; services 349; *see also* competition policy; fiscal policy; industrial policy; monetary policy; trade policy

Government Office Region (GOR) 349, 350, 356

Gowers, A. 309

Gray, B. 284–5

Great Depression 66

Great Universal Stores 265

Green, D. 359

Green Belt 343

green exchange rate 195, 196–7

Greenaway, D. 138, 336

greenfield investment 358

greenhouse gases 182, 183

Gresser, C. 335

Griffiths, J. 250, 253, 254–5

Groom, B. 345, 347, 357, 358

gross domestic expenditure on research and development (GERD) 287–8, 292, 293

gross value added (fuel industries) 175, 177

GTE 335

Gudgin, Graham 343–50, 353
Gulf War 146, 149
Guy 235

Hague, William 376
Halsall, M. 280
Hamilton, C.B. 269
Hargreaves, D. 221, 225–6, 227
'harmonization process' 79–80, 244,
    322–3, 375
Hasselkus, W. 254
Havana Charter 63
Heath, Edward 76
Heckscher–Ohlin theory 33–5
high-definition television (HDTV) 302,
    307, 330
high-technology industries 283–315
Hill, A. 309
Hitachi 312
Hitiris, T. 361
Hogg, Douglas 226, 227
Holberton, S. 160, 162, 163, 181, 182,
    183
Home Condition Survey (1991) 169
homeworkers (in clothing industry) 280,
    281
Honda 249, 250, 252–3, 254–6
'horizontal equity' 356
horizontal integration 264
'hot money' 7
House of Lords 107, 108, 109, 111
household expenditure (on energy) 168
Huby, M. 366
Hufbauer, G.C. 135
Hughes 284
Hussein, Saadam 146
Hyundai 313, 314, 359
hydroelectricity 148, 164, 165

Iberia (of Spain) 327
IBM 112, 113, 114, 115–16, 306, 311,
    328
ICI 264
ICL 114, 115, 306, 309
ICT 113
Ikegami Tsushinki 311
imitation lag 286, 297
imperfect competition 28, 54–6, 57, 60–1
import price, minimum 41, 69, 82, 107,
    111, 190–4, 196, 201, 204, 222, 229
import substitution (agriculture) 188
imports 2–3; anti-dumping duties 41, 58,
    81–2, 89, 91, 111, 279, 309–12, 359,
    373, 375; distribution of (UK) 119–20,
    122; energy sector 123, 124, 144, 146,
    178–9; food/agriculture 188, 190–4,
    196, 201, 204–8, 211–13, 219; motor
    vehicles 239–40, 243, 247–8, 254; non-
    tariff barriers 54–6, 80–2, 115, 302,
    309–12, 318, 373; research and
    development 299, 301, 304–5; services
    sector 319–21; textiles and clothing
    259–60, 262–3, 267, 270–3, 276–8,
    280–1; in trade theory 35–7, 39–40, 45,
    59–61; UK (comparative position) 7, 9,
    21; UK (trade policy) 64–6, 68, 70–6;
    UK trade 125–6, 128–35; *see also*
    generalized system of preferences
    (GSP); quotas; tariffs
incentive effects 40
income: Diamond Report 351, 360–1,
    364–5; elasticity of demand 40, 50, 55,
    59–60, 126; regional disparities 345–7;
    taxation and 359–60, 361–7; trends
    5–6, 19–21
indifference curves 30–2
indirect taxation 28, 69, 75, 96, 167, 183,
    359–60, 361, 368
Industrial Development Certificates 249,
    343
industrial energy consumption 170–1
industrial policy (EU) 105; information
    technology industry 112–17; motor
    vehicles 251–6; steel industry 106–11
Industrial Reorganization Committee
    (IRC) 236
industrial structure of textiles and clothing
    industry 264–6
Industrial Transference Board 343
industry: innovations by 296–301; state
    aid to 358–9; trends 10–14, 25–7
infant industry protection 68, 308
inflation 1, 9, 15, 16, 18, 21–2, 59, 95–6,
    97, 128, 372
Information Technology Agreement (ITA)
    308, 311, 315, 376
information technology industry (EU
    policy) 112–17

ING 336
Inner City Act (1977) 344
innovation (by industry) 296–301
Institute for International Economics
    332
institutional structure of EC 77–9
Integrated Broadband Communications
    (IBC) system 116, 303, 304
integration *see* European integration
intellectual property rights 85, 88
Interconnection Systems 314
interest rate 16, 21, 22, 95, 97, 99, 144–5
internal support (CAP) 223
international agreements (services sector)
    331–3
International Air Transport (AITA) 325,
    333–6, 339
International Civil Aviation Organization
    (ICAO) 323
international context (EU trade) 85–9
International Energy Authority (IEA) 159,
    161, 165, 180–1
international finance system (UK's
    comparative position) 5–27
International Institute of Strategic Studies
    285
International Monetary Fund 8, 9, 195
international pressure (CAP reform)
    219–20
International Radio Consultative
    Committee (CCIR) 307
International Standards Organization
    (ISO) 115, 322
International Telecommunications Union
    (ITU) 115
International Trade Organization (ITO)
    63
international trade theory 28–61
Internet 115, 304
intervention price (in CAP) 190–3, 196,
    201, 203, 207, 220, 222, 223, 226
intra-EC trade (liberalization of) 79–82,
    85–9
investment 7, 16, 19, 96–7; foreign direct
    see foreign direct investment; in high-
    technology 312–14; income (current
    account balance) 141–2; inward 134–5,
    137–40, 248–50, 312–14, 358, 369–70;
    in motor vehicle industry 248–51; ratios

14–15, 20–1, 217; regional policy 344,
    345; trade-related measures 85,
    87–8
inward investment 134–5, 137–40,
    248–50, 312–14, 358, 369–70
Irish Steel 111
Ispat International 111
Italy (clothing industry) 265–6
ITV 330–1

Jack, A. 309
Jaguar 234, 235, 236, 242, 250, 252, 253,
    255
James, S. 361
Japan 81, 138–9, 245, 249–50, 307, 308,
    309
Joint European Submicron Silicon
    Initiative (JESSI) 302
Joint Understanding (CEGB/NCB) 161
Jones, D.T. 240
Jones, P. 288, 289–92
Jones, S. 345
Jonquieres, G. de 333, 358
Josling 72–3, 223
Jowett 235
Jowit, J. 358
just-in-time (JIT) methods 249
JVC 311

Kaldor, N. 72–3, 75
Kampfner, J. 162
Kassim, H. 323, 325–6, 327, 334
Kehoe, L. 307, 313
Kennedy Round 240
Keynesian approach 16, 97
Khanna, S.R. 278
Kiel Institute of World Economics
    105–6
Kindleberger, C.P. 44
Kinetica 163
Kinnock, Neil 339
Kleinwort Benson 335–6
KLM-Northwest Airlines 337, 339
Kohdensha 314
Kohl, Helmut 97
Konica 311
Korean War 15
Krugman, P.R. 20
Krupp-Hoesch 110

labour 68; costs *see* wages; marginal product of 29–30; markets 1, 19, 20–1, 98; supply 34
Labour government 1, 15, 21, 90, 95, 188, 236, 376; energy policy 149–52, 160, 167; regional policy 343, 344, 353, 359; taxation policy 363, 367
lamb (effect of CAP) 215–16
land 29
Lanchester 234
Lapper, R. 328
Lascelles, D. 160
Laspeyres' quantity index 199
Lawson, Nigel 94
LDV 253
Lend-Lease scheme 7
Leonard, R. 67, 71, 78–9
Leontief, W. 34
Lerner assumption 37
Leyland 235, 236, 253
LG Group 313, 314, 358,
liberalization: of energy sector 180–1; of intra-EC trade 79–82, 83; of services sector 80, 318, 322–7, 332, 334, 340; of telecommunications 117, 318, 322–3, 328, 329–30, 340; of textiles and clothing 277–80
Lipsey, R.G. 44
liquified natural gas (LNG) 146, 150
livestock products (effect of CAP) 209–10
living standards 17, 105
Local Employment Acts (1960 and 1963) 344
location of production 57, 58
Lockwood Martin 284
Lomé Agreements 83–4, 263
long run average cost (LAC) 53
Long Term Arrangement (cotton textiles) 260, 261
Lotus 254
Lucas, Joseph (electrics) 235, 254
Luesby, J. 279
Lufthansa 334
Lufthansa–United Airlines 337, 339

Maastricht Treaty 21, 78, 90, 95, 160, 319, 353, 355, 374–5
MAC system 307
McDonnell Douglas 104, 305

MacGregor, Ian 150
McKenna duties 66, 239
McKinlay, A. 235–6
McKinnon, James 169
MacSharry reforms 203, 221–4, 225, 230
Maddison, A. 8
Magnox Electric 160
Magnox reactors 151
Maitland, A. 79, 228
Majmudar, M. 268, 276–7, 280
Major, John 17, 368
Malev (Hungarian airline) 327
Mannesmann 330
Mansell, Ken 2, 65, 119–20
manufactures: employment in 346–7; inward investment 138–9, 140; output 11, 23–4, 25–6, 372; product differentiation 42–3; tariffs on 86–7; trade in (EEC) 68, 75–6; trade in (UK) 2–3, 123, 124, 126–33; UK comparative position 11–13, 23–6
Marcus, Peter 109–10
marginal cost 30, 46, 51, 55, 144, 153–4
marginal product of labour 29–30
marginal rate of substitution (MRS) 31–2, 35, 37
marginal rate of transformation (MRT) 30–1, 32, 37
marginal revenue 51, 55
market access (CAP) 223
market failure (research and development) 301
Marks and Spencer 265, 272
Marrakesh Agreement 85, 89
Marsh, P. 313, 358
Marsh, V. 159
Marshall Plan/Aid 8, 64
Martinson, J. 158
Massell, B.F. 45–6
Matsushita 306, 311, 312
Mattoo, A. 89, 245
Mavroidis, P.C. 89, 245
Maxcy, G. 240
Mayes, D.G. 130
Mazda 255
MCI (US) 328, 335
Mead, D.C. 51
Meade, J.E. 93
Meade assumption 35, 37

Mediterranean countries 83, 376
Members of the European Parliament
    (MEPs) 78, 279
Menon, A. 334
Mercedes-Benz 255
merchandise trade: with US and Western
    Europe 64, 65; visibles 7, 139, 141
Mercury 328, 329
Merger Regulation (1990) 103, 104, 337,
    373
mergers 103, 104–5, 113, 373; energy
    sector 162–3; in motor vehicle industry
    234, 236; services 337, 339, 340; in
    textiles and clothing 264
Messerlin, P.A. 58
Microsoft 115
migration, unemployment and 350–3
milk/milk products (effect of CAP)
    211–15, 225
Miller, Marcus H. 72–4, 75, 76
minimum efficient technical scale (METS)
    55, 56, 107; for car production 234,
    235–6, 238, 251, 253
minimum import price 41, 69, 82, 107,
    111, 190–4, 196, 201, 204, 222, 229
mining and quarrying (output) 24
Ministry of Agriculture, Fisheries and
    Food (MAFF) 198, 228
Ministry of Defence 284, 292
Minolta 311
Mission Energy 159
Mitsubishi 312
Mitter, S. 276
Mitterand, Francois 302
model M (economies of scale) 54–7
model T (economies of scale) 51–4, 56–7
Molyneux, P. 324
Monbiot, G. 170
Monetary Compensatory Amounts
    (MCAs) 195–6
monetary integration (moves towards)
    93–100
monetary policy 9, 90, 93–100
money supply 16
Monopolies and Mergers Commission
    (MMC) 157–8, 162, 181, 339
monopolistic competition 42
monopoly and merger policy 157–8, 162,
    181, 337, 339

Montagnon, P. 85
Moore, L. 121, 127, 129, 240, 260, 266,
    267
Morgan Grenfell 335
Morris 234, 236
most-favoured-nation status 63, 66, 75,
    88, 127, 242, 332
motor vehicles (trade and production)
    234–57
Motorola 306
Muller, P. 283
Mulliners 236
Multi-Fibre Arrangement (MFA) 71, 87,
    261–9 *passim* 271–7, 279–81, 373
multilateralism 63
multinational companies 57, 58, 89, 96,
    307; car industry 253, 254, 256–7
Münchau, W. 98, 314

Nairn, G. 309
Nakamoto, M. 245
national champions 113, 236, 243, 245
National Coal Board 149, 150–1, 153,
    156, 161
National Consumer Council (NCC) 192,
    207, 210, 217–18, 221, 224, 312
National Farmers Union 226
National Insurance Act (1974) 362
National Insurance contributions 246,
    359–61, 362, 363, 366–7, 368, 369
National Microelectronics Institute 313
National Physical Laboratory 283
National Power 159, 161, 162, 163, 182
National Research Development
    Corporation (NRDC) 112
National Union of Mineworkers (NUM)
    150–1
nationalization (energy sector) 149–52
NATO 284, 285
Navaretti, G.B. 263
net effective cost (electricity) 155, 156
networking standards 115
networks: integrated broadband
    communications 116, 303, 304; third-
    party access (TPA) 180; trans-European
    90, 160, 180–2, 309
Neumark Committee 361
New Towns Act (1946) 343
Newbery, D.M. 154

newly industrialized countries (NICs)141, 299

Nicoll, A. 284, 285, 335

NIER 368

Nixdorf 114, 115, 116

Nissan 249–51, 252–3, 254–6

Nobes, C. 361

Nolling, Wilhelm 98

non-tariff barriers 54–6, 80–2, 115, 318, 373; high-technology industries 302, 309–12

non-tradeables 22–3

Norman, P. 97, 106

North American Free Trade Area (NAFTA) 58, 93, 141–2

North of Scotland Hydro-Electric Board 151

North Sea gas 24–5, 34, 123, 148, 151–2, 154, 156–8, 163–5, 169, 176, 183

North Sea oil 1, 24, 25, 27, 34, 138; development 3, 122, 123, 128, 144–85, 345, 369, 372; extraction 152, 163

Northern Development Company 345

Northern REC 162

Northwest Airlines 337, 339

Nouvelles Frontières case 326

NTT 335

nuclear electricity 164, 165

Nuclear Fuels Ltd 160

nuclear power 148, 160, 175, 182, 183

Nuffield 235–6

Nynex 329

o.tel.o, 330

Objective 1 regions 355–6, 357

Objective 2 regions 355–6

Objective 5b regions 355–6

Oce Nederalan 311

Offer 161, 163

offer curves 32–3, 37

Office of National Statistics (ONS) 19, 65, 120, 135, 140, 319, 337–8, 350–2, 356

Ofgas 156, 157–8, 163

OFTEL 328, 329, 330

oil industry 94, 164–5, 175; Conservative policy 156, 157; consumption 24–5, 144–5, 148–9, 168–73; costs 144, 145, 153–4, 176–7; legislation 152, 156–7; prices/pricing 15–16, 24–5, 123, 126, 145–7, 150, 152–4, 163, 170, 176, 179, 372; revenue/tax 150, 166–7; *see also* North Sea oil; Organization of Petroleum Exporting Countries (OPEC)

oilseeds (UK output/consumption) 208–9, 222, 223

oligopoly 42–3, 58

Olivetti 114, 115, 116, 306, 309, 328

Olivetti-Canon 311

Olympic Airways 327

Opel 256

'open systems interconnections' (OSI) 115

'Operation Blue Sky' 334–5

opportunity cost 29, 38, 39, 50, 153

Organization for Economic Co-operation and Development (OECD) 6, 25, 40, 147, 271; agricultural sector 189–91, 215, 217–18, 220, 225; analysis of economic growth (1955–68) 10–22; high-technology sector 283, 286–9, 294–9

Organization for European Economic Co-operation (OEEC) 8, 64, 121

Organization of Petroleum Exporting Countries (OPEC) 138, 146, 363; prices 15–16, 24–5, 123, 152, 176, 179

OSI standards 115

Ottawa Agreements 66, 259

output 2; growth (trends) 10–11, 14, 22–6; manufactures 11, 23–4, 25–6, 372; measurement (research and development) 294–6

outward processing traffic (OPT) 263, 266, 277, 279

overseas trade statistics (OTS) 65, 120, 127–8, 130, 135

Owen, D. 182

Owen, N. 238, 243, 244, 246

ozone layer 182

Paccar 253

Packard Bell 309

Pandolfi, Filippo 116

Parker, G. 345

Parkes, C. 308

part-time employment 351–3

partial equilibrium analysis 30, 37, 38; preferential trade agreements 43–6; of tariffs 39–41, 43–6

patents 294, 295, 296
Pauley, R. 363, 366
Pavitt, K. 303
peace clause (Uruguay Round) 223
'peace dividend' 1, 292, 294
Pearson, M. 368
Peel, M. 249, 250
Peel, Q. 309
Pemberton, M. 246–7
pension schemes 96, 97, 99
perfect competition 28, 29, 30, 33, 35
personal computer 115–16, 117
Peston, R. 100
Peterson, J. 302
petroleum: consumption 173, 174; OPEC
   15–16, 24–5, 123, 138, 146, 152, 176,
   179, 363; revenue tax (PRT) 166
Peugeot 243, 244, 249, 251, 252, 254, 255
Pfaff 276
Pfizer 359
Philips 114, 306, 307, 309,311, 312, 328
Phillips, A.W. (Phillips curve) 15
Piper Alpha disaster 25, 176
'Plan for Coal' 150
Plessey 114, 306
Political and Economic Planning (PEP)
   240
political integration 67, 374
Pollard, S. 8
pollution 182–3
population (comparative positions) 5–6, 11
post, telephone and telegraph companies
   (PTTs) 117, 328–9
Potter, S.J. 137
poverty/poverty trap 3, 361–3, 365–6,
   368–9,
PowerGen 159, 161, 162, 163, 182
Pratten, C. 55, 107, 238, 253
preferential trade agreements 3, 23, 58,
   64, 376; analysis of quotas 49–51;
   enlargement of EU 82–5; partial
   equilibrium analysis 43–6; *see also*
   Commonwealth Preference Scheme;
   European Free Trade Area (EFTA);
   North American Free Trade Area
   (NAFTA)
preferential trading areas 28, 93; impact
   on UK trade 119–42
Pressed Steel 235, 236

price/pricing: agriculture/food 68–9,
   188–98, 201–4, 207, 211, 216, 218,
   220–2, 225, 229–30; differentiation
   42–3, 107–8; elasticity of demand 40,
   50, 55, 59–60, 126; energy 144–7,
   149–50, 153–6; international trade
   theory 31–40, 42–3, 45, 47–61;
   intervention 190–3, 196, 201, 203, 207,
   220, 222–3, 226; minimum import 41,
   69, 82, 107, 111, 190–4, 196, 201, 204,
   222, 229; retail price index 157, 161,
   184, 200; target 68–9, 190, 193, 196,
   207, 211, 222, 225; threshold 69, 190,
   207, 222
primary energy: consumption of 172–4;
   production of 163–4
prior-to-entry production 52–4
privatization 1, 16, 23, 89, 109, 372;
   energy sector 156–63, 176, 183;
   services sector 318–19, 324, 326, 328,
   333–8, 373
producer subsidy 74
producer subsidy equivalent (PSE) 40,
   220, 224–5
producer surplus 38–40, 45, 48
product cycle theory 286
product differentiation 42–3
production 35–6; agriculture/food 197–9,
   203, 208; function 56; location of 57,
   58, of motor vehicles 234–41, 248–57;
   possibility curve 30–2, 33; prior-to-
   entry 52–4; subsidies *see* subsidies
productivity 1, 2, 10–11, 14, 25, 134,
   259
profit maximization 51, 55
protection: of agriculture 64–6; in
   clothing/textile industry 260–1;
   contingent 58, 82, 89, 91; effective rate
   of 43, 64; infant industry 68, 308;
   motor vehicle industry 239–41;
   standards (harmonization process)
   79–80, 244, 322–3, 375; in theory of
   trade 28–61; *see also* non-tariff barriers;
   quotas; tariffs
Proton 254
public procurement 80–1, 115, 319,
   328
public sector borrowing requirements
   (PSBR) 156, 328

public spending 345; gross domestic expenditure on research and development 287–8, 292, 293
purchasing power 30, 95; parity 17, 288

QPL 314
quotas 42, 63, 81; agricultural 207, 211–12, 221; analysis of (under preferential system) 49–51; steel industry 107–8; textiles and clothing 259, 260, 261–3, 267, 269, 270 1, 276–8, 280–1

Racal 329
rail transport 327
Rank Xerox 311
Ravenscraig 106, 109
raw materials 64
Rawsthorn, A. 306
Rayner, A.J. 217
Raytheon 284
rebalancing (under CAP) 223
reciprocity effect 121
Reddaway Report 134, 135–9
Regional Development Grants 344
regional development policy 249, 344
Regional Electricity Companies (RECs) 159, 162–3
Regional Employment Premium 344, 353
regional GDP (sectoral composition) 348–9
regional policy 3; of EC 353, 355–7; inward investment 358; state aid to industry 358–9; of UK 343–53, 354
Renault 243, 244, 245, 255
replacement ratios 368–9
Research in Advanced Communications in Europe (RACE) 114, 303, 304
research and development 55, 56, 105, 107, 359; in Britain 287–301; ESPRIT 113–14, 115, 116, 302–4, 328; EU policy 301–4; EUREKA 302; expenditure 349, 350; high technology industries 283–315; RACE 114, 303, 304
resource allocation 28, 29–30, 35, 89
restrictive agreements 102
retail price index 157, 161, 184, 200
retail trade (clothing and textiles) 265–6

Revell, Jack 134
Rewe-Zentral 79
Rhys, G. 238
Rice, R. 326, 339
Richardson, D. 222, 226
Ricoh 311
Riedinger, Oscar 228
RJB Mining 162, 182
Road Research Laboratory 283
road transport 324–5
Robson, P. 46
Rooke, Denis 154
Rolls-Royce 234, 235, 242, 252, 254
Rootes 234, 235–6
Rover 235, 236, 244, 249–55 *passim*
Royal Commission on the Distribution of Income and Wealth 351, 360–2, 364–5
Royal Dutch Shell 149
Ruhrgas 181
'Rules of Competition' 102–5
rules of origin 44, 70
RWE 330
Ryanair 334
Rybczynski, T.M. 34

Saab 255
Sabena 339
Safeguarding of Industries Act (1921) 66
Samsung 312
Samuelson, P.A. 34
Sanyo 313
Saviotti, P. 302, 304
Scammell 235, 236
Scandinavian Airlines System (SAS) 334, 337, 339
Schneider, V. 328, 329
Science Policy Research Institute (Sussex University) 160
Scientific Veterinary Committee (of EU) 228
Scottish Hydro-Electric 159, 162, 163
Scottish Parliament 98, 345
Scottish Power 159, 163
'screwdriver' firms 313
SEA 113
SEAT 244, 245, 253, 255
Second Banking Directive 324
sectoral composition (regional GDP) 348–9

self sufficiency 37, 38, 39, 46; food
consumption 191–3, 195, 200, 205,
208, 219
Semiconductor Council 309
'sensitive' products/sectors 84, 85, 87,
262, 263, 264, 269, 277
services sector 123–4; employment in
346–7; financial services 319–20, 324,
333, 335–6; General Agreement on
Trade in Services (GATS) 88–9, 332,
375; investment in 139, 140–2, 333–8;
liberalization 80, 318, 322–7, 332, 334,
340; privatization 318–19, 324, 326,
328, 333–8, 373; trade in 76, 85; trends
10–14, 22–3, 25–7
set-aside programme 217, 222, 225, 226,
229, 230–1
Sharp, M. 303
Sharp 311
sheep meat (effect of CAP) 215–16
Shinho Electronic Telecommunication
314
Short Term Arrangement (cotton textiles)
260
Siebert, H. 97
Siemens 112, 114, 115, 116, 306, 311,
313, 314, 358
Silberston, Z.A. 262, 267, 269, 271–3,
275
'Silicon Glen' 313
Simkins, J. 309
Simonian, H. 245, 250, 253
Sinclair Acorn 306
Singer 234, 235–6
Single European Act (1986) 78, 80–1,
114, 302, 318, 323–7
Single European Market (SEM) 23, 28,
55–6, 196, 276, 373; high technology
industries 307, 309; motor vehicle
industry 245, 251, 253, 256; regional
policy 355, 357; services sector 319,
323–8; UK trade policy 81–3, 85, 89
Sizewell (pressurised water reactor) 151–2,
155, 160, 182
Skapinker, M. 104–5, 306, 326, 327,
333–5, 337, 339
Skoda 253, 255
'sluice gate' price 69, 190, 207, 222
Smith, A. 55, 56–7, 241

Smithsonian agreement 15
'Snake' 94, 196
social security 3, 96–9, 246, 360–8, 375
Society of Motor Manufacturers and
Traders (SMMT) 240–1, 248, 252,
255–6
Sonatrach 181
Sony 306, 307, 311, 312
South of Scotland Electric Board 151
Southern Electricity 163
Southey, C. 83, 84, 221, 224, 227,
280
'specialization index' 84
Spottiswoode, Clare 169–70
Sprint 335
stagflation 16
Standard 234, 235–6
standards: computing and
telecommunications 114–15;
harmonization process 79–80, 244,
322–3, 375; high-technology industries
307–8
Star Alliance 334
state aid to industry 358–9
Statoil 181
Steedman, H. 266, 276
steel industry 106–11, 372; ECSC 67,
77–8, 85, 90, 106–7, 110, 146, 355
Stephens, P. 100
sterling 70, 96, 196, 197, 201; devaluation
8, 9–10, 15, 21–2, 23, 95, 226; petro-
currency 94
Stet 114
Stokes, Donald 236
Strategic Defence Initiative (SDI) 302
Stresa Conference (1958) 189
structural funds (EU) 355–6
Stubbs, P. 302, 304
subsidiarity principle 78–9
subsidies 98, 245; agriculture 65, 188,
195, 223, 224; consumer subsidy
equivalent 40, 220, 224–5, 226; cross-
subsidization 153, 158; energy sector
106, 146, 153, 158, 162, 165–7, 176,
191; EU policies affecting trade
105–7, 110–13; producer subsidy
equivalent 40, 220, 224–5; research
(EU policy) 302–4; state aid to industry
358–9

sugar regime 2207–8
supply: elasticities of 43, 44, 46, 60;
    schedule 39–47, 49, 60–1
Swann, D. 107, 146
Swissair 339

Talbot 252
Tangermann, S. 201
target price (agriculture) 68–9, 190, 193,
    196, 207, 211, 222, 225
tariffs 65, 257, 315, 328; Common
    External 16, 44, 46–8, 51, 75, 82–3, 87,
    91, 127, 138, 140, 266, 308, 375;
    Commonwealth Preference Scheme 3,
    63, 66–7, 70, 71, 75, 207, 239, 242,
    259; equivalent (of NTBs) 55–6, 225;
    general equilibrium analysis 35–7;
    generalized system of preferences 71,
    83–5, 264, 266–7; most-favoured-nation
    status 63, 66, 75, 88, 127, 242, 332;
    partial equilibrium analysis 39–41,
    43–6; trade theory 28, 39–41, 43–8,
    50–1, 53, 58–61; *see also* General
    Agreement on Tariffs and Trade
    (GATT)
TAT 334
Tatung 313
Tattersall's Trade Review 121
taxation 3, 98, 345, 357, 362–7, 369;
    agriculture 192, 218, 224, 226, 230;
    direct 359–60, 368; energy sector
    165–7, 176, 182–3; indirect 28, 69,
    75, 96, 167, 183, 359–60, 361,
368
Taylor, C.T. 137
Taylor, Ian 332
Taylor, P. 308, 309, 313
Taylor, R. 353
TCP/IP protocols 115
technical standards 80
technology: gaps 286; high-technology
    industries 283–315; transfer 304–5
telecommunications industry 81, 89;
    alliances 335, 340; EU policy 112–17,
    327–31, 373; liberalization 117, 318,
    322–3, 328, 329–30, 340; WTO
    Agreement 332–3, 376
Telefonica 335
TELEMATICS 303

television 329, 331, 332; high definition
    (HDTV) 302, 307, 330
'Television without Frontiers' Directive
    331, 332
Telewest 329
temporary work 351–2
terms of trade 32, 37
Textile and Clothing Protocol 278
Textile Council 260–1, 265
Textiles and Clothing Agreement 271,
    273, 277, 279–80
textiles and clothing industry 87, 259–81
Thai Airways 334
Thatcher, Margaret 1, 16, 17, 109, 112,
    138, 150–1, 156, 183, 330–1, 368, 372
third-party access (TPA) to networks 180
Thoenes, S. 323
Thomson 114, 306, 307, 311, 312
Thomson-CSF 284, 309
Thomson Multimedia 309
Thornycraft 235
Three Mile Island accident 182
threshold price 69, 190, 207, 222
Thyssen 110
Tighe, C. 313–14
Tinbergen, J. 57
tobacco industry 224
Tokyo Round 80, 307
Toshiba 306, 308, 311, 312
Total 158
total factor productivity growth 20–1
Town and Country Planning Act (1947)
    343
Townsend, D. 322
Toyota 249, 251, 252–3, 254–6
trade: creation 44–8, 54, 73, 93, 111, 125,
    131, 133, 260; deficit 2–3; development
    of UK (impact of preferential trading
    areas) 119–42; diversion 44–8, 50, 53,
    54, 58, 91, 93, 125, 133, 212, 260, 269,
    276, 280–1, 375; effect of CAP on
    188–231; in energy sector 178–80; EU
    policies affecting 102–17; high-tech
    products 304–14; liberalization 64,
    79–82, 85–9; motor vehicles 234,
    241–8; policy (UK) 63–91; related
    intellectual property rights (TRIPs) 85,
    88; related investment measures
    (TRIMs) 85, 87–8; in services 318–40;

textile and clothing 276–80; theory (protection and discrimination) 28–61
trade marks 80, 89
trade unions 15, 16, 56, 150–1, 226, 238, 372
tradeable sectors (output) 23–4
traditional analysis (model T) 51–4
Trans-European Networks 90, 160, 180–2, 319
TransCo 157
transfer cost (of CAP) 218
transfers 7, 73, 139–40, 230–1, 355–6, 357
transport: costs 145, 147, 249; energy consumption 171–2, 174, 185; policy (SEM) 324–7
Transport Directorate 339
Treasury 99, 153, 345
Treaty of European Union (Maastricht) 21, 78, 90, 95, 160, 319, 353, 355, 374–5
Treaty of Paris 67, 106
Treaty of Rome 67, 68, 70, 102–5, 113, 114, 181, 189, 331, 353
Triumph 236, 249
Tucker, E. 79, 99, 104–5, 106, 244–5, 326–7, 330, 339
Turing, Alan 112
Turner, L. 150

UK Atomic Energy Authority 292
UK Continental Shelf (UKCS) 152
UN 144, 145, 146, 323, 336
UNCTAD 71, 84
underemployment 20, 105
unemployment 1, 63, 97–8, 105, 109, 137, 174, 249, 372, 374, 375; benefit 351, 361–3, 366, 367; regional policy 343–5, 350–3, 355–7, 369; UK comparative position 9, 15, 16
Unilever 134
Unisource 335
unit costs (car manufacture) 245–6
United Airlines 334, 339
United States: Lend-Lease scheme 7; Marshall Plan 8, 64; merchandise trade with 64, 65; -Scandinavian Airlines System (SAS) 337, 339
Urry, M. 197

Uruguay Round 58, 64, 85–9, 219–24, 240, 277, 279, 305, 331–2, 375
USAir 334

value added 43, 263
value-added tax (VAT) 28, 69, 75, 96, 167, 183, 361, 368
Van Miert, Karel 106, 111, 117, 339
Varig (of Brazil) 334
Varity 254
Vauxhall 137, 234, 235, 252–3, 255–6
veal 210–11
Veba 330
vegetables and fruit (CAP reform) 224
Venables, J. 55, 56–7, 241
Vernon, R. 286
vertical integration 284: energy sector 160, 162–3; motor vehicle industry 235; textiles and clothing 264
Viag/Viag Interkom 330
Vickers 254
Vickers, J. 151, 152, 153–4, 156–7, 326
Videotron 329
Viner, J. 44
Virgin Express 327, 334
visible trade 7, 139, 141
Viyella International 264
Volkswagen 106, 242–3, 244, 245, 253, 254–5
voluntary export restraints (VERs) 42, 58, 66–7, 81–2, 89, 91, 111, 240–1, 245, 249, 259, 264, 270, 309, 372–3, 375
Volvo 242, 255

wages 97, 98, 150, 153, 193; motor industry 246–7, 250; regional differences 353–4, 369; textile/ clothing industry 259, 260, 267–8
Wagner, K. 266, 276
Wagstyl, S. 249, 250, 313–14, 339, 358–9
Wall Street Crash 66
Walter, I. 107
Wang, Z.K. 83, 279
water sector 22–3
welfare: effects 73–4, 75, 76, 134; gains 56; loss 40, 42, 54, 73–4, 75, 76
Welsh Assembly 98, 345
Western Europe: integration 67–71; merchandise trade with 64, 65

Weston, C. 162
Weyman-Jones, T. 155–6
Wheat Act (1933) 65
White, L.J. 238, 240, 245
Wighton, D. 162, 358
Williams, F. 82, 308, 309, 332–3
Williams, T.I. 149, 154
Wilson, Harold 112
windfall tax 160
Wingas 181
Winters, L.A. 83, 126, 131–3, 279
Wolffe, R. 267, 358, 369
Wonnacott, R.J. 83
World-Com 335
World Bank 8, 147
World Partners 335

world prices (agriculture) 191, 192, 193, 201
World Trade Organization 80, 83–8, 147, 219, 240, 301, 304, 308–9; Financial Services Agreement 333 *see* Information Technology Agreement (ITA); Telecommunications Agreement 332–3, 376; Textiles and Clothing Agreement 271, 273, 277, 279–80

Yarrow, G. 151, 152, 153–4, 156–7, 326
Yom Kippur War 15–16, 146
Young, S.Z. 71

Zenith Data Systems 309